COOKING THE WHOLE FOODS WAY

COOKING THE WHOLE FOODS WAY

Your Complete, Everyday Guide to Healthy,
Delicious Eating with 500 Recipes, Menus, Techniques,
Meal Planning, Buying Tips, Wit & Wisdom

Christina Pirello

Illustrations by Christina Pirello

HPBooks

HPBooks
Published by The Berkley Publishing Group
200 Madison Avenue
New York, NY 10016

Cover design by James R. Harris
Cover photograph by Anthony Loew
Interior illustrations copyright © 1997 by Christina Pirello.

First edition: March 1997

Published simultaneously in Canada.

The Putnam Berkley World Wide Web site address is
http://www.berkley.com/berkley

Library of Congress Cataloging-in-Publication Data

Pirello, Christina.
    Cooking the whole foods way : your complete, everyday guide to
healthy, delicious eating with 500 recipes, menus, meal planning,
techniques, buying tips, wit, and wisdom / Christina Pirello. — 1st ed.
        p.   cm.
    ISBN 1-55788-262-2
    1. Cookery (Natural foods)   2. Natural foods.   3. Macrobiotic
diet—Recipes.   I. Title.
TX741.P564 1997
641.5'63—dc20   . 96-23176
                                                                   CIP

Printed in the United States of America

10 9 8 7 6 5 4 3 2 1

Thirteen years ago, my life changed course forever. I was diagnosed with terminal cancer and thought my life was, indeed, over. But instead, I met my husband, Robert Pirello, and my life has never been the same. This book is for him—my teacher, my love, my partner and my life.

Contents

Acknowledgments

There are so many people to thank in connection with this book that I could ramble on for days . . . but don't worry, I'll be brief.

First, to my mother, who taught me to cook from my soul—and to my father, who always thought I could do anything. To my brothers and sister, who endured countless experimental recipes as I evolved, but especially to my brother Tom, for being the best big brother a girl ever had.

To my high school art teacher, John Sebes, who introduced me to vegetarianism.

To my many teachers—Michio and Aveline Kushi, your work with macrobiotics enabled me to save my very life; Diane Avoli, Wendy Esko, Mary Kett, Carry Wolf and Geraldine Walker, your depth of understanding of food helped shape the cook I claim to be today; Tom Monte, for author encouragement and friendship; and William Tara, your enduring encouragement and mentoring taught me to listen to my heart.

To my many computer troubleshooters, for bailing me out every time my illiteracy got me in hot water—Diana and Dave, for your endless patience; Jim, who could teach an idiot how to operate a computer—and in this case, did just that.

To Sharon and Patty, for their patient proofreading and honesty.

To Christopher, for letting me pick his writer's brain more often than I care to admit.

To my numerous students and friends who have taught me so much over the years about keeping my mind open to the learning process and who acted as willing guinea pigs for recipe after recipe.

To the macrobiotic community of Philadelphia, for all your support, friendship and well-wishing.

To my special women friends—that little group of strong, beautiful women who not only helped me get through the rough spots of this work, but who loved and supported me, unconditionally. Barbara (both of you), Cyn, Elaine, Sheryl, Lynn, Sue, Donna, Nongo, Sharon, Diana, June, Robin, Susan, Kay, Lisa—I know, I know, I said I'd be brief . . . you know who you all are . . . you have my undying love and friendship.

To Barbara, Lisa, Patrick and Andrew, for the body work that kept me sane when the stress nearly did me in. Your magic hands and healing hearts are much appreciated.

To Ray, for telling me over and over and over that I could do this.

To Richard, for all the work and friendship and faith and trust put into this effort . . . Tuscany is getting closer every day.

To Steve Feinberg, for getting this ball rolling in the first place.

To Jeanette, my editor, and to everybody at Putnam/Berkley who made this work possible, especially John. Thanks for making this novice look and sound so good.

And finally, again, to my husband, Robert. Without your love and encouragement—and support—I am not sure that I would have accomplished half of what I have in this last year . . . or in this life, for that matter. It's true what they say—behind every great woman . . . I love you.

Thank you all.

Foreword

Over the past thirty years, there has been a revolution in the way Americans relate to their food. As a nation, we now know all about the dangers of fats, the risks of food additives and the hazards of sugar. What we often don't know is what to do about it. Even though we are educated on what's wrong, we lack practical guidance on the steps necessary to establish a way of eating that is healthy, delicious and practical. That's why I have long been a supporter of Christina Pirello's cooking classes and am so pleased that she has now put her refreshing approach to natural foods cooking in a book.

In my work as a health educator, I have seen the idealism of the natural foods movement of the '60s and '70s absorbed into the American culture. For the most part, this is a good thing; we can now buy tofu and organic vegetables in many supermarkets. But many of the most important messages of healthy eating are getting lost in the shuffle. It is still the truth that changing food patterns would bring down the rise of degenerative disease faster than any other single thing we could do. The increased use of fast food is a sad testimony to the fact that we still don't get the message. It is going to take a continued effort and education till we get the good news about the health benefits of freshly prepared food out of the fringes of society and into the mainstream. Using organic foods, grown without the use of chemicals, is just as much about social responsibility and environmental awareness as it is about personal health. This idea is basic to appreciating this book.

Christina understands the importance of food as a center of family and community. Her kitchen is a mecca for friends, and great food is always on the way for her lucky guests. Hundreds of people in Philadelphia have come to count on the community dinners she and her husband, Robert, sponsor. These dinners serve not only as a source of a great meal, but also feature after-dinner lectures on health care, nutrition and personal development. Her powerful recovery from serious disease through the use of nutrition has shaped her respect for the healing power of food, which lies at the foundation of this book.

I have eaten many meals with Christina and Robert. I have seen her whip up leftovers into a tasty meal or create gourmet treats that rival anything you would be served in the best of restaurants. Creativity and care are always present. She knows that if people are going to make any significant change in their diet, the food better fill our needs for taste and variety. Christina has crafted a book that takes natural whole foods cooking out of the arena of stuffy self-righteousness and into the mainstream. She has done it without sacrificing a bit of concern for the quality of ingredients or healthful preparation.

I invite you to take this journey into Christina's kitchen. What you will find there is a fresh look at recreating a kitchen that is truly a source of health and joy. Enjoy.

BILL TARA
Boulder, Colorado

COOKING THE WHOLE FOODS WAY

INTRODUCTION

You are what you eat. A tired cliché or the simple truth? Over the years, this little axiom has been bandied about, commercialized, bastardized and, even worse, trivialized to the point where most of us laugh when we hear it. But the fact is, nothing could be closer to the truth. Food creates who we are, how we feel, how we act—and react.

The kitchen is the true heart of any home. It is also a place of transformation—where the food prepared creates the people that consume it. Cooks bring together ingredients, transform them into meals, and create the energy that people take into the world with them. Never thought of food in those terms? Well, the reality of the situation is just that. Food creates us and all that we are and will become.

When I discovered macrobiotics, I was in a health crisis of mammoth proportions. I was twenty-six years old and had been diagnosed with an acute form of leukemia; I was what doctors call terminally ill. At best, with all manner of experimental protocols, I was given three to six months to live. I have to tell you, nothing gets your attention quite so quickly as five doctors telling you that your life is virtually over.

I will never forget the day I was diagnosed. It was a lovely spring day, sunny and fragrant with the blossoming buds of the season. I was going to what I thought was a routine follow-up visit to a physical exam I had recently had—part of my new lease on life after the death of my mother.

In retrospect, I should have seen this coming, seen the signs in my own health, but more important, I should have gauged the somber mood in the doctor's office as a portent of the bad news that was to come. But I was so filled with the spirit of the season that I blithely followed the receptionist to the conference room, fully expecting to be declared in relatively good health, although anemic, a condition that had plagued me since early childhood. I was, instead, diagnosed with terminal cancer.

I remember standing in the elevator, counting the floors of my descent, fighting back my panic by memorizing the pattern in the carpet on the floor. Passing through the lobby, I remember staring into a mirror and thinking that this was not the face of a dying person.

Stepping into the street, I was blinded by the sunlight and assaulted by the life that surrounded me: people going about their business as though nothing bad could happen in their lives. I wanted to scream. Instead, I returned home to my quiet apartment to examine my options.

After a sleepless night, I had reached at least one decision. I would not be returning to the doctors' offices—not on their terms, anyway. There had to be another way to approach this. I couldn't believe that my only options were devastating, experimental chemotherapies, followed by certain death.

The next day dawned clear and warm—another perfect spring day—almost mocking me, or rather, I know now, daring me. Walking to work, I decided to take the challenge. I would beat this disease, on my own, my way—no doctors, no chemical treatments. Just to get the diagnosis, I had been pushed, poked and injected in places I didn't even know I could be pushed, poked and injected. Once resolved, I realized that I was absolutely clueless as to where to start. Undaunted, I prayed for guidance and found it in the most surprising place.

Steve Feinberg was the quintessential advertising man. I was new to Philadelphia, and Steve had made it his personal business to see that my acclimation to my new home was enjoyable and easy. In a short time, we had become the best of friends.

I told him about my illness and we sat in my cluttered office for what seemed like hours, not speaking. Finally, after the longest time, Steve looked up, a grin lighting up his face. Declaring himself the answer to my prayers, he told me about a friend of his who ate this strange diet—a macrobiotic diet—that could cure cancer. I remember thinking that as much as I loved my friend, he was nuts. Next thing I knew, I would be jetting off to Barcelona to have my blood boiled at a Jesuit monastery. Steve met my resistance by phoning his friend and arranging for us to meet.

To say that I was leery of this meeting is an understatement. I stopped at a local natural foods store, asking what, in fact, macrobiotics was. The owner's cavalier reply was that the macrobiotic diet was some sort of fanatical approach to vegetarianism. Just great. I had been a vegetarian since I was about fourteen years old and had developed cancer, so what possible good would this diet do me? But, Steve was so enthusiastic, I resolved not to disappoint him and decided to hear this fellow out. I truly had nothing to lose, after all.

My first meeting with Robert Pirello centered around the meal he had painstakingly prepared for me. His gentle manner put me instantly at ease and his confidence in the macrobiotic approach to health was infectious. My first macrobiotic meal consisted of simple miso soup with onions and daikon, a rice salad dotted with colorful blanched vegetables, arame (a sea vegetable) with sautéed carrots and onions, grilled tempeh with a light mustard sauce, corn on the cob (finally, something I recognized) and steamed collard greens. Finding the food interesting at best, I left Robert with mixed feelings about all this. He had given me a book to read, *The Cancer Prevention Diet* by Michio Kushi, with only one request—that I read it with an open mind. No commitment, no decision. Just read.

So I did. I began with the section on leukemia, but then I read more and more and more—all night, in fact. The more I read, the more amazed I became. Finally, as the sun rose, I slammed the book shut, thinking that this was either the best kept secret in the world, or the biggest hustle I had ever come across. I really hadn't decided which at that point.

My mind was made up the next day during lunch with Robert. While he assured me that he would help me along, with everything from the shopping to showing me a few cooking tricks, what sold me was his observation that my other options were extremely limited—namely none. Laughing in spite of my predicament, I agreed to try out the macrobiotic approach to regaining my health.

And so I began my journey. Robert took me shopping at the neighborhood natural foods shop, loading my cart with foods I didn't recognize and whose names I could barely pronounce. Now, I love a challenge as much as the next person, but we were talking about my life here. How was I ever going to learn to prepare foods that I was completely unfamiliar with—foods that were supposed to save my life—when I couldn't even identify most of them?

At first, I read everything I could get my hands on, and tried recipe after recipe, mostly failing miserably, preparing tasteless, burnt, or undercooked meals. I grew quite disheartened and my health continued to decline. Robert constantly encouraged me and offered help, but I was determined to do this on my own. Then I read a book by George Ohsawa, the "father of macrobiotics," and discovered that the key to my health was in keeping things simple. So I consulted Robert, got a few quick cooking lessons from him, and pared down my diet to include only the most basic, simple ingredients: whole grains, steamed greens, miso soup, small amounts of beans and sea vegetables and an occasional root vegetable dish to keep my strength up. I read cookbooks like novels and began studying macrobiotics as though my life depended on it—which it did. I cooked and cooked and read and read. I mastered all the basics. Robert and I had endless discussions about what I was doing. He became my guide and my mentor. (We also fell completely in love, but that was later.) I began to see changes in my health, all positive at first—more vitality, more strength, incredible changes in my blood work—changes that prompted my doctors to say that I was in remission. Every blood test I took indicated incredible improvements in all of my counts—platelets, hemoglobin, white cells.

To make a long story short, I recovered my health completely; much to the shock and disbelief of my doctors. After a long, torturous thirteen months of cooking, improving my condition and struggling with the discharge of toxins that encompassed everything from severe nausea to blinding headaches to itchy rashes, my blood was declared perfectly normal, totally free of leukemic cells—cancer free.

That was thirteen years ago. Since then, my life has been transformed—in my kitchen. Oh, the things I have discovered, not only about my own health, but about life, about the universe, about all things great and small, to turn a familiar phrase. It's as though layers of fog lift from my consciousness as I discover more and more. But the greatest gift I have received from macrobiotics has been the ability to become responsible for my own life and health.

And it all began in the kitchen. Looking back, I transformed my life and health in that room. As I struggled with my cooking, I struggled with my health. My health and cooking abilities improved simultaneously. I discovered that the key to good health is so simple that most people miss it. The single element in our lives over which we have the most control is the food we eat. The quality and quantity of the food we eat directly determines the kind of people we become. We create ourselves—our personalities, our outlook, how we act and interact and react to what life sends our way. Okay, I admit that there are other factors that contribute to who we are, but food creates a strong foundation upon which we can build.

I began to study the art of food in earnest; reading, cooking classes, and, most important, cooking. I mean, I had cooked all of my life, but now I began to learn about the effect food has on us. As I studied, I learned that human beings are products of Mother Nature, products of our environment; that we don't live on nature but are part of nature; and that through an understanding of this, we can reveal our true selves and understand our deepest nature. We begin to create the life we live in our kitchen.

See, there is more to food than food. There is the cook—the person who transforms ingredients into the food we eat, transforms us into the people we become. Think about it. We combine fresh, tender lettuce with crisp cucumbers and peppery radishes to create refreshing salads to cool our bodies in the summer months. Hearty winter stews give us vitality and warming strength to face the chilling temperatures of winter. Food and the way we prepare it, the wholeheartedness of spirit that we bring to each meal is what nurtures us through our lives.

When I began my cooking, I was taught mostly by my family, some of the most masterful, intuitive chefs with whom I have ever worked. There wasn't a cook in my family who could give ingredient amounts or cooking times. They never tasted as they cooked. All my questions were met with the same response: "Listen to the food—cook with your eyes and ears and nose, not just your stomach."

"How can you tell when something is done?" I would ask my mother. "Why do you think we have forks?" was her response. My mother taught me commonsense cooking: if a sauce cooks down too much, add liquid; if an ingredient for a recipe is missing, substitute something else.

Today, people have moved away from cooking because it is so complicated. We have become so locked into cookbooks and recipes that understanding and spontaneity have been lost. It's no wonder that cooking, menu planning or dinner parties turn people into nervous wrecks, trying to orchestrate the meals and praying that dishes turn out right. Develop an understanding of food and how ingredients work together, and cooking becomes an act of pure joy: How can the act of nourishment be anything but?

All it really takes to make cooking an exhilarating experience is an understanding of food and its energy and a mastery of a few basic cooking techniques. Becoming a student of life and listening to your intuition teaches you to create food that always turns out right—more often than not better than when you follow someone else's idea. Understanding food as energy, along with mastering some basic cooking techniques, will open up a whole new culinary world. You will find that most really great whole foods cooking comes from stretching the imagination and developing a personal style of working with the most humble ingredients. You will stop thinking about recipes and begin thinking in terms of ingredient and flavor combinations.

This is the beginning of freedom in the kitchen—and the end of cooking as a chore. Following simple techniques, using the freshest ingredients, following your taste and intuition, cooking with simplicity and common sense—these are the chief characteristics of whole foods cuisine that make life in the kitchen a joy.

I fell in love with cooking at the age of four. I remember my birthday present that year was a stool that my dad made so that I could reach the countertops to work with my mother in the kitchen. As I grew up, I read cookbooks like most people read novels. I loved everything about the art of nourishing, from shopping for ingredients to preparing the food and even cleaning up—a time I used to reflect on the meal I had just served.

To this day, I love every aspect of cooking. As an artist, I find it one of the most creative outlets I know. But the real reward of cooking is that while most artistic skills require years of practice and study, cooking yields rewards immediately. And the more you cook, the greater your skills and the deeper your understanding of the energy of what you are creating.

In one corner of my kitchen, I have a floor-to-ceiling bookcase holding my prized collection of international cookbooks and magazines; everything from simple macrobiotic books to the epitome of gourmet cuisine from the greatest chefs in the world. I keep my books close at hand, because, while my own diet and understanding of food has changed dramatically, my cookbooks still serve me as constant sources of inspiration. Since learning that food is energy, that food creates who we are and how we act, these books have become more valuable to me than ever. I have learned to see recipes with new eyes, adapting and changing ingredients to create the energy I desire.

This cookbook is designed to help you understand what I have been rambling on about—understanding that the energy of food unlocks an entire world of culinary adventure. It makes cooking a natural extension of your life, not a burden to be dealt with as quickly and painlessly as possible . . . or worse yet, something to let someone else handle for you. I would never want to give anyone that much power over my destiny. I love being responsible for each day, each adventure, each challenge or difficulty.

Filled with delicious recipes and ideas for creating wonderful, healthy meals, this book is also a book that hopefully will make you think about what you are feeding yourself and your family. I offer you what I have discovered on my journey and hope that this volume encourages you to make your own discoveries as you make your own journey. Remember that there is more to cooking than meets the eye.

Oh, one more thing. My family used to say that the best food you could ever eat is the food you prepare in your own home. So when you prepare food, see with more than your eyes, hear with more than your ears, and taste with more than your appetite. Cook with respect and gratitude for all the abundance that our Mother has provided. Keep a peaceful, harmonious mind and cook wholeheartedly. To cook is to live. Enjoy all of it.

WHAT IS MACROBIOTICS?

Macrobiotics or whole foods cuisine carries with it a lot of baggage; a lot of misconceptions and myths surround its practice. Is it a religion? Is it Oriental? Is it a deprived, nutritionally deficient diet practiced by old hippies? Or is it that rice and seaweed diet? And the most widespread myth, that macrobiotics is complicated to practice, clouded with exotic ingredients, bound up by all manner of rules with little flexibility. Well, once and for all, let's clear up what the practice of macrobiotics is all about. Macrobiotics is a life-style that hearkens back to a more traditional way of living and eating.

No matter what that tradition may be—Italian, Polish, Irish, Jewish, Greek, Asian—every culture is steeped in traditions that are based on a connection with nature, with the environment in which we live. So don't be trapped in misconceptions.

Macrobiotics is simply about living naturally in harmony with everything around us, about realizing that we are part of everything around us. Macrobiotics is an understanding that food is energy, that everything that we eat becomes part of us and helps create who we become. An understanding of food as energy makes it easy to create delicious, healthful meals. An understanding of food frees us from any rules because there is no more mystery. The macrobiotic approach to cooking is joyous and free of restrictions that make cooking a chore.

Whole foods cooking is about freedom. It's not about the rigid techniques and rules that make cuisine more like an institution in some cultures. Whole foods cooking is about intuition, about listening to that little voice inside you that tells you the truth. You know the voice, the one that society has trained us to ignore; the one that, when ignored, leads invariably to regret. With understanding, that voice is the only guide, guru, mentor or teacher that we will ever need.

Ingredients are at the core of good natural cooking. My theory is that cooking begins with the shopping. The freshness and quality of your ingredients are just as important as your cooking technique. The final outcome of the dish depends on that fact. Shopping itself should be a pleasure. I remember shopping with my grandmother.

She never shopped with a list. Availability and freshness of foods dictated our menus for each meal. She and I would go to the market, see what looked best, and plan our meals around these things.

THE BASICS

There are foods, recipes and techniques that compose the basic understanding of food energy. Whenever I teach a beginning cooking class, I liken the basics to learning the art of pottery making. Before you can become truly creative at this, or at any other art or craft, you need to master some basic techniques, understand concepts and learn to work with new ingredients. If you never learn how to center a pile of clay on the potter's wheel, you can never truly branch off into wild, creative outpourings of your talents. The same goes for cooking.

Macrobiotic or whole foods cooking is truly unique. With a selection of simple, natural ingredients, delicious, nutritionally balanced meals can be created. The cook determines the impact of various dishes, creating the energy that will nourish the household. Strong cooking, with more salt, fire, time and pressure will concentrate the effects of foods, while lighter, fresher foods will produce a more relaxed, gentle energy quality in foods. A masterful, intuitive cook will manage these energies according to the needs and desires of those he or she cooks for.

Variety is the key to good whole foods cooking. A wide selection of foods, chosen from whole grains, beans and bean products, all manner of seasonal vegetables from land and sea, fresh seasonal fruits, nuts, seeds and other food choices, are the ingredients that will compose your diet. Various cooking methods, from boiling and blanching, to sautéing and roasting as well as cutting styles will all be combined to create certain dishes. Of course, seasoning and condiments create supplemental flavors to support and enhance the natural tastes of your ingredients, changing the energy inherent in any food.

Variety extends past cooking styles and ingredients—all the way to the seasons. Seasonal cooking is as basic to healthy cooking as any organic ingredient you may use. In a temperate climate (the typical four-season weather with which we are most familiar), conditions vary from cool to cold to warm to hot. As a result, our cooking needs to change as frequently as the seasons. Spring and summer cooking, as you might guess, is lighter, fresher, taking greater advantage of the seasons' abundance of fruits and vegetables. There seems to be no end to fresh salads, dressings and quick-cooked dishes to accommodate our tastes and give us plenty of time to enjoy the outdoors. Autumn and winter focus more on heartier soups, stews and casseroles; longer-cooked grain and bean dishes, drawing from the harder, stronger root vegetables, sweet winter squash, whole beans and grains. While spring and summer take us out of the kitchen and into the garden, picking freshly grown produce and cooking it as little as possible, autumn and winter bring us back to the hearth, stewing, simmering and baking hearty, warming dishes to shield us from the harsh cold outdoors.

Now all of that is just great, if you live in one of the heavily populated temperate climates of our world. But what if you choose the world of suntans and sandals—life in a tropical region? Well, if that is the case, then you would adjust your cooking accordingly. Sure, you would focus more consistently on lighter, fresher foods, but you would also need to employ enough strong, cooked foods to keep you hale and hearty. You would choose from the foods indigent to your home and culture. You would work with what is native to your environment.

Sound complicated? Truly, it's not. It is simply a matter of understanding that food is energy and that the energy of food creates the energy that fuels us in our lives.

As I have said before (about a million times by now, I think), a healthy whole foods diet is centered around the use of whole cereal grains. These grains are supplemented by the use of fresh, seasonal vegetables, beans and bean products, sea vegetables, fresh fruits and soups.

A balanced whole foods macrobiotic diet consists of 50 to 60 percent whole cereal grains, 30 percent fresh vegetables (choosing from leafy greens, root and round, ground vegetables), 5 percent soups and sea vegetables, 10 to 15 percent beans and bean products. Any other foods, fresh fruits, nuts and seeds and fish are generally taken as supplemental foods, in small amounts on occasion.

GETTING STARTED

I know what you're thinking. Easy for someone who has been cooking since she was four years old and she not only loves cooking, but she does it for a living. But what about those of us who can barely get a meal on the table after a day of work? She wants us to create new recipes when we can hardly get the shopping done from week to week. Well, relax. This section of the book is designed to help ease the burden of making the transition to a healthier, whole foods–based diet, from shopping to menu planning.

Shopping

Now some of you may be thinking that this could make shopping more difficult. Not true. Isn't shopping for clothing or books fun? We enjoy wandering through the shops, carefully choosing our purchases. When something looks or feels right, we know it. Simply think that way when shopping for food as well. This attitude toward food helps you to rediscover the freedom and pleasure of shopping for food. Always remember that you are nourishing yourself. Don't you deserve the very best? Aren't we worth it?

My mother would talk to me while we did the family grocery shopping. Never buy food that comes prewrapped or precut, she would say. It's not fresh, so it will taste flat. She went from farmers' market to farmers' market, shopping only where she could touch, feel and smell the vegetables and fruits; where she knew the fish and meat was fresh. I tell you this, not to reminisce, but to illustrate that shopping this way adds pleasure to thinking about and preparing your meals.

Natural foods cooking seems to be shrouded in mystery, reputed to employ strange, exotic ingredients cooked in bizarre ways. Well, the fact is you can purchase most basic whole foods in your neighborhood supermarkets. You may need to supplement your weekly shopping with occasional trips to a natural foods store, but for the most part, you'll be able to find all that you'll need in your local market.

In larger supermarkets and gourmet stores, you'll find a wide variety of whole grains and grain products, like brown rice, barley, oats, polished rice, corn grits, cornmeal, whole-wheat pastas and whole-grain flours. Even buckwheat (kasha), couscous and bulgur wheat can be found in gourmet sections of markets. Dried beans abound in supermarkets, everything from lentils, to chick-peas, to black and white beans, to split peas and kidney beans, even tofu. And while these foods may not always be organic, they will nourish you and yours quite nicely.

You also don't need to go on a quest to purchase good-quality oils and condiments. Most supermarkets carry extra-virgin olive oil and other cold-pressed, unrefined oils. Nuts and seeds are readily available. You can even find some good-quality mustards, pickles, spices and herbs. Just read labels and try to avoid foods with preservatives or any chemical ingredient that you can't pronounce!

In terms of seasonings, my advice is to make that trip to the nearest natural foods store. You always want to use the best-quality seasonings, especially salt and salt products like miso and soy sauce. For your salt, you will want to choose a white, slightly moist, unrefined sea salt over any commercial brand. Why? Sea salt is simply dried from the sea, with all its nutrients intact, while commercial brands have been chemically processed, laced with sugar to ensure pourability and re-enriched with minerals that were stripped away during processing. Soy sauce is a naturally fermented soybean and salt condiment. Commercial brands have been artificially fermented, colored and processed, making it quite difficult to digest and assimilate the salt. Natural soy sauces, on the other hand, have been traditionally fermented, ensuring that the salt and soybeans have been completely broken down for better digestion and superior taste. Miso can only be purchased in natural foods stores or Oriental markets. I prefer the brands found in natural foods stores, because more often than not, the brands found in Oriental markets have been processed with sugar, which I choose not to eat.

And, of course, fresh produce, now featured at all markets, is one department that is fast growing because the demand for fresh fruits and vegetables is on the rise. Just take care when choosing produce to pick items that are unwrapped and unwaxed; these will always be fresher.

I think that you should become familiar with your neighborhood natural foods store. There is a whole community of people to consult for help, support, and all manner of information. Many natural foods stores sponsor cooking classes and product demonstrations and provide recipe handouts to familiarize people with certain products.

The quality of food available in natural foods stores is usually superior to that of anything available in regular supermarkets. Organic grains, beans, and produce not only taste better (really!), but they retain far more of their vital life force than other foods, and so are superior to standard fare. Choosing certified organic products is a way in which you can avoid eating foods laced with pesticides and fungicides.

If you choose to dive into healthy cooking, you'll need to stock your pantry with a variety of fresh fruits and vegetables, of course. But you'll also need a few other staples to get started. Short-grain brown rice, barley, millet and oats are grains that you'll want on hand at all times. A variety of dried beans, including lentils, chick-peas, azukis and black beans will give you a good start. Finally, stock your cupboards with good-quality soy sauce, extra-virgin olive oil, cold-pressed sesame and corn oil, sea salt and some good-quality herbs and spices, like basil, dried chiles and rosemary. Barley or brown-rice miso, umeboshi vinegar, brown-rice vinegar and balsamic vinegar should round out your pantry nicely. With these basics you can walk into the kitchen at any time and create a simple yet delicious meal in no time. I told you the transition would be painless. A well-stocked pantry allows you to grocery shop without a plan, to buy what looks freshest, to purchase on instinct—with your appetite—and plan your meals accordingly.

Equipping Your Kitchen

Any kitchen, from compact, efficient ones with barely enough room for a cutting board, to gadget-laden, spacious culinary heavens, pours forth nourishment based on the cook who works in it. The kitchen is where food is literally transformed. The warmth and love that exist in these simple rooms make us who we are. All it takes for any kitchen to be productive is organization and order.

Whether a novice in the kitchen or a seasoned chef, you will need a bit of reorganization to make a smooth transition to healthier cooking. First, clean the kitchen thoroughly. This kind of ritual will help you create a new atmosphere of respect for yourself and the food you will be preparing.

And besides, there is nothing better to work in than a clean, orderly, pleasant environment. I personally find cooking to be much more relaxing when everything is in its place.

Create a space in which to organize your ingredients. Empty a cabinet or pantry section to accommodate your dried foods. Try to create a place where your foods can be organized together, making your job easier. Store dried foods such as grains and beans in glass jars with good seals to maintain their freshness. As much as possible, keep your ingredients close at hand, in one place, so that looking for ingredients while cooking doesn't cause you stress. I have found it easiest to keep like ingredients together—all the grains on one shelf in the pantry, beans in their own section, condiments and oils all together—so that everything is easy to locate.

Lucky for us, whole foods cooking requires very few fancy appliances. The best cookware is stainless, cast iron, stoneware or porcelain-covered cast iron. Aluminum is not a great choice for cookware because its soft texture can cause toxic elements to leach into the food. Some of the basic tools you will need to cook easily and well include a great vegetable cutting knife—your most important tool (stainless steel or carbon steel)—a sharpening steel or stone, a large wooden cutting board (not a postage-stamp-sized one), a vegetable brush for scrubbing, a colander and a strainer. Pots that you will find indispensable include a large soup pot, a heavy pot or pressure cooker for grain and bean cooking, a couple of flame deflectors, a large and small skillet—either stainless or cast iron, preferably one of each—a couple of medium and small saucepans. Rounding out

your basic equipment list are wooden spoons of various shapes and sizes, spatulas, a whisk, a vegetable peeler, a ginger grater, a steamer basket, a wok, mixing bowls, measuring cups, a food processor, a food mill and any other kitchen gadget that makes you feel comfortable.

PUTTING IT ALL TOGETHER

Working in the kitchen is an art, one that is cultivated with practice and time. One of the basic skills you will need to function smoothly is organization. A bit of planning can take away the anxiety that oftentimes surrounds whole foods meals, especially when you are new to this style of cooking. Let me walk you through a typical day in my kitchen to show you how you just a bit of forethought can make cooking a part of life.

Our day begins early, around 6:30 in the morning. Robert and I get up and toss a coin for who makes breakfast, but he usually takes on the task willingly. Breakfast is usually a simple meal of miso soup for him, and a soft, cooked porridgelike grain, with or without vegetables, and a side of lightly cooked green vegetables for both of us. Once the meal is cooking, Robert jumps in the shower and gets ready for work, while I put the finishing touches on breakfast and quickly put together lunch for us—usually leftovers from dinner the night before with a quick freshly cooked vegetable dish added. As we leave for work, I quickly decide if I will need to soak beans for that evening's meal and check the refrigerator for any produce I might want to pick up on the way home.

I arrive home well before my husband, around 5:00 P.M. Before I even think about cooking for us (remember, I spend my days cooking), I take a relaxing shower to help wash away the day and calm my nerves so that I can cook with a clear mind and relaxed heart. The last thing I want to do is incorporate any stress from my day into our evening meal, the time of day we unwind and relax together.

The average dinner in our home consists of a simple soup of fresh vegetables, sometimes with beans and grains, sometimes not. Our main meal will include a whole-grain dish of some type—brown rice, millet with vegetables, barley stew, corn polenta with a simple sauce or whole-grain noodles. I round out the meal with two or three simple vegetable dishes: a root vegetable stew, fresh steamed greens, oven-roasted winter squash and onions, perhaps a sautéed sea vegetable and, two or three times a week, a vegetable and bean stew or tofu stir-fry, and all kinds of salads in the summer months.

Variety is most important to me. It is the key to vitality. However, I don't have the time to cook seven or eight dishes each time I prepare dinner. So I focus on creating different dishes each evening. While I might only prepare soup, grain, and one or two other dishes, they always incorporate different ingredients and different cooking styles to ensure that we eat a wide variety of foods and get adequate nutrients as a result.

Preparing an average dinner in my home usually takes a bit over an hour, time well spent in my opinion. When we are properly nourished with good-quality food, freshly cooked, we become much more adept at handling all the adventures life throws at us. So when planning menus, I try to incorporate a whole grain; some kind of protein dish such as beans, tofu, or tempeh; and a variety of seasonal vegetables, drawing from leafy greens, root veggies, and sweet ground vegetables, combining them in a few simple dishes.

Leftovers and cooking ahead play a part in my cooking. I prefer to cook food fresh as much as possible, but I do not discount the value of having a container of cooked chickpeas, lentils, or other beans to use as a base to create another dish. And bean soups always seem to taste better the next day. Leftover grains can easily be resteamed or cooked with fresh vegetables to create a quick, simple stew or stir-fry. And I never underestimate the value of tofu and tempeh as bases for quick protein dishes.

THE BEGINNING

My best advice to novice whole foods chefs is this. Master a few basic techniques and recipes, and cook these until you are comfortable. Keep your meals simple and delicious. One or two truly satisfying dishes will go a long way toward making a smooth transition to healthier foods. After you have mastered a few techniques and have become familiar with your ingredients, let your imagination and intuition be your teacher. Relax and create.

I know what you are thinking. All this sounds great, but how exactly do you go about planning a menu? What makes a balanced meal, now that animal protein is not the featured entree?

Dinner is always the greatest challenge for cooks—and the easiest trap to fall into, especially now, living in the age of fast-food take-outs. However, I also realize that it is difficult to face the task of preparing a meal from scratch every day, which is where planning comes in. Simply starting grains or beans in the morning or the evening before can simplify the act of getting dinner on the table in less than an hour, without becoming a nervous wreck.

I'm trained as a chef, so for me, timing is everything. One of my most valued skills is knowing what cooking times are required for what foods, so that my meal comes together, all dishes being ready at the same time, more or less. So, obviously, long-cooking dishes, like grains and beans start cooking first, with the lighter, fresher dishes being cooked as meal preparation progresses. I know that only seems like common sense—and it is—but it is one of those overlooked facts that people often forget.

I know I said that leftovers play only a small part in my cooking, but I should clarify that a bit. When I cook a meal from scratch, sometimes, there is something leftover. I use those foods to create other dishes in subsequent meals. Very often, leftover cooked beans get refried and wrapped in tortillas or stewed vegetables serve as the base for a hearty soup. The most important thing to remember about leftovers is to add some fresh ingredient. Do something with the food; don't just take leftovers from the refrigerator and eat them. Add some life to them by creating a fresh dish with the leftover foods as the base. By themselves, leftovers lack vitality and can make you tired. Adding fresh ingredients infuses leftover food with new vitality.

Many people who work long hours have told me that their saving grace is carving out a block of time, usually on weekends, to cook a variety of food in batches—pickles, condiments, a big pot of beans or soup. Then on subsequent nights, these cooked foods become everything from croquettes, to burgers, to stews to stir-fry dishes. Filling in the gaps with quick-cooking foods like couscous, bulgur, tofu, and tempeh, nicely balanced with lightly cooked fresh vegetables, goes a long way to helping you put a balanced meal on the table without a lot of fuss. Don't forget the value of noodles: many is the night that I have put a hearty meal on the table in about half an hour with noodles as the base, rounded out with fresh vegetable dishes and crusty bread.

Another tip I'd like to pass along, not only to beginning chefs but to anyone who loves to cook, is that food doesn't have to be complicated to be delicious. The taste comes with the skill of the cook. All whole foods have a character of their own just waiting to be brought forth in any variety of dishes. By keeping recipes simple, with not too many ingredients, your success is virtually ensured. Traditional grain and bean combinations, for instance, serve as inspiration for many contemporary dishes. Can you think of a more satisfying dinner than red bean and vegetable chili served over moist corn bread or rice with freshly cooked vegetables and a light soup? Delicious foods need not be spice-laden, cooked to death or smothered in heavy, complicated sauces to be truly delicious.

Of course, I encourage you to be as creative as you wish. Combine foods as your taste dictates. Draw recipes from other parts of the world, and put them together to create an international meal. Don't be trapped by recipes or rigid plans. I never know how a final menu will turn out. I make a grocery list, but usually it consists of staple items that are running low in my pantry. The availability and freshness of various items will dictate what I will ultimately buy and cook. The sign of a confident cook is flexibility and the ability to adapt. Practice until you get this confidence. It is truly liberating, with delicious rewards for your efforts.

I have found that the best way to minimize cooking stress and to avoid obsessing about what to cook is to keep my pantry and refrigerator well-stocked. At any given time, you should be able to walk in the door and pull together a meal. Careful shopping once or twice a week really helps.

MENU PLANNING

How do you put a balanced meal together? Here are a few basic menu ideas you can use to create some simple whole foods meals on your own. These are designed to give you a place to begin building your own repertoire. The foundation of a whole foods diet is whole cereal grains. Around these foods, I build the rest of my menus. Bean soups or stews, hearty casseroles and light, fresh vegetable dishes complete the picture.

When preparing menus, keep in mind that the concentration should be more on grain and vegetable carbohydrates, rather than proteins from beans or fish or even nuts. Keep protein dishes to a small amount per day, and limit them to only one type of protein. For instance, I don't prepare a bean dish and a dish that includes nuts in the same meal. I wouldn't make a bean soup in a meal that featured a fish entree. Prepare a wide variety of seasonal vegetables in different ways, employing long-

and short-cooking dishes, with an occasional crisp, fresh raw salad thrown in for variety and lighter energy.

When I began cooking, one of the most valuable habits I developed was jotting down my evening menus. The resulting diary not only helped me learn how to balance a meal—grains, beans, varieties of vegetables, soup—but created for me a collection of winning menu combinations that I return to when inspiration is in short supply in the kitchen or when I just want to refresh myself with some old tried and true dishes. And finally, when cooking, remember that whole, natural foods have innate, delicious flavors of their own. They need very little help to release their flavors. So keep seasoning light and delicate to bring forth the true richness of these foods.

The following menu suggestions are all based on recipes that are included in this book. I hope they aid you on your journey toward a healthier way of eating.

Breakfast

Breakfast is literally breaking our overnight fast. Foods eaten for breakfast, as a result, need to help you balance your day. The body needs a gentle nudge in the morning, foods that are easy to digest, not heavy foods that require a lot of work to assimilate. Whole-grain cereals, prepared as soft, creamy porridge are one of the healthiest ways to start the day. Breakfast in our house rarely, if ever, includes heavy, baked flour products like bagels, muffins, or even, toast. These foods are hard and dry, make the body work very hard, and can make us very tired and short on vitality in the long run.

With a little forethought, a healthy breakfast can be ready in the time it takes *you* to get ready. By simply rinsing and soaking grain overnight—or in cold weather, cooking grain all night over low heat—breakfast porridge can be ready in roughly thirty minutes or less. Oatmeal, corn grits, millet, kasha or cracked wheat can be cooked into creamy, nutritious breakfast foods in no time. Served with lightly cooked vegetables and on rare occasions, cooked fruit, like applesauce, breakfast is an easy task.

On those mornings that we have a bit more time, I like to cook whole-grain cereals for a longer period of time to release a more vitalizing energy. Add five parts water to one part oats, barley, rice or any combination of whole grains and cook for about one hour to create a hearty grain porridge. These are the mornings that I might supplement this porridge with scrambled tofu and vegetables or a lightly cooked vegetable dish. Oh, and weekends, those are the mornings for mochi waffles or whole-wheat pancakes with a sweet, fruity sauce.

Of course, there are those inevitable mornings when there is no time for anything—or maybe just a few minutes to pull together an almost-instant breakfast. On those occasions, I might make a quick dish of noodles simmered in a miso broth with vegetables or a quick porridge with leftover cooked grain with some vegetables or some quickly pan-toasted mochi. Bottom line? If you have ten or fifteen minutes, you can have breakfast that doesn't have to be a dry bagel on the run.

You may have noticed by this point, that fruit plays a very small part in my breakfast meals. Fruit contains a great deal of liquid and simple sugars. In general, I have found that these foods are best consumed in small amounts, but especially at breakfast. The simple sugar present in fruits wreak havoc with our blood sugar, creating mood swings and perpetuating hypoglycemia. Lots of fruit and fruit juice in the morning set you up for a roller coaster ride of emotional and energetic ups and downs for the day.

Lunch

Usually a light and simple meal, lunch is easy. You can put together a really satisfying noontime feast from foods you prepared for dinner the evening before. These are the meals most preferred by my husband. A distance runner, he loves to sit down at lunchtime to a full meal composed of a whole-grain dish, lots of fresh vegetables and sometimes a small bean dish.

Many people, however, prefer a simpler lunchtime meal. A bowl of homemade soup and a sandwich can be most satisfying. A sandwich packed with fried tofu or tempeh, smothered with sautéed onions, lettuce, sprouts and spicy mustard, coupled with corn chowder or mushroom-barley soup compose some of my favorite lunches. Some days find me sitting down to a simple lunch of hearty lentil soup with a lightly cooked salad of fresh broccoli, cauliflower, carrots and leafy green vegetables. Other days find me fixing simple lunches of chick-pea hummus with crisp vegetable sticks or toasted pita bread triangles. And whole-grain noodles, simmered in a delicate miso broth laden with vegetables makes a lunch to satisfy the most hearty appetite.

Dinner

Dinner presents a bit more of a challenge than other meals of the day. The family is coming home from a busy day—and they are hungry. It is up to the cook to create meals that nourish and satisfy. Not as difficult a task as you would think. Here is a week's worth of menus, typical of my own household. Pick and choose from these meals to create your own winning combinations.

Pay attention to the way that foods reappear in various dishes on different nights, using up leftover foods to create fresh meals. Note that soups and vegetable dishes are fresh just about every day. That's an effort worth making. The vitality and energy in these foods when cooked fresh are invaluable.

A Week of Dinner Menus

SUNDAY

Pureed squash bisque

Pressure-cooked brown rice with millet

Black bean feijoada

Stewed root vegetables with kombu

Blanched watercress and Chinese cabbage

Creamy orange custard

MONDAY

Miso vegetable soup with noodles

Brown rice and millet croquettes

Oven-baked squash and onions

Sea palm salad

Steamed leafy greens

Lemon-daikon pickle

TUESDAY

Corn chowder

Boiled brown rice with barley

Refried black beans in corn tortillas

Braised vegetable stew

Brussels sprouts with chestnuts and onions

Boiled kale and carrot matchsticks

Stewed apple slices with raisins

WEDNESDAY

Lentil-vegetable soup

Millet with squash and corn

Dried daikon with kombu, carrot and onions

Skillet-steamed broccoli

Whole red onions with rosemary

THURSDAY

Millet-sweet vegetable soup

Brown and wild rice pilaf with corn

Grilled tofu with sweet ginger marinade

Sautéed arame with carrots and onions

Sweet and sour cabbage salad with tart apples

Steamed leafy greens

Italian biscotti

FRIDAY

Italian minestrone soup with white beans

Basil pesto noodles

Sautéed broccoli rapini with yellow summer squash

Miso vegetable soup

Pressure-cooked brown rice with dried

  sweet corn

Sukiyaki vegetables

Tempeh stroganoff

Simple boiled salad with balsamic

  vinaigrette

Apple-cranberry pie

Menu Tips

Creating variety in daily cooking by employing a variety of ingredients is not as hard to handle as it may seem. We are all busy. We don't live in a perfect world where we can spend countless hours in the kitchen creating fresh, delicious meals from scratch. Here are a few tips that I employ on a daily basis in my own kitchen.

I usually make one soup each day and use it for two meals, with a fresh bit of something added to change it and freshen it for the second meal—like another vegetable, an herb, a change in garnish.

Leftover, lightly cooked green vegetables can be tossed with pickles or with vinegar to create a lightly pickled vegetable dish. Stewed or baked vegetables most often find their way into a hearty soup or stew, or can be pureed and seasoned to create a rich sauce for another dish.

Cooked grains are easily incorporated into other dishes, simply resteamed with fresh condiments, stir-fried with vegetables, cooked in a rich stock with root vegetables to create a hearty stew or made into croquettes, nori rolls, rice balls or even grain and vegetable burgers.

Pasta is easy. One meal serves up noodles with a rich vegetable sauce or gravy and the leftover, undressed pasta is served smothered in a delicate, vegetable-laden broth, making a fabulous one-dish meal. Leftover beans are used in soups, stews, stir-fries; pureed into flavorful pâtés and dips; and combined with veggies and a sauce to make delicious casseroles.

What I am really trying to say here is that you can create a whole range of dishes with leftovers, when you need to do that. I must say again that I still advocate fresh cooking wherever and whenever possible, but leftovers can be a valuable tool when used properly. Just take care that the majority of your diet isn't comprised of leftover food. Nothing replaces the vitality of fresh foods, and leftovers are only meant to supplement fresh cooking. Face it, there is no escape from cooking if you wish to achieve optimum health. But by adding fresh ingredients here and there to leftover foods, you can create different energies to nourish yourself and your loved ones.

HOW MUCH DO I COOK?

This guide will provide you with a base to work from. These guidelines indicate how many people, on average, certain amounts of foods will feed. While these may vary slightly based on people's activity level and appetite, I have found the quantities to be sound in determining the quantities I need to prepare to sufficiently nourish those I cook for.

Whole grains	1 cup uncooked	3 people
Noodles	8 ounces	2 people
Morning porridge	1 cup grain cooked in 5 cups water	3–4 people
Soup	1 cup	1 person
Whole beans	1 cup	4 people
Tofu	1 pound	4–5 people
Tempeh	8 ounces	2–3 people
Lightly cooked leafy green vegetables	1 cup, raw	1 person
Stewed root vegetables	2 cups raw = 1 1/2 cups cooked	2 people
Pressed salads	3 cups raw = 1 1/2 cups pressed	2–3 people
Sea vegetables	1/2 cup, dried	2–3 people
Garnishes	1/2 to 1 teaspoon	as desired

GLOSSARY

I can practically hear your sigh of relief when you found this section. Some of the natural ingredients I use may sound mysterious and exotic to you, but don't panic. While they may be new to you, it may be comforting to remember that most of the strange ingredients used in my recipes are, in fact, very traditional foods which have been used in various cultures for many, many years. Draw from these cultures to develop your own style in your healthy kitchen.

Become familiar with the more exotic foods you find in these pages. The more you cook, the more fun you will have experimenting with different foods and flavors. Preparing natural foods can be a wonderful culinary adventure. This section can help you to understand what it is you are buying and how to use it to create delicious, healthy meals.

Agar-agar Also called "kanten" in Oriental shops, agar is a gelatinlike food made from various types of red algae. The algae fronds are harvested, dried and boiled in iron kettles. The resulting liquid is allowed to set and is then placed in the sun to dry and bleach. This process takes about ten days. After drying, the flaky gelatin is finally packaged in bars.

Agar flakes are made from another type of sea vegetable. A more modern product, agar flakes are easier to process and use, with more concentrated bonding properties.

Almonds Fruit kernels of the almond tree. They keep best when purchased in their thin brown skins, which protect their freshness and flavor.

Amaranth A very tiny, brownish-yellow seed, high in protein and lysine. It has an earthy, nutty flavor and cooks quite quickly.

Amasake A fermented sweet rice drink with the texture of milk. It is a creamy base for custards, puddings and frostings, not to mention a wonderfully satisfying drink on its own.

Anasazi beans A native American burgundy and white bean, similar in taste and texture to pinto beans. Their slightly sweet taste makes them ideal in Mexican-style bean dishes.

Arame A large-leaf sea vegetable, arame is finely shredded and boiled before drying and packaging for selling. Since it is precooked, it requires far less cooking time than other sea vegetables. One of the milder-tasting sea plants, it is a great source of protein and minerals like calcium and potassium.

Arrowroot A high-quality starch made from a tropical tuber of the same name, used for thickening much the same way as cornstarch is used. Arrowroot has virtually no taste and becomes clear when cooked, making it ideal as a thickener for puddings, gravies, and sauces. Less expensive than kuzu, it can be used interchangeably in recipes.

Azuki beans Azuki beans are small and very compact, with a deep, reddish-brown color. These tiny beans are a staple in the Far East. Originally cultivated in Japan and revered for their healing properties, these small red beans are quite low in fat and reputed to be more digestible than most other beans as well as a good source of vitamin B-12, potassium and iron.

Baking powder A leavening agent made up of baking soda, cream of tartar, and either cornstarch or arrowroot. Double-acting powder releases carbon dioxide on contact with liquid, creating the air pockets responsible for the light texture in baked goods. Always try to purchase nonaluminum baking powder so that sodium aluminum sulfate is not released into your foods, possibly compromising your health.

Baking powder is more perishable than you might think, not lasting much beyond the expiration date on the can. Store in a cool, dry place for the best shelf life.

Balsamic vinegar Italian vinegar made from white Trebbiano grapes. The vinegar becomes a deep, rich amber color during aging in wooden barrels. The best balsamic vinegars are syrupy, a bit sweet, and a little more expensive than other vinegars, but well worth it.

Bancha (See *Kukicha*)

Barley Said to be the oldest cultivated grain, barley is native to Mesopotamia, where it was mainly used to make bread and ferment beer. Used by ancient cultures since the dawn of time, barley even served as currency in Sumeria. In Europe, barley has been replaced by wheat and rye but is still the staple grain of many countries in the Far and Middle East, Asia, and South America. In modern cultures, barley serves to make everything from livestock feed to malted whisky to tea to miso. However, by itself, barley is a great, low-fat grain, chock full of nutrients. Delicious when cooked with other whole grains and in soups and salads.

Barley malt A sweetener or grain honey made from sprouted barley that is cooked into a sweet syrup. The barley is simply steeped in water and germinated. The sprouted or malted barley is then heated to bring out the flavor and cooked until a thick syrup forms. The syrup contains dextrin, maltose, various minerals and protein. It adds wonderful depth to baked beans, roasted squash and savory baked goods.

Beans (See individual listings)

Black-eyed peas Medium-size beans with an oblong shape, they have a distinctive black spot on their ivory surface. In the same family as yard-long beans, the pods can grow three feet in length. Native to Africa, black-eyed peas were brought to Europe and North America where they became a staple in cooking, being paired with collard greens for a most delicious supper, nicely complemented with hearty corn bread.

Black soybeans Rounder and more plump than black turtle beans, black soybeans are renowned in Asia for their restorative effects on the reproductive organs. Incredibly sweet and rich, but requiring soaking or roasting and long cooking time, these beans are well worth the extra effort.

Black turtle beans A sturdy, very satisfying common bean. Earthy and mildly sweet, these beans go well with stronger seasonings, like those commonly used in Brazilian, Caribbean and Mexican dishes, and make great, creamy soups.

Bran A fiber-rich layer just beneath the hull of whole grains that protects the endosperm or germ. Bran is a great source of calcium, carbohydrates and phosphorous and is the main reason for eating grains in their whole form.

Brown rice vinegar A vinegar traditionally made by the agricultural communities of Japan, it is composed of brown rice, cultured rice (*koji*), seed vinegar from the previous year and well water. The vinegar is then fermented for nine to ten months. Brown rice vinegar has a sharp taste and is used for everything from salad dressings to preserving vegetables. It is also commonly used in sushi rice for flavor and for its preservative properties.

Buckwheat (Kasha) Also known as Saracen corn, buckwheat was reportedly brought to Europe by the Crusaders, although it originated in the Himalayan mountains. In botanical terms, buckwheat is not really a grain; it is actually a member of the rhubarb family, with its fruit or groats that resemble tiny, dark-colored nuts.

Grown under adverse conditions in cold weather, buckwheat is very strengthening and warming, containing more protein than most other grains as well as iron and B vitamins. A natural source of rutic acid, which aids in arterial and circulatory problems, buckwheat is used by many homeopaths for high blood pressure and other circulatory difficulties.

Cooked by itself, buckwheat makes a great porridge, grain dish or even a salad. A very traditional recipe involves sautéing onions and noodles and then tossing together with cooked kasha. Ground into flour, buckwheat is the chief ingredient used to make traditional Japanese soba noodles.

Bulgur (Cracked wheat) Made from whole-wheat berries that are cracked into pieces, enabling it to cook quite quickly. A great breakfast cereal, bulgur is most commonly associated with tabouleh, a marinated bulgur salad combining tomatoes, onions and cucumbers with an aromatic olive oil dressing.

Burdock A wild, hearty plant from the thistle family. According to traditional medicine, this long, dark brown root is renowned as one of nature's finest blood purifiers and skin clarifiers. A strong, dense root vegetable, burdock has a very centering, grounding energy, and is most commonly used in stews and long-simmered sautés.

Cannellini beans Creamy white oval beans most commonly used in the Italian dish *pasta e fagioli*. Their creamy texture makes them ideal for purees, dips, and creamy soups.

Canola oil Expressed from rape seeds, this light oil is substantially lower in saturated fats than any other oil and also contains Omega-3 fatty acids. Virtually tasteless, this is a good oil choice for baking and salad dressings, but kind of bland for sautéing.

Capers Little pickled flower buds, most commonly used in Mediterranean cooking. Salty and briny in taste, they really add flavor to sauces and salads. If they taste too strong for you, simply rinse lightly before use.

Caraway seeds Traditionally used in rye bread, caraway seeds have a distinctive, hearty taste, making them ideal for seasoning savory stews and other vegetable dishes. Their pungent taste is quite strong, so use sparingly.

Carob Renowned as a substitute for chocolate by natural foods enthusiasts, carob truly doesn't taste much like chocolate, so true devotees are rarely fooled. Carob is most commonly used in powdered form, which is made from grinding roasted, tropical pods. Its natural sweet taste and dark, rich color are what gained it its reputation as a substitute for chocolate. It is higher in simple sugars than chocolate; I don't really recommend it.

Cashews A tropical nut quite high in fat, with a rich, luscious flavor for creams and nut milks.

Chervil An aromatic herb with lacy, fernlike leaves that tastes quite like tarragon. It tastes best when used fresh.

Chestnuts Their rich texture and taste belie the fact that chestnuts are in fact quite low in fat, making them an ideal ingredient in many recipes. At their peak in the fall, fresh chestnuts are a wonderful addition to soups, stews and vegetable dishes, and their natural sweet taste makes them a great dessert ingredient. Dried chestnuts are available year-round and, with presoaking, achieve as creamy and sweet a taste and texture as their fresh counterparts.

Chick-peas (Garbanzo beans) Beige round beans with a wonderful nutty taste and creamy texture when cooked. Traditionally used when making hummus, a creamy spread, combining chick-peas with olive oil, lemon juice and a bit of garlic. Also wonderful in bean dishes combined with sweet vegetables or corn as well as in soups and stews.

Chiles Available fresh and dried, they range from mildly spicy to blazing hot. Remember that the real "heat" comes from the seeds, so removing them reduces the "fire." I recommend you wear rubber gloves when removing seeds so the oil, containing capsaicin, doesn't get on your hands—and then into your eyes when you rub them. It takes several hours, even with washing, to remove this oil, so trust me on this one. Ancho, chipotles and jalapeños are the most common varieties used in cooking today.

Chili powder A powdered blend of ground chiles, ranging from mild to hot, combined with oregano, cumin, garlic and salt. Add it slowly to dishes, adjusting the spicy taste as you go along, so your dish doesn't get too hot. The hot taste increases as you cook it.

Chocolate Do I really need to define chocolate? I suppose not, but perhaps I should define its rare appearances in this book. Energetically, chocolate is highly stimulating and agitating, giving the consumer a great high followed by a very depressing crash of blood sugar. Chocolate also loves stealing minerals from our organs and cells, forcing them to pull minerals from our blood for nourishment, causing everything from cravings to overeating. I reserve the use of chocolate for very special occasions.

Corn Native to South America, corn has been used for over ten thousand years. It has become the staple grain for the entire North American continent. Today, corn is cultivated worldwide and is one of the most popular grains used in cooking.

Corn requires hot summer sun and rain to flourish and grows quickly. Often eaten by itself, the popular corn on the cob has practically limitless other culinary uses—flour, meal, grits, tortillas, corn syrup, corn oil, bourbon, and popcorn (from one variety of the grain).

Corn grits A cracked form of dried corn. Corn grits make a great polenta, creamy breakfast cereal or texturizer for soups.

Cornmeal Dried field corn ground into a coarse flour. Used to make creamier polentas, this flour is most commonly used in cornbreads, tortillas and corn chips.

Corn oil A golden-colored oil with a rich, buttery taste, ideally suited to whole grain baking. Its full-bodied texture and light taste give baked goods a moist crumb.

Couscous A staple of North Africa, this rolled durum wheat product has been stripped of its bran and germ, made into a thick paste, steamed and then dried in the form of small granules. It cooks quite quickly and its starchy texture makes it a great ingredient for loaves, patties and soups.

Daikon A long, white radish root with a refreshingly clean, peppery taste. Commonly used in salads and side dishes, soups, and stews. Frequently served in Asian restaurants with fish or oily dishes, since it is reputed to aid in the digestion of fat and protein as well as to help the body to assimilate oil and cleanse organ tissue. Also available in dried, shredded form to be used in various stews and hearty vegetable dishes.

Dulse Dried dulse has a rich, red color, is high in potassium and comes packaged in large, wrinkled leaves. Its salty rich taste makes it a great snack right out of the package. Because it is so delicate, it actually requires little or no cooking, just a quick rinse to remove any debris on the leaves. It adds depth of flavor to hearty soups, stews and bean stews.

Fava beans Available both fresh and dried, favas are used extensively in Mediterranean cooking. These large, chunky beans have a rich, earthy flavor that will remind you of split peas, but they do not get quite as creamy; they retain a soft, potatolike texture.

Flageolets Light ivory beans with a very subtle taste. Highly esteemed in French cooking, these beans are best in simple recipes, which showcase their delicate flavor.

Flax seeds Richer than soybeans in Omega-3 fatty acids and rich in vitamin E, they have a sweet, nutty flavor. When boiled and whipped with apple juice, they make a good binder and leavener in baked goods, in place of eggs. On their own, flax seeds have a laxative effect on the body and so should be consumed in moderation.

Flour Flour is any ground meal of whole grains. Try to choose only whole-grain flours, since these retain a bit of germ and bran and therefore are not completely devoid of nutrients. Also look for stone-ground flours, as these are not processed with extreme heat, which also can destroy nutrients. For the best shelf life, store flour in tightly sealed containers in either the refrigerator or freezer.

Fu A meat substitute developed by vegetarian Buddhist monks, fu is made of dried wheat gluten. A good source of protein, fu can be used in various soups and stews by simply reconstituting it in water.

Ginger A golden-colored, spicy root vegetable with a variety of uses in cooking. It imparts a mild, peppery taste to cooking and is commonly used in stir-fries, sautés, sauces and dressings. Shaped like the fingers of a hand, ginger has the reputation of stimulating circulation with its hot taste. A very popular remedy in Oriental medicine for helping with everything from joint pain to stomachaches.

Gluten The protein found in wheat, although it is also found in smaller amounts in other grains like oats, rye and barley. When kneaded in dough, gluten becomes elastic and holds air pockets released by the leavener helping bread to rise.

Gluten is also used to prepare *seitan*, a meat substitute made from wheat gluten.

Great Northern beans Medium-size white beans, they hold their shape very well in cooking, making them ideal ingredients in bean salads as well as in heartier bean dishes that complement their subtle flavor.

Hato mugi barley Also known as "Job's Tears," this grain is large pearl barley with a beige, translucent skin. A good source of iron, protein, and calcium, hato mugi is reputed in the Orient to create beautiful, flawless skin, due to its ability to cleanse the blood and remove hard fat desposits from beneath the skin.

Hazelnuts (Filberts) Shaped like a large chick-pea, hazelnuts have a very bitter outer skin that needs to be removed before eating. These guys love chocolate.

Herbs Simply defined, herbs are the leaves and stems of certain plants used in cooking because of their unique, aromatic flavors. Available fresh or dried, herbs add rich, full-bodied taste to soups, stews and salad dressings among other things. When using fresh herbs, remember to use three to four times the amount of dried, as drying concentrates their natural flavor. Try to buy your herbs in natural foods stores, since you can be assured that these herbs are not irradiated, as most commercial brands are.

Hiziki (Hijiki) Sold in its dry form, hiziki resembles black angel hair pasta. It is one of the strongest-tasting of all sea plants, so soaking it for several minutes before cooking can gentle its briny flavor. Lightly sautéing it in sesame oil before stewing can really bring forth its inherent sweet taste. It is a great companion food to vegetables like carrots, corn, squash and onions, but is a bit strong for delicate soups.

Horseradish A root vegetable known for its sharp, hot taste. Actually a member of the mustard family, horseradish adds real zing to any dish. It is truly wonderful freshly grated and stirred into bean dishes or grain salads or served with fish.

Kidney beans Available in a variety of shapes and colors, kidney beans are most commonly recognized in their deep-red All-American shape. Full-flavored and hearty, kidney beans hold up incredibly well in chilies, stews, soups, salads and casseroles.

Kombu (Kelp) A sea vegetable packaged in wide, dark, dehydrated strips that will double in size upon soaking and cooking. Kombu is a great source of glutamic acid, a natural flavor enhancer, so adding a small piece to soups and stews deepens flavor. It is also generally believed that kombu improves the digestibility of grains and beans when added to these foods in small amounts.

Kukicha A Japanese tea made from the stems and twigs of the tea bush.

Kuzu (Kudzu) Kuzu is a high-quality starch made from the root of the kuzu plant. A root native to the mountains of Japan (and now in the southern United States), kuzu grows like a vine with tough roots. Used primarily as a thickener, this strong root is reputed to strengthen the digestive tract.

Legumes A large plant family including beans, lentils, peanuts and peas.

Lentils An ancient legume that comes in many varieties, from common brown-green lentils to red lentils to yellow lentils to lentils *le puys* (a tiny sweet French variety that is great in salads). Very high in protein and with a full-bodied, peppery taste, lentils are good in everything from stews and soups to salads and side dishes.

Lima beans Also known as "butter beans," these popular white beans are most commonly used in their dried form, although

fresh lima beans are exquisite. Lima beans have a very delicate outer skin, so they seem to do best when cooked in salted water (unlike other beans), which helps hold their skin in place. Once the skins loosen, the limas turn to mush—although then you can use them to cream soups or make dips.

Baby lima beans are simply smaller, with tougher skins and a sweeter taste.

Maple syrup A traditional sweetener made by boiling sugar maple sap until it becomes thick. The end product is quite expensive because it takes about 35 gallons of sap to produce 1 gallon of maple syrup. The syrup is available in various grades of quality from AA to B: AA and A are quite nice for sauces and dressings, but I use grade B in baking. I have found the higher grades can result in hard baked goods.

I do not often use maple syrup, since it is a simple sugar, releasing quickly in the bloodstream, thus wreaking havoc with blood sugar.

Millet Native to Asia, millet is a tiny grain that once equaled barley as the chief staple of Europe. It was very popular in Japan before the cultivation of rice and is still the staple grain of China, India, and Ethiopia.

Millet is a tiny round grain grown in cold weather. An effective alkalizing agent, it aids spleen and pancreas function as well as stomach upset.

Millet is very versatile, making delicious grain dishes, creamy soups, stews and porridges, stuffings and loaves. With its sweet, nutty taste and beautiful yellow color, millet complements most foods well, but goes best with sweet vegetables like squash and corn.

Mirin A Japanese rice wine with a sweet taste and very low alcohol content. Made by fermenting sweet brown rice with water and koji (a cultured rice), mirin adds depth and dimension to sauces, glazes and various other dishes.

Miso A fermented soybean paste used traditionally to flavor soups but prized in the Orient for its ability to strengthen the digestive system. Traditionally aged miso is a great source of high-quality protein. Available in a wide variety of flavors and strengths, the most nutritious miso is made from barley and soybeans, and is aged for at least two years—this is the miso used most extensively in daily cooking. Other varieties of misos are used to supplement and to create different tastes in different dishes.

Miso is rich in digestive enzymes, but these enzymes are quite delicate and should not be boiled. Just lightly simmering miso activates and releases their strengthening qualities into food.

Mochi Mochi is made by cooking sweet brown rice and then pounding or extruding it to break the grains, a process that results in a very sticky substance. Flat packages of mochi can be purchased in most natural foods stores. Mochi can be used to create creamy sauces, to give the effect of melted cheese, to make dumplings in soups, or it can be simply cut into small squares and pan fried, creating tiny turnoverlike puffs.

Mung beans Tiny pea-shaped, deep-green beans, these are most popular in their sprouted forms, although they cook up quickly, making delightful soups, purees and various dishes. Mung bean sprouts are a delicious addition to any salad or stir-fried dish.

Mustard Mustard in a jar is made by blending dried mustard seeds with vinegar and various spices. The best-quality mustards are Dijon or those that have been stone ground; these are made from coarse seeds and have a rougher texture.

Navy beans Also called pea beans, these are cream-colored, egg-shaped beans that are the quintessential baked bean. They generally require long, slow cooking, but hold up well in the pressure cooker. I have found that they do not have a substantial enough flavor for salads, so I use other white beans for those dishes.

Noodles (Pasta) Pasta or noodles are made by combining flour, salt, and water into limitless shapes and sizes. Try to choose pastas made from organic flours, preferably whole-grain. These are made from the endosperm of the wheat and contain protein and carbohydrates as well as essential fiber, minerals and B vitamins. However, even refined semolina pastas have a place in a whole foods diet, lending light taste and texture when desired.

Nori (Sea layer) Usually sold in paper-thin sheets, nori is a great source of protein and minerals like calcium and iron. Most well-known as a principal ingredient in sushi, nori has a mild, sweet flavor, just slightly reminiscent of the ocean. Great for garnishing grain and noodle dishes or floating in soup.

Nut butters Thick pastes made from grinding nuts. While rich in fiber and protein, nut butters are also quite high in fat. Nut butters have intense, rich flavors and are great in sauces, dressings and baked goods.

Nuts (See also individual listings) Nuts are true powerhouses of energy. Bear in mind that, in most cases, nuts have the strength to grow entire trees, so imagine what impact they have on us. But they are wonderful in small amounts for taste and richness.

Oats Native to Central Europe and used since Neolithic times, oats are rich in B vitamins and contain one of the highest amounts of protein of any grain in addition to iron and calcium. Reputed to have a high fat content (which they do), oats contain soluble gums which bind cholesterol in the intestines, preventing its absorption by the body.

Most commonly used in modern cultures as oatmeal, a process by which the oat groats are rolled or steel cut, oats are the most delicious when used in their whole state. I use oatmeal flakes mostly to cream soups and thicken sauces as well as in breads, cookies and croquettes.

Ocean ribbons A brownish-green sea vegetable in the kelp family, normally packaged in long, thin strips—ribbons. It has a sweeter taste than kombu and cooks a bit more quickly.

Oil Oils are rich liquids extracted from nuts, seeds, grains, and olives (the only real fruit oil around). A highly refined food source, oils add a rich taste to foods, making dishes more

satisfying and creating a warming, vitalizing energy and soft, supple skin and hair. Try to choose oils that are expelled or cold pressed, since these oils were extracted by pressing and not by extreme heat, which can render oil carcinogenic. I try to limit my oil use to only a few of the more digestible varieties, like toasted sesame, light sesame, corn and olive oil (usually only extra virgin, which is the oil extracted from the first pressing of the olives, and therefore the best quality), occasionally adding safflower and canola oil to a recipe. Oils should be stored in a cool place, but it is not necessary to refrigerate oils to prevent rancidity.

Olives Olives are native to semitropical climates and are used sparingly in cooking to add an appealing punch to grain, vegetable and bean salads. There are almost limitless varieties available, so you can satisfy your taste by choosing anything from the intensely flavored, oil-cured ripe olives, to purple Greek Kalamata olives, to green Spanish olives.

Peanuts Although considered a nut, peanuts are in fact legumes and are a good source of protein. Unlike other legumes, peanuts are very high in fat. Since peanuts are one of the most chemically treated of all crops, try to choose organic peanuts for use. Peanuts are also prone to a carcinogenic mold called *aflatoxin*, especially if they are stored under humid conditions, so choose peanuts from the arid climate of the Southwest, like Valencia peanuts, to minimize this risk.

Pecans Among the highest in fat, these nuts are one of the most delicious for baking in cookies, pies and cakes.

Pignoli (Pine nuts) Incredibly luscious nuts that are quite expensive, due to the labor-intensive process involved in their harvesting from pinecones. High in oil and rich in taste, pine nuts add great depth to pasta and grain pilafs. Roasting them enhances their rich taste, making them delightful in any dish.

Pinto beans The most famous Southwestern bean, pintos were actually named by the Spanish, who used the word meaning "painted" for them, because of the red-brown markings on their beige surface. Their nutty taste holds up well in stews, chilies and baked bean dishes.

Quinoa A tiny seedlike grain native to the Andes mountains. Pronounced *"keen-wah,"* this small grain packs a powerhouse of protein and numerous amino acids not normally found in large amounts in most whole grains. Quinoa grains are quite delicate, so nature has coated them with an oily substance called *saponin.* If the grain isn't rinsed well, it can have a bitter taste. Quinoa has a lovely, nutty taste and cooks quickly; qualities that make it a great whole-grain addition to your menus.

Rice The staple grain of most whole foods diets, rice is low in fat and rich in vitamins and minerals, like calcium, protein, iron and B vitamins. Rice as we know it was reportedly cultivated in India, spreading from there to Asia and the Middle East.

In its whole form, rice is a near perfect food. High in moisture, rice acts as a gentle diuretic, balancing the moisture content of the body and encouraging the elimination of any excess. Polished or white rice, while delicious on occasion, is pretty much devoid of nutrition and should be enjoyed occasionally, with whole rice as the staple grain.

The most common strains of rice include short grain, medium grain and long grain. Short grain, the hardest and most compact variety, is best suited to cooler, temperate climates, while medium- and long-grain rice are used in warmer climates and during the summer months. Other gourmet varieties of rice have become popular in today's cooking. These include arborio, basmati, texmati, wehani, black japonica and red rice. Sweet brown rice, a glutinous variety of brown rice, is commonly used not only as a grain dish but also in *mochi,* a cake formed by pounding and drying cooked sweet rice.

There are limitless uses for rice in daily cooking; it can be pressure cooked, steamed, boiled, fried, baked, roasted, sautéed and used in breads, sushi, casseroles, sautés, pilafs or stuffings.

Rice milk A creamy liquid made by cooking 10 parts water to one part rice for 1 hour, the resulting rice is pressed through a cheesecloth creating "milk." It is also packaged commercially.

Rice syrup (Brown rice syrup, Yinnie, Rice malt) The Japanese call this "liquid sweetness." Rice syrup is a thick, amber syrup made by combining sprouted barley with cooked brown rice and storing it in a warm place. Fermentation begins and the starches in the rice convert to maltose and some other complex sugars, making this syrup a wonderfully healthy sweetener. Complex sugars release slowly into the bloodstream, providing fuel for the body rather than wreaking havoc on the blood sugar.

Rice syrup's wonderful, delicate sweetness makes it ideal for baked goods and other desserts.

Risotto A generic term for a creamy, almost soupy rice dish native to Northern Italy. Traditionally made with a specific short-grain white rice called *Arborio* rice, the perfect risotto is creamy and soupy, while the rice retains a bit of chewy texture.

Rye The Romans began cultivating this Asian grain, thought to be a weed by the Greeks. By the Middle Ages, rye was a staple grain in most of Europe.

As opposed to use in its whole form, rye is most commonly used in flour form to make rich, hearty breads. Similar to wheat in composition, rye is a bit less glutinous and, like wheat, can be used by itself to make breads. Rye is, however, completely delicious when cooked with rice and makes a great whole-grain dish.

Salt All salt is not a good thing. The quality of the salt we use is quite important. The best quality of salt to use is white, unrefined sea salt with no additives. Unrefined salts are rich in the trace minerals that are destroyed in processed salt.

Sea vegetables The exotic vegetables that are harvested from the sea coast and rocks along the coast are high in protein and rich in minerals. Readily available in natural foods stores in dehydrated form, sea vegetables are not yet widely used in American cooking, but are growing in popularity for their nutritional benefits and interesting taste.

Seeds In a word, seeds are powerhouses. (Remember that they are the source of entire plants, even trees in some cases.) That's a lot of energy in a little seed. They are good sources of protein and calcium, but because of their high oil content, seeds perish relatively quickly and keep best refrigerated. The most popular seeds in natural foods cooking include pumpkin seeds (pepitas), poppy seeds, sunflower seeds and sesame seeds.

Seitan (Wheat gluten) Most commonly called "wheat meat," seitan is made from wheat gluten. Made by kneading the bran and starch out of flour, raw seitan is rather bland, so most commercial brands are simmered in savory broth before sale. A wonderful source of protein, it is low in calories and fat and is very popular in Oriental "mock meat" dishes as well as in hearty stews and casseroles.

Sesame tahini A thick, creamy paste made from ground hulled sesame seeds that is used for flavoring everything from sauces to salad dressings to dips, spreads and baked goods. Available in natural foods stores and Middle Eastern markets, this spread has a delicate nutty flavor that adds luxurious taste to any recipe.

Shiitake mushrooms Gaining popularity over the last several years for their power to lower cholesterol and cleanse blood, shiitake mushrooms can be found in just about any natural foods store and gourmet shop. They have an intensely earthy taste, so a few go a long way. It is necessary to soak them until tender, about 15 to 20 minutes before cooking, and I usually trim off the stem to avoid bitter flavor. They are wonderful in soups, stews, gravies and sauces and as bouillon flavoring.

Shiso (Beefsteak leaf) A lovely herb with large, reddish leaves. A very popular staple in Japanese cooking, shiso is often used in pickling, most commonly in umeboshi plum pickling. Shiso is rich in calcium and iron.

Shoyu (Soy sauce) A confusing term because it is the generic term for Japanese soy sauce as well as the term for a specific type of traditionally made soy sauce, the distinguishing characteristic of which is the use of cracked wheat as the fermenting starter, along with soybeans. The best shoyu is aged for at least two years. A lighter seasoning than tamari.

Soba A noodle made from buckwheat flour. Some varieties contain other ingredients, like wheat flour or yam flour, but the best-quality soba are those made primarily of buckwheat flour.

Somen Japanese angel hair. A very fine, white-flour noodle that cooks very quickly, somen are traditionally served in a delicate broth with lightly cooked fresh vegetables.

Soybeans The base bean for many natural foods products, from miso to soy sauce to tofu and tempeh to soy milk to soy flour. On their own, soybeans are rather bland and hard to digest, and so are more commonly used in other products. However,

when cooked on their own—long and slow cooking is the only way—soybeans can be most delicious.

Soyfoods A catchall term for the wide range of foods that have soybeans as their base, including soy milk, tofu, soy flour, tempeh, soy sauce, tamari, shoyu, miso, soy cheese, soy oil, etc.

Soy sauce Traditional soy sauce is the product of fermenting soybeans, water, salt and wheat. Containing salt and glutamic acid, soy sauce is a natural flavor enhancer. The finest soy sauces are aged for one to two years, while commercial soy sauce is synthetically aged in a matter of days, producing a salty, artificially flavored condiment.

Spices Spices are highly aromatic seasonings that come from the seed, root, bark and buds of plants, while herbs are obtained from the leaves and stems. Spices generally give food a very strong taste and energy, and should be used sparingly and wisely, as overuse can overstimulate the nervous system, causing irritability and excessive aggression. They can numb the taste buds. However, sparing use of spices can be very helpful in getting energy moving when stagnant or stuck. Spices become stale when kept for more than six months, so it is advisable to buy them in small quantities that you will use in that time period. Store spices and herbs in well-sealed containers in a cool, dark place to retain potency.

Split peas These dried peas, most commonly available in yellow or green, make wonderful creamy soups.

Tamari A fermented soy sauce product that is actually the liquid that rises to the top of the keg when making miso. This thick, rich flavor enhancer is nowadays produced with a fermentation process similar to that of shoyu, but the starter is wheat-free. Tamari is richer, with a full-bodied taste, and contains more amino acids than regular soy sauce. I prefer the heavier taste of tamari for heartier, winter cooking.

Tempeh A traditional, Indonesian soy product created by fermenting split, cooked soybeans with a starter. As the tempeh ferments, a white mycelium of enzymes develops on the surface, making the soybeans more digestible as well as providing a healthy range of B vitamins. Found in the refrigerator or freezer section of natural foods stores, tempeh is great in everything from sandwiches to salads to stews to casseroles.

Toasted sesame oil An oil extracted from toasted sesame seeds that imparts a wonderful, nutty flavor to sautés, stir-fries and sauces.

Tofu (Soybean curd) Fast becoming a popular low-fat food in our fat-crazed world, tofu is a wonderful source of protein and is both inexpensive and versatile. Rich in calcium and cholesterol-free, tofu is made by extracting curd from coagulated soy milk and then pressing it into bricks. For use in everything from soups and stews to salads, casseroles and quiches or as the creamy base to sauces and dressings.

Udon Flat whole-wheat noodles, much like fettuccine. Udon comes in a variety of blends of flours, from all whole wheat to

brown rice to unbleached white flour. I prefer the whole wheat.

Umeboshi plums (Ume plums) Japanese pickled plums (actually, green apricots) with a fruity, salty taste. Pickled in a salt brine and shiso leaves for at least one year (the longer, the better), ume plums are traditionally served as a condiment with various dishes, including grains. Ume plums are reputed to aid in the cure of a wide array of ailments—from stomachaches to migraines—because they alkalize the blood. These little red plums (made red from the shiso, which add vitamin C and iron) make good preservatives. The best-quality plums are the most expensive ones, but they are used in small amounts, so one jar will last a long time.

Umeboshi plum paste A puree made from umeboshi plums to create a concentrated condiment. Use this sparingly, as it is quite salty, but it is a great ingredient in salad dressings and sauces.

Umeboshi plum vinegar A salty liquid left over from pickling umeboshi plums. Used as a vinegar, it is great in salad dressings and pickle making.

Vanilla (Pure vanilla extract) A smoky, smooth flavoring made by extracting the essence from vanilla beans and preserving it in alcohol and water, although nowadays you can obtain vanilla preserved without alcohol. Pure vanilla extract is a bit expensive, but a small bit goes a long way, so splurge and get the best. By the way, inexpensive, artificial vanilla is made from vanillin, a by-product of paper making—appetizing, no?

Vegetable stock A flavorful broth made by simmering any variety of finely cut vegetables until they release their flavor and nutrients into the water. A great base for soups and sauces, a good stock is usually made from a combination of vegetables and small quantities of herbs to create a full-bodied broth.

Vinegar A fermented condiment familiar to most people. There is an entire world of vinegars to explore—and a variety of uses for them, way beyond salad dressings. While lots of vinegars exist, they can be very acidic, so I keep my use to brown rice vinegar, sweet brown rice vinegar (both made from fermented brown rice and sweet brown rice), umeboshi vinegar, balsamic vinegar and, occasionally, a fruity vinegar, like raspberry or champagne vinegar.

Wakame (Alaria) A very delicate member of the kelp family, wakame is most traditionally used in miso soups and tender salads. It requires only a brief soaking and short cooking time and has a very gentle flavor, so it is a great way to add sea vegetables to your diet.

Wasabi A very potent root, comparable to horseradish in taste. Rather fiery, wasabi adds quite a kick as a condiment or as an ingredient, so use it sparingly until you become familiar with its potency.

Wheat Called the "staff of life," wheat has been the mainstay of foods in temperate climates since the dawn of time. As long ago as 4000 B.C., Egyptians were cultivating yeast and baking exotic breads for their royalty. From there, wheat spread throughout the Roman Empire and eventually the rest of the world.

There are many strains of wheat, classified according to hardness or softness, which reflects the percentage of protein. Hard winter wheat is high in gluten and is best for breads, while softer wheats work best in cakes and pastries. Hard durum wheat and its by-product, semolina, are the principal ingredients in most pasta and macaroni. White flour, bleached and unbleached, has been stripped of most of its nutritional value and makes the soft, puffy pastry and bread commercially produced today.

Couscous is made from refined cracked wheat; bulgur is a wheat that has had the outer bran removed and is then boiled and cracked.

Whole-wheat berries are difficult to digest in their whole form but can be soaked and cooked with other whole grains to create delicious dishes.

Whole-wheat flour A flour ground from whole-wheat berries that is high in gluten. Good, stone-ground flour retains much of its germ and bran, and thus much more of its nutrients than its unbleached white counterpart, making it a healthier choice for bread baking.

Whole-wheat pastry flour A flour ground from a softer strain of wheat that is low in gluten. It is more finely milled than regular whole-wheat flour, making it an excellent choice for pastry, cookie, cake, and muffin baking.

Zest Also called the peel, the zest is the thin, colored layer of skin on citrus fruit that imparts a fragrant essence of the fruit into cooking.

THE BASICS

There are some dishes basic to macrobiotic, whole foods cooking. These dishes encompass the very foundation of food energy—the most central theories surrounding macrobiotic cooking—of how food creates who we are and how we act. Mastering these dishes and understanding their energy is the basis upon which you can build an entire whole foods repertoire. Only in understanding can you find true freedom.

When you truly understand the effects of food and cooking, in terms of energy, you can branch out and use foods to create the person you want to be, achieving what it is

nutritive properties are retained. Pressure cooking imparts a strength to whole grains that can't be achieved by using any other method. Cooking grains under pressure, over strong fire for a long period of time creates a great vitality in us. Pressure cooking combines great contracting energy in the bottom of the pot with balanced energy midpot and expanded, light energy at the top of the pot, where the steam is contained.

This particular method of pressure cooking is the one I have found most strengthening for my family. There are many twists on pressure cooking, and I recommend you try a variety of them to see which method suits you best.

1 cup organic short-grain brown rice   Pinch of sea salt
1 1/4 cups spring or filtered water

Rinse rice by placing it in a bowl with enough water to cover. Gently swirl with your hands to loosen any dust. Pour through a fine strainer to drain.

Combine rice and the 1 1/4 cups water in a pressure cooker and cover loosely. Bring to a boil over medium heat. Add salt and seal the lid. Increase the heat to high and bring the pot to full pressure. Allow the pot to cook at full pressure 30 to 60 seconds. Reduce heat to low, place over a flame deflector and cook over low heat 50 minutes. Remove pot from heat and allow pressure to reduce naturally. Stir rice well and transfer to a serving bowl. Makes 4 servings

VARIATION One method of pressure cooking rice that yields a wonderfully light result, while still retaining its energetic strength, is handed down to us by George Ohsawa, the father of macrobiotics in this country. Follow the recipe above, but cook the grain over low heat only 25 minutes. Then remove the pressure cooker from the heat and allow to stand, undisturbed, another 20 to 25 minutes. Stir well and transfer to a serving bowl.

Nishime-style Vegetables

Nishime, or braising vegetables, calls for large pieces or chunks of vegetables that cook for a relatively long time over low heat. The steam generated in this method of cooking allows the veggies to cook in their own juices, eliminating the need for more than just a little added water. A light seasoning toward the end of cooking brings out their full-bodied flavor and natural sweetness. Vegetables cooked in this manner are very soft and juicy, giving us a very warming, strengthening energy. A great dish for creating vitality.

Nishime-style stew is generally made up of sweet root vegetables cut into large pieces and cooked in a tiny bit of water. A small piece of kombu in the bottom of the pot brings out the sweetness of the veggies, naturally tenderizes them by virtue of its glutamic acid and lightly mineralizes the dish.

Nishime dishes may be very simple, consisting of one root vegetable braised to sweet perfection to hearty stews made up of any number of vegetables. Here is one of my favorites, with a few variations to get you started. ◎

1 (1-inch) piece kombu
1 onion, cut into thick wedges
1 cup (1-inch) cubed winter squash

1 carrot, cut into large chunks
Spring or filtered water
Soy sauce

In a heavy pot, place kombu and layer the vegetables in order listed above or arrange the vegetables in a pot in individual sections. Add enough water just to cover the bottom of the pot and bring to a boil over medium heat. Reduce heat to low, cover, and cook until vegetables are just tender, about 25 minutes. Season vegetables lightly with soy sauce and simmer 10 minutes more, until all liquid has been absorbed into the vegetables. If water evaporates too quickly during cooking, add a little more and reduce the heat; it is cooking too quickly. Transfer to a bowl and serve. ◎ Makes 4 servings

VARIATIONS Other nishime combinations that are real winners include: carrot, burdock and onion; onion, Brussels sprouts and corn-on-the-cob pinwheels; leek, parsnip and turnip; onion and squash; onion, squash and green cabbage wedges; daikon and lotus root. Most often I add the small piece of kombu, but it is okay to leave it out on occasion.

Squash, Azuki Beans & Kombu

A very strengthening dish, especially for the kidneys. The small red azuki beans are extremely low in fat, while power-packed with potassium and other valuable nutrients. Combine them with mineral-packed kombu and the natural sweet squash to help stabilize the blood sugar, and you have a dish that creates great vitality and strength. ✐

1 (1-inch) piece kombu
1/2 cup azuki beans, sorted, rinsed
and soaked 4 to 5 hours

2 cups spring or filtered water
1 1/2 cups cubed winter squash
Soy sauce

Place kombu in the bottom of a heavy pot. Top with beans and spring water. Bring to a boil over high heat and cook, uncovered, about 10 minutes. Reduce heat to low, cover, and cook until beans are about almost done, 50 to 60 minutes.

Add squash and cook, covered, until squash and beans are tender, about 25 minutes. Season lightly with soy sauce and simmer until all liquid has been absorbed by the beans. Transfer to a serving bowl and serve. ✐ M a k e s 4 s e r v i n g s

VARIATIONS Add or substitute other vegetables like onions, carrots, or parsnips—any sweet root vegetable will do. And when the weather is particularly chilly, I add a bit of fresh, grated ginger juice for added zing and warmth. The sweet taste can be accented with 1 to 2 teaspoons barley malt when seasoning the dish.

Dried Daikon with Vegetables

A deep-cleansing dish. Fresh daikon has the energy to help the body assimilate and discharge excess fluids, fats, and proteins. Dried daikon concentrates that energy, aiding deeper organs in their cleansing process. The sweet taste of the carrot and onion in this dish helps create a calming, strengthening energy, gently mineralized by ever-faithful kombu. ✐

Place kombu in the bottom of a small skillet. Top with onion, carrot, mushrooms, and daikon. Add water to half cover ingredients, using a combination of soaking and fresh water. Bring to a boil, cover, and cook over low heat 35 minutes. Season lightly with soy sauce and simmer about 10 minutes more. Remove the cover and simmer until any remaining liquid has been absorbed into the dish. Transfer to a serving bowl before serving. ✒ M a k e s 4 s e r v i n g s

1 (3-inch) piece kombu, soaked about 5 minutes or until tender and sliced into thin strips

1 small onion, cut lengthwise into thin slices

1 carrot, cut into thin matchsticks

1 or 2 dried shiitake mushrooms, soaked until tender and thinly sliced

1/2 cup dried daikon, soaked about 10 minutes or until tender

Spring or filtered water

Soy sauce

Pressed Salad

A quick pickle dish that gives you the freshness of raw salad, it is processed just enough with salt or vinegar to break down the tough outer cellulose layer that can make raw vegetables so difficult to digest. Use 1/2 teaspoon sea salt or umeboshi vinegar per cup of vegetables. Pressing also eliminates a lot of the excess liquids in raw vegetables that can make us feel very cold during winter months. The secret to this dish is slicing the vegetables as thinly as you can. This helps them press quickly, so that they retain their fresh quality. ✒

1 cup finely shredded Chinese cabbage

1 to 2 red radishes, thinly sliced

1/2 cucumber, thinly sliced, peeled, if desired

1 carrot, cut into thin matchsticks

2 to 3 green onions, cut into thin diagonal slices

1 teaspoon sea salt or umeboshi vinegar

Place all vegetables in a medium bowl and toss well with salt or vinegar, rubbing the vegetables through your fingers to work the salt into their surfaces. Either transfer salad to a pickle press or another bowl. If using a press, screw on the lid of the press and set aside about 30 minutes. If using a bowl, place a plate on top of the salad with a weight on top and press 30 minutes.

Squeeze out the fluid that accumulates in the salad and, if the salad is too salty, gently rinse to gentle the taste. ✒ M a k e s 4 s e r v i n g s

Kinpira

Kinpira is an incredible dish whose name means "sauté and simmer." Vegetables are sautéed over high heat and then simmered to tender perfection. Kinpira-style cooking is very vitalizing. Burdock is the most strengthening root vegetable known to man. Other plants do not grow within a 4-foot radius. If burdock encounters rock in its growth path, it grows right through it, and is thus by nature a very centering, strengthening vegetable. Burdock helps us focus and take aim at our goals. Very strong, burdock needs the gentle, sweet taste of carrots to balance its strength. ✒

1 teaspoon dark or light sesame oil
1 cup matchstick pieces burdock
Sea salt

1 cup matchstick pieces carrot
Spring or filtered water
Soy sauce

Heat sesame oil in a heavy skillet over medium heat. Add burdock and a pinch of salt and cook, stirring, until coated with oil, about 2 minutes. Spread burdock evenly over skillet and top with carrots. Do not stir. Add water to just cover burdock only, cover and cook over medium-low heat about 10 minutes. Season lightly with soy sauce and simmer until any liquid that remains has been absorbed, about 10 minutes. Stir well before transferring to a serving platter. ✒ M a k e s 4 s e r v i n g s

Nabe Cooking

Nabe, pronounced "*na*-bay," is a quick and fresh style of cooking that involves actually cooking at the table, usually in a large open ceramic or metal nabe pot. This style of cooking has lots of advantages: it is easy on the cook and as fresh as you can possibly get. Your food certainly can't lose much vitality when you are cooking it just as you eat it. This style of fresh cooking not only is delicious but also imparts a terrific vitality.

The great majority of nabe meals involve thinly sliced vegetables, including a small portion of cooked grain dishes on the side. I usually choose lighter veggies for these meals—anything from sliced, leafy greens, Chinese cabbage, head cabbage, leeks, dandelion greens, broccoli, rapini, mushrooms, green beans, sugar snap peas, snow peas, Brussels sprouts, green onions, chives and onions. However, I can't resist adding veggies like thin slices of winter squash, daikon, carrot and corn pinwheels, because they are so incredibly sweet when cooked this way. And on occasion, I add small pieces of fresh tofu or tempeh, mochi, or fu. Sound like a lot of food? Well, nabe can be as simple or as complicated as you like. The greater the variety of ingredients you choose, however, the greater the vitality you will receive from this type of meal. And actually, the only real work involved here is in slicing and dicing the vegetables and cooking an accompanying grain dish.

So to put a nabe meal together, simply cook a grain side dish. While the grain is cooking, begin preparing your vegetable platter for the meal. Then fill the nabe pot with fresh spring or filtered water and one or two shiitake mushrooms. (Sometimes I add a small piece of kombu as well, but no other seasoning for this broth.) When the mushrooms are soft, slice them thinly and return them to the broth.

When everything is ready, bring your nabe broth to a boil and begin adding sliced vegetables to the pot, cooking each one for anywhere from several seconds to a couple of minutes. You want the veggies to be just tender, not too soft. Don't add so many vegetables to the pot that you lose the boil, just add a few pieces at a time. Take a small amount of grain, a bowl of dipping sauce, and eat to your heart's content!

The final touch to this elegant, and social, meal is to create a simple dipping sauce for your freshly cooked vegetables. The dipping sauces you create are the seasoning for nabe meals, so don't be afraid of them. Give them interesting strong flavors. I like to use a wide variety of dipping sauces, from hot to spicy to citrusy to hearty. Some dipping sauces I use on a regular basis include tamari broth with grated gingerroot, miso broth with lemon juice and sesame seeds, tamari broth with hot chiles, leftover miso soup with green onions and grated daikon and, during the summer months, umeboshi vinegar combined with fresh orange juice is really refreshing. Use the proportions that taste good to you and experiment to find your favorite.

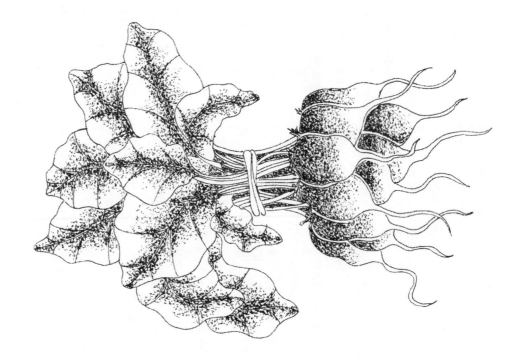

AMAZING GRAINS

G rain. It's interesting how even the word evokes feelings of simplicity, elegance, beauty and humility. Simply stated, whole grains and grain products are the cornerstone of any healthy, whole foods diet. There is an old saying, "Man can not live by bread alone." But he sure can live well on grain! Yes, we need to supplement whole grains with fresh fruits and vegetables, beans, nuts and seeds, and even a small amount of fish, if you so desire. With the abundant variety of grains available to us, however, we could, in theory, survive on whole grains alone. Grains are the link between the plant and animal kingdoms from which we, as humans, draw life.

So are grains the all-around perfect food? Just about. The majority of nutrients that the human organism needs to sustain life are fully present in whole grains. Water, protein, vitamins, minerals, carbohydrates, fats, and fiber compose this miraculous food that not only reproduces itself a thousand times over (with little assistance from us), but can be stored and transported literally without damage or spoilage.

In traditional cultures, grain was always associated with the fruitful forces of Mother Nature. To these peoples, grain was the key to opening consciousness, carrying the force of life through its deep roots in the earth up through its stem to its fruit, opened to the heavenly force of the sun. In modern botanical thinking, there are about eight thousand species of grasses that are categorized as "grain." Of these, human beings eat only a few, although we have come to think of other plant varieties as "grains" because of the similarities in their characteristics and energetic qualities.

What does *whole grain* mean anyway? This name refers to a seed's anatomical structure—the pericarp, endosperm and germ. So, any reference to whole grains means that the entire grain structure is being used; there has been no polishing, rolling, purling or stripping of the seed. All of the nutritive parts of the grain are intact for consumption.

When shopping for whole grains, look for well-shaped, uniform (size, shape and color) grains. I personally prefer organic grains to commercial varieties, because grain is such an important part of a healthy diet, it only makes sense to obtain the very best quality. And since grain absorbs so much from the soil, any pesticide residue present in the earth will find its way into our grains.

Once purchased, I advise storing grains in tightly sealed glass jars in a cupboard or pantry—or any cool and dry place. I have gotten into the habit of adding a whole bay leaf to each jar to discourage grain moths. At first, with so many grains available to us, you may wish to label each jar, so you will remember what is what until grains become familiar to you.

In general, cooking styles for grains will vary—amounts of water, cooking time, etc. You will see many different methods employed in the following recipes. What remains constant is rinsing grains. Grains will develop a light dust over their surface as they sit because of naturally occurring oxidation. A light rinsing process will ensure the natural, sweet, nutty taste of your cooked grains. First, quickly sort through the grain for any tiny stones or debris. Then, simply place the grain in a bowl, cover with water, swirl gently with your fingers to loosen dirt and pour through a fine strainer. You may wish to repeat the process a couple of times if the water is particularly cloudy.

The energy and spirit of whole grains keep me enchanted almost more than the delicious flavors. They possess an inner strength that comes from the harmony of water, earth, sun and air—nature's basic elements of life. By utilizing the whole grain, these powerful energetic qualities are passed on to us, nourishing us completely and restoring us to that same harmony with nature.

A diet centered around the grain family will awaken our spirits and open our consciousness to all that the universe has to provide. Our instinct and intuition will guide our choices, making our lives happier and healthier and free from the petty stresses of daily living that seem to so debilitate people these days.

Looking at grains, we see a great variety available to us. I dare say that, to a newcomer, a natural foods store with row after row of grain products can be quite daunting. But instead of giving in to anxiety, let this abundance reawaken the very essence of humanity in you—your creativity. And again, always choose organic grains over commercially grown and processed ones whenever possible. Organic foods nourish us better because they are allowed to flourish naturally, and they also support the earth that gives them life . . . and it is always better to choose life.

Let these recipes serve only as your inspiration. All that follows are simply tools to create dishes to nourish the body and spirit. For more information on the vast varieties of grains available to us, check the Glossary.

Mochi

Made from sweet brown rice, mochi is so versatile you can use it in sauces, stews, casseroles and soups; as a cheese alternative; and on its own. While you can purchase it packaged, nothing compares to homemade mochi. Make the effort; it really is worth it. 🌿

2 cups sweet brown rice, rinsed	**2 pinches of sea salt**
2 1/2 cups spring or filtered water	**Rice flour**

Place rice and water in a pressure cooker and soak 6 to 8 hours. Bring to a boil, loosely covered. Add salt, seal, and bring to full pressure. Place over a flame deflector, reduce heat to low and cook 45 minutes. Remove pot from heat and allow pressure to reduce naturally. Transfer grain to a heavy clay or wooden bowl.

Take a large pestle and moisten it. Begin pounding the cooked rice, periodically dipping the pestle in water to prevent the rice from sticking. Continue pounding about 1 hour, until all the grains of rice appear to be broken and the rice is very sticky. Sprinkle a baking sheet with rice flour and spread mochi evenly over the sheet. Cover with a straw mat and allow to dry 1 to 2 days before cutting into pieces and wrapping in plastic. Mochi will keep, refrigerated, about 10 days. 🌿 Makes about 10 ounces

VARIATION Place freshly pounded mochi in a moistened plastic container. Cover and refrigerate. The mochi will be a little softer, but just as good.

Short-Grain Brown Rice with Squash
This is a staple in our house during the fall and winter, when the squash is so sweet that you'd swear it was sugared if you didn't know better. A delicious breakfast dish when cooked soft, it creates very warming energy, which nourishes our middle body organs, like the spleen, pancreas and stomach, but it will also liven up any evening meal very nicely. 🌿

2 cups short-grain brown rice, rinsed	1 tablespoon barley miso
1 cup cubed winter squash	Slivered nori sheets or minced
3 cups spring or filtered water	parsley, for garnish
2 pinches of sea salt	

Combine rice, squash, and water in a pressure cooker and cook over medium heat, uncovered, until mixture comes to a boil. Add salt. Seal and bring to full pressure. Place over a flame deflector, reduce heat to low, and cook 50 minutes.

Meanwhile, puree miso in a small amount of water and simmer it 3 to 4 minutes. When the rice is cooked, remove it from heat and allow pressure to reduce naturally. Stir pureed miso into hot rice and transfer to a serving bowl. Serve garnished with nori or parsley. 🌿 Makes 5 or 6 servings

Fried Rice & Vegetables

A familiar favorite. This vegetarian version relies on an abundance of fresh vegetables and flavorful seasoning to create a low-fat, delicious alternative to the oily and salty standard. ✍

1 to 2 teaspoons dark sesame oil	1 to 2 cups cooked short-grain
3 or 4 slices gingerroot, cut into thin matchsticks	brown rice
	1 to 2 stalks broccoli, broken into flowerets
Sea salt	
1/4 cup *each* sliced onion, carrot matchsticks, burdock matchsticks, thinly sliced button mushrooms and shredded cabbage	Soy sauce
	Brown rice vinegar
	Parsley sprigs, for garnish

Heat oil in a skillet. Add gingerroot and a pinch of salt and cook, stirring, until golden. Add onion and another pinch of salt and cook, stirring, until onion is translucent, about 5 minutes. Add carrot, burdock, mushrooms and another pinch of salt and cook, stirring occasionally, until coated with oil. Finally, stir in cabbage and another pinch of salt and cook until cabbage begins to wilt, about 5 minutes.

Spread vegetables evenly over the skillet and top with cooked rice, then broccoli. Sprinkle lightly with soy sauce. Gently add about 1/8 inch of water to allow everything to steam together, cover and cook over medium heat about 10 minutes, until all liquid is absorbed and broccoli is cooked. Turn off heat and season to taste with rice vinegar. Stir well, transfer to a serving bowl and garnish with parsley sprigs. ✍

Makes 4 or 5 servings

Millet & Veggie Burgers

This is such an easy dish to put together for lunches or snacks or on those nights when you would love to just send out for a pizza instead of cooking a well-balanced, healthy meal. These burgers satisfy the cook's need for ease of preparation, without compromising your food choices. ✒

1 to 2 teaspoons light sesame oil, plus
    additional for pan-frying
3 to 4 slices gingerroot, cut into thin
    matchsticks
Sea salt
1 cup millet, rinsed

3 cups boiling water
1/2 cup *each* diced carrot, onion
    and celery
1/4 cup minced fresh parsley
1/2 cup cornmeal, plus additional
    for dredging

Heat 1 to 2 teaspoons sesame oil in a pot over medium heat. Add gingerroot and a pinch of salt and cook 2 to 3 minutes. Remove ginger from oil. Add millet and cook, stirring, until millet is coated with oil and gives off a nutty fragrance. Add boiling water, season lightly with salt and reduce heat to low. Cover and simmer 35 minutes. Add carrot, onion and celery, re-cover, and simmer about 5 minutes. Remove from heat and stir in parsley and cornmeal. Allow mixture to stand 10 to 15 minutes before forming into burgers.

Shape millet mixture into thick patties. Dredge in cornmeal to coat. Heat about 1/8 inch sesame oil in a skillet over medium heat. Fry patties until golden, about 3 minutes on each side. Remove from skillet and drain on paper towels to absorb any excess oil. Serve as you would any conventional burger. ✒ Makes 4 or 5 servings

Chilled Oriental Rice

It may sound like just another brown rice and tofu salad, but this delicious take on Oriental traditional fare contains less salt and fat than its restaurant counterpart. It is a great, easy recipe for using up leftover grain as well. ◇

8 ounces extra-firm tofu, cubed

Marinade (opposite)

7 or 8 snow peas, cut into thin slices

1 celery stalk, diced

1/2 red bell pepper, roasted, diced

2 cups cooked medium- or long-grain brown rice

2 tablespoons minced, pan-roasted walnut pieces (page 417)

Sliced green onions, for garnish

MARINADE

1 to 2 teaspoons light sesame oil

Juice of 1 lemon

Juice of 1 lime

2 cloves garlic, minced

Fresh ginger juice (page 242)

Soy sauce

Brown rice vinegar

Spring or filtered water

Place cubed tofu in a shallow dish. Mix together marinade ingredients, combining a little ginger juice, soy sauce, and vinegar with enough water to create a thin marinade. The flavors in the marinade can be as mild or strong as you like; because the tofu takes on the flavors of the marinade, err to the mild side on the taste here. Pour marinade over tofu and allow to stand 10 to 15 minutes.

Combine vegetables, rice, walnuts, tofu and marinade. Serve garnished with green onions. ◇ M a k e s 4 o r 5 s e r v i n g s

Quinoa Salad

Quinoa is far from a new grain. Dating back to Native American cooking, this delicious, nutty grain is quite high in protein, cooks quickly and has a very cooling effect on the body, making it a great summer grain, although I use it year-round. Available at most natural foods stores, quinoa is an inexpensive addition to your grain repertoire. ✒

2 cups spring or filtered water

Pinch of sea salt

1 cup quinoa, rinsed well

1 cup fresh corn kernels

1 cup fresh green peas

1 cucumber, peeled, seeded and diced

1 to 2 celery stalks, diced

Juice of 1 lemon

Juice of 1 orange

7 or 8 fresh mint leaves, minced

3 to 4 fresh basil leaves, minced

Soy sauce

2 tablespoons extra-virgin olive oil

Bring water and sea salt to a boil over medium heat. Add quinoa and bring back to a boil. Cover, reduce heat, and simmer about 30 minutes or until all the liquid is absorbed and the quinoa is fluffy.

Bring water to a boil in a pot over high heat. Add corn and boil 2 minutes. Remove with a slotted spoon and cool in iced water. Drain and set aside. Add peas to boiling water and boil 30 seconds. Drain and cool in iced water. Drain and set aside. Toss the quinoa with corn, peas, cucumber, and celery in a large bowl.

Whisk together the lemon and orange juice, mint and basil to taste, soy sauce to taste and the olive oil in a small bowl. Pour dressing over hot quinoa mixture and toss to combine. Serve immediately or the quinoa will take on too much moisture and become soggy. ✒ M a k e s   4   o r   5   s e r v i n g s

Roasted Vegetable & Corn Chili

This thick, rich, elegant-tasting version of a classic recipe employs corn grits as an unusual alternative to the beans usually found in vegetarian versions of chili without meat. Serve with crusty whole-grain bread and lightly boiled or steamed veggies to round out your meal. ✒

1 to 2 yellow squash, cut into cubes

1 red bell pepper, diced

1 Portobello mushroom, cut into cubes

1 to 2 cups chopped button mushrooms

Extra-virgin olive oil

Sea salt

1 yellow onion, diced

3 cloves garlic, diced

Generous pinch *each* of ground cumin and powdered ginger

2 to 3 fresh plum tomatoes, diced

1/2 cup fresh corn kernels

Spring or filtered water

Generous pinch of chili powder

1 cup corn grits

Preheat oven to 450F (220C). Toss the squash, bell pepper and mushrooms in a little olive oil. Spread on a baking sheet and sprinkle lightly with salt. Roast about 20 minutes, tossing occasionally, until lightly browned. Remove from oven and set aside.

Heat 2 teaspoons olive oil in a large, heavy Dutch oven (enamel-covered cast iron is great) over medium heat. Add the onion, garlic and a pinch of salt and sauté until fragrant, 2 to 3 minutes. Stir in cumin and ginger and cook 1 to 2 minutes more. Add tomatoes, corn, 3 cups of water, a pinch of salt and chili powder to taste. (The flavor of chili powder gets stronger as it cooks, so err to the mild side in the beginning. You can always spice things up later.) Fold in corn grits and roasted vegetables, cover partially and simmer, stirring occasionally, over low heat until thick, about 1 hour. Add water as needed as the chili cooks. The finished product should be creamy and thick, but not pasty. ✑ Makes 4 or 5 servings

Sweet & Sour Corn Salad

The quintessential symbol of summer, this wonderful summer grain is packed with vitamins, minerals and protein. Growing high and proud, it is at its best during the warmest summer weather. The high "fire" energy it contains gives us great vitality and helps us adapt more smoothly to the warm temperatures of the season. This salad is a different take on the use of corn: the mustard-flavored sweet and sour sauce enhances the sweet taste of the corn just perfectly. It is great served over a bed of lightly steamed leafy greens. ✑

SWEET & SOUR SAUCE

1 teaspoon rice syrup
1/2 teaspoon umeboshi vinegar
2 tablespoons spring or filtered
  water
Soy sauce
2 tablespoons brown rice vinegar
3 to 4 teaspoons prepared mustard
1 teaspoon extra-virgin olive oil

4 ears of fresh corn, kernels removed
1 red bell pepper, roasted over a
  flame, peeled, seeded and diced
1/2 cucumber, seeded and diced, but
  not peeled (unless it has been
  waxed)
3 to 4 green onions, cut into thin
  diagonal slices
1/4 cup minced fresh parsley

Bring a small pot of water to a boil and add the corn kernels. Return to a boil and drain. (This will enhance the sweet flavor of the corn and make it tender.) Toss together the corn, bell pepper, cucumber, onions and parsley in a large bowl.

Combine the sauce ingredients in a small bowl and whisk until blended. Stir sauce into the vegetables and allow to marinate about 30 minutes so the flavors can develop.
Makes 4 or 5 servings

Rice Pilaf

No grain section would be complete without a pilaf recipe. This popular style of serving whole grains is a chewy, crunchy symphony of flavors, textures and colors.

1 teaspoon light sesame oil
1 onion, diced
Sea salt
2 tablespoons slivered almonds
1 cup thinly sliced button mushrooms,
  brushed clean

1 cup fresh corn kernels
1 carrot, diced
1 cup long-grain brown rice
1/4 cup wild rice
2 1/2 cups spring or filtered water
Parsley sprigs, for garnish

In a deep, heavy pot, heat the oil over medium heat. Add the onion and a pinch of salt and cook until fragrant, 2 to 3 minutes. Add the almonds and cook, stirring, until coated with oil. Stir in the mushrooms, corn, carrot and a pinch of salt and cook 1 to 2 minutes more. Spread the vegetables evenly over the bottom of the pot and top with the rices.

Gently add the water and bring to a boil. Add 1 or 2 pinches of salt. Reduce heat, cover, and simmer over low heat about 45 minutes, until all the liquid is absorbed and the rices are fluffy. Remove pot from heat and allow to stand, covered, 5 minutes. Stir well and transfer to a serving bowl. Garnish with parsley sprigs.

Makes 4 or 5 servings

Cynthia's Chili with Polenta Croutons

Meatless meals have predominated cooking throughout most, if not all, cultures. This peasant cuisine is again becoming fashionable as modern people discover that vegetarian meals are satisfying and simple to prepare. I worked as head chef a number of years ago in a natural foods restaurant where this chili recipe was developed by the owner, Cynthia Tice. It is the best I have ever tasted. Its thick texture and authentic, spicy flavor will win raves. Trust me, no one will miss meat in this meal. Serve with crusty whole-grain bread and lightly cooked vegetables.

1 (1-inch) piece kombu

1/2 cup *each* pinto beans and kidney beans, soaked together 6 to 8 hours and drained

Spring or filtered water

Generous pinch of cumin powder

1 to 2 teaspoons chili powder

1/2 cup *each* diced onion, celery, winter squash and carrot

1 cup millet, rinsed

Soy sauce

About 2 teaspoons extra-virgin olive oil

1 recipe Old World Polenta (page 75), cut into 1-inch squares

Place kombu in the bottom of a pressure cooker. Add beans and 3 cups fresh water. Bring to a boil, uncovered, over medium heat and cook at a rolling boil about 10 minutes. Seal and bring to full pressure. Reduce heat to low and cook 40 minutes. Remove pot from heat and allow pressure to reduce naturally. Open the pot, stir in cumin and chili powder to taste and simmer 5 minutes, uncovered.

In a soup pot, layer the onion, celery, squash, carrot, millet and, finally, the cooked beans. Add water to generously cover all ingredients and sprinkle lightly with soy sauce. Cover and bring to a boil over medium heat. Reduce heat and cook 35 minutes, until millet is creamy and chili is thick and "meaty."

Heat enough olive oil in a skillet over medium heat to cover the bottom. Add polenta squares and cook, turning, until golden brown on both sides. Garnish each bowl of chili with a few polenta squares and serve. ✑ M a k e s 5 o r 6 s e r v i n g s

VARIATION You may also use canned organic beans instead of cooking your own to save cooking time in this recipe.

Bulgur with Skillet Veggies A simple and satisfying one-dish meal. Serve with a fresh salad and a light soup to round out a refreshing summer repast. ✑

1 to 2 teaspoons light sesame oil

1 onion, diced

1 clove garlic, minced

Sea salt

1 cup bulgur wheat

2 cups spring or filtered water

2 cups thinly sliced fresh crimini or
    button mushrooms brushed clean

1 cup small cauliflowerets

1 carrot, cut into thin matchsticks

7 or 8 Brussels sprouts, halved
    and thinly sliced lengthwise

Soy sauce

Generous pinch of dried rosemary

1 tablespoon kuzu, dissolved in a
    little cold water

2 tablespoons slivered almonds,
    pan-toasted (page 65), for
    garnish

Heat sesame oil in a skillet over medium heat. Add onion, garlic and a pinch of sea salt and sauté until translucent, 2 to 3 minutes. Add bulgur and cook, stirring constantly, about 2 minutes. Gently add water and a pinch of salt and bring to a boil. Cover, reduce heat, and cook 15 minutes, until liquid is absorbed.

In another skillet over medium heat, arrange mushrooms, cauliflower, carrot and Brussels sprouts around the skillet, each in its own section. Add enough water to half cover, sprinkle lightly with soy sauce, and bring to a boil. Cover, reduce heat, and simmer until cauliflower is crisp-tender, about 6 minutes. Add rosemary to taste and stir in dissolved kuzu. Cook, stirring, until liquid is slightly thickened. Transfer bulgur to a serving bowl and top individual servings with vegetables and almonds.

Makes 4 or 5 servings

Barley & Corn Salad

A lovely summer combination, this salad joins the cooling, dispersing energy of barley with the energizing power of fresh summer corn, all generously dressed in a refreshing lime vinaigrette.

2 cups spring or filtered water

Sea salt

1 cup pearl barley, sorted and rinsed

1 to 2 ears fresh corn, kernels removed

1 small red onion, diced

1 small cucumber, peeled, seeded
and diced

1/4 cup minced fresh parsley

1/4 cup extra-virgin olive oil

2 to 3 tablespoons umeboshi
vinegar

2 teaspoons rice syrup

Juice of 1 lime

1 to 2 tablespoons prepared
mustard

Bring water and a pinch of sea salt to a boil in a medium saucepan over medium heat. Slowly add barley. Cover, reduce heat to low, and cook 40 to 45 minutes, until barley is tender and water is absorbed. Transfer to a bowl and allow to cool.

Bring water to a boil in a pot over high heat. Add corn and boil 2 minutes. Remove with a slotted spoon and cool in iced water. Drain and set aside. Add onion to boiling water and boil 1 minute. Drain and cool in iced water. Drain and mix together with the corn, cucumber and parsley in a large bowl.

In a small bowl, combine the oil, umeboshi vinegar, rice syrup, lime juice, mustard and a little salt. Whisk until blended. The dressing should have a refreshing, yet spicy taste. Toss the barley, vegetables, and dressing together. Allow the salad to marinate in the refrigerator about 30 minutes before serving. Makes 4 or 5 servings

Wild Rice with Apples

Wild rice is not actually a whole grain but an aquatic grass seed still harvested by hand. It has a wonderful, nutty flavor. Mix in crisp, tart apples and a warm orange dressing for a taste sensation. This dish is a particularly lovely complement to a holiday meal.

1 cup wild rice, rinsed well
1 cup brown basmati rice, rinsed well
2 1/2 cups spring or filtered water
2 pinches of sea salt
1/2 cup fresh orange juice
1 tablespoon olive oil

2 teaspoons rice syrup
Grated peel of 1 orange
Juice of 1 lemon
1 tart apple (such as Granny Smith), cored and diced
1 celery stalk, diced

Place both rices and water in a pressure cooker and bring to a boil, uncovered, over medium heat. Add salt, seal and bring to full pressure. Place over a flame deflector, reduce heat to low and cook 45 minutes. Remove pot from heat and allow pressure to reduce naturally. Transfer rice to a serving bowl.

While the rice is cooking, warm the orange juice, olive oil, rice syrup, orange peel and a pinch of salt in a small pan over low heat. Remove from heat and stir in lemon juice and diced apples. Toss rice and celery with apple and orange dressing and serve warm. Makes 4 or 5 servings

Oriental-style Millet

Millet is one of the natural wonders of the culinary world. It is one of the most versatile grains, with a delicious, nutty flavor. It cooks up creamy and stewlike or you can simply pan-roast it to make it fluffy and light, enhancing and supporting the other flavors in the dish, as in this elegant, exotic grain dish. ✍

1 cup millet, rinsed

3 cups spring or filtered water

Soy sauce

1 to 2 teaspoons dark sesame oil

3 to 4 slices gingerroot, minced

2 cloves garlic, minced

1 small carrot, finely diced

2 to 3 green onions, cut into thin diagonal slices

1 teaspoon fresh ginger juice (page 242)

1 teaspoon brown rice syrup

1 tablespoon brown rice vinegar

2 tablespoons shelled peanuts, pan-toasted (page 417)

Heat a deep, dry skillet over medium heat. Drain millet well before toasting so that it toasts evenly and doesn't burn. Add to skillet and toast about 5 minutes, until millet puffs and begins to pop. Add water and a sprinkle of soy sauce and bring to a boil. Reduce heat, cover, and simmer 30 minutes or until the liquid is nearly absorbed. Remove from heat and allow to stand, covered, 10 minutes. Fluff with a fork and transfer to a serving bowl.

Heat sesame oil in a skillet over medium heat. Add ginger and garlic and cook 2 to 3 minutes. Add carrot and green onions and cook until tender, 2 to 3 minutes. Sprinkle with a little soy sauce and stir in ginger juice and rice syrup. Remove from heat and stir in rice vinegar and peanuts. Fold into hot millet. Serve warm, as millet tends to stiffen as it cools. ✍ Makes 4 or 5 servings

Amaranth & Corn

An ancient grain revisited. It was cultivated by the Aztecs, but was also widely used in China and in South and Central America. Commonly ground into flour, amaranth is also a wonderful whole-grain dish, but it only recently came back into vogue as a grain. It has a strong, earthy, sweet flavor that matches perfectly the sweetness of fresh corn. Its unique flavor and texture make it a delicious alternative to the more commonly used whole grains. ✑

1 cup amaranth, rinsed and drained
    through a very fine strainer
1/2 cup fresh corn kernels

2 1/4 cups spring or filtered water
Pinch of sea salt

Combine amaranth, corn and water in a medium pan over medium heat and bring to a boil. Add salt. Cover, reduce heat and simmer 30 to 35 minutes, until all the liquid is absorbed and the grain is creamy. ✑ Makes 4 or 5 servings

VARIATION This grain dish combines very well with hato mugi barley, also known as Job's Tears. Cooked in the same manner as the recipe indicates, you simply add 1/4 cup barley to the amaranth and increase the water by a little over 1/2 cup.

Quinoa with Tempeh & Cilantro

Truly a fast food, quinoa cooks up very quickly, unfolding like a spiral as it cooks. As in this recipe, quinoa partners very well with more cooling vegetables and helps to create some wonderful, nutty grain dishes. ✑

1 cup quinoa
2 cups spring or filtered water
Pinch of sea salt
Safflower oil for deep-frying
1 (8-oz.) package tempeh, cubed
1 teaspoon extra-virgin olive oil
1 clove garlic, minced

6 or 7 green onions, cut into thin
   diagonal slices
Soy sauce
2 celery stalks, diced
Juice of 1 lime
1/4 cup cilantro, minced

Place quinoa in a fine strainer and rinse well. This is especially important because the grains are covered with a coating of a substance called saponin, which protects the delicate grains. If not rinsed off, this substance can make your cooked grain taste bitter. Place in a pot with water and bring to a boil. Add salt. Cover, reduce heat, and simmer about 30 minutes, until liquid is absorbed and quinoa is fluffy. Set aside.

Heat about 1 inch of safflower oil in a heavy skillet or pan over medium heat. Test the oil temperature by dropping in a piece of tempeh. If it sinks and comes immediately back to the top, the oil is hot enough to deep-fry properly. (Remember the point of deep-frying is to add richness to your diet and to give you the strong kind of energy present only in cooking foods over high heat, very quickly.) Deep-fry the tempeh cubes until golden brown. Drain on paper towels and set aside.

Heat olive oil in a skillet over medium heat. Add the garlic, green onions and a little soy sauce and cook until onions are bright green, about 3 minutes. Stir in celery, quinoa, and tempeh and toss well. Remove from heat and stir in lime juice and cilantro. Serve warm. ✑ M a k e s   4   o r   5   s e r v i n g s

Brown Rice & Millet Croquettes

Tired of simply resteaming leftover grain, putting it into soup or, even worse, throwing it away after a few days? Well, this recipe is for you. All you need to make croquettes is some cooked grains, some oil and about a half hour to prepare the dish. The amounts suggested are really just a guide. Grain ratios may vary, depending on what you have available. The same goes for vegetables.

1/2 cup cooked brown rice

1/2 cup cooked millet

1/4 cup combined diced onion and
    carrot

1/4 cup fresh corn kernels (optional)

Fine yellow or white cornmeal

Safflower oil for deep-frying or
    shallow frying

Combine grains and vegetables in a large bowl. With moist hands, form the croquettes into small rounds, thick discs or oblong fingers. Pour some cornmeal onto a plate and gently pat croquette until completely coated. This will hold the croquette together as well as give it a crispy outer coating.

To deep-fry, heat about 1 inch of oil in a heavy skillet or pan over medium heat. Deep-fry each croquette until golden brown. Drain well on paper towels to remove excess oil. If shallow-frying, heat about 1/4 inch of oil in a skillet over medium heat. Fry the croquettes on each side until golden. Drain well on paper towels.

These are great served with Creamy Sesame Dressing (page 413), Garlic, Mushroom & Leek Sauce (page 423) or a simple dipping sauce consisting of soy sauce, water and fresh ginger juice or lemon juice.   Makes 4 or 5 servings

VARIATIONS Don't be limited to this combination. Any cooked whole or cracked grains will make delicious croquettes. Rice with bulgur, millet with couscous, barley and corn—the list is virtually endless.

Bulgur, Mushroom & Greens Salad In the
summer months, it is really nice to lighten things up a bit with quick-cooking cracked grains on occasion. This delicious salad combines a variety of flavors to create a nutty, sweet and sour medley.

2 cups spring or filtered water

Sea salt

1 cup bulgur

2 tablespoons extra-virgin olive oil

1/2 cup diced onion

1 cup button mushrooms, brushed clean and thinly sliced

6 or 7 leaves kale or collard greens, rinsed

1 cup seedless grapes

Juice of 1 lemon

2 tablespoons slivered almonds, pan-toasted (See note, below)

Bring water and a pinch of salt to a boil in a medium pan over medium heat. Add bulgur, cover, and reduce heat. Cook 20 minutes or until water is absorbed and bulgur is fluffy.

Heat oil in a skillet over medium heat. Add onion and a pinch of salt and cook until translucent, about 5 minutes. Add mushrooms and sauté until limp. Slice greens into small pieces, add to the skillet and cook 10 minutes or until greens are deep green. Add grapes and stir well. Remove from heat and stir in lemon juice. Toss with bulgur and almonds and transfer to a serving bowl. Makes 4 or 5 servings

NOTE Pan-toast almonds in a dry skillet over medium heat, stirring constantly, until fragrant, about 5 minutes.

Nutty Rice & Broccoli

Another take on a basic grain dish.

See? The variations really are endless . . .

2 cups brown rice, rinsed

2 1/2 cups spring or filtered water

2 pinches of sea salt

2 cups broccoli flowerets

1/4 cup diced carrot

1/4 cup diced red onion

1/2 cup walnut pieces

1 teaspoon barley miso, dissolved in a little water

Grated peel of 1 lemon

Combine rice and water in a pressure cooker. Bring to a boil, loosely covered, over medium heat. Add salt, seal, and bring to full pressure. Place over a flame deflector, reduce heat to low, and cook 45 minutes. Remove from heat and allow pressure to reduce naturally.

While the rice is cooking, bring a pan of water to a boil. Separately, cook broccoli, carrot and onion in boiling water until crisp-tender, cool in iced water and drain. Mix vegetables together in a medium bowl. Set aside.

Heat a dry skillet over medium heat. Add the walnuts and pan-toast until fragrant, about 5 minutes, stirring. Puree walnuts and miso until a coarse paste forms. Stir vegetables, walnut paste, and lemon peel into rice. Transfer to a serving bowl. 🌿 M a k e s 6 o r 8 s e r v i n g s

Brown Rice Risotto

Traditionally made in northern Italy from a glutinous white rice, this risotto is a whole-grain version. A few alterations in ingredients and cooking methods result in a rich and creamy dish, much like the classic version. 🌿

1 1/2 cups medium-grain brown rice

2 teaspoons light sesame oil

Sea salt

1/4 cup mirin

3/4 cup spring or filtered water

5 cups Vegetable Stock (page 96)

1/4 cup leek, rinsed well and
thinly sliced

1/2 cup diced carrot

Soak rice in water to cover 6 to 8 hours. Drain and discard the soaking water. Heat 1 teaspoon of the oil in a deep skillet over medium heat. Add rice and a pinch of salt and cook, stirring, until coated with oil. Stir in mirin and water, cover and cook, stirring frequently, over medium heat. As soon as rice absorbs the liquid, begin adding vegetable stock in 1/2-cup amounts, stirring frequently, but cooking rice covered, instead of the traditional method of cooking risotto in an uncovered pan. As rice absorbs liquid, continue adding stock until all the stock has been used, 40 to 45 minutes. Taste the rice to be sure that it is tender before removing from heat.

Heat the remaining oil in a skillet over medium heat. Add leeks and a pinch of salt and cook, stirring, until limp. Add carrots and a pinch of salt and cook until tender. Stir vegetables into the risotto. Serve warm. 🌿 M a k e s 5 o r 6 s e r v i n g s

Basic Risotto

Rather than pasta, rice is the dominant grain in the cuisine of northern Italy. Risotto is traditionally made with Arborio rice, a white, glutinous grain. Its name refers to the cooking method as well as to the dish itself. The trademark creamy texture is achieved by slowly adding liquid, usually a savory stock, in small increments, cooking the rice over medium heat and stirring constantly. Straying from these basics can result in tough, uncooked risotto or gluey, sticky risotto—neither of which is desirable. ✒

4 cups Vegetable Stock (page 96)
1 tablespoon extra-virgin olive oil
1 to 2 cloves garlic, minced
1 small onion, diced

Pinch of sea salt
1 cup Arborio rice, rinsed well
1 cup white wine or spring water

Warm stock over low heat and keep warm. Heat oil in a deep skillet over medium heat. Add garlic, onion and salt and cook, stirring, until onion is softened, about 3 minutes. Add rice and cook, stirring, 2 to 3 minutes. Add wine and, stirring often, cook until absorbed into rice.

In 1/2-cup amounts, slowly add warm stock mixture to rice and cook, stirring constantly, until liquid is absorbed. Continue this process until all stock mixture is used and rice is creamy and tender, about 25 minutes. ✒ M a k e s   4   o r   5   s e r v i n g s

Butternut Squash Risotto

The squash adds a rich golden color and delightful sweet taste to basic risotto. ✿

1 medium butternut squash, seeds removed and cut into 8 pieces

5 cups Vegetable Stock (page 96)

1 tablespoon extra-virgin olive oil

3 shallots, peeled and minced

Soy sauce

1 cup Arborio rice, rinsed

1/2 cup white wine (or 1/4 cup mirin plus 1/4 cup water)

Generous pinch of grated nutmeg

Fresh basil, minced, plus several whole leaves, for garnish

Steam the squash over boiling water 10 to 15 minutes or until soft. Scoop meat out of skin and mash. Set aside. Heat stock in a large pot and keep warm over low heat.

Heat olive oil in a heavy, deep skillet over medium heat. Add the shallots and a little soy sauce and cook, stirring, 2 to 3 minutes. Add rice and cook, stirring, 2 to 3 minutes. Stirring constantly, add wine and cook until wine is almost absorbed. Stir in squash puree. In 1/2-cup amounts, slowly add warm stock to rice and cook, stirring constantly, until liquid is absorbed. Continue this process until all of stock is used and rice is creamy and tender, about 25 minutes. Add nutmeg and minced basil to taste. Serve hot, garnished with fresh basil leaves. ✿ M a k e s 4 o r 5 s e r v i n g s

Mushroom-Leek Risotto

The mushroom flavor is enhanced by the homemade stock and fresh mushrooms. ✿

5 to 6 cups Mushroom Stock (page 97)

1 tablespoon extra-virgin olive oil

1 or 2 cloves garlic, minced

1/2 small leek, rinsed well and thinly sliced

Sea salt

1 cup thinly sliced button mushrooms, brushed free of dirt

1/2 cup thinly sliced porcini mushrooms, brushed free of dirt

1 cup Arborio rice, rinsed

1 cup white wine or 1/2 cup water and 1/2 cup wine or mirin

1/4 cup minced fresh parsley

Heat stock in a large pot and keep warm over low heat. Heat about half of the olive oil in a deep skillet over medium heat. Add garlic and sauté 2 to 3 minutes. Add leek and a pinch of sea salt and cook, stirring, until leek is bright green and softened. Add mushrooms and a pinch of sea salt and cook until softened. Transfer mixture to a small bowl and set aside.

In the same skillet, heat remaining oil over medium heat. Add the rice and cook, stirring, 2 to 3 minutes. Stirring constantly, add the wine and cook, stirring, until wine is almost absorbed. In 1/2-cup amounts, slowly add warm stock to rice and cook, stirring constantly, until liquid is absorbed. Continue this process until all of stock is used and rice is creamy and tender, about 25 minutes. Stir in sautéed vegetables and minced parsley. Serve hot. M a k e s 4 o r 5 s e r v i n g s

Corn & Shallot Risotto This is a perfect summer dish when corn is at its peak.

5 cups Corn Stock (page 70)

1 tablespoon extra-virgin olive oil

2 to 3 shallots, peeled and minced

2 cloves garlic, minced

Sea salt

1 cup Arborio rice, rinsed

1/4 cup mirin

1/2 cup water

2 ears of corn, kernels removed

Fresh rosemary leaves and sprigs

Heat stock in a large pot and keep warm over low heat. Heat the olive oil in a deep skillet over medium heat. Add shallots, garlic, and a pinch of sea salt and sauté 2 to 3 minutes or until fragrant. Add rice and cook, stirring, 2 to 3 minutes. Stir in mirin and water and cook, stirring constantly, until liquid is absorbed.

In 1/2-cup amounts, slowly add warm stock to rice and cook, stirring constantly, until liquid is absorbed. Continue this process until all of stock is used and rice is creamy and tender, about 25 minutes.

Meanwhile, add corn to boiling water and bring back to a boil to bring out its sweetness; drain. Stir corn and about 1/8 teaspoon fresh rosemary leaves into rice. Serve hot, garnished with rosemary sprigs. Makes 4 or 5 servings

CORN STOCK

1 teaspoon corn oil

1 onion, diced

Sea salt

3 to 4 ears of corn, kernels removed

8 to 9 cups spring or filtered water

2 bay leaves

Make stock: Heat oil in a large pot over medium heat. Add onion and a pinch of salt and cook, stirring, 2 to 3 minutes. Add corn kernels and cook, stirring, until coated with oil. Add water, corn cobs, and bay leaves and bring to a boil. Reduce heat and simmer 1 hour. Season lightly with salt and simmer 10 minutes. Strain the stock, pressing as much liquid as possible from the vegetables before discarding them. Makes about 6 cups

Baked Risotto with Italian Herbs

A variation on the stovetop theme . . . great rich taste with no stirring.

5 to 6 cups Vegetable Stock (page 96)

1 tablespoon extra-virgin olive oil

1 small onion, minced

2 cloves garlic, minced

Sea salt

1 cup Arborio rice

Equal amounts (about 1/2 teaspoon each) of fresh parsley, basil, rosemary and oregano

1/2 cup spring or filtered water

1/2 cup white wine

Preheat oven to 350F (175C). Lightly oil a shallow baking dish. Heat stock in a large pot and keep warm over low heat. Heat the olive oil in a skillet over medium heat. Add onion, garlic and a pinch of sea salt and sauté 2 to 3 minutes or until softened. Add rice and cook, stirring, 2 to 3 minutes. Stir in herbs. Spoon into prepared dish. Combine water, wine and stock and pour over rice mixture. Stir well, cover and bake 25 to 30 minutes or until liquid is absorbed and rice is tender. Remove from oven and allow to stand, undisturbed, 5 minutes. Stir well and serve hot. ❧ M a k e s 4 o r 5 s e r v i n g s

Hato Mugi Stew

Hato mugi, or Job's Tears barley, has been revered in the Orient for centuries for its ability to restore the complexion to flawless vitality. I learned this recipe from Aveline Kushi, whose skin simply glows with perfection. The energy of this dish is amazing. Its cleansing properties are present in each ingredient: hato mugi and daikon to remove excess fat and protein from organs, shiitake mushrooms to cleanse the blood, lotus root to promote respiratory clarity, onion to sweeten, kombu to help in the absorption of the protein and fat in the dish, and celery, a natural mild diuretic. All these ingredients combine to help improve the quality of blood that feeds each organ and ultimately nourishes our skin. ❧

1 (1-inch) piece of kombu
1/2 cup dried daikon, soaked until
    tender and diced
2 dried shiitake mushrooms, soaked
    until tender and diced
2 or 3 slices dried lotus root, soaked
    until tender and diced

2 cups hato mugi, sorted and
    rinsed well
1 small onion, diced
Spring or filtered water
Soy sauce
2 or 3 celery stalks, diced

Place kombu in the bottom of a pressure cooker. Reserving all soaking waters, place daikon, mushrooms, lotus root, hato mugi and onion on top of kombu. Measure the soaking water and add enough fresh water to make 4 cups. Add water to the pressure cooker. Add a little soy sauce, seal, and bring to full pressure. Place over a flame deflector, reduce heat to low, and cook 35 minutes. Remove pot from heat and allow pressure to reduce naturally before opening. Stir celery gently into cooked grain and transfer to a serving bowl. Serve hot. ❧ M a k e s 6 t o 8 s e r v i n g s

Millet-Tofu Stew

Truly one of the great comforting dishes of all time with its creamy texture laden with sweetly satisfying squash, laced with tiny cubes of tofu, and wrapped in the nutty taste of millet.

1 cup millet

1 cup cubed winter squash

1/2 cup small cubes tofu

5 cups spring or filtered water

1 teaspoon barley miso

Nori, green onions or parsley, for garnish

Millet tends to hold on to dust, so be sure to rinse it: Place millet in a bowl, cover with water, and gently swirl with hands to loosen any dirt. Drain and repeat 2 or 3 times or until the water is relatively clear. Layer squash and then tofu in a heavy pot and top with millet. Gently add water, cover, and bring to a boil over medium heat. Reduce heat and cook about 30 minutes, until liquid is absorbed and millet has a creamy texture. Dissolve miso in a small amount of warm water and gently stir into millet. Simmer 2 to 3 minutes. Remove from heat and stir briskly. Squash will break apart and disperse throughout the millet. Serve hot, garnished with shredded nori, green onions, or minced parsley.

Makes 4 or 5 servings

Smashing Corn Casserole

This truly deluxe casserole is a snap to make and a hit with everyone who has tasted it. It blends the sweet taste of fresh corn, tangy roasted red bell peppers, rich sesame tahini and the nutritional kick of tofu.

1 (1-lb.) package firm tofu

1/3 cup sesame tahini

Soy sauce

About 1/2 cup yellow cornmeal

Pinch of sea salt

Spring or filtered water

2 ears of corn, kernels removed and outer husks reserved

1 red bell pepper, roasted over an open flame, peeled, seeded and diced

Cooking the Whole Foods Way

Preheat oven to 375F (190C). Lightly oil a deep casserole dish. Mix the tofu and tahini together until blended and season lightly with soy sauce. Set aside. In a medium bowl, mix cornmeal, salt, and enough water to make a thick paste. You will need about 1 1/2 cups of this mixture. Fold in corn kernels. Set aside.

Line the prepared casserole dish with several clean corn husks, allowing them to hang over the sides a bit. Begin layering by spreading some cornmeal mixture on the husks. Next, add some of the tofu mixture and sprinkle with some of the bell peppers. Continue layering until the dish is full, but be sure to end with cornmeal mixture on the top. Fold the husks over the casserole and press into the topping to hold them in place. Cover and bake 35 minutes or until firm. Remove the cover and return to oven to brown the top slightly. Serve immediately. ℘ Makes 4 or 5 servings

Grain Medley

This simple combination is just one of literally thousands you can come up with for mixing various whole grains. I love this particular one for its complementary flavors—the sweetness of rice is nicely set off by the slight sour taste of barley and wheat berries. And the stickiness of the sweet rice rounds out the rich contrasting textures of the whole medley. ℘

1/4 cup *each* short-grain brown rice, sweet brown rice, whole-wheat berries, and whole barley

2 1/2 cups spring or filtered water

Pinch of sea salt

Rinse grains by combining them in a bowl and adding water. Gently swirl the grains in the water with your fingers to loosen any dust; drain. Place grains and water in a pressure cooker, cover loosely, and bring to a boil over medium heat. Add salt, seal the lid, and cook over low heat 20 minutes. Increase the heat to high and bring to full pressure. Place over a flame deflector, reduce heat to low, and cook 45 minutes. Remove pot from heat and allow pressure to reduce naturally before opening and stir well before transferring to a serving bowl. ℘ Makes 5 or 6 servings

Millet-Corn Loaf

This is a really unique way to serve this lovely grain. Millet takes on a delightful, creamy texture that will cause the grain to set up as it cools—ideal for a loaf like this.

1 small onion, diced
1 small carrot, diced
1 ear of corn, kernels removed
1 1/2 cups millet, rinsed
6 cups spring or filtered water

Sea salt
2 to 3 green onions, thinly sliced
2 tablespoons umeboshi vinegar
3 tablespoons sesame tahini

In a heavy pot, place diced onion, carrot, corn and millet. Add water and a pinch of sea salt. Cover and bring to a boil over medium heat. Reduce heat and simmer 25 to 30 minutes. Season lightly with salt and simmer 5 minutes. Stir in green onions and remove from heat.

Preheat oven to 300F (150C). Lightly oil a loaf pan. Whisk together umeboshi vinegar and tahini and stir into cooked millet. Press mixture into prepared pan and bake, uncovered, 15 minutes. Allow to cool slightly before slicing so the loaf can set up.

To serve, cut into slices and serve with a light sauce or lightly pan-fry before serving.
Makes 5 or 6 servings

Old World Polenta

I hated polenta as a child. Well, okay, it wasn't the polenta I actually hated, but the process. My mother liked to make it the old-fashioned way—stirred literally for hours over low heat while it thickened and finally pulled away from the pan and could be turned out to set. And yes, you guessed it. All us kids got to do the stirring. Sure, the resulting dish was delicious, but we were exhausted! Well, I have since learned that you can make an equally delicious polenta just as light and airy in no time at all.

5 cups spring or filtered water
Sea salt
1/2 cup fresh corn kernels
1 cup yellow corn grits
Fresh basil (optional), minced

....

Extra-virgin olive oil
Fresh Basil Pesto (page 426), Creamy
   Mushroom Sauce (page 420),
   Roasted Pepper Sauce (page
   424), or other sauce (optional)

Lightly oil a shallow casserole dish. In a deep pot, bring water and salt to a rolling boil. Add corn kernels and then whisk in corn grits and cook, whisking constantly, until the mixture returns to a boil. Reduce heat to very low and cook, stirring frequently, until the center of the polenta "burps," about 25 minutes. Stir in basil, if using, and a splash of olive oil and whisk vigorously to blend. Turn into prepared dish and allow to stand until set, about 30 minutes. Slice and serve with sauce, if using.   Makes 5 or 6 servings

VARIATIONS If serving the polenta with a sauce, I usually omit the herbs, so that flavors don't compete. If I want a smooth, airy, almost quichelike polenta, I omit the corn kernels. However, if I am serving polenta on its own, then I cook it with not only the herbs and corn, but also some finely diced green onion and minced parsley.

Buckwheat Salad

Because buckwheat's nature is to create warmth in the body, it is not usually thought of in the context of summer grain salads, but it makes a wonderful nutty base to build on for this simple recipe.

2 cups buckwheat groats, rinsed
4 cups boiling water
Pinch of sea salt
2 to 3 stalks celery, diced
3 to 4 red radishes, thinly sliced

1 cup sauerkraut, drained
3 to 4 green onions, sliced thinly on the diagonal
Parsley sprigs for garnish

Lightly pan-toast buckwheat in a dry skillet over medium heat 5 to 7 minutes or until fragrant. This will cause the grain to hold its shape, creating a more desirable texture for a salad.

Bring water to a boil and add buckwheat and salt. Cover, reduce to low and cook 15 to 20 minutes or until water is absorbed and buckwheat is tender. Remove from heat and transfer to a large bowl. Fluff with a fork.

Bring a small pot of water to a boil and quickly boil the celery and radishes separately, about 30 seconds each. Toss together the buckwheat, sauerkraut, celery, radishes, and onions until combined. Serve garnished with parsley sprigs. ✐

Makes 4 or 5 servings

Fried Wheat & Rye

This incredibly unique flavor combination will surely wake up your taste buds! Deliciously rich and chewy, it will also stick to your ribs. ✐

1 cup whole-wheat berries, soaked 6 to 8 hours and drained
1/4 cup whole rye berries, soaked 6 to 8 hours and drained
2 cups spring or filtered water
Pinch of sea salt

1 to 2 teaspoons dark sesame oil
1/4 cup diced onion
Soy sauce
1/4 cup diced celery
1 small carrot, diced

Place the soaked grains in a pressure cooker with the water. Cover loosely and bring to a boil. Add salt, seal the lid and bring to full pressure over medium heat. Place over a flame deflector, reduce heat to low, and cook 50 minutes. Remove pot from heat and allow pressure to reduce naturally. ✍ Makes 4 or 5 servings

Heat oil in a skillet over medium heat. Add onion and a little soy sauce and cook until onion is translucent, about 5 minutes. Add celery, carrot and more soy sauce and cook, stirring occasionally, until softened. Spoon cooked grain over vegetables, sprinkle lightly with soy sauce and cover. Simmer until vegetables are tender. Stir well and serve.

Savory Barley Stew

The flavor of barley is surpassed only by its energizing properties. Creating wonderful dispersing energy in the body, barley not only keeps you cool in warmer weather, but regular consumption can help in ridding the body of excess fats and protein. This simple and delicious stew employs a layering style of cooking, which brings to the dish two things: ease of preparation and the energy of layering— a gathering of the ingredients' characters that provide us with great strength. ✍

1 (1-inch) piece kombu
1 small onion, diced
1 cup diced button mushrooms, brushed clean
1 to 2 celery stalks, diced
1 carrot, diced

1 1/2 cups whole barley, rinsed and soaked 6 to 8 hours
3 cups spring or filtered water
Soy sauce
Sliced green onion, for garnish

Place kombu on the bottom of a pressure cooker and layer the onion, mushrooms, celery, carrot and, finally, barley on top. Slowly add water, trying not to disturb the layering. Add a sprinkle of soy sauce, seal the lid, and bring to full pressure. Place over a flame deflector, reduce heat to low, and cook 45 minutes. Remove pot from heat and allow pressure to reduce naturally. Season lightly with a little soy sauce and simmer 5 to 7 minutes more. Stir well and transfer to a serving bowl. Serve garnished with green onion. ✍ Makes 4 or 5 servings

Miso-Millet Stew

A hearty, warming breakfast dish, this is sure to get your day off to a great start.

1/2 teaspoon light sesame oil
1 small onion, diced
1 small parsnip, diced
Sea salt
1 cup millet, rinsed and drained

1/4 cup dried sweet corn
5 cups spring or filtered water
2 1/2 teaspoons barley miso
Mirin

Heat oil in a heavy pot over medium heat. Add onion and a pinch of salt and cook, stirring, until onion is translucent, about 2 minutes. Add parsnip and a pinch of salt and cook, stirring, until coated with oil. Top with millet and dried corn and slowly add water. Cover and bring to a boil. Reduce heat and simmer 25 to 30 minutes. Dissolve miso in a small amount of water, stir into stew and simmer, uncovered, 4 to 5 minutes. Remove from heat and stir in a little mirin. Transfer to a serving bowl and serve.

M a k e s   4   o r   5   s e r v i n g s

Mochi Melt

Miss melted cheese? Try this incredibly rich and easy-to-make alternative. Sure to cure the dairy blues . . .

1 teaspoon dark sesame oil
1/2 leek, rinsed well and thinly sliced
1 cup thinly sliced button mushrooms
1 carrot, cut into thin matchsticks
1 parsnip, cut into thin matchsticks
1 cup matchsticks daikon

1/2 cup finely shredded green cabbage
1 cup cauliflowerets
Soy sauce
1 cup broccoli flowerets
1 to 2 cups thin strips Mochi (page 49)
1/2 cup spring or filtered water

Heat oil in a large skillet over medium heat. Add vegetables (except broccoli) and stir-fry in the order listed in the recipe until tender, but not quite cooked through, seasoning lightly throughout cooking with soy sauce. Spread the vegetables evenly over the bottom of the skillet and top with broccoli. Begin placing thin strips of mochi over the entire surface. When the vegetables are completely covered with mochi, gently pour water down the side of the skillet to allow everything to steam. Cover and cook over medium heat about 10 minutes, until mochi melts completely. Serve immediately.

M a k e s   4   o r   5   s e r v i n g s

Kasha with Noodles

A very traditional recipe cooked in a very healthy manner. It is so wonderful to go back and find all of these traditional foods that work so well in our return to a more natural style of cooking. ✺

1 cup blonde kasha, rinsed and drained

2 cups spring or filtered water

Pinch of sea salt

1 small onion, halved through stem end and thinly sliced crosswise

1 cup uncooked whole-grain noodles, spirals, bow-ties or elbows

Fresh sauerkraut, for garnish

Add kasha to a large dry pot over medium heat and pan-roast, stirring occasionally, until darker golden in color and very fragrant, about 2 to 3 minutes.

Bring water and salt to a boil. Add onion and simmer 2 minutes. Pour water and onion over kasha and return to a boil. Reduce heat to low, cover, and cook until liquid is absorbed, about 15 minutes. Remove from heat and allow to stand, undisturbed, 5 minutes.

While the kasha is cooking, bring a pot of water to a boil and cook noodles until just tender. Drain well.

Toss kasha and onions with noodles, mix well, and transfer to a serving bowl. Serve garnished with sauerkraut. ✺ M a k e s 4 o r 5 s e r v i n g s

Nori Maki

I remember the first time I attempted to make this traditional Japanese dish. Trying to follow very complicated and confusing instructions, I ended up rolling the bamboo sushi mat into the roll. I gave in to defeat that time and did not attempt to make this easy-to-assemble (really!) rice dish until my husband showed me how. Let's see if I can instruct you more clearly—I have certainly made all the mistakes you can make . . . . ✏

2 to 3 sheets of nori
About 1 cup cooked brown rice
Filling (opposite)
Pickled ginger or dipping sauce

FILLING

2 to 3 blanched carrot spears
2 to 3 thinly sliced green onion spears
Prepared mustard
Fresh sauerkraut

Take either a bamboo sushi mat or a cotton dish towel and place it in front of you on a dry work surface. If using a mat, make sure that the bamboo pieces are horizontal (so it can roll up). Next, place the nori, shiny side down, on the mat. (If nori is toasted, simply take it from the package and use it. If you purchased untoasted nori, toast it over an open flame until it turns a deep green.)

Press rice evenly and firmly over nori sheet, leaving about 1 inch of nori exposed at the edges closest to and farthest from you. Make sure the rice covers the nori completely from side to side. Rice should be about 1/4 inch thick.

Place filling ingredients on the rice on the edge closest to you. A thin line of filling will suffice: a carrot and onion spear, a thin line of mustard and sauerkraut. Then, using the mat as a guide, roll the nori maki, jelly-roll style, completely encasing the rice and filling in nori.

When completely rolled, wrap the mat around the maki and gently press to seal the roll. Remove the mat and with a sharp, wet knife, slice the nori roll, crosswise, into 8 nori rounds, about 1 inch thick. Arrange on a serving platter and serve with pickled ginger or a mild dipping sauce made of soy sauce, water, ginger, and diced green onion. ✏

M a k e s   4   o r   5   s e r v i n g s

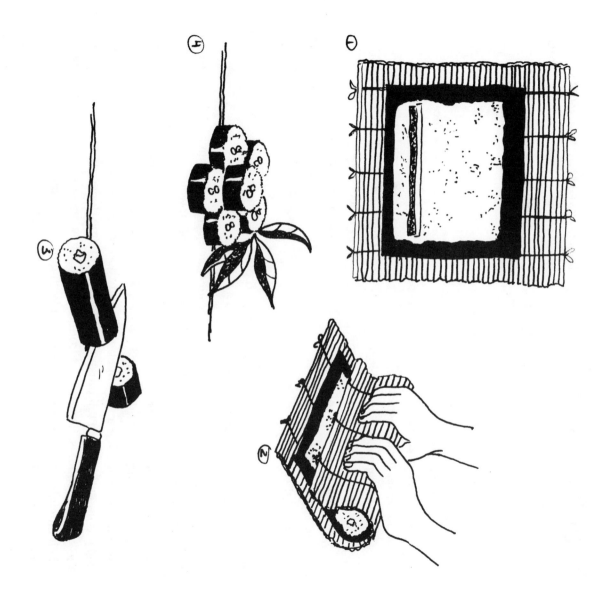

Spanish Paella

I love to play with traditional recipes, making them work for me within my own understanding of cooking and food energy. This delicious version of paella has no meat, fowl or fish, but is packed with flavor. You won't miss anything . . . This hearty rice dish can stand on its own as a meal with some lightly steamed vegetables on the side. ✑

1 1/2 cups short-grain brown rice, rinsed and drained

Safflower oil for deep-frying

4 ounces tempeh, cut into 1/4-inch cubes

1 teaspoon extra-virgin olive oil

1 to 2 cloves garlic, minced

1 onion, diced

1 or 2 celery stalks, diced

1 carrot, diced

1 cup diced fresh burdock

2 cups spring or filtered water

Soy sauce

Minced fresh parsley

Freshly grated gingerroot and juice (page 242)

Add rice to a dry skillet over medium heat and pan-roast, stirring occasionally, until light brown and fragrant, about 2 to 3 minutes. Set aside.

Heat 1 inch of safflower oil in a deep saucepan over medium heat. Add tempeh and deep-fry until golden brown. Set aside to drain on paper towels.

Heat olive oil in a pressure cooker over medium heat. Add garlic and onion and cook, stirring, until fragrant, about 3 minutes. Add celery, carrot and burdock and stir to combine. Top with rice and tempeh and gently add water. Sprinkle lightly with soy sauce, seal the lid and bring to full pressure. Place over a flame deflector, reduce heat to low, and cook 45 minutes. Remove pot from heat and allow pressure to reduce naturally. Open carefully, stir in parsley, to taste, and fresh ginger juice and pulp to taste and transfer to a serving bowl. ✑ M a k e s 5 o r 6 s e r v i n g s

Sweet Rice with Chestnuts

Winter cooking just wouldn't be the same without chestnuts. In desserts, soups, bean and grain dishes or on their own, lightly roasted, they impart a delicate sweetness that brings a smile to everyone's lips. In this dish, combining chestnuts with sweet rice creates a comfortable warming energy just right for cold winter months, not to mention that this combination nourishes the middle organs of the body—the stomach, spleen, and pancreas—helping to alleviate symptoms of hypoglycemia.

1/2 cup dried or fresh chestnuts (see Note below)	2 1/2 cups spring or filtered water
1 1/2 cups sweet brown rice, rinsed well	Pinch of sea salt per cup of grain and chestnuts

If using dried chestnuts, dry-roast them in a dry skillet over medium heat until fragrant and then soak them 6 to 8 hours before using. This extra bit of effort ensures their sweetness.

Place chestnuts and the rice in a pressure cooker with water. Cover loosely and bring to a boil over medium heat. Add 2 pinches of salt, seal the lid, and bring to full pressure. Place over a flame deflector, reduce heat to low, and cook 45 minutes. Remove pot from heat and allow pressure to reduce naturally. Gently stir to combine grain and chestnuts. Transfer to a serving bowl. Makes 4 or 5 servings

NOTE If using fresh chestnuts for this dish, cut a cross in the flat side of each and roast in a 350F (175C) oven about 20 minutes. Allow to cool enough to handle and peel. You may also boil the chestnuts 15 minutes before peeling.

Millet "Mashed Potatoes"

I am not much into disguising healthy foods to look like their conventional counterparts: you know, tofu lasagna, etc. The diner is always disappointed, and more than that, our approach to food will never change if habits don't change. So while this grain dish is very unlike mashed potatoes as you may know them, its creamy, rich texture and mellow flavor make it a wonderful alternative to its cream and fat-laden counterpart.

1 onion, diced
1 cup cauliflowerets
1 cup millet, rinsed

4 to 5 cups spring or filtered water
1 teaspoon sweet white miso
1/4 cup minced fresh parsley

Place onions on the bottom of a heavy pot. Add cauliflower and then millet. Gently add water, trying not to disturb the layers. The layering effect allows the flavors of the vegetables to cook up into the grain without stirring. Cover and bring to a boil. Reduce heat and cook over low heat about 25 to 30 minutes, until liquid has been absorbed and millet is soft. Dissolve the miso in a small amount of water. Stir mixture into millet and simmer 3 to 4 minutes more. Whisk briskly to create creamy texture, fold in minced parsley and serve topped with your favorite gravy. We love this dish smothered in Creamy Mushroom Sauce (page 420). Makes 4 or 5 servings

Holiday Rice

Nothing spices up a vegetarian holiday meal more than a deliciously festive whole-grain entree. This combination of fragrant basmati, tangy tangerines, and aromatic pine nuts creates something so good that you know it's a triumph. The dressing should be a light essence added to the cooked rice. A small amount will go a long way.

1 1/2 cups brown basmati rice, rinsed
1/2 cup wild rice, rinsed
2 1/2 cups spring or filtered water
Sea salt
1/4 cup fresh tangerine juice
1/2 cup dried currants

2 tangerines
2 tablespoons pine nuts
2 to 3 tablespoons extra-virgin olive oil
2 tablespoons sweet brown rice vinegar

Combine both rices in a pressure cooker with water. Cover loosely and bring to a boil. Add salt, seal the lid, and bring to full pressure. Place over a flame deflector, reduce heat to low, and cook 50 minutes.

Meanwhile, heat the tangerine juice in a small saucepan until hot and pour it over the currants to soften them. Peel and section the tangerines, being careful to remove all the skin and threads to avoid a bitter taste. Lightly pan-toast the pine nuts in a dry skillet over medium heat 2 to 3 minutes until fragrant and set aside.

When the rice is cooked, remove pot from heat and allow the pressure to reduce naturally. Open the lid and stir in currants and juice, tangerine segments, olive oil and rice vinegar. Stir well and transfer to a serving bowl. Just before serving, stir in pine nuts.

❧ M a k e s   5   o r   6   s e r v i n g s

Corn-Squash Pudding

This hearty side dish is great and easy to make. The combination of sweet, chewy corn and tender squash is so satisfying. ❧

2 ears of corn, kernels removed

1/4 to 1/3 cup yellow cornmeal

8 ounces firm tofu

1 to 2 green onions, finely diced

1 to 2 teaspoons white miso, dissolved in 2 tablespoons water

Spring or filtered water

1/2 cup cooked pinto beans

1 small yellow summer squash, diced

Whole-wheat bread crumbs

Preheat oven to 350F (175C). Lightly oil a deep casserole dish. In a large bowl, combine fresh corn with enough cornmeal to coat the kernels and create a crumbly texture. In a blender or food processor, puree tofu, green onions, white miso to taste and enough water to create a thick paste.

Mix beans and squash with the tofu and cornmeal mixtures until combined. Spoon into prepared dish and top with bread crumbs. Cover and bake 40 minutes. Remove cover and return to oven to brown the top. Allow to stand, undisturbed, 10 minutes before serving. ❧ M a k e s   4   o r   5   s e r v i n g s

Polenta with Mushroom Ragout

A more traditional style of polenta, this version is a thick creamy mixture served in bowls. Top it off with this thick, reduced vegetable sauce for a real winning combination. A bit time-consuming to make, however, the sauce can be made up to two days in advance and refrigerated. It may thicken, so you may need to thin it with water when reheating for use.

1 to 2 teaspoons extra-virgin olive oil

1 or 2 cloves fresh garlic, minced

1 or 2 small carrots, finely diced

2 celery stalks, diced

1/2 red bell pepper, roasted, peeled, seeded, and finely diced

Sea salt

1 to 2 cups 1/4-inch-thick slices button mushrooms, brushed free of dirt

3 or 4 dried shiitake or porcini mushrooms, soaked in warm water until tender, liquid reserved and diced

POLENTA

5 cups spring or filtered water

Sea salt

1 cup yellow cornmeal

Heat the olive oil in a deep skillet over medium-high heat. Add garlic and cook until fragrant, 1 to 2 minutes. Add carrots, celery, bell pepper and a generous pinch of salt and cook, stirring, about 3 minutes. Add fresh mushrooms, reduce heat to medium, and cook until mushrooms exude liquid. Add dried mushrooms and cook, uncovered, until all the liquid evaporates, about 10 minutes. Add mushroom soaking water, plus some additional water to almost half-cover the vegetables. Cover pan and bring to a boil. Reduce heat and simmer about 2 hours, stirring occasionally, until the sauce thickens.

Meanwhile, to prepare polenta, bring the 5 cups water and a generous pinch of salt to a boil in a deep pot over medium heat. Slowly add cornmeal, through your fingers (like rain, my grandmother would say), stirring constantly. Cook, stirring constantly, until polenta becomes very thick and pulls away from the sides of the pan, usually 20 to 30 minutes but up to 1 hour. Ladle into individual serving bowls. Ladle ragout over polenta and serve hot. Makes 5 or 6 servings

Corn with Green Onions & Bell Peppers

We really don't use many peppers in macrobiotic cooking; they belong to the nightshade family, a group of vegetables that create a highly acidic internal condition, which can aggravate certain health problems, create indigestion and, in general, wreck havoc. But in some dishes, you simply can't substitute any other vegetable to get that delicious, strong, smoky taste. So, occasionally, indulge yourself . . .

⁓

1 red bell pepper
1 yellow bell pepper
1 to 2 teaspoons extra-virgin olive oil

1 to 2 green onions, minced
Soy sauce
4 ears of fresh corn, kernels removed

Place whole peppers over an open flame and roast until the outer skin turns completely black. Place them in a paper sack, seal tightly and allow to steam about 10 minutes to loosen the skin. Then rub the peppers gently between your fingers to remove the skins. Seed the roasted peppers and finely dice.

Heat oil in a skillet over medium heat. Add green onions and cook 1 minute. Add bell peppers and a little soy sauce. Add corn and a little soy sauce and cook 10 minutes, stirring occasionally. Transfer to a bowl and serve hot. *⁓*

Makes 4 or 5 servings

Spicy Oriental Rice

Rice and Oriental spices are a natural combination. A tart, gingery dressing really adds pizzazz to this whole-grain side dish.

2 cups organic brown basmati rice

2 1/2 cups spring or filtered water

Sea salt

1 carrot, cut into thin matchsticks

1 cup thin matchsticks fresh daikon or red radish

2 celery stalks, cut into thin diagonal slices

6 or 7 fresh snow peas, trimmed and strings removed

Juice of 1 lemon

2 to 3 tablespoons freshly grated ginger-root, squeezed for juice (page 242)

2 to 3 tablespoons brown rice vinegar

Green onions, sliced, for garnish

Rinse rice by placing in a bowl and covering with water. Gently swirl grain around with your fingers to loosen any dust. Drain by pouring through a strainer. You may need to repeat this process two to three times, depending on how dusty the rice has become. Combine rice and water in a pressure cooker, cover loosely, and bring to a boil over medium heat. Add 2 pinches of salt, seal the pressure cooker, and bring to full pressure. Reduce heat to low and cook on a flame deflector 45 to 50 minutes. Remove pot from heat and allow pressure to reduce naturally.

Place carrot, daikon, celery, and snow peas in a bamboo steamer, arranging them so each one is in its own section. Cover steamer, place over a pot of boiling water and steam vegetables until snow peas are bright green, but still crispy. Remove from heat and set aside.

Prepare the dressing by combining the lemon juice with ginger juice and rice vinegar to taste. Stir together the dressing, vegetables, and rice. Serve hot, garnished with green onions. Makes 6 to 8 servings

Barley with Winter Vegetables

I know, I know, I told you that barley has great dispersing energy and can help to keep you cool in warm weather. So why am I pairing it with warming winter vegetables? Well, the energies harmonize very well to create a very warming stew that's not too heavy and balances with the heavier, well-cooked foods that make up winter cooking. That's why. ✍

2 (1-inch) pieces kombu

2 cups whole barley, rinsed and
soaked 6 to 8 hours

6 cups spring or filtered water

Sea salt

1 onion, chopped

1/2 cup 1/2-inch cubes rutabaga

1/2 cup 1/2-inch cubes turnip

1 small carrot, cut into 1/2-inch
cubes

1/2 cup thinly sliced fresh burdock

2 to 3 dried shiitake mushrooms,
soaked and thinly sliced

2 stalks celery, thinly sliced

Place kombu in a heavy pot and add barley and water. Cover and bring to a boil over medium heat. Reduce heat to low, add salt and cook 40 minutes. Add the vegetables, layering on top of the barley in the order listed. Re-cover pot and cook 40 to 45 minutes, until barley is creamy and vegetables are soft. Stir in celery and transfer to a serving bowl. Serve hot. ✍ Makes 5 or 6 servings

Kasha Croquettes with Creamy Mushroom Sauce

Talk about a stick-to-your-ribs grain dish. Serve this on the coldest winter days to keep you and yours toasty warm. ✑

1 cup buckwheat groats (kasha),
  pan-toasted
2 cups spring or filtered water
Pinch of sea salt
1/4 green cabbage, finely diced
1 onion, finely diced
2 stalks celery, finely diced

Safflower or canola oil
Cornmeal
Whole-wheat pastry flour
1 recipe Creamy Mushroom Sauce
  (page 420)
Minced fresh parsley, for garnish

In a hot, dry skillet, lightly toast the kasha, stirring occasionally, about 2 to 3 minutes or until fragrant to bring out its natural, nutty flavor.

Bring water and salt to a boil, add kasha, and return to a boil. Cover, reduce heat, and simmer 15 to 20 minutes, until all liquid has been absorbed. Remove from heat and stir gently to fluff grain. Stir in the diced vegetables.

Heat about 1/2 inch of oil in a deep skillet over medium heat. With moist hands, press a small amount of kasha mixture into rounds or ovals (or any other shape you'd like), pressing firmly to ensure that the croquette holds together. Mix together equal parts of cornmeal and flour. Dredge each one in flour mixture and pan-fry until golden, 2 to 3 minutes on each side. Drain well on paper towels and serve on a pool of Creamy Mushroom Sauce, garnished with parsley. ✑ M a k e s 4 o r 5 s e r v i n g s

Millet Pie

Millet takes on a creamy texture when cooked, and, upon cooling, it is easily molded into shapes, lending itself nicely to a variety of uses. One delicious way to add millet to your diet is to create a pie crust for a rich vegetable filling.

MILLET CRUST

3 cups spring or filtered water

Pinch of sea salt

1 cup millet, rinsed and drained

VEGETABLE FILLING

1 to 2 teaspoons extra-virgin olive oil

1 or 2 cloves garlic, minced

2 to 3 shallots or 1 onion, diced

Soy sauce

1 carrot, diced

1/2 cup diced daikon

1/2 cup diced rutabaga or turnip

1/2 cup diced winter squash

1 to 2 cups cauliflowerets

2 cups peeled and diced broccoli stems

1 cup broccoli flowerets

1 cup fresh or frozen corn kernels

Spring or filtered water

Generous pinch of fresh or dried ground rosemary

3 to 4 leaves fresh leafy greens (kale, collards, etc.), finely chopped

1 tablespoon kuzu, dissolved in 2 tablespoons water

To prepare the crust, bring water and salt to a boil, add the millet, and return to a boil. Reduce heat, cover, and simmer until creamy, about 30 minutes. Remove from heat and whisk briskly to increase creaminess. Allow to cool only enough to be able to handle it, stirring frequently to prevent the millet from setting up. When cool enough to handle, press the millet into a lightly oiled pie plate, taking care to create an even crust on the bottom and sides. Set aside while preparing the filling.

Preheat oven to 375F (190C). To prepare the filling, heat olive oil in a skillet over medium heat. Add garlic, shallots and a sprinkle of soy sauce and cook until limp, about 3 minutes. Add carrot, daikon, rutabaga, squash, cauliflower and broccoli stems and cook 2 or 3 minutes. Add broccoli flowerets, corn and about 1 cup water. Add rosemary and sprinkle with soy sauce. Cover and cook over medium-low heat about 10 minutes. Add chopped greens and simmer, covered, until bright green, about 5 minutes. Stir in dissolved kuzu and cook, stirring, 3 minutes or until a thin glaze forms over the vegetables.

Spoon the filling into the crust and bake about 30 minutes, until the filling is set and the millet crust turns a nice golden color. Serve warm.

Makes 6 to 8 servings

SAVORY SOUPS & STEWS

Soup making has always been a kind of ritual in my kitchen. I can remember the aromas coming from the bubbling pots on my mom's stove. She had a way of combining the most humble ingredients to make the most delicious soups and stews. She understood that the key to really good soup is determined by the quality and freshness of what goes into the pot—never any limp, old veggies for her. I learned well.

I find it interesting that meals begin with soup. Have you ever wondered why? It is a symbolic return to the sea, where life began. Also, a bowl of soup is soothing and relaxing. It stimulates the appetite and relaxes our digestive system in preparation for the meal to come.

Soup creates the atmosphere for the entire meal. An ideal soup complements the meal with its taste, texture, aroma and color. If a meal is hearty and complex, it is always a pleasure to begin the meal with a simple, elegant broth or clear soup. A light and simple meal might be given some substance by beginning with a thick vegetable, bean or grain stew.

Seasonal balance also plays a large role in soup making. In cooler weather, I tend more toward warming soups that include a greater portion of root vegetables, richer ingredients, and stronger seasoning. During the warmer months of the year, I make more cooling soups, even chilled soups, to complement the weather. Lighter ingredients, like noodles, leafy greens and delicately cut vegetables, along with lighter seasoning and reduced cooking time will actually help to beat the heat.

The variety of soups we can prepare is virtually limitless. There are a few basic, yet essential techniques that, if mastered, will give you the confidence you need to really experience the pleasure of making soup. Remember that repetition is our greatest teacher. Find a few favorite recipes and make them a few times to build your confidence. Then, change ingredients around. Vary the beans and vegetables. Add whole or cracked grains. Season with any variety of herbs. Sauté the vegetables before adding water. The possibilities of soup are endless. Scavenging around the refrigerator, you will come up with enough fresh ingredients to make a wonderfully delicious soup.

SOME BASIC TECHNIQUES

Soups need to begin with base or foundation flavors. I begin a lot of my soups by either sautéing or simmering onions, shallots or leeks, and occasionally a bit of garlic. A pinch of sea salt at this point seals in the vegetables' flavors while drawing out some vegetables' juices, thereby creating a richer flavor.

When seasoning soups, don't wait until the last minute. Herbs, spices, and salty seasonings need time to develop and blend with the other flavors in the soup. You may even want to add seasoning several times during cooking so that the flavors gradually mature until they are exactly as you desire. Common choices for seasoning are good-quality soy sauce or sea salt, both of which I simmer for at least 7 minutes to develop the flavors. Fresh herbs and garnish will serve you best if added just prior to serving.

Generally, miso is added only toward the end of cooking—the last 3 to 4 minutes to be exact. Miso adds a full-bodied taste to any soup, but its real benefits come from its delicate enzyme content. These beneficial enzymes are good for intestinal and immune system strength. However, the enzymes are delicate. When seasoning with miso, take care not to boil the soup; the enzymes need heat to activate, but boiling will destroy them, so instead just simmer miso about 4 minutes.

I don't often add wine or mirin to soups, but occasionally these more exotic ingredients can add a depth to soup that is impossible to achieve any other way. I save this type of seasoning for special occasions.

I mostly begin my soups with fresh spring or filtered water, but sometimes I like to make stocks. They give the soup a full-bodied taste that is simply amazing. When adding stock to soup, go slowly. Adding stock gradually ensures that the soup will retain its richness and texture. A too-thin soup can be flavorless and flat. Remember that even simple brothlike soups should have a full flavor.

Soups based on beans or whole grains can be hearty or incredibly light. It all depends on the seasoning and quantities of ingredients. I usually cook bean soups for a long time, unseasoned, adding vegetables gradually so that I can achieve a variety of vegetable textures—some very tender, some just tender, some a bit crispy for lightness. The key to good bean soup is cooking the beans long enough. The softer the better; even mushy is good. A bay leaf or two or some fresh herbs will transform the bean cooking water into a delicious broth. Bean soups are one exception to the seasoning rule. Season toward the end of cooking, so that the beans become very tender. If you salt beans too early in the cooking, they will contract and resist moisture, remaining hard.

Whole grains add hearty flavor and creamy texture to soups, making them the world's greatest comfort foods. Pasta, rice, barley, and millet add delicious flavors as well. I usually cook pasta separately so that my broth doesn't get too starchy or overly thick with pasta. Whole grains are added to soups during cooking, depending on the time required for each grain to soften. While grains cook in soups, their natural starches bind the broth, giving the soup body and a creamy consistency. Remember that grains expand during cooking, so use them sparingly so that you don't end up with a pot of soft grain mush instead of a hearty soup.

Last, invest in a few really good soup and stockpots. They will come in handy more often than you can imagine. And get a food mill. This simple kitchen gadget will become indispensable. It's great for smoothing the texture of soups. I use mine all the time in place of a food processor. The soups that come through a food mill are so smoothly elegant.

STOCKS

Stock is the full-bodied broth that ties a soup together, complementing the ingredients and making the soup whole. I work mostly with three different stocks, going from one to the next to build a variety of soups: a mushroom stock, an onion stock and a basic vegetable stock. I don't always begin soup with a stock. Many times, I like to begin fresh with water and work from there, but occasionally I like the variety in tastes you can achieve with stock.

To make a good stock, remember that the broth will taste exactly like the ingredients you are using, so stock is not the place to use up stale, limp vegetables that you just can't bear to discard. Flavorful, fresh vegetables are essential for a delicious broth. Trim away any dry or yellowed bits on vegetables and do not use onion skins and roots in the stock. They can turn the broth bitter. However, keep the papery skin on garlic cloves to keep the flavor gentle. Herbs can be used, stems and all, to get the full benefit of their delicate tastes. And of course, vegetables that are cut to expose the greatest surface area will make the most flavorful broth, so dicing or slicing into very thin pieces will work best.

When I start the stock, I simmer onions or leeks in a small amount of water or sauté them in oil or water with a pinch of salt to enrich their flavor. Then I add the balance of ingredients and water, bring the mixture to a boil, reduce the heat, and simmer it, uncovered, about one hour to develop and concentrate the flavors.

Stock will keep, refrigerated, for a day or two. After that, it can turn sour. However, stocks will keep almost indefinitely in the freezer. Just allow any frozen stock to thaw and then warm it before using. Cold stock can inhibit the cooking process of the soup and compromise the flavors. Personally, I prefer not freezing anything, as I think that the food's vital life forces also become frozen, minimizing the benefit we receive.

Vegetable Stock   This serves as the foundation of many of my soups. It

is quite versatile, as I vary the vegetables, seasonings and herbs, but the technique remains constant. I usually avoid members of the cabbage family because their strong flavors can create a stock that will overpower rather than support your soups. ℘

1 onion, cut lengthwise into thin slices

Several green onions or a small leek, cleaned and diced

2 cloves garlic, unpeeled

Sea salt

8 or 9 cups spring or filtered water

1 or 2 carrots, diced

2 celery stalks, diced

1 cup diced button mushrooms, brushed clean and left whole

1 or 2 bay leaves

2 fresh parsley sprigs

Fresh or dried basil or rosemary sprigs (optional)

Add onions, garlic, salt and about 1/2 cup of the water to a soup pot over low heat. Simmer about 15 minutes. Add the remaining water and other ingredients and bring the stock to a boil. Reduce heat to low and cook, uncovered, about 1 hour. Pour the stock through a strainer, pressing as much liquid as you can from the vegetables before discarding them. ∕ M a k e s   a b o u t   6   c u p s

VARIATION Sauté the onions in olive or sesame oil instead of simmering them in water.

Mushroom Stock

This is a rather strong-tasting stock. Use it for heartier soups and for sauces or gravies as well as for some grain dishes. Dried mushrooms give the stock tremendous flavor. Fresh mushrooms on their own will make a weak-flavored stock. ∕

1 onion, cut lengthwise into thin slices

8 or 9 cups spring or filtered water

Several green onions or a small leek, cleaned and diced

2 or 3 dried shiitake mushrooms, soaked until tender and thinly sliced

Sea salt

2 cups button mushrooms, thinly sliced

1 carrot, diced

2 bay leaves

2 fresh parsley sprigs

Combine onion and about 1/2 cup of the water in a soup pot over low heat and simmer 1 to 2 minutes. Add green onions and shiitakes and soaking water with a pinch of salt and simmer 15 minutes. Add the remaining water and other ingredients and bring to a boil. Simmer, uncovered, over low heat about 1 hour. Strain the stock, pressing as much liquid as possible from the vegetables before discarding them. ∕ M a k e s   a b o u t   6   c u p s

Onion Stock

This sweet stock can be delicate or strong, depending on the quantity and freshness of the onions used. Remember that stale onions will give your stock a strong and bitter taste instead of a delicately sweet, aromatic flavor. The corn cobs add sweetness. 🍃

1/2 teaspoon extra-virgin olive oil

6 or 7 onions, cut lengthwise into thin slices

1 leek, cut in half lengthwise, rinsed well and diced

Sea salt

8 to 9 cups spring or filtered water

2 or 3 corn cobs (optional), corn kernels removed

2 or 3 celery stalks, diced

2 bay leaves

Fresh parsley sprigs

Heat olive oil in a soup pot over medium-low heat. Add onions and leek with a pinch of salt and cook, stirring occasionally, until translucent and fragrant, about 5 minutes. Add a small amount of the water and simmer over low heat 15 minutes. Add remaining water and other ingredients and bring to a boil. Reduce heat to low and simmer, uncovered, about 1 hour. Strain the stock, pressing as much liquid as possible from the vegetables before discarding them. 🍃 M a k e s a b o u t 6 c u p s

Neptune's Delight A sea vegetable lover's dream. 🍃

1/2 teaspoon light sesame oil

1 onion, cut lengthwise into thin slices

1 carrot, cut into thin matchsticks

1 cup thin matchsticks daikon

1/2 cup sea palm, soaked until tender and diced

1 (2-inch) piece kombu, soaked until tender and diced

1 (2-inch) piece wakame, soaked until tender and diced

4 to 5 cups spring or filtered water

Soy sauce

Green onions, thinly sliced, for garnish

Heat oil in a soup pot over medium-low heat. Add onion and cook until translucent, about 5 minutes. Add carrot and daikon and cook, stirring occasionally, until coated with oil. Add sea palm, kombu and wakame and cook 2 or 3 minutes. Gently add water and bring to a boil. Reduce heat, cover and simmer 20 minutes. Season very lightly with soy sauce and simmer 10 minutes more. Serve garnished with green onions.

M a k e s   4   s e r v i n g s

Wheat Berry Soup

This wonderful soup is a virtual treasure-trove of flavor. Whole wheat berries give the soup great body.

1 (1-inch) square kombu	5 to 6 cups Vegetable Stock (page 96)
1 cup chick-peas, soaked 6 to 8 hours	1 or 2 turnips, diced
3 cups spring or filtered water	Sea salt
1/2 teaspoon extra-virgin olive oil	Generous pinch of dried rosemary
1 onion, diced	Several fresh parsley sprigs, minced, for garnish
1 stalk celery, diced	
1/2 cup wheat berries, soaked 6 to 8 hours	

Combine kombu, chick-peas and water in a soup pot and bring to a boil. Cook over high heat, uncovered, 10 minutes. Reduce heat to low, cover and cook until chick-peas are soft, 45 to 60 minutes. Drain and set aside.

Heat oil in a separate soup pot over medium-low heat. Add onion and cook until translucent, about 4 minutes. Add celery and cook, stirring, until coated with oil. Stir in wheat berries and cook 2 to 3 minutes. Gently add stock and bring to a boil over high heat. Add turnips. Reduce heat to low, cover and cook until wheat berries are tender, 40 to 45 minutes. Season lightly with salt and stir in rosemary to taste. Simmer 10 minutes more. Serve garnished with fresh parsley.   M a k e s   4   s e r v i n g s

Creamy Parsnip Soup

This is a delicious winter soup. Its smooth and creamy consistency lends quite an elegant touch to a holiday or any other meal. 🌿

4 to 5 cups spring or filtered water
2 or 3 shallots, peeled and diced
2 cups diced or diagonally cut parsnips

2 teaspoons white miso
2 or 3 green onions, thinly sliced, for garnish

Bring 1 cup of the water to a boil in a soup pot over medium-low heat. Add shallots and simmer 4 to 5 minutes. Add parsnips and the remaining water and bring to a boil. Reduce heat, cover and cook over low heat 25 minutes.

Remove a small amount of broth, add miso and stir until dissolved. Stir mixture into soup and simmer 3 to 4 minutes. Put soup through a food mill or puree in a food processor until a creamy consistency. Serve garnished with green onions. 🌿 **M a k e s   4   s e r v i n g s**

Creamy Squash Bisque

Any sweet winter squash works in this recipe. This bisque is so satisfyingly sweet that you could serve it for dessert. 🌿

2 to 3 pounds winter squash
(butternut, delicata or buttercup)
5 cups Vegetable Stock (page 96)
1/2 cup apple juice
1 teaspoon fresh ginger juice
(page 242)

Pinch of grated nutmeg
Sea salt
Fresh dill sprigs, for garnish

Preheat oven to 450F (230C). Halve the squash, place on a baking sheet, cut side down, and bake until tender when pricked with a fork, 35 to 45 minutes.

Cool squash slightly. Remove and discard seeds. Puree pulp in a food mill or food processor. Gradually stir in stock. Transfer to a soup pot over low heat and add apple juice, ginger juice and nutmeg. Lightly season with salt and simmer, covered, 10 minutes. Serve garnished with fresh dill sprigs. 🌿 **M a k e s   4   s e r v i n g s**

Winter Vegetable–Bean Stew

Any beans work well in this hearty recipe, but I think that white beans are the prettiest. I love to serve this stew on cold nights with crusty whole-grain bread and lightly cooked vegetables for a warming easy-to-make meal. ◊

1 teaspoon extra-virgin olive oil
1 leek, halved lengthwise, well rinsed
   and sliced into 1-inch pieces
2 tablespoons whole-wheat pastry
   flour
1 (1-inch) piece kombu
1 cup cubed winter squash
1 small sweet potato, cubed
2 carrots, cut into small irregular pieces
1 cup diced turnip

2 parsnips, cut into small irregular
   pieces
1 cup cauliflowerets
5 cups Vegetable Stock (page 96)
2 to 3 teaspoons white miso
1/2 cup white beans, cooked without
   seasoning until tender
1 cup broccoli flowerets
1 or 2 green onions, thinly sliced,
   for garnish

Heat olive oil in a soup pot over medium-low heat. Add leek and cook 2 minutes. Slowly stir in flour and cook, stirring constantly, until leeks are coated. Add kombu, squash, sweet potato, carrots, turnip, parsnips and cauliflower and gently add stock. Bring to a boil. Reduce heat to low, cover and cook 35 to 40 minutes. Remove a small amount of broth, add miso and stir until dissolved. Stir mixture into soup. Add beans and broccoli and simmer until broccoli turns bright green, about 4 minutes. Serve garnished with green onions. ◊ Makes 4 servings

Millet–Sweet Vegetable Soup

This deliciously satisfying soup is comfort in a cup. The creamy texture of stewed millet combined with the delicate sweet taste of the vegetables gives this soup ability to center and ground us by stabilizing our blood sugars. 🌿

1/2 cup millet
1/4 cup *each* finely diced onion, green cabbage, winter squash and carrot

5 cups spring or filtered water
2 teaspoons barley miso
1 or 2 green onions, thinly sliced, for garnish

Rinse millet by placing in a glass bowl and covering with water. Gently swirl grain with your hands to loosen any dust. Drain well.

Layer onion, cabbage, squash, carrot and then millet in a soup pot. Add enough water to just cover, being careful not to disturb layering. Cover and bring to a boil over medium heat. Add remaining water. Reduce heat to low and simmer soup 30 minutes. Remove a small amount of broth, add miso and stir until dissolved. Stir mixture into soup and simmer 3 to 4 minutes. Serve garnished with green onions. 🌿 Makes 4 servings

Minute Miso Soup

Okay, so it really takes 6 minutes to make this soup, but it's still quick and easy. 🌿

3 cups spring or filtered water
1 (3-inch) piece wakame, soaked and diced
1 small onion, cut lengthwise into thin slices

1 1/2 teaspoons barley miso
Small handful fresh parsley, minced

Bring water to a boil in a medium saucepan over medium heat. Add wakame ar simmer 1 minute. Add onion and simmer 1 to 2 minutes more. Remove a small of broth, add miso and stir until dissolved. Stir mixture into soup and simmer 3 to minutes more. Serve garnished with fresh parsley. ✍ M a k e s 4 s e r v i n g s

French Onion Soup

Without cheese, I achieve richness in this soup by sautéing the onions until nearly caramelized, sometimes for as long as 25 minutes. It's well worth the effort. ✍

1 teaspoon extra-virgin olive oil	
8 to 10 onions, thinly sliced lengthwise	
Pinch of sea salt	Soy sauce
4 to 5 cups spring or filtered water	2 tablespoons minced fresh parsley
Several pieces brown rice mochi, cut into 1/4-inch cubes	Sourdough bread croutons (see Note below)

M a k e s 4 s e r v i n g s

Heat olive oil in a soup pot over low heat. Add onions and sea salt. Cook, stirring occasionally, until lightly browned and reduced in bulk, 25 to 30 minutes. Gently add water and bring to a boil. Reduce heat, cover and cook about 15 minutes. Add mochi cubes. Season lightly with soy sauce and simmer about 7 minutes more, until mochi melts and becomes creamy. Serve garnished with parsley and a few croutons. ✍

NOTE The best croutons are made from slightly stale bread that is cubed and dried in a warm oven until crispy. Or deep-fry the bread cubes just before serving the soup.

Sunny Buckwheat Soup

This unique soup combines sweet vegetables with the nutty flavor of buckwheat groats, whose creamy consistency gives this soup a full-bodied taste and texture sure to please. ✒

1/2 cup buckwheat groats	2 cups finely diced green cabbage
4 to 5 cups spring or filtered water	1 carrot, diced
1 small onion, diced	2 tablespoons minced fresh parsley
Sea salt	

Pan-toast the buckwheat in a dry skillet over medium heat until fragrant and lightly browned, about 2 to 3 minutes.

Bring a small amount of the water to a boil in a soup pot over medium heat. Add onion with a pinch of salt and cook 3 to 4 minutes. Add remaining water and vegetables, except parsley, and bring to a boil. Add buckwheat. Return to a boil, cover and cook over low heat 15 minutes or until creamy. Season to taste with salt and simmer 10 minutes more. Serve garnished with parsley. ✒ M a k e s   4   s e r v i n g s

Creamy Celery Soup

This traditional European soup is a delicate beginning to any meal; however, it is especially refreshing, served either warm or chilled, during the summer months. ✒

6 cups spring or filtered water	2 tablespoons kuzu, dissolved in
1 onion, minced	1/4 cup cold water
6 stalks celery, diced	1 or 2 green onions, thinly sliced
2 tablespoons sesame tahini	for garnish
Sea salt	

Bring a small amount of water to a boil in a soup pot. Add onion and simmer 3 to 4 minutes. Add remaining water and bring to a boil. Add celery, cover and cook over low heat about 10 minutes. Remove a small amount of broth. Add sesame tahini, stir until dissolved and stir mixture into soup. Lightly season with salt and simmer 7 minutes more. Stir in dissolved kuzu, and cook, stirring, until the soup thickens slightly. Serve garnished with green onions. ✑ M a k e s 4 s e r v i n g s

Buckwheat Noodle Soup Round out your meal with some

lightly steamed green vegetables or a fresh salad. ✑

1 teaspoon light sesame oil	3 or 4 Brussels sprouts, quartered
1 small onion, diced	2 teaspoons white miso
4 to 5 cups spring or filtered water	6 ounces buckwheat noodles (soba),
1 cup thin rounds daikon	cooked until al dente
1 carrot, cut into thin rounds	Green onions, thinly sliced, for
1 cup shredded Chinese cabbage	garnish

Heat oil in a soup pot over medium-low heat. Add onion and cook, stirring, 3 to 4 minutes. Gently add water and bring to a boil. Add vegetables. Return to a boil, cover and cook over low heat 10 minutes. Remove a small amount of broth, add miso and stir until dissolved. Stir mixture into soup and simmer about 4 minutes more.

Divide noodles among individual soup bowls and ladle soup over noodles. Serve garnished with green onions. ✑ M a k e s 4 s e r v i n g s

Creamy Chestnut Soup

A tradition on our holiday table. Simple and rich at the same time, this soup is so good, you'll have trouble moving your guests to the next course! 🍃

1/2 pound fresh chestnuts

1 teaspoon corn oil

1 onion, diced

4 to 5 cups spring or filtered water

2 or 3 celery stalks, diced

Dried basil

1/2 cup soy or rice milk

Sea salt

2 or 3 teaspoons mirin

Fresh parsley sprigs, for garnish

Cut a slit in the flat side of the chestnuts and place in a saucepan. Add enough spring or filtered water to almost cover and boil 20 to 30 minutes or until tender. Drain chestnuts and cool slightly. Remove outer shells and skins from the chestnuts. Set aside.

Heat oil in a soup pot over medium-low heat. Add onion and cook until limp, about 3 minutes. Add the 4 to 5 cups water and bring to a boil. Add celery, a sprinkle of basil and soy or rice milk and return to a boil. Add chestnuts, cover and cook over low heat 20 minutes. Season lightly with salt and simmer 10 minutes more.

Remove pot from heat and puree soup in a food processor until smooth and creamy. Add mirin and simmer 3 to 4 minutes. Serve garnished with fresh parsley sprigs. 🍃

M a k e s   4   s e r v i n g s

Jim's Lemon–Zucchini and Leek Soup

This lovely soup was adapted by a good friend of mine from a recipe in *Gourmet* magazine. Healthful, delicious versions of rich recipes are his trademark. ✎

1 teaspoon extra-virgin olive oil

2 or 3 fresh garlic cloves, minced

1 onion, diced

Sea salt

1 pound leeks, sliced lengthwise,
   rinsed well and cut into
   1/4-inch pieces

1 pound zucchini, cut into
   1/4-inch-thick rounds, then halved

3 to 4 cups spring or filtered water

1 (2-inch) piece kombu, soaked
   briefly and diced

4 ounces tofu, crumbled

2 tablespoons sweet white miso

Juice of 1 lemon

Lemon slices, for garnish

Heat olive oil in a soup pot over medium-low heat. Add garlic and onion with a pinch of salt and cook 3 to 4 minutes. Add leeks, zucchini and a pinch of salt and sauté until just tender, about 5 minutes. Add enough water to just cover the veggies, add kombu and bring to a boil over high heat. Cover and cook over low heat 30 minutes. Add remaining water and crumbled tofu and simmer 10 minutes more. Puree soup until smooth and return to pot. Remove a small amount of hot broth, add miso and stir until dissolved. Stir mixture into the soup and simmer 3 to 4 minutes more. Remove from heat and stir in lemon juice to taste. Serve warm or chilled, garnished with lemon slices. ✎

M a k e s   4   s e r v i n g s

Mushroom Barley Soup

A hearty, rich soup that can be a meal all by itself. The creamy consistency of barley balanced by the smoky natural flavor of mushrooms makes a lovely combination. I love to serve this soup on chilly autumn days with crusty whole-grain bread and a freshly cooked vegetable medley. ✒

1 cup whole barley

1 teaspoon light sesame oil

1 onion, cut lengthwise into thin slices

5 to 6 cups Mushroom Stock (page 97)

4 or 5 dried shiitake mushrooms, soaked until tender and thinly sliced

1 cup button mushrooms, brushed clean and thinly sliced

Soy sauce

2 celery stalks, thinly sliced

Green onions, thinly sliced, for garnish

Rinse the barley by placing it in a bowl and covering with water. Swirl gently with your hands and drain. Soak in water to cover 6 to 8 hours. Drain and discard the soaking water.

Heat oil in a soup pot over medium-low heat. Add onion and cook, stirring, until translucent, about 5 minutes. Add stock and barley and bring to a boil over high heat. Stir in mushrooms, reduce heat and cook, covered, about 40 minutes, until barley becomes soft and creamy. If the soup begins to stick, you may need to cook the soup on a flame deflector. Season lightly with soy sauce and simmer 10 to 15 minutes more. Stir in celery for some crunch and serve garnished with green onions. ✒

Makes 4 servings

VARIATION Use pearled barley, a cracked form of the whole grain that does not require soaking and cooks more quickly. It will create as creamy a soup as the whole-grain version in half the cooking time.

Fresh Corn Chowder

If you love corn, don't miss this one. Jam-packed with succulent corn, this soup is the epitome of light summer cooking.

1/2 teaspoon corn oil

1 small onion, diced

5 cups spring or filtered water

3 to 4 ears fresh corn, kernels removed and cobs reserved

2 or 3 small turnips, diced

Sea salt

2 to 3 teaspoons kuzu, dissolved in 4 tablespoons cold water

Several sprigs fresh parsley

Heat oil in a soup pot over medium-low heat. Add onion and cook, stirring, until translucent, about 5 minutes. Add water and corn cobs and boil 3 to 4 minutes. Remove the cobs from the soup and discard. Add corn kernels and turnips and return the soup to a boil. Reduce heat, cover and cook over low heat 15 to 20 minutes. Season lightly with salt and simmer 5 minutes more. Stir in dissolved kuzu and cook, stirring, until soup thickens slightly. Serve garnished with fresh parsley. ❧ M a k e s 4 s e r v i n g s

VARIATION Create a soup with a velvety texture by partially pureeing the soup.

Creamy Carrot Bisque

A creamy, sweet beginning to any meal. Serve it any time of the year; it is delicious warm in cool weather and refreshing chilled and garnished with fresh lemon slices to help beat the heat of summer. ❧

1 teaspoon extra-virgin olive oil

1 clove garlic, minced

3 to 4 shallots, peeled and diced

Sea salt

3 to 4 cups diced carrots

4 to 5 cups spring or filtered water

2 tablespoons white miso

Fresh dill sprigs, for garnish

Heat olive oil in a soup pot over medium-low heat. Add garlic and shallots with a pinch of salt and cook, stirring, 3 to 4 minutes. Add carrots, another pinch of salt and cook, stirring, until coated with oil. Add water and bring to a boil over high heat. Reduce heat, cover and simmer over low heat until carrots are tender, 20 to 25 minutes. Put soup through a food mill or puree in a food processor until smooth and return to the pot. Remove a small amount of broth, add miso and stir until dissolved. Stir mixture into soup and simmer 3 to 4 minutes more. Serve garnished with fresh dill sprigs. ❧ M a k e s 4 s e r v i n g s

Japanese Noodle Soup with Tofu

Oriental-style soup that is easy to make and quite delicious. A traditional

4 cups spring or filtered water

1 (2-inch) piece kombu

1 dried shiitake mushroom

Soy sauce

1 cup 1/4-inch cubes tofu

4 to 6 ounces udon or somen
noodles, cooked al dente, drained
and rinsed

1 or 2 green onions, cut into thin
diagonal slices

1/2 sheet nori, shredded

Bring water to a boil in a soup pot. Add kombu and shiitake, cover and simmer 10 minutes. Remove kombu and mushroom and season lightly with soy sauce. You have just made a traditional Japanese broth called *dashi*, which is used as a soup base or dipping sauce in many recipes. Stir in tofu cubes. Simmer 10 minutes more. Divide cooked noodles among individual soup bowls and ladle soup over noodles. Serve garnished with green onions and shredded nori. Makes 4 servings

VARIATION If desired, thinly slice the kombu and shiitake and add back to the soup.

Sweet & Sour Soup

Another favorite from the Orient. My version is rich in flavor, not fat and salt. I like to serve this soup with homemade dumplings or wontons. ✒

1 teaspoon dark sesame oil

1 onion, diced

4 to 5 cups Vegetable Stock (page 96)

3 celery stalks, cut into thin diagonal slices

1 carrot, diced

2 stalks broccoli, cut into small flowerets with stems peeled and diced

1 tablespoon brown rice syrup

2 tablespoons mustard powder

Sea salt

1 tablespoon brown rice vinegar

1 to 2 green onions, thinly sliced, for garnish

Heat oil in a soup pot over medium-low heat. Add onion and cook until translucent, about 5 minutes. Add stock and bring to a boil. Add celery, carrot and broccoli stems. Reduce heat, cover and cook over low heat 10 minutes. Stir in rice syrup, mustard powder and a light seasoning of salt. Add broccoli flowerets and simmer 5 minutes more. Remove from heat and stir in rice vinegar. Serve garnished with green onions. ✒

Makes 4 servings

VARIATION If serving this soup with wontons or dumplings, add them just before the last 5 minutes of cooking, so they are soft, but not doughy.

Fresh Corn on a Green Field

I discovered this recipe quite a long time ago in an out-of-print cookbook, *Cooking for Life* by Michel Abeshara, a long-time macrobiotic teacher and counselor who wrote one of the loveliest cookbooks I have ever used. I hope you enjoy it as much as I have over the years. ✒

1 teaspoon light sesame oil

1 leek, sliced lengthwise, rinsed well
    and diced

Sea salt

4 to 5 cups spring or filtered water

2 ears fresh corn, kernels removed
    and cobs reserved

1 (2-inch) piece wakame, soaked
    briefly and diced

2 or 3 celery stalks, diced

2 cups finely sliced kale

1 tablespoon kuzu, dissolved in
    4 tablespoons cold water

Small handful fresh parsley,
    minced, for garnish

Heat oil in a soup pot over medium-low heat. Add leek with a pinch of salt and cook, stirring, 3 to 4 minutes. Add water and bring to a boil. Add corn cobs and boil 3 to 4 minutes. Carefully remove cobs and discard. Add corn kernels, wakame and celery, cover and cook over low heat 15 minutes. Season lightly with salt and simmer 5 minutes more. Add kale and stir in dissolved kuzu. Cook, stirring, until soup thickens slightly. Serve garnished with fresh parsley. 🌿 Makes 4 servings

Sweet Rice & Azuki Bean Soup   I love hearty

winter soups—thick and rich. You know the ones, comfort in a bowl. This one combines sweet brown rice and tiny, nutty-flavored red azuki beans with fresh vegetables. A bit more glutinous than short-grain brown rice, sweet brown rice has more protein and a great strengthening effect. And these beautiful red beans are not only delicious, but low in fat and high in protein. 🌿

1 (2-inch) piece kombu, soaked until
    tender and diced

1/2 cup azuki beans, soaked 6 to
    8 hours

1/2 cup sweet brown rice

1 cup diced daikon

6 cups Vegetable Stock (page 96)
    or spring or filtered water

1 tablespoon barley miso

1 cup finely sliced kale

1 or 2 green onions, thinly sliced,
    for garnish

Place kombu in a pressure cooker. Top with beans, rice, daikon, and stock and bring to a boil, loosely covered. Seal the lid and bring to full pressure over high heat. Reduce heat and simmer 45 minutes, maintaining pressure. Remove pot from heat and allow pressure to reduce naturally.

Remove a small amount of broth, add miso and stir until dissolved. Stir mixture into soup with kale and simmer 4 minutes more. Serve garnished with green onions. ✑

M a k e s   6   t o   8   s e r v i n g s

Cantaloupe Soup with Blueberries

If you love fruit, this summer refresher is for you. Serve as a starter for a brunch or as the finishing touch to any summer feast. ✑

1 ripe peach, peeled, pitted and diced	Juice of 1 lemon
1 cantaloupe, peeled, seeded and diced	1 teaspoon pure vanilla extract
1 cup apple juice	Fresh mint leaves, for garnish
Pinch of sea salt	Fresh blueberries, for garnish

Place peach and cantaloupe in a soup pot with apple juice and salt. Cook over medium heat, covered, about 10 minutes. Remove from heat. Transfer to a food processor and puree until smooth. Stir in lemon juice and vanilla, pour into a bowl and cover. Chill thoroughly before serving, about 2 hours. Serve garnished with fresh blueberries and mint leaves. ✑ M a k e s   4   s e r v i n g s

Zuni

A simple soup, it is traditionally served in Japan on the New Year for good fortune. ✐

4 to 5 cups spring or filtered water
1 (3-inch) piece wakame, soaked until tender and diced
1 cup thin rounds daikon
4 to 6 (1-inch) brown rice mochi cubes
2 teaspoons barley miso
1 or 2 green onions, thinly sliced, for garnish

Bring water to a boil in a small soup pot over medium-low heat. Add wakame and simmer over low heat 3 to 4 minutes. Add daikon and mochi and cook over low heat, covered, until mochi has softened, about 7 minutes. Remove a small amount of broth, add miso and stir until dissolved. Stir mixture into soup and simmer 3 to 4 minutes more. Serve garnished with green onions. ✐ M a k e s 4 s e r v i n g s

Italian Minestrone

My mom used to make this hearty soup; it was one of my dad's favorite dishes. I can still see him sitting at the head of the table, a heel of bread in one hand, spoon in the other, intent on not leaving a drop behind. ✐

1 (1-inch) piece kombu
1/4 cup *each* dried chick-peas, kidney beans and white beans, soaked together 6 to 8 hours
9 cups spring or filtered water
1 teaspoon extra-virgin olive oil
2 cloves garlic, minced
1 onion, diced
2 celery stalks, diced
1/2 cup diced winter squash
Generous pinch of dried basil
Generous pinch of dried rosemary
Sea salt
1 cup tiny pasta (orzo, acini, pastina), cooked and rinsed
Several leaves broccoli rapini, diced

Place kombu and beans in a heavy pot with 3 cups of the water. Bring to a boil and cook, uncovered, over high heat about 10 minutes. Reduce heat to low, cover and cook until beans are tender, about 1 hour.

Heat oil in a soup pot over medium-low heat. Add garlic and onion and coo[k] 3 minutes. Add celery, squash, herbs and a generous pinch of salt. Cook, stirring, coated with oil. Add cooked beans and remaining water. Bring to a boil, cover a[nd cook] over low heat until vegetables are tender, about 35 minutes. Season again with herbs and salt to taste and simmer 10 minutes more. Stir in cooked pasta and rapini, simmer 1 minute to cook greens, and serve hot. ✐ M a k e s 8 t o 9 s e r v i n g s

VARIATION I cook the pasta separately for this soup, because my mother believed that cooking pasta in the soup made the broth too starchy and the pasta too mushy. But you may cook it in the broth, if you wish. The resulting soup will be much thicker.

Clear Daikon Consommé

This elegant soup is the ideal starter for a rich meal that may contain heartier foods, like long-cooked beans, a fish entree or perhaps some foods cooked with rich sauces or oils. Daikon helps the body to assimilate and process fat and protein, so this light broth can be more than just a delicious beginning to your meal. ✐

4 cups spring or filtered water
1 cup thinly sliced fresh daikon
1 to 2 tablespoons umeboshi vinegar
1 or 2 green onions, thinly sliced, for garnish

Bring water to a boil in a soup pot over medium heat. Add daikon, cover and simmer over low heat until daikon is tender, 7 to 10 minutes. Remove from heat and season to taste with umeboshi vinegar. Serve garnished with green onions. ✐ M a k e s 4 s e r v i n g s

NOTE This soup is delicious served hot or chilled during the summer, when, in fact, it can really help you beat the heat, because of the alkalizing effect of the umeboshi vinegar, along with the cooling effect of the daikon.

Creamy Rutabaga Soup

A lightly sweet and very creamy bisque. I prefer to use smaller rutabagas for this dish because they have a more delicate flavor than the larger ones. Peel the rutabagas only if they have been waxed. 🌿

1/2 teaspoon corn oil

1 onion, diced

Sea salt

2 celery stalks, diced

4 to 5 cups Vegetable Stock (page 96)

1 cup cooked brown or white rice, pureed to a smooth paste

2 cups cubed rutabagas

1/2 cup cubed winter squash

1 tablespoon sweet white miso

Fresh parsley sprigs, for garnish

Heat oil in a soup pot over medium-low heat. Add onion and a pinch of salt and cook, stirring, until translucent, about 5 minutes. Add celery and another pinch of salt and cook, stirring, 1 to 2 minutes more. Gently add stock and bring to a boil. Stir in pureed rice, rutabagas and squash and return to a boil. Reduce heat to low, cover and cook until vegetables are tender, about 30 minutes.

Transfer the soup to a food mill or food processor and puree until smooth. Return to the pot. Remove a bit of hot soup, add miso and stir until dissolved. Stir mixture into soup and simmer 3 to 4 minutes more. Serve garnished with fresh parsley sprigs. 🌿

M a k e s   5   o r   6   s e r v i n g s

Flageolet Bean Soup

Flageolet beans are French white beans found in most gourmet shops. They have the loveliest subtle flavor. However, you may make an equally delicious soup with white navy beans. I like to serve this very pretty, delicately flavored soup in the spring and early fall. ✑

1 (1/2-inch) piece kombu	3 to 4 cups Vegetable Stock (page 96)
1 onion, diced	Sea salt
1 clove garlic, minced	3 or 4 slices whole-grain sourdough
1/2 cup white flageolet beans, soaked	bread, cubed
6 to 8 hours	1/2 teaspoon extra-virgin olive oil
Dried rosemary leaves	1 cup diced fresh tomato for garnish
2 bay leaves	(optional)
Spring or filtered water	2 tablespoons minced fresh parsley

Place kombu in a heavy pot and top with onion, garlic, beans, a generous pinch of rosemary, bay leaves and enough water to just cover ingredients. Boil 10 minutes. Reduce heat to low, cover and cook until beans are tender, about 1 hour. Drain away any remaining liquid and puree the beans and vegetables in a food mill or food processor until smooth. Return mixture to the pot and whisk in stock until you achieve the consistency you desire. Season to taste with salt and simmer 10 minutes more.

Meanwhile, preheat the oven to 300F (150C). Arrange bread cubes in a single layer on an ungreased baking sheet and bake until dry and crisp, about 10 minutes.

Heat oil in a skillet. Add bread cubes and cook, stirring occasionally, until cubes are light golden. Drain on paper and set aside.

Serve the soup hot, garnished with diced tomatoes, fresh parsley, and several sourdough croutons. ✑ Makes 4 to 6 servings

Simple Vegetable Soup

This basic vegetable soup makes a great lunch when partnered with a sandwich and some lightly cooked vegetables. More than just an energizing meal, soup can be a quick-to-fix solution to menu planning in our busy lives. Mixing and matching soups and sandwiches is a great way to add variety to your noontime meals.

1/2 cup thinly sliced onion
4 cups Mushroom Stock (page 97) or spring or filtered water
1 carrot, cut into thin diagonal slices
1 cup thinly sliced daikon
1/2 teaspoon light sesame oil
1 cup button mushrooms, brushed clean and thinly sliced
1/2 red bell pepper, sliced into thin pieces
1/2 teaspoon powdered ginger
Soy sauce
4 to 6 snow peas, sliced into thin matchsticks

Combine onion and enough stock to just cover in a soup pot and simmer 3 to 4 minutes. Add remaining stock and bring to a boil. Stir in carrot and daikon, cover and cook over low heat about 5 minutes.

Meanwhile, heat oil in a skillet over medium-low heat. Add mushrooms and bell pepper and cook until just tender, about 4 minutes. Add vegetables to soup, season with ginger and soy sauce and simmer 5 minutes more. Serve garnished with snow pea slices.

Makes 5 or 6 servings

Florentine Rice Soup

When I lived in Tuscany several years ago, I discovered that rice is much more popular there than pasta. I spent a lot of time with the people I worked with, and one of our favorite things to do together was, yes, you guessed it, cook! This fabulous soup has changed and evolved over the years, but I still get nostalgic for life in Italy whenever I make it.

1 cup white rice
Sea salt
2 1/2 cups spring or filtered water
1/2 teaspoon extra-virgin olive oil
2 cloves garlic, minced
3 to 4 shallots, minced
4 to 5 cups Vegetable Stock (page 96)
3 or 4 kale leaves, minced

Rinse rice very well to prevent it from becoming sticky when it is cooked: Simply place rice in a bowl with enough water to cover and gently swirl with your hands. Drain through a strainer and repeat process until water rinses away relatively clear.

Place rice in a pot with a pinch of salt and water and bring to a boil, uncovered. Cover pot and return to a boil. Reduce heat to low and cook until liquid has been absorbed, about 30 minutes. Transfer rice to a bowl, cover and set aside.

In a soup pot, heat oil over medium-low heat. Add garlic and shallots and cook 3 to 4 minutes. Add stock and bring to a boil. Cover and simmer over low heat about 10 minutes. Add cooked rice, season lightly with salt and simmer 5 minutes more. Stir in kale and simmer 1 to 2 minutes just before serving. ✎ Makes 5 or 6 servings

Chilled Cucumber Bisque
A quick and easy, light summer soup. A great addition for an outdoor summer buffet. ✎

1 teaspoon corn oil

1 small leek, sliced lengthwise, rinsed well and diced

2 to 3 cups peeled, seeded, and diced cucumber

Fresh dill, minced (about 1 tablespoon or to taste)

Sea salt

2 cups spring or filtered water

1 cup soy or rice milk

2 tablespoons kuzu, dissolved in 4 tablespoons cold water

Juice of 1 lemon

Fresh lemon slices, for garnish

Dill sprigs, for garnish

Heat oil in a soup pot over medium-low heat. Add leek and cook, stirring, 2 to 3 minutes. Add cucumber, some minced dill and a pinch of salt and cook 2 to 3 minutes more. Add water and soy or rice milk and bring to a boil. Cover and cook over low heat until vegetables are tender, about 5 minutes. Stir in dissolved kuzu and cook, stirring, until soup thickens slightly, about 3 minutes. Remove from heat and stir in lemon juice. Chill thoroughly, about 2 hours, before serving garnished with fresh lemon slices and dill sprigs. ✎ Makes 4 or 5 servings

Greek Lentil Soup

I spent only three days in Greece, but realized immediately that you only need three minutes to fall completely in love with the country, the culture, the people, and the food. I got this recipe from an elderly Greek chef during my brief stay. The changes I have made over the years have kept the essence of this lovely, saffron-scented soup intact. 🌿

1 teaspoon extra-virgin olive oil

1 onion, diced

1 small leek, sliced lengthwise, rinsed well and diced

2 celery stalks, diced

1 carrot, diced

1/2 cup green lentils, sorted and rinsed well

5 cups spring or filtered water

1 (1-inch) piece kombu

About 1 teaspoon saffron

Sea salt

Juice of 1 lemon

Grated peel of 1 lemon

1 cup whole-grain sourdough croutons (see Note, page 103)

Heat olive oil in a soup pot over medium-low heat. Add onion and leek and cook 3 to 4 minutes. Add celery and carrot and cook 3 to 4 minutes more. Top with lentils and stir briefly, just to coat the lentils with oil. Add water and kombu and bring to a boil. Cover and cook over low heat until lentils are soft, about 35 to 40 minutes. Season to taste with salt and saffron (a little goes a long way, so use saffron sparingly) and simmer 20 minutes more. Remove from heat and stir in lemon peel and juice. Serve garnished with several croutons per bowl. 🌿 M a k e s 6 t o 8 s e r v i n g s

Arroz con Chícharos

This Mexican recipe is also known as *sopa seca*, which means "dry soup," because much of the broth is soaked up by the rice, making a thick, rich stew. Serve with tortilla chips and a fresh salad for a very satisfying meal. 🌿

1 to 2 teaspoons light sesame oil

1 onion, cut lengthwise into thin slices

2 carrots, diced

2 to 3 teaspoons chili powder or to taste

1 1/2 cups long-grain brown rice, rinsed well

5 cups spring or filtered wat[er]

Sea salt

1 cup fresh or frozen green peas

1 cup diced fresh tomatoes, for garnish (optional)

Heat oil in a soup pot over medium heat. Add onion and cook, stirring, until translucent, about 2 minutes. Add carrots and chili powder and cook, stirring, until all vegetables are coated. Stir in rice. Gently pour in water and bring to a boil. Cover and cook over low heat until rice is soft and the consistency is creamy, 40 to 45 minutes. Season lightly with salt, stir in peas and simmer 5 minutes more. Serve garnished with diced tomatoes. ✑

M a k e s 6 t o 8 s e r v i n g s

Chick-pea Stew

A thick and creamy stew that is a meal on its own. On chilly days I usually serve this stew followed by a simpler meal of sautéed noodles and vegetables. ✑

1 onion, diced

1 clove garlic, minced

5 cups Vegetable Stock (page 96)

1/2 cup yellow corn grits

1/2 cup cooked chick-peas

1 cup finely shredded green cabbage

2 teaspoons white miso

1 or 2 green onions, thinly sliced, for garnish

Combine onion, garlic, and a small amount of stock in a soup pot over medium heat. Bring to a boil, reduce heat, and simmer 3 to 4 minutes. Add remaining stock and return to a boil. Stir in grits, chick-peas and cabbage, cover and cook over low heat 40 minutes, stirring frequently to prevent corn grits from scorching. Remove a small amount of broth, add miso and stir until dissolved. Stir mixture into soup and simmer 3 to 4 minutes. Serve garnished with green onions. ✑ M a k e s 5 o r 6 s e r v i n g s

Red Lentil–Corn Chowder

Adding fresh vegetables and tiny pasta makes this a fabulous change from the lentil soup we all knew and loved growing up. ✑

1 teaspoon extra-virgin olive oil

3 to 4 shallots, peeled and minced

Several pinches of ground cumin

1 cup dried red lentils, rinsed well

5 to 6 cups spring or filtered water

1 medium zucchini, diced

1/2 red bell pepper, roasted, diced

2 cups fresh corn kernels

1 cup cooked tiny pasta (orzo, pastina, acini)

2 tablespoons barley miso

1 tablespoon umeboshi vinegar

Small handful minced fresh parsley

Fresh parsley sprigs, for garnish

Heat oil in a soup pot over medium-low heat. Add shallots and cumin and cook, stirring, 3 to 4 minutes, until shallots are limp. Add lentils and water and bring to a boil. Add vegetables, cover and cook over low heat 20 minutes, until lentils are very soft.

While soup simmers, cook pasta in boiling salted water according to package directions until al dente. Drain pasta.

Remove a small amount of broth from soup, add miso and stir until dissolved. Stir mixture into soup and simmer 3 to 4 minutes more. Remove soup from heat and stir in cooked pasta, vinegar and minced parsley. Serve garnished with fresh parsley sprigs and a side of crusty whole-grain bread. ✑ M a k e s 6 t o 8 s e r v i n g s

Anasazi Bean Stew

I love to serve this unique stew with cornmeal dumplings. It is so savory and rich that I usually round out the meal with some lightly cooked vegetables and a simple grain dish. ✑

1 (1-inch) piece kombu

3/4 cup anasazi beans, rinsed well

5 cups spring or filtered water

1 small leek, sliced lengthwise,
   rinsed well and diced

2 celery stalks, diced

1 medium carrot, diced

1 cup diced daikon

1 cup diced winter squash

2 or 3 bay leaves

Dried rosemary leaves

2 or 3 ripe tomatoes, diced (optional)

Sea salt

Balsamic vinegar

Cornmeal Dumplings (recipe follows)

Layer kombu, beans and 3 cups of the water in a soup pot and bring to a boil over high heat. Boil, uncovered, 10 minutes. Add vegetables, bay leaves and a generous pinch of rosemary. Return to a boil, cover and cook over low heat until beans are very tender, about 45 minutes. Stir in remaining water and tomatoes and season lightly with salt. Simmer 10 minutes more. Remove from heat and stir in a light sprinkle of vinegar. Ladle stew into individual soup bowls and serve topped with dumplings.

Makes 5 or 6 servings

CORNMEAL DUMPLINGS

1/2 cup whole-wheat pastry flour

1/2 cup cornmeal

Pinch of sea salt

1/4 teaspoon baking powder

4 ounces tofu

Combine flour, cornmeal, salt and baking powder in a medium bowl. Puree tofu with a small amount of water until a smooth paste forms. Fold into cornmeal mixture until ingredients are well incorporated and the dough gathers easily into a thick batter.

Bring a pot of spring or filtered water to a boil. Drop dumpling batter, by large spoonfuls, into the pot and simmer about 10 minutes over low heat. Test for doneness by removing a dumpling and slicing it in half. The inside should be moist and breadlike.

Orange Squash Soup

This is the sweetest, most delicious squash soup. The delicate zest of fresh orange makes this an attention-getting starter. ✎

1/2 teaspoon corn oil
1 onion, diced
Sea salt
Grated zest of 1 orange
1 or 2 small butternut squash, seeded, peeled and diced

Spring or filtered water
1 to 2 tablespoons sweet white miso
    (1/2 teaspoon for each cup of soup)
Juice of 1 orange
Fresh orange slices, for garnish

Heat oil in a soup pot over medium-low heat. Add onion and a pinch of salt and cook, stirring, until translucent, about 5 minutes. Stir in zest and squash and cook, stirring, 3 to 4 minutes until coated with oil. Add enough water to just cover and bring to a boil. Cover and cook over low heat until squash is tender, about 20 minutes.

Transfer soup to a food mill or food processor and puree until smooth. Remove a small amount of soup, add miso and stir until dissolved. Stir mixture into soup and simmer 3 to 4 minutes more. Whisk in more water, if necessary, to create a thinner soup. Remove from heat and stir in orange juice while soup is still hot. Serve garnished with fresh orange slices. ✎ M a k e s 4 o r 5 s e r v i n g s

Chili Noodle Soup

Not quite a chili, not just a soup, it makes a completely satisfying meal with cooked vegetables and warm bread. ✎

1 teaspoon extra-virgin olive oil
3 to 4 shallots, minced
2 cloves garlic, minced
1 teaspoon ground cumin
2 teaspoons chili powder
2 to 3 ripe tomatoes, diced
4 to 5 cups Vegetable Stock
    (page 96)

2 celery stalks, diced
1/2 red bell pepper, roasted, diced
1 carrot, diced
Sea salt
1 (8-oz.) package capellini, cooked
    al dente and drained
Green onions, thinly sliced on the
    diagonal, for garnish

Heat oil in a soup pot over medium-low heat. Add shallots, garlic, cumin and chili powder and cook, stirring, 3 to 4 minutes. Stir in tomatoes and cook 1 to 2 minutes more. Add stock and bring to a boil. Add celery, bell pepper and carrot. Cover and cook over low heat about 25 minutes. Season lightly with salt and simmer 5 to 7 minutes more, until vegetables are tender. Divide cooked capellini among individual soup bowls and ladle soup over capellini. Serve garnished with green onions. ⌇

Makes 6 or 7 servings

Dulse and Leek Soup

I learned this soup from my Irish grandmother. I remember she found it quite amusing when I discovered dulse, a sea vegetable that Irish cooks have been using for thousands of years. So much for re-inventing the wheel . . . ⌇

1 small leek, sliced lengthwise, rinsed well and diced	2/3 cup rolled oats
4 to 5 cups spring or filtered water	2 tablespoons white miso
1/2 cup dried dulse (page 26)	Green onions, thinly sliced, for garnish

Combine leek and enough water to just cover in a soup pot over medium heat. Bring to a boil and simmer over low heat 3 to 4 minutes. Add remaining water and bring to a boil.

Sort through dulse and shred. Do not soak. Add dulse and oats to boiling broth, cover and cook over low heat 15 minutes. Remove a small amount of broth, add miso and stir until dissolved. Stir mixture into soup and simmer 3 to 4 minutes more. Serve garnished with green onions. ⌇

Makes 5 or 6 servings

VARIATION During winter weather, I cook this soup about 1 hour using whole oats, instead of rolled oats, to create a more warming, hearty soup.

Italian Vegetable Stew

This Tuscan specialty is really lovely. I make it with everything: during the summer, fresh fava beans make a most delicious soup; in cooler weather, dried lima beans. My vegetarian version gets its full-bodied flavor from a rich vegetable stock. ✐

1 teaspoon extra-virgin olive oil

1 cup dried lima beans, soaked 6 to 8 hours

1/2-pound brick tofu, cut into tiny cubes

1 pound fresh or frozen green peas

1 onion, diced

5 to 6 cups Vegetable Stock (page 96)

2 bay leaves

1/4 cup mirin

Soy sauce

Juice of 1 lemon

3 or 4 leaves of kale, finely chopped

Heat oil in a soup pot over medium-low heat. Add beans and tofu cubes and cook, stirring, 3 to 4 minutes. Stir in peas and onion, add stock and bay leaves and bring to a boil. Add mirin, cover and cook over low heat until beans are soft, about 45 minutes. Season lightly with soy sauce and simmer 10 minutes more. Remove from heat and stir in lemon juice and chopped kale. Serve hot. ✐ M a k e s 6 o r 7 s e r v i n g s

Italian Cabbage Soup

This lovely peasant soup is another jewel from my mother's kitchen. Although, as kids, we didn't quite see it that way; a simple soup like this was an indication of just how limited our resources were that week. It was only later in life that I learned that I get the most pleasure from simple things. ✐

1 teaspoon extra-virgin olive oil

2 cloves garlic, sliced

1 onion, diced

Sea salt

1 cup very finely shredded green cabbage

4 to 5 cups spring or filtered water

1/2 cup yellow corn grits

Fresh parsley sprigs, for garnish

Heat oil in a soup pot over medium-low heat. Add garlic and cook until dark brow not burned. Remove from oil and discard. Add onion and a pinch of salt and coo stirring, until translucent, about 5 minutes. Stir in cabbage and a pinch of salt and cook, stirring, until coated with oil. Next, gently add enough water to just cover ingredients and boil gently 3 to 4 minutes. Add remaining water and return to a boil. Stir in corn grits, whisking constantly. Reduce heat to low, add a pinch of salt, cover and cook, stirring very frequently to prevent scorching, about 35 minutes. The soup will take on a very creamy consistency. Season lightly with salt and simmer 5 to 7 minutes more, stirring frequently. Serve garnished with fresh parsley sprigs. ✍ Makes 5 or 6 servings

BEANS, BEANS, BEANS

I have to be honest and tell you that I put off writing this section of the book for as long as I could. Not that I don't love beans; I do, but as a culture, we're protein maniacs. I hear the same lament more times than I care to relate: "Where do vegetarians get their protein?" "Am I getting enough protein if I give up meat?" Well, I am here to tell you that in all the years I have been vegetarian, I have never met a protein-deficient person—ever.

Truth is, all grains, vegetables, nuts, seeds and, yes, beans contain protein. The best news is that all the protein is vegetable-quality, which means that we can assimilate it easily and utilize it completely. Something else, in our vitamin-obsessed thinking: we have lost sight of the fact that we require only a small amount of protein to satisfy our bodies' needs. In traditional cuisines, protein-rich foods, like animal food or even beans, were used in small amounts, composing less than 10 percent of daily intake, as supplemental food or luxury food. These foods were added to the diet for richness and for the strength they naturally give. People labored physically harder than we do and required that particular kind of stamina. But the people of these cultures knew instinctively that only small amounts of these foods were required to obtain the desired effects. It is only in our modern culture that we have centered our daily diet around protein-rich animal foods, so much so, that when we consider eliminating animal protein from our diet, we become fearful of protein deficiency and loss of strength.

Beans have been cultivated around the world since ancient times. It seems that, along with vegetables, they have always been served as a traditional complement to whole cereal grains. For example, in South and Central America, cooked beans wrapped in corn tortillas were a dietary staple. In India, *dahl*, a thick sauce made from dried peas or lentils, was served with rice or *chapatis*. Far Eastern cuisine traditionally pairs whole-grain rice with azuki, soy or mung beans. In Africa, chick-peas and black-eyed peas are served as accompaniments with couscous or cracked wheat. And in Europe, broad beans and lentils are the natural companions of barley and rice.

Modern culture has turned its back on most traditional cuisines in favor of convenient, quick foods. The result has been that we, as a species, have become weaker and have more difficulty digesting food, especially whole food. This is manifested by the great number of people who have difficulty assimilating whole beans and bean products. We need to understand that animal foods and dairy foods are very taxing to our digestive tract, leaving it weak and flaccid. So sometimes the change to a whole foods diet can result in digestive trouble, especially when those whole foods are beans.

What is the best way to handle this problem of digesting beans? Do we just grin and bear it until we become a bit stronger? Do we eliminate beans from our diet? (A grim thought . . .) Or are there ways of preparing beans to make them easier on our digestion, while still preserving the benefits of these nutrient-rich foods? Of course there are. We'll get to them.

Why eat beans in the first place? Beans and bean products are proportionately higher in fat and protein than whole cereal grains and lower in carbohydrates. So combined with grains, beans make a complete protein, providing all of the amino acids needed by the body to function properly. Beans are also quite high in nutrients like calcium, phosphorous, iron, niacin, thiamin and vitamin E. While relatively low in vitamin A, legumes contain phosphatides, which increase our absorption of beta-carotene (the precursor to vitamin A found in yellow and orange vegetables and considered a strong anticancer factor), making vegetable and bean combinations an ideal food.

Beans are completely cholesterol free and contain only unsaturated fat. Also high in minerals, tofu, for example, which is a soybean product, contains about the same amount of calcium by weight as milk. And recent studies have shown that a diet including beans and bean products greatly reduces arteriosclerotic lesions and high cholesterol levels. European doctors have reported that patients eating a diet high in soy foods significantly reduced the risk of heart disease. And tempeh, which contains the microorganism *bacillus subtilis*, has strong antibiotic effects.

Beans and bean products have another benefit as well. They provide slow, steady energy—fuel, if you will—by releasing nutrients slowly into the bloodstream. The result is that the quality of the blood is strengthened, as well as the lymph and other body fluids. Remember that the blood nourishes every organ and organ system in the body; so if blood quality is good and strong, it only follows that the body will be strong, too.

BUYING BEANS

Before we talk about cooking beans, let's consider which characteristics we should look for when buying them. Quality is important, and since beans are often rotated with other crops, it is important to consider the quality of the growing soil. So in my opinion, organic beans are always the best choice; they are not grown in chemically depleted soil and thus give us more strength and nutrients, drawn from the earth.

After harvest, beans are cleaned, dried and packaged. Good processing loses only about 10 percent to damage. Once at the market, you should look for beans that are well formed, uniform in size and shape, smooth skinned, full-bodied and shiny. Any deformities like spots, wrinkles, flecks, cracks and pits mean that the beans have lost their vitality. And if you don't believe me, take a cracked or broken bean and try to sprout it. It will not grow; no life force exists. Dried beans should also be hard, shattering when bitten into. If the beans only dent, they have not been properly dried and will not yield a hearty taste.

After purchase, store beans in tightly sealed glass jars and keep in a cool, dry place like a pantry. Preserved and stored in this manner, beans will retain their vitality for many years. Different varieties of beans should be stored separately from one another.

So what are the best types of beans to purchase for regular use? Generally, I like to choose smaller beans that are lower in fat for daily use, supplementing with larger, broader beans more occasionally. As an additional supplement, I use bean products like tofu and tempeh. For more information about individual beans, check the listings in the glossary.

COOKING BEANS

Okay, so now you've made the decision to include more beans and bean products in your diet. You've gone out and bought a variety of beans and stocked your pantry. So now what? Well, here are some of the most common methods for cooking beans for the best flavor and digestibility.

Before cooking beans, quickly sort through them to remove any stones or damaged beans that are easily visible. (Don't get crazy with this, just a quick sort to remove debris.) Then gently rinse the beans in a colander to remove any surface dust.

To improve their digestibility and soften their hard exteriors, most beans should be soaked for several hours prior to cooking. (The exception is lentils.) Soaking time depends on the kind and quality of bean, but general guidelines are that small beans, such as azuki, pinto, navy, great northern, baby lima and black turtle, need to soak 2 to 4 hours, while larger, fatter beans, such as chick-peas, soybeans and red kidney beans, need to soak 6 to 8 hours before cooking. To save on soaking time, one shortcut I use is to soak beans in hot (just below the boiling point) water, which cuts the soaking time in half. Do not add salt to the soaking water, as it will cause the beans to contract and resist opening to moisture.

When ready to cook the beans, discard the soaking water and begin the cooking process with fresh water. This small step helps to eliminate much of the gas problem associated with eating whole beans. Next, take a deep, heavy pot and place a 1-inch piece of kombu per cup of beans on the bottom. This small piece of sea vegetable mineralizes and softens the beans, rendering the fat and protein more digestible. Add the beans and water and bring the pot to a rolling boil. The last step in making beans most digestible is to allow the beans to boil rapidly 10 minutes before covering and cooking over low heat until done. This final precaution helps cook away any remaining gas from the beans.

Following these simple steps prior to cooking beans can really help alleviate the digestive problems commonly associated with beans. The last step in your insurance policy comes when the beans are fully prepared. Chew them very well. That exercise is the very best advice I can give you for bean eating. Saliva secreted during chewing is the best aid to digestion.

So, now, what are the methods of cooking beans that work best? Well, in order for beans to thoroughly cook inside and out, it is best to cook beans for as long as possible over low heat. There is a wide variety of seasonings, including miso, soy sauce, sea salt, mirin, barley malt and sometimes a bit of oil, depending on what taste you want in the final dish. Sometimes I add vegetables at the beginning of cooking to create a creamy stew; other times I add the vegetables toward the end of cooking so that each retains its own character and holds its shape. Or I may use dried vegetables in a bean stew. Finally, I frequently serve bean dishes garnished with something a bit spicy or hot, such as grated daikon, gingerroot or horseradish, diced green onions or chives. And many times I will separately sauté a variety of vegetables, possibly with cumin or other spice, and stir them into completely cooked beans for yet another type of bean dish. So, you see, preparing beans is still another area of creativity in the kitchen.

Some of the more common methods for cooking whole beans properly include:

Shock Method

Shocking, a traditional method for cooking beans, comes to us from the Orient. Place soaked beans in a heavy, cast-iron pot with 2 1/2 cups of water for each 1 cup of soaked beans. Cook the beans over low heat, uncovered, until they boil. After a few minutes at a boil, set a drop lid (a lid that sets loosely inside the pot) inside the pot on top of the beans. After the beans are covered, the water will return to a strong boil, causing the cover to jiggle. Remove the lid and add cold water down the side of the pot until the boiling stops, then replace the lid. Repeat the process each time the beans return to a boil until they are about 80 percent cooked. At that point, remove the lid, add any desired vegetables and allow the beans to cook over medium heat until they and the vegetables are tender. Season to taste and simmer away any remaining liquid. This method brings out the natural sweet taste of beans, giving you perfectly tender and delicious beans every time.

Boiling

Beans can be boiled after soaking. Add 3 to 3 1/2 cups water to 1 cup soaked beans. After bringing beans to a boil, cover them and cook over low heat until tender. Season and continue cooking until completely done.

Pressure Cooking

The fastest method for cooking beans is to pressure-cook them, although some of their delicate sweet taste is sacrificed. This method is a great time-saver, giving great energy to the dish, but remember that beans like to cook slowly, and speeding up the process diminishes their great natural flavors.

CANNED BEANS

If cooking beans simply cannot fit into your busy schedule, there are canned organic beans now available in most natural food stores. Granted, they won't be quite as delicious as beans cooked from scratch, but in a pinch, they do quite nicely. Before use, rinse the beans free of the liquid in the can, as this fluid can give the beans a stale taste. Any whole-bean recipe here can be made with canned beans: simply eliminate the bean-cooking steps in the cooking process.

Crispy Pea Fritters

This recipe is based on a Cuban delight that I loved when I lived in Miami. Called *bollitos de caritas* (little face fritters), these black-eyed pea treats were sold by just about every street vendor and shopkeeper in Little Cuba. I love them served with a hot dipping sauce. They have a truly vitalizing effect—from hot onions, aromatic garlic and the strong fire of frying—with a steady energy base provided by the beans.

1 (1-inch) piece kombu
1 cup dried black-eyed peas, rinsed and sorted
3 cups spring or filtered water
1 red onion, diced
2 or 3 cloves garlic, minced

1/4 cup minced fresh parsley
1/2 to 1 teaspoon sea salt
1/4 cup whole-wheat pastry flour
1/4 cup yellow cornmeal
1 teaspoon baking powder
Safflower oil for frying

Place kombu in a heavy pot and add peas and water. Bring to a boil over medium heat and boil, uncovered, 10 minutes. Reduce heat, cover and simmer until peas are tender, about 45 minutes. Drain the peas and transfer to a food processor or hand grinder and puree to a mashed potato consistency. Spoon into a bowl and fold in onion, garlic and parsley. Add salt and mix well.

In a small bowl, combine flour, cornmeal and baking powder. Stir into the pea mixture, making a stiff dough. Form the mixture into small, thick rounds, like silver-dollar pancakes.

Heat about 1/4 inch oil in a deep skillet over medium heat and pan-fry each fritter until golden brown in color, turning. Remove from oil and drain on paper towels before arranging on a platter. Serve hot as a side dish or as a snack with a spicy dipping sauce.

Makes 4 or 5 servings

Sautéed Broad Beans

My grandfather loved fresh fava beans fixed this way. Hard to come by these days, fresh fava beans can be found in ethnic markets, although frozen, shelled fava beans are available in most supermarkets. This dish imparts a lovely, steady energy that is enhanced by the freshness and lighter tastes of the vegetables.

1 tablespoon extra-virgin olive oil

Several leaves fresh basil, minced, or generous pinch dried basil

1 leek, cut lengthwise, rinsed well and thinly sliced

1 clove garlic, minced

2 cups fresh shelled fava beans

Spring or filtered water

1 red bell pepper, roasted, diced

1 or 2 small zucchini, diced

1 or 2 tomatoes, coarsely diced

Sea salt (optional)

1/4 cup minced fresh parsley

Heat oil in a saucepan over medium heat. Add basil, leek and garlic and sauté 1 to 2 minutes. Add beans and cook, stirring, to combine. Add water to cover and bring to a boil. Reduce heat to low, cover and simmer until beans are tender, about 15 minutes. Add bell pepper, zucchini, tomatoes and a light seasoning of salt. Cook 15 to 20 minutes. Remove from heat and stir in parsley. Transfer to a bowl and serve hot.

Makes 4 or 5 servings

Savory Black Beans with Squash

A rich and savory stew, nicely scented with lots of garlic and ginger and brimming with sweet winter squash. It has a warm, vitalizing energy to make you feel strong and steady.

1 (1-inch) piece kombu

1 cup dried black turtle beans, sorted, rinsed and soaked 6 to 8 hours

3 cups spring or filtered water

2 teaspoons light sesame oil

5 or 6 cloves garlic, minced

4 or 5 slices gingerroot, minced

3 or 4 shallots, minced

Generous pinch of cumin

2 or 3 celery stalks, diced

2 or 3 cups cubed winter squash

Spring or filtered water

1 tablespoon barley miso

4 or 5 green onions, thinly sliced, for garnish

Place kombu in a heavy pot and add beans and water. Bring to a boil over medium heat and boil, uncovered, 10 minutes. Reduce heat, cover and simmer until beans are tender, about 45 minutes. Transfer to a heat-resistant bowl, draining away any remaining cooking liquid.

In the pot used for cooking the beans, heat oil over medium heat. Add garlic, ginger, shallots and cumin and cook, stirring, 3 to 4 minutes. Add celery and squash. Add enough water to just cover and simmer, covered, until squash is tender, about 10 minutes. Add cooked beans. Do not stir. Remove about 1 tablespoon cooking broth and mix with miso until dissolved. Stir mixture into the bean stew and simmer, uncovered, about 4 minutes. Remove from heat and fold in green onions. Transfer to a bowl and serve hot. ✒ M a k e s 4 o r 5 s e r v i n g s

Black Soybean Relish

The great thing about black soybeans is that as they cook, they create their own gravy. In addition to being a deliciously satisfying stew, this dish has celery and dried daikon, which, coupled with the beans, create cleansing energy. In traditional cultures, this dish was believed to have the ability to cleanse stagnated fat and mucus from the reproductive organs. ✒

1 cup dried black soybeans, sorted,
  rinsed and towel-dried
1 (1-inch) piece kombu
3 to 4 cups spring or filtered water
1 onion, diced
2 or 3 celery stalks, diced
1/2 cup dried daikon, soaked until
  tender and diced
2 or 3 tablespoons barley miso
1/4 cup minced fresh parsley

In a hot, dry skillet, dry-roast soybeans over medium heat, stirring occasionally, until slightly puffed and skins have split, 4 to 5 minutes.

Place kombu in a heavy pot and add beans and water. Bring to a boil over medium heat and boil, uncovered, 10 minutes. If a thick foam appears, simply skim it from the pot with a slotted spoon. Reduce heat, cover, and simmer until beans are slightly tender, about 1 to 1 1/2 hours. Add vegetables to the top of the pot. Re-cover and cook 30 minutes. Remove about 1 tablespoon cooking broth and mix with miso until dissolved. Stir mixture into beans and cook, uncovered, until any excess liquid has been absorbed and beans are creamy, stirring often. Remove from heat and stir in fresh parsley. Spoon into a bowl and serve hot. ⟿ Makes 4 or 5 servings

Kidney Bean Casserole

Simple to make and delicately scented with herbs, this bean casserole will satisfy even the most finicky appetites. An interesting energy is created in a dish like this—steady, grounded energy from the beans and the baking, with a shot of light, fresh energy, courtesy of the herbs. ⟿

1 (1-inch) piece kombu
1 cup dried kidney beans, sorted,
  rinsed and soaked 6 to 8 hours
3 to 4 cups spring or filtered water
1 bay leaf
Generous pinch of dried rosemary
Generous pinch of dried basil
2 teaspoons toasted sesame oil

1 red onion, diced
2 or 3 cloves garlic, minced
2 or 3 celery stalks, diced
2 tablespoons red or barley miso,
  dissolved in 2 tablespoons warm
  water
2 teaspoons stone-ground mustard

Place kombu in a heavy pot and add beans and water. Bring to a boil over medium heat and boil, uncovered, 10 minutes. Add bay leaf and herbs. Reduce heat, cover, and simmer until beans are just tender, about 45 to 60 minutes. There should be very little liquid remaining in the pot. If too much liquid remains, allow the beans to cook, uncovered, until liquid evaporates.

Meanwhile, heat oil in a skillet over low heat. Add onion and garlic and cook, stirring occasionally, 2 or 3 minutes. Add celery and cook 1 minute.

Preheat oven to 375F (190C). Lightly oil a casserole dish. Stir vegetables into cooked beans. Stir miso mixture and mustard into the bean mixture. Spoon into prepared dish. Cover and bake about 40 minutes, until the beans are bubbling and appear creamy. Serve hot. ✆ M a k e s   4   o r   5   s e r v i n g s

Spicy Black Beans & Peppers

Another take on black beans from my life in Florida, this dish was originally a Spanish recipe. Cuban cuisine added a bit of ginger and spice to produce a real attention-getter . . . and a great dish for creating strong, fiery energy. ✆

1 (1-inch) piece kombu
1 cup dried black turtle beans, sorted, rinsed and soaked 3 to 4 hours
3 cups spring or filtered water
1/2 to 1 teaspoon soy sauce
2 teaspoons extra-virgin olive oil
2 onions, diced

4 or 5 slices gingerroot, minced
3 cloves garlic, minced
1 to 2 chiles, seeded and minced
1 teaspoon umeboshi vinegar
2 red bell peppers
1/4 cup minced fresh parsley

Place kombu in a heavy pot and add beans and water. Bring to a boil over medium heat and boil, uncovered, 10 minutes. Reduce heat, cover, and simmer until beans are tender, about 1 hour. Season with soy sauce to taste and simmer 10 minutes. If too much liquid remains, allow the beans to cook, uncovered, until liquid evaporates.

Meanwhile, heat oil in a skillet over medium heat. Add onions, gingerroot, garlic and chiles and cook, stirring, 4 to 5 minutes or until softened. Season with soy sauce and cook 1 to 2 minutes. Remove from heat and toss veggies with umeboshi vinegar.

Place whole peppers over an open gas flame until the outer skin is charred black. Transfer to a paper sack, seal tightly and allow peppers to steam. Gently rub charred skin from peppers, removing all black from the peppers. Cut in half and remove seeds. Dice peppers and toss with vegetables.

When beans are completely cooked, simply toss with vegetables and minced parsley. Transfer to a serving bowl and serve hot with corn tortillas or with crisp corn chips for dipping. ✒ Makes 4 or 5 servings

Red Lentil–Walnut Pâté

This is a great dip for parties. I love to serve it with toast points or toasted pita bread chips. Lightly toasted walnuts give this dish such a rich taste that you'd best make a lot; it's usually the first dish to disappear. Full of energizing qualities, this dish will make for an active social gathering.

For this recipe, I always pan-toast the nuts instead of oven-roasting them. They have a much nicer flavor when cooked that way. ✒

2 cups dried red lentils, sorted and
  rinsed well

1 (2-inch) piece wakame, soaked and
  diced

4 cups spring or filtered water

Soy sauce

1 teaspoon extra-virgin olive oil

1 onion, diced

2 to 3 cloves garlic, minced

Generous pinch dried basil

1 1/2 cups walnut pieces, lightly
  pan-toasted (page 417)

1/4 cup minced fresh parsley

Umeboshi vinegar

Balsamic vinegar

Place lentils, wakame, and water in a heavy pot over medium heat. Bring to a boil and boil, uncovered, 10 minutes. Reduce heat, cover and simmer 20 minutes, until lentils are very creamy. Season lightly with soy sauce and simmer 5 minutes.

Meanwhile, heat oil in a skillet over medium heat. Add onion, garlic, and basil and cook, stirring, 3 to 4 minutes or until softened. Set aside.

Transfer cooked beans, vegetables, walnuts, parsley and a dash of soy sauce to a food processor. Puree until smooth and creamy. Spoon into a serving bowl and lightly sprinkle with umeboshi and balsamic vinegars. Mix well and serve surrounded with toast points. 🍃 Makes 6 to 8 servings

Vitality Stew

This black soybean stew is like rocket fuel in a pot. I have based this recipe on a dish I learned from Aveline Kushi during my studies of macrobiotic cooking and food energy. Filled with strengthening root and dried vegetables, which complement the beans, and pressure-cooked on top of it all, this stew creates great strength and vitality. This dish is a bit of work, but worth the effort. 🍃

1 cup dried black soybeans, rinsed
    and towel-dried

1 (1-inch) piece kombu

3 cups spring or filtered water

1/4 cup dried daikon, soaked until
    tender and diced

2 or 3 pieces dried tofu, soaked until
    tender and diced

1/2 cup diced fresh daikon

1 carrot, diced

1/4 cup diced fresh lotus root

1/4 cup diced burdock

2 tablespoons barley miso

Fresh ginger juice (page 242)

4 or 5 green onions, thinly sliced

In a hot, dry skillet, pan-toast soybeans over medium heat until slightly puffed and the skins split, about 3 to 4 minutes. Place kombu in a pressure cooker and add beans and water. Bring to a boil and cook 5 minutes, uncovered. Seal pressure cooker and bring to full pressure. Cook over low heat 35 minutes. Remove from heat and allow pressure to reduce naturally.

In a heavy pot, place dried daikon, then dried tofu. Open pressure cooker and, reserving cooking liquid, add beans, using a slotted spoon, to dried vegetables. Add fresh daikon, carrot, lotus root, then burdock. Using cooking liquid, add enough liquid to the pot to half cover ingredients. Bring to a boil, cover, and cook over low heat until vegetables are tender, about 30 to 40 minutes.

Makes 4 or 5 servings

Remove about 1 tablespoon cooking broth and mix with miso until dissolved. Stir into stew with ginger juice to taste and simmer 5 to 10 minutes, until all liquid has been absorbed. Stir in green onions, transfer to bowl, and serve warm. ✑

Lentils with Squash

A simple bean stew, but a welcoming dish to come home to on a chilly night. The peppery lentils are nicely balanced by the deliciously sweet squash and onion, all simmered together in a bubbling stew, creating a warming, comforting dish. ✑

1 (1-inch) piece kombu	
1 cup dried lentils, sorted and rinsed	
3 cups spring or filtered water	
1 onion, diced	
2 to 3 cups 1/2-inch cubes winter squash	
Soy sauce	
Balsamic vinegar	

Place kombu in a heavy pot and add lentils and water. Bring to a boil over medium heat and boil, uncovered, 10 minutes. Cover and cook over low heat 35 minutes. Add onion and squash and cook until squash is tender, about 15 minutes. Season lightly with soy sauce and simmer 10 minutes. All liquid should be absorbed and the stew should be creamy. Remove from heat and sprinkle lightly with vinegar. Mix well, transfer to a bowl, and serve hot. ✑ Makes 4 or 5 servings

Azuki Beans with Dried Chestnuts Naturally

sweet, azukis are the perfect companion for the delicate sweet taste of the dried chestnuts. The energy of this combination provides stamina and an even temper.

1/2 cup dried chestnuts
1 (1-inch) piece kombu
1 cup dried azuki beans, sorted and
    rinsed

3 1/2 cups spring or filtered water
2 tablespoons barley malt
1 tablespoon barley miso

In a hot dry skillet, pan-toast chestnuts over medium heat until fragrant, about 4 minutes. Remove from skillet and soak 6 to 8 hours before use. These two steps ensure the sweetness of the chestnuts. Discard the soaking water. Soak beans 6 to 8 hours and drain.

Place kombu in a heavy pot and add beans, water, and chestnuts. Bring to a boil over medium heat and boil, uncovered, 10 minutes. Reduce heat, cover and simmer 30 minutes. Add barley malt and cook 30 minutes or until beans are soft. Remove about 1 tablespoon cooking broth and mix with miso until dissolved. Stir mixture into beans and simmer, uncovered, until all liquid has been absorbed. Transfer to a bowl and serve hot.

⌐ Makes 4 or 5 servings

Baked Chick-pea Casserole I don't usually bake

beans; it can create very heavy, dense energy, making us lethargic, but this is a great winter dish. The brown rice mochi gives it a creamy, cheeselike consistency, making a really hearty casserole. ⌐

1 (1-inch) piece kombu
1 cup dried chick-peas, sorted, rinsed
    and soaked 6 to 8 hours
3 cups spring or filtered water
2 or 3 cloves garlic, minced
1 onion, diced

1 carrot, cut into small irregular pieces
2 cups 1/2-inch cubes winter squash
3 tablespoons sweet white miso
2 tablespoons brown rice syrup
1 cup grated brown rice mochi

Place kombu in a pressure cooker and add chick-peas, water, and garlic. Bring to a boil over medium heat and boil, uncovered, 10 minutes. Seal pressure cooker and bring to full pressure. Cook over low heat 30 minutes. Remove from heat and allow pressure to reduce naturally.

Preheat oven to 375F (190C). Lightly oil a casserole dish. Mix the cooked beans with vegetables. Whisk together the miso and rice syrup. Stir mixture into beans and vegetables and spoon into prepared casserole dish. Add about 1/4 inch of water and top with grated mochi. Make a loose tent over top of the casserole with foil, being careful not to touch the mochi or it will stick to the foil. Bake 35 minutes. Remove cover and increase oven temperature to 450F (230C). Bake 10 to 15 minutes or until mochi browns. Serve hot, while mochi is soft. ∅ Makes 4 to 6 servings

Baked Beans with Miso & Apple Butter

A sweet and savory bean casserole, inspired by Ann Marie Colbin. Lightly spiced with stone-ground mustard and dotted with sweet vegetables, it is a real treat anytime. ∅

1 (1-inch) piece kombu
1 cup dried pinto beans, sorted and
  soaked 4 hours
3 cups spring or filtered water
1 red onion, diced
1 red bell pepper, roasted, diced

2 tablespoons barley miso
1/3 cup apple butter
3 teaspoons stone-ground mustard
2 tablespoons brown rice syrup
1 tablespoon brown rice vinegar

Place kombu in a heavy pot and add beans and water. Bring to a boil over medium heat and boil, uncovered, 10 minutes. Reduce heat, cover, and simmer 45 minutes. Drain, reserving 1 cup cooking liquid.

Preheat oven to 350F (175C). Lightly oil a deep casserole dish. In a small bowl, combine remaining ingredients and reserved cooking liquid. Stir cooked beans into apple butter mixture until combined. Spoon into prepared casserole dish, cover, and bake 1 1/2 hours. Remove cover and return to oven 10 minutes to set casserole. Serve hot. ∅ Makes 5 or 6 servings

Kidney Bean Stew

A sweet and savory, hearty winter bean dish, cooked to creamy perfection and filled with lots of sweet vegetables. I love to serve this stew on those days when I need a bit of comfort . . . the steady, grounding energy of beans and sweet vegetables makes me feel better every time.

1 (1-inch) piece kombu
1 cup dried red kidney beans, soaked 6 to 8 hours
3 to 4 cups spring or filtered water
2 teaspoons extra-virgin olive oil
2 cloves garlic, minced

1 onion, finely chopped
1 to 2 carrots, diced
1 to 2 cups cubed winter squash
2 tablespoons barley miso
2 to 3 tablespoons barley malt
1/4 cup minced fresh parsley

Place kombu in a pressure cooker and add beans and water. Boil 5 to 7 minutes over high heat, uncovered, skimming any foam that accumulates over the surface of the beans. Seal pressure cooker and bring to full pressure. Reduce heat and cook over low heat 1 hour.

Meanwhile, heat oil in a skillet over medium heat. Add garlic and onion and cook, stirring, 2 to 3 minutes. Add carrots and squash and cook 2 or 3 minutes. Add about 1/4 inch of water, cover skillet, and cook over low heat until vegetables are tender, but not mushy, about 15 minutes. Remove the cover and allow any remaining liquid to be absorbed. Set aside.

Remove beans from heat and allow pressure to reduce naturally. Remove about 1 tablespoon cooking broth and mix with miso until dissolved. Stir dissolved miso and barley malt into beans and cook, uncovered, until all liquid has been absorbed and beans are soft. Stir vegetables and minced parsley gently into cooked beans. Serve hot.

Makes 4 or 5 servings

Lentils with Braised Vegetables & Thyme

Peppery lentils are nicely offset by sweet, braised winter vegetables and delicately scented with thyme, providing the kind of energetic boost everyone wants. ✍

1 (1-inch) piece kombu

1 cup dried lentils, sorted and rinsed

1 onion, diced

1 carrot, diced

3 cups spring or filtered water

1 bay leaf

Soy sauce

1 tablespoon extra-virgin olive oil

4 or 5 cloves garlic, minced

4 or 5 shallots, peeled and diced

Several sprigs fresh thyme or a few
  generous pinches of dried

----

1 cup matchstick-size pieces winter
  squash

7 or 8 button mushrooms, brushed
  clean and thinly sliced

2 or 3 zucchini, cut into thin
  matchsticks

1 or 2 celery stalks, cut into thin
  diagonal slices

1 cup Vegetable Stock (page 96) or
  spring or filtered water

1 to 2 tablespoons balsamic vinegar

Green onions, sliced, for garnish

Place kombu in a heavy pot and add lentils, onion, carrot, and water. Bring to a boil over medium heat and boil, uncovered, 10 minutes. Add thyme and cook 1 minute. Stir in winter squash, mushrooms, zucchini, and celery and cook 2 to 3 minutes. Gently add stock and cook over low heat, uncovered, until all liquid has been absorbed and vegetables are tender. Remove from heat and stir in vinegar. Cover and set aside 10 to 15 minutes so flavors can develop.

Meanwhile, heat oil in a heavy skillet over medium heat. Add garlic and shallots and sauté until fragrant, 2 to 3 minutes. Add thyme and cook 1 minute. Stir in winter squash, mushrooms, zucchini, and celery and cook 2 to 3 minutes. Gently add stock and cook over low heat, uncovered, until all liquid has been absorbed and vegetables are tender. Remove from heat and stir in vinegar. Cover and set aside 10 to 15 minutes so flavors can develop.

Just before serving, stir braised vegetables into cooked lentils and serve warm, garnished with green onions. ✍ M a k e s 4 t o 6 s e r v i n g s

Frijoles Borrachos

Here is another Cuban recipe adapted from my days in Miami. I guess you can tell by now that I loved the Latin influence in Florida. There is a vibrancy and exuberance in all aspects of Latin life, especially in the cuisine, that I have always found irresistible. The name of this recipe translates to mean "drunken beans," because they are simmered in beer for a long time. Combined with crisply sautéed tempeh (bacon in the original version) and vegetables, this dish goes well with crunchy tortilla chips. 🍃

1 tablespoon extra-virgin olive oil

2 to 3 cloves garlic, minced

1 onion, diced

1 hot chile, seeded, finely minced

4 ounces tempeh, crumbled

1 cup dried pinto beans, soaked 4 hours

1 (1-inch) piece kombu

1 (12-oz.) bottle dark beer

1 cup spring or filtered water

Generous pinch of oregano

Generous pinch of cumin

Soy sauce

3 or 4 green onions, minced

Heat oil in a heavy pot over medium heat. Add garlic and onion and cook, stirring, 2 to 3 minutes. Add chile and tempeh and cook until tempeh is golden brown and crispy. Add beans and push kombu to the bottom of the pot. Slowly add beer, water, and herbs. Boil, uncovered, 10 minutes. Reduce heat, cover, and simmer over low heat until beans are very tender, 1 1/2 to 2 hours. Season lightly with soy sauce and simmer 10 minutes. The beans should be very creamy, almost pureed. Gently stir in green onions and transfer to a bowl. Serve warm with tortilla chips. 🍃 M a k e s 4 o r 5 s e r v i n g s

Hoppin' John

This old Carolina dish dates back as far as the 1700s, when "Carolina Gold" was considered the finest rice in the modern world. Developed by Sarah Rutledge, the original recipe was not concerned with dietary fats; it contained 1 pound of bacon. Equally tasty, this version is quite a bit safer for our arteries . . . . ∽

1 (1-inch) piece kombu

1 cup dried black-eyed peas, sorted and rinsed

3 cups spring or filtered water

1 to 2 teaspoons light sesame oil

3 or 4 cloves garlic, minced

1 onion, diced

2 red bell peppers, roasted over an open flame, peeled, seeded, and diced

2 or 3 fresh tomatoes, minced

1 cup long-grain brown rice

2 cups Vegetable Stock (page 96) or spring or filtered water

4 ounces tempeh, cut into 1/4-inch cubes, deep-fried until golden (page 161)

Soy sauce

3 or 4 green onions, minced

Place kombu in a heavy pot and add peas and water. Bring to a boil over medium heat and boil, uncovered, 10 minutes. Reduce heat, cover, and cook over low heat 20 minutes. Drain and set aside. Peas will still be a bit tough.

In a large Dutch oven or heavy pot, heat oil over medium heat. Add garlic and onion and cook, stirring, 2 to 3 minutes. Add bell peppers and tomatoes and cook 5 minutes. Add rice and cook 1 minute, stirring to combine. Add stock and bring to a boil. Add tempeh and partially cooked peas. Cover and cook over low heat until liquid has been almost absorbed and the peas are tender, about 40 minutes. Season lightly with soy sauce and simmer 5 minutes, until liquid is completely absorbed. Stir in green onions, transfer to a bowl, and serve immediately. ∽ M a k e s 4 o r 5 s e r v i n g s

Baked Lentil & Veggie Stew

Nothing sticks to your ribs on a frigid winter night quite like a baked lentil casserole. Creamy, peppery lentils and vegetables, served over brown rice with a side of lightly cooked vegetables, provide a centered energy that lets us approach life's many adventures with a clear head. ✿

1 cup dried lentils, sorted and rinsed
1 to 2 cups Brussels sprouts, quartered
1 leek, sliced lengthwise, rinsed well,
    and diced
1 carrot, diced
1 small rutabaga, diced
1 turnip, diced

1 cup cubed winter squash
2 or 3 bay leaves
3 cups spring or filtered water
2 tablespoons fresh ginger juice
    (page 242)
Soy sauce
1/4 cup minced fresh parsley

Preheat oven to 350F (175C). Lightly oil a deep casserole dish.

Combine lentils and vegetables and spoon into casserole. Insert bay leaves deep into mixture and gently add water and ginger juice. Cover and bake until lentils are tender, about 45 minutes, adding water midway through the cooking, if necessary. Remove casserole from oven and stir in a little soy sauce. Cover and return to oven for 10 minutes. Remove cover and return to oven for 5 to 10 minutes to allow the casserole to set. Stir in parsley and serve hot. ✿ M a k e s 4 t o 6 s e r v i n g s

Red Lentil Loaf

One taste of this savory loaf and you will forget all about meat loaf. ✐

1 cup dried red lentils, sorted and rinsed well	1 carrot, diced
2 cups spring or filtered water	2 celery stalks, diced
1 (1-inch) piece wakame, soaked briefly and minced	Generous pinch of dried basil
2 teaspoons extra-virgin olive oil	Soy sauce
2 to 3 shallots, minced	1 cup organic rolled oats
	1 teaspoon umeboshi vinegar
	1 to 2 teaspoons balsamic vinegar

Combine lentils, water, and wakame in a saucepan. Bring to a boil over medium heat and boil, uncovered, 10 minutes. Reduce heat, cover, and cook over low heat until liquid is absorbed and lentils are creamy, 20 to 25 minutes.

Meanwhile, heat oil in a skillet over medium heat. Add shallots and cook, stirring, 2 to 3 minutes. Add remaining vegetables and cook, stirring, 3 to 4 minutes. Stir in basil and season lightly with soy sauce. Simmer 2 to 3 minutes and remove from heat.

Preheat oven to 350F. Lightly oil an 8 × 4-inch loaf pan. Combine cooked lentils with cooked vegetables and rolled oats, reserving a small amount of oats to sprinkle on top of the loaf. Season to taste with vinegars and press mixture into oiled loaf pan. Sprinkle remaining oats on top and bake 20 to 25 minutes, until the loaf is firmly set. Remove from oven and allow to stand 5 to 10 minutes before slicing. Serve warm or at room temperature on a pool of your favorite sauce with a whole-grain dish and lightly cooked vegetables or as a pâté with toast points. ✐ M a k e s 6 t o 8 s e r v i n g s

Red Bell Peppers Stuffed with Black Beans

I like to serve these peppers with a side of mildly hot salsa and a crisp fresh salad for a delicious, easy-to-make lunch or brunch. Beans with the zip of hot flavor lift our energy and make us more outgoing as well as stronger. ✐

1 (1-inch) piece kombu

1 cup dried black turtle beans, sorted, rinsed and soaked 4 hours

3 cups spring or filtered water

Soy sauce

5 red bell peppers

1 to 2 teaspoons extra-virgin olive oil

1 red onion, diced

1 to 2 teaspoons chili powder

Generous pinch *each* of powdered cumin and basil

1 cup cooked short-grain brown rice

1 to 2 teaspoons balsamic vinegar

3 or 4 green onions, minced

Place kombu in a heavy pot and add beans and water. Bring to a boil over medium heat and boil, uncovered, 10 minutes. Reduce heat, cover, and cook over low heat until beans are tender, about 45 minutes. Season lightly with soy sauce and cook 10 minutes.

Cut bell peppers in half lengthwise and remove seeds and tops. Place in a skillet with 1/2 inch water and steam until crisp-tender, about 5 minutes. Rinse under cold water and set peppers aside.

Preheat oven to 350F (175C). Lightly oil a baking sheet. Heat oil in a skillet over medium heat. Add onion and cook until translucent, about 5 minutes. Add chili powder, a little soy sauce, and herbs and cook 3 to 4 minutes. Stir in rice until ingredients are well incorporated. Add beans and balsamic vinegar and stir well.

Fill the pepper halves with the rice and bean mixture. Place on prepared baking sheet and bake until peppers are tender, about 15 minutes. Arrange on a platter and serve hot. ⚘ Makes 5 servings

Black Bean Tacos

Back we go to Miami or perhaps Mexico, although the Cuban version of these spicy tacos was always my favorite. ⚘

1 tablespoon extra-virgin olive oil

4 to 5 cloves garlic, minced

1 hot chile, seeded and minced

1 red onion, diced

Generous pinch of dried basil

1 carrot, diced

1 to 2 cups button mushrooms, brushed clean and thinly sliced

2 cups cooked dried black turtle beans

1/2 to 1 teaspoon chili powder

Spring or filtered water

2 tablespoons barley or red miso, dissolved in 2 tablespoons water

Several chapati breads, lightly steamed, or taco shells

Shredded Romaine lettuce

Heat oil in a deep skillet over medium heat. Add garlic, chile, and onion and cook, stirring, 2 to 3 minutes. Add basil, carrot, and mushrooms and cook, stirring, 2 to 3 minutes. Partially mash beans and add to skillet with chili powder. Add about 1/8 inch of water, cover, and simmer over low heat 15 minutes. Stir miso mixture into beans. Simmer 3 to 4 minutes more. Spoon beans into chapati or taco shells and garnish with shredded lettuce. Serve warm. ✒ M a k e s 5 o r 6 s e r v i n g s

Baked Pinto Beans in Dijon Mustard Sauce

A spicy take on baked beans. This creamy casserole is smothered in a sweet Dijon mustard sauce and laced through with summer vegetables. A great summer picnic dish, with just the right touch of freshness to keep it light for summer weather. ✒

1 **(1-inch) piece kombu**
1 **cup dried pinto beans, sorted, rinsed and soaked 4 to 6 hours**
3 **cups spring or filtered water**
1 **small onion, diced**
2 **or 3 celery stalks, diced**
1 **cup fresh corn kernels**

DIJON SAUCE
1/4 **cup prepared Dijon mustard**
1/4 **cup sesame tahini**
2 **tablespoons brown rice syrup**
1 **tablespoon barley malt**
1 **teaspoon umeboshi vinegar**
2 **teaspoons barley miso**

Place kombu in a heavy pot and add beans and water. Bring to a boil over medium heat and boil, uncovered, 10 minutes. Reduce heat, cover, and cook over low heat until beans are tender, about 45 to 60 minutes. Drain beans, reserving 1 cup of the cooking liquid.

Preheat oven to 350F (175C). Lightly oil a deep casserole dish. Combine beans, onion, celery, and corn in a bowl. Next, whisk together the sauce ingredients with the reserved bean liquid. Stir into beans and spoon the mixture evenly into the oiled casserole dish. Cover and bake 1 1/2 hours. Remove cover and bake until beans are creamy and set, about 15 minutes. Serve warm or hot. ✒

M a k e s 5 o r 6 s e r v i n g s

Lima Bean Succotash

My Irish grandmother used to make this dish whenever we went to visit her at the New Jersey shore during the summer. Loaded with summer veggies, it tasted great whether warm or chilled. ✑

1 (1-inch) piece kombu
1 cup dried baby lima beans, sorted, rinsed and soaked 2 hours in lightly salted water
3 cups spring or filtered water
1 tablespoon extra-virgin olive oil
1 red onion, diced
1 red bell pepper, roasted, diced

2 celery stalks, diced
1 to 2 cups fresh corn kernels
Generous pinch of dried basil or several fresh basil leaves, minced
Soy sauce
Balsamic vinegar
Juice of 1 lemon
1/4 cup minced fresh parsley

Place kombu in a heavy pot and add beans and water. Bring to a boil over medium heat and boil, uncovered, 10 minutes. Reduce heat, cover, and cook over low heat until beans are tender but not mushy, about 45 minutes. Drain and set aside.

Meanwhile, heat oil in a skillet over medium heat. Add onion and sauté until translucent, about 5 minutes. Add bell pepper, celery, corn, and basil, season with a little soy sauce, and cook until vegetables are crisp-tender, about 4 minutes.

Gently toss vegetables with cooked beans, seasoning lightly with balsamic vinegar and fresh lemon juice. Fold in minced parsley and serve warm or chilled with a light grain dish and fresh vegetables for a great summer meal. ✑

Makes 4 or 5 servings

Sweet & Sour White Beans

I learned this recipe from Melanie Waxman, a truly wonderful whole foods cook whose creative approach and delicate sense of taste has made her a leading chef and instructor. And she writes great children's stories, too . . . ∽

1 (1-inch) piece kombu
1 onion, cut into large dice
1 to 2 celery stalks, cut into large dice
1 carrot, cut into bite-size irregular chunks
4 pieces dried tofu, soaked until soft and diced
1 cup dried white beans, sorted, rinsed and soaked 4 hours

Spring or filtered water
Soy sauce
1 to 2 tablespoons barley malt
Umeboshi vinegar
Juice of 1 lemon
3 or 4 green onions, sliced, for garnish

Layer kombu, onion, celery, carrot, dried tofu and beans in this order in a pressure cooker. Add enough water to just cover ingredients; bring to a boil and cook, uncovered, 10 minutes. Seal pressure cooker and bring to full pressure. Cook over low heat 45 minutes. Remove from heat and allow pressure to reduce naturally.

Open pressure cooker and season bean mixture lightly with soy sauce and barley malt. Return to heat and simmer 7 to 10 minutes. Remove from heat and gently stir in vinegar and lemon juice. Transfer to a bowl and serve warm, garnished with green onions. ∽ M a k e s 4 o r 5 s e r v i n g s

Plantain-Bean Casserole

On a trip to St. Thomas, I taught a cooking class using native Caribbean produce to create a whole foods meal. It was quite a challenge, using foods that I was completely unfamiliar with in old, standard recipes, but incredible fun. This recipe is based on a very traditional bean stew that is truly delicious . . . and a great balance of stamina and freshness—perfectly suited to a tropical clime. ✑

2 teaspoons extra-virgin olive oil

6 cloves garlic, minced

1 onion, diced

1 cup cooked chick-peas

1 cup cooked pinto beans

2 cups cubed winter squash

2 small chayote, cubed

2 cups diced celery root

2 cups peeled and diced yucca

6 plum tomatoes, coarsely diced

Soy sauce

3 to 4 cups spring or filtered water

1/4 cup minced cilantro (optional)

Preheat oven to 350F (175C). Lightly oil a casserole dish. Heat oil in a skillet over medium heat. Add garlic and onion and cook, stirring, 2 to 3 minutes. Mix together chick-peas, beans, onion mixture, winter squash, chayote, celery root, yucca, tomatoes, and a little soy sauce. Add water and sprinkle with cilantro, if using. Spoon into casserole and cook, uncovered, 3 hours, stirring gently every half hour and adding water as needed, or until creamy and thick. Serve hot over a cooked whole grain with a side of lightly cooked vegetables and crusty whole-grain bread. ✑

M a k e s 5 o r 6 s e r v i n g s

Polenta-Topped Kidney Bean Casserole

Crispy polenta tops a creamy kidney bean casserole, laden with savory vegetables and scented with spices. ✑

2 teaspoons extra-virgin olive oil

2 to 3 garlic cloves, minced

1 red onion, diced

Several sun-dried tomatoes, soaked until tender and diced

1 red bell pepper, roasted over an open flame, peeled, seeded, and diced

1 yellow bell pepper, roasted over an open flame, peeled, seeded, and diced

2 chiles, seeded and minced

2 zucchini, diced

2 cups cooked kidney beans, partially mashed

Generous pinch of dried rosemary

Soy sauce

Polenta Topping (see below)

Spring or filtered water

POLENTA TOPPING

2 1/2 cups spring or filtered water

Pinch of sea salt

1/2 cup yellow corn grits

1/2 cup fresh or frozen corn kernels

Preheat oven to 375F (175C). Lightly oil a deep casserole dish.

Heat oil in a deep skillet over medium heat. Add garlic and onion and cook, stirring, 2 to 3 minutes. Add sun-dried tomatoes, bell peppers and chiles and cook, stirring, 2 minutes. Add zucchini and cook, stirring, 2 minutes. Top cooked vegetables with beans, rosemary and a light seasoning of soy sauce. Stir well until ingredients are well incorporated. Set aside.

Meanwhile, prepare polenta: Bring water and salt to a boil in a heavy pot. Whisk in corn grits and corn and cook over low heat until polenta pulls away from the pan and the middle "burps," about 25 minutes, stirring frequently to prevent sticking.

Spoon bean mixture into casserole dish and add about 1/4 inch of water. Spoon polenta evenly over beans and vegetables and bake, uncovered, about 30 minutes, until casserole is bubbling and thick and the polenta is golden and crispy. Serve hot. ✑

Makes 5 or 6 servings

Pum Buk

This is a traditional Chinese side dish served around the New Year for good fortune. Sweet and satisfying, this dish will make you so steady, you will have no choice but to have good luck. 🌿

1/2 cup dried chestnuts, soaked 6 to 8 hours

1/2 cup dried azuki beans, soaked 4 hours

1 cup sweet brown rice, rinsed well

3 cups cubed winter squash

2 1/2 cups spring or filtered water

Pinch of sea salt

Combine all ingredients in a pressure cooker. Seal lid and bring to full pressure over medium heat. Reduce heat, place over a flame deflector, and cook over low heat 50 minutes. Remove from heat and allow pressure to reduce naturally. Stir briskly to create a creamy texture, transfer to a bowl, and serve immediately. 🌿 Makes 5 or 6 servings

TASTY TOFU, TEMPEH & SEITAN

Soybeans, long associated with healthful eating, have always, in traditional cuisine, been processed in some way or another before consumption by humans, because they are so difficult to digest. It actually takes more effort by our bodies to digest these beans than the energy provided by the beans. The result gives us a wide variety of delicious, versatile products, including tofu and tempeh.

TOFU

Tofu or bean curd are the names given to the pressed curd of the soybean. Processing involves adding a coagulating agent to cooked soybeans, which causes the curd to separate and rise to the top of the cooking pot. The curd is then removed and pressed to the desired firmness. Tofu can be found in a variety of firmness, from silken and soft to extra firm.

A rather bland character, tofu is virtually packed with nutrition. High in protein, calcium, choline, and phyto-estrogens, tofu has the reputation for being effective in building strong bones and teeth, improving memory, relieving symptoms of PMS and helping to create strong bone mass before menopause—not to mention helping to regulate estrogen levels after menopause.

This important food has little personality by itself, but when combined with stronger oils, seasonings, or vegetables, it immediately comes to life, bursting with flavor. It seems to wait for stimulation through other foods with more defined characteristics.

Tofu by nature has a cooling effect on the body, making it very helpful in reducing fever, inflammations—like sprains and swelling—and as a topical remedy for minor burns and abrasions. It holds coldness much longer than any ice, effectively reducing any inflammation symptoms; it is not only a great food, but an essential member of your first aid kit. However, remember that with its cooling effect, too much tofu can dampen or cool your energy, so you don't want to overuse it in your cooking, serving it only once or twice a week.

TEMPEH

Coming to us by way of Indonesia, tempeh is a whole fermented soy food with a chewy, delectable and quite unique flavor. Its meaty texture makes for a most satisfying entree for a meatless meal.

Eating tempeh has many benefits. Containing a microorganism called *bacillus subtilis*, tempeh has been found effective in relieving symptoms of cirrhosis of the liver, diabetes, intestinal disorders and iron-deficient blood. Because it is fermented, tempeh is especially helpful in promoting healthy digestion, which in turn strengthens the quality of the blood, lymph, and other body fluids.

Tempeh can be stewed, fried, steamed, or roasted. Combined with grains and vegetables, tempeh makes a great foundation for any number of stews, stir-fries, kabobs, sandwiches or salads.

Actually, seitan is a wheat product, not a bean product. So why is it in the chapter that features mostly soybean products? Well, the truth is, no one is really sure how to categorize seitan. Though it has wheat as its source, after its processing, seitan is such a great source of concentrated protein that you would not want to serve it as a grain dish, but rather as your protein or bean dish in a meal. Hence, most cooks, me included, usually place seitan recipes with other beans and bean product recipes.

Seitan is made from hard whole-wheat flour, which is combined with water to create a dough not unlike bread dough. Then, alternating between warm and cool water, the dough is kneaded under water until all of the germ and bran of the flour is rinsed away, leaving only a ball of gluten. This gluten is then cooked in a savory broth, creating the product we recognize as seitan.

Very meaty in texture and rich in flavor, seitan goes well in any number of recipes, but seems to shine in stews, oven-baked casseroles—when it is grilled or broiled—or when sautéed with onions for a great sandwich filling.

Tofu "Cream Cheese"

This is a great alternative to dairy products. Completely cholesterol-free and low in fat, this version retains all of its creamy texture and rich taste without it. I love to serve it at brunches with toasted bagels or whole-grain toast. ✒

1 pound soft tofu	
2 teaspoons umeboshi paste	1 or 2 celery stalks, diced
1 teaspoon sesame tahini	1 carrot, grated
2 or 3 green onions, minced	1/4 cup fresh minced parsley
	Juice of 1 lemon

Makes 4 to 6 servings

Bring a pot of water to a boil, add tofu, and cook 5 minutes. Drain tofu and process in a food processor with umeboshi paste and tahini until smooth. Fold in vegetables, parsley and lemon juice, transfer to a serving bowl, and chill thoroughly before serving. ✒

Tofu Vegetable Roll

A great appetizer. I love to serve it chilled as a starter to a summer meal. It's light and refreshing, pretty on a serving platter and, best of all, a breeze to make. ✑

1 pound extra-firm tofu
1/2 red bell pepper, roasted over an open flame, peeled, seeded, and minced

1 small carrot, minced
1/2 bunch watercress, minced
Soy sauce

Puree tofu in a food processor to a smooth, thick paste. Fold in bell pepper, carrot, watercress and soy sauce to taste and mix well.

Using a bamboo sushi mat, spread tofu mixture about 1/4 inch thick directly on the mat, leaving 1 inch exposed on the side of the mat furthest from you and also the one closest to you. With the mat as a guide, roll the tofu into a tight cylinder, wrapping the mat completely around the roll, but not into it. Place in a bamboo steamer over boiling water and steam 10 to 15 minutes. Unroll the mat and slice the tofu roll into 1-inch-thick rounds. Repeat process until all ingredients are used up. Arrange rolls on a serving platter and serve at room temperature or chilled. ✑ M a k e s   4   t o   6   s e r v i n g s

Creamy Olive Dip

Strong and aromatic, this dip is great served with toast points or pita chips. Its salty, rich taste makes for an active, social get-together. ✑

1/4 cup extra-virgin olive oil
3 or 4 cloves garlic, minced
8 ounces firm tofu, boiled 5 minutes and drained
Juice of 1 lemon

Pinch of sea salt
10 to 12 oil-cured olives, pitted and minced
1/8 cup capers, drained well

Heat oil in a small skillet over medium heat. Add garlic and cook until fragrant, 1 to 2 minutes. Place tofu, oil with garlic, lemon juice, and salt in a food processor and puree until smooth. Transfer to a mixing bowl and gently fold in olives and capers. Chill thoroughly before serving. ✑ M a k e s   4   t o   6   s e r v i n g s

Chinese Firecrackers

I love to serve this hot and spicy appetizer at parties. The energy of the ground chiles makes for animated conversation and a most lively gathering! ◌

Safflower oil for deep-frying

1 pound firm tofu, cut into 1/2-inch cubes and patted dry

Firecracker Sauce

Green onions, sliced, for garnish

FIRECRACKER SAUCE

3 tablespoons soy sauce

2 tablespoons brown rice syrup

2 tablespoons brown rice vinegar

1 tablespoon chili powder

Scant pinch of cayenne

Scant pinch of powdered ginger

1 cup spring or filtered water

1 tablespoon kuzu, dissolved in small amount cold water

Heat about 3 inches of oil in a deep saucepan over medium heat. Add tofu cubes and deep-fry until golden brown and crispy. Drain on paper towels and set aside while preparing the sauce.

Prepare sauce: Combine soy sauce, rice syrup, rice vinegar, chili powder, cayenne, ginger and water in a small saucepan over medium heat. When warmed through, stir in dissolved kuzu and cook, stirring, until sauce is thick and clear. Stir in tofu cubes until well coated with sauce and serve garnished with green onions. ◌

Makes 4 servings

Tofu Cheese

If you hate the thought of giving up cheese, this recipe is for you. Rich, creamy, and savory, this sharp-tasting, pickled tofu can stand on its own in place of any cheese in recipes ranging from creamy white sauces to thin squares on a cracker, to whipped cream cheese, without the negative effects of dairy products. You have to experience this one for yourself . . . .

About 1 to 1 1/2 cups white miso

....

1 pound extra-firm tofu

Spread about 1/4 inch of miso on a plate. Press tofu on top of miso. Cover the rest of the tofu with a 1/4-inch-thick coating of miso, covering it completely. (Any tofu left exposed will spoil.) Cover with cheesecloth and set aside in a cool place to ferment (not in the refrigerator). Tofu may pickle anywhere from 12 hours to 4 days, depending on how strong you would like the flavor to become. During fermentation, there will be a delicate beerlike aroma around the tofu. This means that the fermentation process is active. When the tofu cheese is ready, simply scrape miso completely from the tofu, reserving the miso to use in sauces or salad dressings. Rinse tofu gently under cool water to remove any remaining miso residue and use as you wish as a cheese substitute in any recipe. Experiment with different misos to create an incredible variety of flavors.

Makes 1 pound

Broiled Tofu with Walnut-Miso Sauce

Delightfully easy to make and sinfully rich tasting, this dish will change your mind about tofu . . . .

1 pound firm tofu, cut into 6
(1/2-inch-thick) slices

1/2 cup walnut pieces

....

3 tablespoons barley miso

3 tablespoons spring or filtered water

1 teaspoon brown rice syrup

Preheat broiler. Lightly oil a baking pan. Lay tofu slices on a dry kitchen towel and pat dry. Next place slices in pan, place pan under broiler and cook until golden on one side, 4 to 5 minutes. Turn and repeat on the other side. Remove from baking pan and set aside to cool.

Prepare the sauce by lightly pan-toasting the walnuts in a dry skillet over medium heat until fragrant, about 4 minutes. While warm, grind into a fairly fine meal in a food processor. Add miso, water, and rice syrup and process to a thick paste. Spread a thin layer of walnut sauce over each slice of tofu and return to the broiler 1 minute. Serve warm or at room temperature. ✒ Makes 6 servings

VARIATION I like to spread the walnut sauce on 3 tofu slices, top with the remaining 3 slices, making "sandwiches." Then wrap a thin vegetable strip (blanched leek or green onion strip) around each one to make packages.

Mushroom Broccoli Quiche

Real men do eat quiche, especially this one. This is so creamy and rich, you won't believe it's tofu. Laced through with fresh broccoli and smoky mushrooms, this quiche is a meal in itself. ✒

Whole-Wheat Crust (opposite)

2 teaspoons extra-virgin olive oil

2 cloves garlic, minced

1 onion, diced

1 cup mushrooms, brushed clean and
   thinly sliced

1 to 2 stalks broccoli, cut into small
   flowerets

1 1/2 pounds extra-firm tofu

3 tablespoons sesame tahini

2 tablespoons umeboshi vinegar or
   fresh lemon juice

1 teaspoon brown rice syrup

Soy sauce

2 tablespoons black or tan sesame
   seeds, for garnish

WHOLE-WHEAT CRUST

1 1/2 cups whole-wheat pastry flour

1/4 cup corn oil

Pinch of sea salt

1/4 cup cold spring or filtered water

Prepare the crust: Preheat oven to 350F (175C). Combine flour, oil and salt with a fork until the mixture is sandy in texture. Add water and continue to mix until the dough begins to form a ball. Do not overmix or use your hands during this stage of dough preparation as it can result in a tough, heavy crust. Gather dough between hands and knead 3 to 4 times to shape into a ball. Roll dough out between 2 sheets of waxed paper or pastry cloth into a thin crust. Transfer to a 9-inch pie plate and, without stretching the dough, press it into the pan. Trim away any excess crust, leaving about 1/4 inch hanging over the edge of the pie plate. Fold the excess back toward the inside of the pan, pinching between thumb and fingers to create a scalloped edge around the crust. Prick the crust with a fork several times over the surface. Bake 15 to 17 minutes or until dough is set. Set aside to cool while preparing the filling.

Heat oil in a skillet over medium heat. Add garlic and onion and cook, stirring, 2 to 3 minutes. Add mushrooms and cook, stirring, until limp. Set aside. Bring a small pot of water to a boil and quickly cook broccoli until bright green but still crispy, 1 to 2 minutes. Drain and set aside. Place tofu, tahini, vinegar, rice syrup, and a generous dash of soy sauce in a food processor and puree until smooth. Transfer to a bowl and fold in broccoli and sautéed vegetables. Spoon mixture evenly into prebaked pie shell, sprinkle sesame seeds lightly around the rim of the quiche and bake until quiche is firm and edges are light golden, about 30 minutes. Remove from oven and allow to stand about 15 minutes before serving. ✒ M a k e s 5 o r 6 s e r v i n g s

Stuffed Tofu Agé

This is a traditional Oriental way to serve tofu.

Pretty ingenious, too, I might add. What you do is deep-fry the tofu and then, to remove any excess oily taste, the pockets are simmered in a savory broth. Talk about rich flavor! The stuffing is up to you. I serve them smothered in Sweet & Sour Sauce. Fabulous . . .

1 pound firm tofu, cut into 8 triangular wedges
Safflower oil for deep-frying
Spring or filtered water
Soy sauce
1 (2-inch) piece kombu

4 or 5 slices gingerroot
About 1/2 cup sautéed, curried vegetables, pickled sea vegetables, sautéed corn and shallots, or sautéed mushrooms for filling
Sweet & Sour Sauce (page 56)

Make a slit along the longest side of each tofu wedge for the stuffing. Be careful not to slice all the way through. Heat oil in a saucepan over medium heat. Add tofu, 2 at a time, and deep-fry until deep golden brown. Drain on paper towels.

Bring a medium pot of water to a boil, season lightly with soy sauce, and add kombu and ginger. Carefully drop tofu wedges into broth and simmer over low heat, uncovered, 30 minutes. Drain tofu wedges and discard broth.

Allow tofu to cool enough to touch, while preparing filling. When wedges have cooled enough to handle, gently pull open slits and press stuffing inside. Arrange on a serving platter and just before serving, ladle warm Sweet & Sour Sauce over each pocket.

Makes 4 servings

Steamed Tofu Rolls

This is a really pretty dish with round white pinwheels of tofu, dotted with sautéed, diced vegetables. Wrapped in thin sheets of rich, black nori, these beauties are as much fun to eat as they are to serve. A light energy provided by the tofu and lightly cooked veggies, makes this an ideal summer side dish.

2 teaspoons light sesame oil
4 or 5 slices gingerroot, minced
1 onion, finely diced
1 carrot, finely diced
1 cup button mushrooms, brushed clean and finely diced

1 pound extra-firm tofu
Soy sauce
Nori, toasted

Heat oil in a skillet over medium heat. Add ginger and onion and cook, stirring, 3 to 4 minutes. Add carrot and mushrooms and cook, stirring, 2 to 3 minutes or until vegetables are limp. Crumble tofu into a fine meal into a bowl. Stir in sautéed vegetables and a little soy sauce.

Place a sushi mat on a flat surface and lay a sheet of nori, shiny side down, on top. Gently spread tofu mixture 1/4 inch thick evenly over surface of nori, leaving 1 inch of nori exposed at the far end to help seal the roll. Using the mat as a guide, gently but firmly roll the tofu roll, jelly-roll style, sealing it at the end with the exposed nori. Remove mat and place roll in a bamboo steamer over a pot of boiling water and steam over high heat, uncovered, 10 to 12 minutes. Remove roll from heat and cool 5 to 10 minutes before slicing into 1-inch-thick rounds. Arrange on a platter and serve at room temperature or chilled. Makes 4 to 6 servings

Tofu-Millet Stew

Real comfort food. A creamy, golden stew, with tiny cubes of tofu throughout. We love to serve this for breakfast, especially on chilly fall and winter mornings, when the warming energy of millet is especially nice to have around . . . .

1 cup yellow millet, rinsed well
8 ounces firm tofu, cut into 1/4-inch cubes
1 cup cubed winter squash

5 cups spring or filtered water
Pinch of sea salt
Green onions, for garnish (optional)

Combine all ingredients in a heavy pot and bring to a boil. Cover and cook over low heat until all liquid is absorbed and millet has a creamy consistency, about 30 minutes. Remove from heat and stir briskly. Transfer to a bowl and serve immediately, perhaps garnished with sliced green onions.

Any leftover stew can be pressed into a loaf pan and, when set, sliced and lightly pan-fried. ☙ M a k e s 4 t o 5 s e r v i n g s

Yu-Dofu

Since tofu is a traditional staple food in the Orient, it's no wonder so many tofu recipes have an Asian flair to them. This is a very traditional one-dish meal that is usually served family style, with everyone dipping into the pot as they eat. It makes for a very social, active meal. ☙

1 pound firm tofu, cut into 1-inch cubes	**4 dried shiitake mushrooms, soaked**
1 cup finely shredded Chinese cabbage	**until tender and thinly sliced**
1 (2-inch) piece kombu, soaked briefly	**Spring or filtered water**
and cut into thin matchsticks	**Soy sauce**
1 carrot, cut into thin matchsticks	**1 small bunch watercress, rinsed and**
1 cup matchstick-size pieces fresh	**drained**
daikon	

In a wide pot or deep skillet, arrange tofu and each vegetable, except watercress, in its own section. Add water to generously half-cover ingredients, cover, and bring to a boil over medium heat. Reduce heat and simmer, covered, over low heat 10 minutes. Season lightly with soy sauce and simmer, covered, 5 to 7 minutes more. Remove from heat, add watercress, cover, and allow to stand 3 to 4 minutes, cooking watercress in the heat of the pot. Serve at once with a side dish of cooked whole grain or noodles. ☙

M a k e s 5 o r 6 s e r v i n g s

VARIATION Sometimes, in really cold weather, I deep-fry the tofu before proceeding with the yu-dofu.

Oden

Another Oriental tradition. A simple, clean-tasting dish with just enough richness to make you sigh with satisfaction after eating. ✑

6 (4-inch) pieces kombu, soaked until
    tender

2 teaspoons toasted sesame oil

6 to 8 (1/2-inch-thick) slices firm tofu

2 cups (1/2-inch-thick) rounds fresh
    daikon

4 or 5 shiitake mushrooms, soaked
    until tender and halved

Spring or filtered water

Soy sauce

Tie kombu pieces into small knots and set aside. Heat oil in a skillet over medium heat. Add tofu slices and cook until golden on each side. Drain on paper towels and set aside.

Arrange kombu, daikon, tofu, and mushrooms in a deep skillet, each in its own section. Add water to half cover and bring to a boil. Reduce heat, cover, and cook over low heat until daikon is translucent, about 20 minutes. Remove cover and season lightly with soy sauce. Simmer, uncovered, until all remaining liquid has been absorbed. Transfer to a platter and serve immediately. ✑ M a k e s   5   o r   6   s e r v i n g s

Sweet Marinated Tofu with Spicy Peanut Sauce

I love tofu dishes. They are so good and with tofu's neutral nature, a simple sauce can transform it into a most delicious dish. And they have a cooling, relaxing energy that is ideal for us in our stress-filled lives. I like to serve this tofu dish with the marinated slices on a pool of thick sauce, garnished with green onion slices. 🍃

1 pound extra-firm tofu, cut in half and then into 1/2-inch-thick slices

2 tablespoons soy sauce

2 or 3 teaspoons brown rice syrup

1/4 cup toasted sesame oil

2 teaspoons prepared mustard

2 tablespoons fresh ginger juice (page 242)

3 or 4 cloves garlic, crushed

1 cup spring or filtered water

SPICY PEANUT SAUCE

2 teaspoons toasted sesame oil

1 tablespoon grated onion

1 clove garlic, minced

2 teaspoons chili powder

1 cup unsweetened peanut butter

Soy sauce

1 tablespoon brown rice syrup

Juice of 1 lemon

Spring or filtered water

Place tofu slices on a dry kitchen towel and pat excess water off the surface. Whisk together remaining ingredients for a marinade and pour into a small saucepan. Bring to a boil, reduce heat, and simmer, uncovered, 10 minutes. Place tofu pieces in a shallow dish and spoon hot marinade over top, covering completely. Allow to marinate at least 1 hour before serving or up to 12 hours in the refrigerator.

Prepare sauce: Heat sesame oil in a small pan. Add onion, garlic, and chili powder and cook, stirring, over medium heat 2 to 3 minutes. Add peanut butter, a dash of soy sauce, and rice syrup. Stir well and simmer over very low heat 5 minutes. Remove from heat, stir in lemon juice and enough water to make the sauce as thick or thin as you desire. Serve tofu at room temperature with sauce. 🍃 M a k e s   4   s e r v i n g s

Tofu Pot Pie

I learned this recipe from Sarah LaPenta, a cooking instructor from Massachusetts. I was assisting her in a cooking class on fun foods at a conference. This is an easy-to-make family casserole that will win you raves. 🌿

2 recipes Whole-Wheat Crust (page 164)	1 cup fresh corn kernels
4 teaspoons light sesame oil	1 cup fresh or frozen green peas
1 pound extra-firm tofu, cut into 1/2-inch cubes	1 cup cauliflowerets
1 cup diced onion	Soy sauce
1 carrot, diced	1 to 2 cups spring or filtered water
1 to 2 cups broccoli flowerets	2 tablespoons kuzu, dissolved in small amount cold water
	Generous pinch of powdered ginger

Prepare pastry dough and roll each one between waxed paper. Set aside.

Heat 2 teaspoons oil in a skillet over medium heat. Add tofu cubes and cook, turning as needed, until browned. Set aside.

Heat remaining 2 teaspoons oil in another skillet over medium heat. Add onion and cook, stirring, 2 to 3 minutes. Add remaining vegetables and cook, stirring, until crisp-tender, 2 to 3 minutes. Add tofu cubes, season lightly with soy sauce, and add water. Bring to a boil over medium heat and stir in dissolved kuzu. Cook, stirring, until a thin glaze forms over the entire mixture, about 3 minutes. Stir in powdered ginger and set aside.

Preheat oven to 350F (175C). Place 1 crust in pie plate and without stretching dough, press into pan. Prick surface with a fork in several places. Spoon filling into pie shell and lay second crust over top. Crimp edges of both crusts between fingers and thumb, creating a crimped edge. Pierce the top crust in several places to allow steam to escape. Bake 40 to 45 minutes, until crust is golden and filling is bubbling. Serve hot.

🌿 M a k e s   5   t o   6   s e r v i n g s

Tofu Chili

Frozen tofu creates a texture that is similar to that of ground meat in traditional chili con carne. Coupled with lots of beans and vegetables in a savory chili broth, this Southwestern-style dish is a real winner, with a rich, strengthening energy. ✍

1 pound extra-firm tofu
Soy sauce
2 tablespoons natural peanut butter
2 cloves garlic, minced
Generous pinch of ground cumin
Scant pinch of powdered ginger
1 tablespoon extra-virgin olive oil
1 red bell pepper, roasted, peeled, seeded, and diced
1 small hot chile, seeded and diced
1 teaspoon chili powder

1 red onion, diced
1 carrot, diced
1 cup diced winter squash
1 or 2 celery stalks, diced
1 cup cooked pinto beans
1 cup cooked red kidney beans
1 to 2 cups Vegetable Stock (page 96)
Sea salt
1/4 cup minced fresh parsley, for garnish

Cut tofu into 1/2-inch-thick slices and place on a tray in the freezer until firmly frozen, about 2 hours. Thaw tofu pieces, squeeze out the fluid, and coarsely crumble.

Preheat oven to 375F (175C). Lightly oil a baking sheet. Mix together a dash of soy sauce, peanut butter, garlic, cumin, and ginger. Stir tofu into peanut butter mixture until sauce is completely absorbed. Spread tofu evenly on oiled baking sheet and bake about 20 minutes. Stir well and bake another 10 minutes. Set aside.

Heat oil in a soup pot over medium heat. Add bell pepper, chile, chili powder and onion and cook, stirring, 3 to 4 minutes. Add balance of vegetables and sauté 2 to 3 minutes more. Add beans and enough stock to just cover ingredients. Bring to a boil, season to taste with salt and stir in baked tofu. Cover and simmer over low heat 10 to 15 minutes more. Serve hot, garnished with fresh minced parsley. ✍

Makes 5 or 6 servings

Tropical Tempeh Grill

When I was in St. Thomas, the native produce was so lush and so abundant that I simply could not resist it. So I didn't. I looked through lots of local cookbooks and discovered so many ways to incorporate all of these exotic, delicious foods into my own recipes. 🌿

Juice of 2 or 3 limes

1/4 cup plus 2 tablespoons brown
   rice syrup

Generous dash of soy sauce

2 to 3 tablespoons extra-virgin
   olive oil

2 cloves garlic, minced

2 teaspoons powdered ginger

8 ounces tempeh, cut into 1-inch-thick
   slices

1 onion, finely chopped

1 cup cubed fresh pineapple

1 cup cubed fresh papaya

1 red bell pepper, roasted, minced

Pinch of sea salt

Spring or filtered water

1 to 2 tablespoons kuzu, dissolved in
   small amount cold water

Generous dash of umeboshi vinegar
   or fresh lemon juice

Rice, cooked, to serve

Whisk together lime juice, 1/4 cup rice syrup, soy sauce, oil, garlic and ginger. Pour mixture over tempeh and marinate 35 minutes. Drain tempeh. Heat a griddle over medium heat. Add tempeh and cook, turning, until golden on both sides, about 3 minutes. Drain on paper towels and set aside.

Combine onion, pineapple, papaya, bell pepper, remaining 2 tablespoons rice syrup, and salt in a saucepan. Add enough water just to cover and bring to a boil. Cover and cook over low heat until fruit is soft, but not mushy, 5 to 7 minutes. Stir in dissolved kuzu and cook, stirring, until slightly thickened. Remove from heat and stir in vinegar and tempeh. Transfer to a bowl and serve over rice. 🌿 M a k e s   4   o r   5   s e r v i n g s

Tempeh with Corn & Onions
Tempeh is delicious deep-fried and then stewed in a rich sauce. It forms a crispy, outer coating with a moist,

chewy center. In this recipe, I combine the distinctive flavor of tempeh with stewed onions and fresh sweet corn. Because it's fermented, tempeh makes digesting protein so easy. ❧

Safflower oil for deep-frying
8 ounces tempeh, cut into 1-inch cubes
2 onions, cut into thick wedges
2 cups fresh corn kernels
2 cups spring or filtered water

Soy sauce
1 teaspoon powdered ginger
1 1/2 tablespoons kuzu, dissolved in small amount cold water

Heat 3 inches of oil in a heavy pot over medium heat. Add tempeh, increase heat to high, and deep-fry until golden brown. Drain on paper towels and set aside.

In a soup pot, layer onions, corn, and then tempeh. Add water and bring to a boil. Reduce heat, cover, and cook over low heat until onions are very soft, about 5 minutes. Season lightly with soy sauce and ginger and simmer 5 minutes. Stir in dissolved kuzu and cook, stirring, until slightly thickened. Transfer to a bowl and serve immediately.

❧ M a k e s 4 s e r v i n g s

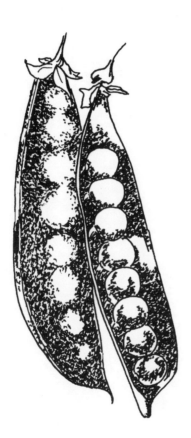

Tender Tempeh with Basil

Indonesia meets Italy in this recipe. Combining the distinctive flavor of tempeh with the delicate taste of fresh basil makes for an explosion of sensations in your mouth as well as a light energy that will put pep in your step. ❧

4 teaspoons extra-virgin olive oil

8 ounces tempeh, crumbled

2 cloves garlic, minced

1 red onion, diced

1 carrot, diced

1 or 2 celery stalks, diced

1 red bell pepper, roasted over an
open flame, peeled, seeded, and diced

2 cups button mushrooms, brushed
clean and thinly sliced

4 or 5 leaves fresh basil, minced, or
generous pinch of dried basil

Sea salt

Spring or filtered water

1 tablespoon kuzu, dissolved in small
amount cold water

Pasta, cooked, to serve

1/4 cup minced fresh parsley, for
garnish

Heat 2 teaspoons oil in a skillet over medium heat. Add tempeh and cook, stirring occasionally, until golden and crispy.

In the same skillet, heat remaining 2 teaspoons oil. Add garlic and onion and cook, stirring, 2 to 3 minutes. Add carrot, celery, bell pepper, mushrooms and basil and cook 3 to 4 minutes. Sprinkle with salt to taste. Add tempeh and enough water to half-cover ingredients and bring to a boil. Reduce heat, cover, and cook over low heat 15 minutes. Stir in dissolved kuzu and cook until slightly thickened, about 3 minutes. Serve over pasta, garnished with fresh minced parsley. ✐ M a k e s 4 o r 5 s e r v i n g s

Tempeh Brochettes
Marinated tempeh is perfect for grilling. Its own distinctive flavor is enhanced by the variety of flavors in the marinade and then it is grilled to golden perfection and skewered with fresh summer veggies. A cookout dish to die for . . . ✐

2 to 3 teaspoons soy sauce
1/3 cup mirin or white wine
1/3 cup fresh orange juice
2 tablespoons toasted sesame oil
1 tablespoon brown rice syrup
1 or 2 cloves garlic, crushed
Generous pinch of powdered ginger
Generous pinch of red pepper flakes
8 ounces tempeh, cut into 1-inch cubes
1 red bell pepper, cut into
    1-inch pieces

1 yellow bell pepper, cut into
    1-inch pieces
1 red onion, cut into 6 wedges
2 zucchini, cut into 1-inch-thick rounds
2 yellow summer squash, cut into
    1-inch-thick rounds
7 or 8 button mushrooms, brushed
    clean and left whole
1 to 2 cups 1-inch cubes cantaloupe

For marinade, whisk together soy sauce, mirin, orange juice, sesame oil, rice syrup, garlic, ginger, and pepper flakes. Arrange tempeh in a shallow dish, cover with marinade and allow to stand at room temperature about 1 hour, stirring occasionally.

Preheat grill. Thread tempeh, veggies and melon alternately on skewers, leaving a tiny space between each piece to allow for quicker, more even cooking. When brochettes are complete, brush lightly with marinade.

Arrange the brochettes on grill rack with a small space between them. Grill 7 to 8 minutes, turn each brochette, brush with marinade and grill the other side 7 to 8 minutes. Brochettes are ready when edges of the tempeh and vegetables are crispy and beginning to blacken. Serve hot. ✐ Makes 5 or 6 servings

Steamed Spring Rolls with Citrus Mustard Sauce

No one handles tempeh quite like Indonesia, and lightly steamed spring rolls have a freshness about them that makes this a protein dish that won't weigh you down. ✐

2 teaspoons toasted sesame oil

8 ounces tempeh, cut into 2 × 1/4-inch strips

1/2 cup mung bean sprouts

4 green onions, cut into 3-inch pieces

1/2 cup finely shredded Chinese cabbage

1/2 red bell pepper, roasted over an open flame, peeled, seeded, and cut into 3-inch strips

Juice of 1 lemon

8 dried rice-paper spring roll wrappers

CITRUS & MUSTARD SAUCE

3 tablespoons prepared Dijon mustard

3 to 4 tablespoons sesame tahini

2 green onions, minced

Juice of 1 lime

Juice of 1 orange

1 teaspoon brown rice syrup

Dash of soy sauce

2 teaspoons toasted sesame oil

Generous pinch of powdered ginger

Heat sesame oil in a skillet over medium heat. Add tempeh and cook, turning, until golden brown on all sides. Drain and set aside. Toss sprouts, green onions, cabbage, and bell pepper with lemon juice in a medium bowl.

Soften rice wrappers by soaking in cold water 5 minutes or by moistening with a wet sponge until pliable. Lay rice wrappers with one corner pointing toward you. Arrange one-eighth of vegetables (about 3 tablespoons) and a strip of tempeh close to the middle of the wrapper. Fold over the corner near you, then the two side corners. Gently roll toward the far corner. The spring roll wrapper will seal itself as you roll it. Arrange rolls in a bamboo steamer basket and steam over boiling water 10 minutes. Transfer rolls to a serving platter and set aside while preparing the sauce.

Combine all sauce ingredients in a small saucepan over low heat. Cook 3 to 5 minutes, or until warmed. Serve sauce in individual bowls for dipping either warm or chilled if made ahead. ℐ Makes 4 servings

White Chili
An Indonesian stew, actually, this traditional dish is served over rice and has a soupy consistency. However, a thicker version can be achieved simply by

cooking the chili the day before you wish to serve it, allowing the flavors to develop fully and the stew to thicken naturally. ✒

2 teaspoons extra-virgin olive oil

2 or 3 cloves garlic, minced

1 red onion, diced

1 red bell pepper, roasted over an open flame, peeled, seeded, and diced

Generous pinch of ground cumin

2 to 3 cups Vegetable Stock (page 96)

8 ounces tempeh, cut into 1-inch cubes

4 or 5 slices gingerroot, minced

2 to 3 cups button mushrooms, brushed clean and thinly sliced

2 cups cooked white beans (navy, Great Northern, flageolet)

Soy sauce

Rice, cooked, to serve

Heat oil in a soup pot over medium heat. Add garlic, onion, bell pepper, and cumin and cook, stirring, 3 to 4 minutes or until softened. Add 1 cup stock and tempeh and simmer about 10 minutes. Add ginger, mushrooms, beans, soy sauce to taste, and enough additional stock for a thin or thick stew, as you desire. Cover and simmer over low heat 15 to 20 minutes. Serve hot over cooked rice. ✒ Makes 5 or 6 servings

Tempeh Stroganoff

A hearty winter bean dish. Aromatic tempeh, crispy deep-fried and smothered in a creamy white mushroom sauce, is just about as unbeatable a combination as I can imagine. Oh, and do yourself a real favor and serve this dish over fettuccine with a side dish of lightly cooked green vegetables—a fabulous warming winter supper. ✒

Safflower oil for deep-frying

8 ounces tempeh, cubed

2 teaspoons light sesame oil

1 or 2 cloves garlic, minced

4 or 5 slices gingerroot, minced

1 onion, cut lengthwise into thin slices

2 to 3 tablespoons whole-wheat
    pastry flour

6 to 8 dried shiitake mushrooms,
    soaked until tender and thinly
    sliced

5 or 6 button mushrooms, brushed
    clean and thinly sliced

2 cups spring or filtered water

Soy sauce

Wide noodles, cooked, to serve

Heat 3 inches of safflower oil in a deep pot over medium heat. Add tempeh and deep-fry until golden and crispy. Drain on paper towels and set aside.

Heat sesame oil in a skillet over medium heat. Add garlic, ginger and onion and cook, stirring, 3 to 4 minutes or until softened. Stirring constantly, slowly add flour to skillet. Add mushrooms and stir well. Slowly add water, stirring constantly so it doesn't get lumpy. Add tempeh, season lightly with soy sauce, cover, and simmer over low heat 25 minutes, stirring occasionally to prevent sticking. The sauce will thicken as it simmers, forming a rich, creamy sauce. Remove skillet from heat and stir gently. Arrange cooked noodles on a serving platter and top with stroganoff. Serve hot.   🌿 M a k e s   4   s e r v i n g s

Tempeh-Stuffed Cabbage Rolls   This is a

delicious, easy dinner dish. Smothered in a rich, mushroom gravy and filled with savory tempeh and melted mochi, this version of cabbage rolls will become a standard in your mealtime repertoire, providing stamina and energy from that winning combination of grain and beans. 🌿

8 ounces tempeh, steamed 10 minutes and crumbled

1/2 cup minced onion

1 carrot, minced

About 8 large cabbage leaves, lightly blanched

4 ounces brown rice mochi, thinly sliced into 1-inch pieces

Spring or filtered water

5 or 6 button mushrooms, brushed clean and thinly sliced

Soy sauce

1 teaspoon kuzu, dissolved in small amount cold water

Crumble tempeh into a bowl. Stir in onion and carrot. Lay each cabbage leaf flat and spoon a small amount of tempeh filling (about 1/4 cup) onto the center of the leaf. Top filling with 2 or 3 pieces mochi. Roll the cabbage, folding in the edges to seal the roll. Repeat until all leaves and filling are used up.

Arrange cabbage rolls in a skillet, packed tightly together. Add enough water to half-cover rolls, top with a layer of mushroom slices and bring to a boil. Reduce heat, cover, and cook over low heat 10 minutes. Season lightly with soy sauce and simmer 5 minutes.

Gently lift cabbage rolls from pan, leaving mushrooms behind as much as possible, and arrange rolls on a serving platter. Stir dissolved kuzu into remaining cooking liquid and mushrooms and cook, stirring, until slightly thickened, about 3 minutes. Spoon sauce over cabbage rolls and serve hot. ❖ M a k e s 4 s e r v i n g s

Tempeh Melt

Move over, tuna melt . . . ❖

8 ounces tempeh, coarsely crumbled

Spring or filtered water

Soy sauce

4 ounces grated brown rice mochi

2 teaspoons light sesame oil

1 red onion, diced

1 red bell pepper, roasted, diced

1 or 2 small zucchini, diced

1 cup finely shredded green cabbage

Heat oil in a deep skillet over medium heat. Add onion and bell pepper and cook, stirring, 3 to 4 minutes or until softened. Add zucchini and cabbage and cook until cabbage is limp, about 5 minutes. Sprinkle tempeh over vegetables, add 1/16 inch of water, and season lightly with soy sauce. Cover and cook over low heat 10 minutes. Sprinkle grated mochi over tempeh and vegetables, re-cover, and simmer over low heat until mochi has melted and water is absorbed, 5 to 7 minutes. Serve hot. ❖ M a k e s 4 s e r v i n g s

Tempeh Maki

These take a bit of practice, but they make the most beautiful party appetizers. The key to this recipe is steaming the tempeh just enough: not too little, not too much. It needs to be tender enough to roll, but not so soft it crumbles. They are truly worth the effort. ✐

8 ounces tempeh
Prepared stone-ground mustard
1/2 cup alfalfa or mung bean sprouts

1 carrot, cut into thin sticks
1 or 2 green onions, cut into thin
pieces

Slice tempeh carefully into thin, even sheets, about 4 sheets per piece of tempeh. Place tempeh on a bamboo steamer basket over a pot of boiling water and steam 5 or 6 minutes, until tempeh is flexible, but not too soft. Remove from heat and set aside on a flat surface to cool.

Place a dish towel on a flat surface and lay a piece of tempeh on top. Spread a thin layer of mustard over the tempeh and top with a small amount of sprouts. At the end closest to you, place a carrot stick and 1 or 2 green onion pieces. Using the towel as a guide, firmly roll the tempeh, jelly-roll style, into a cylinder. When rolled, press gently but firmly to secure the roll. Secure with wooden picks, if needed. Set aside and repeat until all tempeh and filling are used. Slice each roll into 1-inch rounds and arrange on a serving platter. Serve at room temperature with the dipping sauce of your choice. ✐

Makes 4 servings

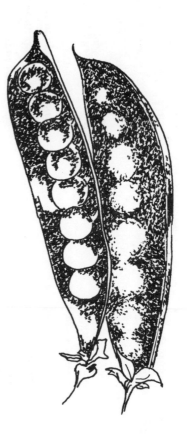

Tempeh-Mushroom Sauce

Over noodles or rice, with a side of fresh, crisp salad greens or cooked veggies, this saucy stew makes a wonderfully simple supper or a fabulous weekend lunch. I love to prepare this dish on a cold, winter weekend afternoon and curl up with Robert and a great book or old sentimental movie.

1 tablespoon extra-virgin olive oil
1 or 2 cloves garlic, sliced into matchsticks
8 ounces tempeh, cut into 1/4-inch cubes
2 cups Vegetable Stock (page 96)
1 red onion, cut lengthwise into thin slices

2 to 3 cups button mushrooms, brushed clean and thinly sliced
Generous pinch of dried basil
2 tablespoons white miso
2 teaspoons kuzu, dissolved in small amount cold water
Cooked noodles, to serve

Makes 4 servings

Heat oil in a skillet over medium heat. Add garlic and cook until dark brown. Remove garlic from oil and discard. Add tempeh cubes to skillet and cook until golden brown on all sides, stirring as needed. Drain on paper towels and set aside.

Bring stock to a boil in a pot. Add onion, mushrooms, basil and tempeh and return to a boil. Reduce heat, cover, and cook over low heat until mushrooms are soft, about 15 minutes. Remove about 1 tablespoon cooking broth and mix with miso until dissolved. Stir into sauce and simmer 3 to 4 minutes. Stir dissolved kuzu into sauce and cook, stirring, until slightly thickened, about 3 minutes. Serve hot over noodles.

Winter Seitan Pie

My inspiration for this pot pie came from Meredith McCarty, one of the most talented whole foods cooks in the world, in my humble opinion. She has an intuitive cooking style that has created some of the richest, most delicious whole foods dishes I have ever tasted.

	CRUST
4 cups spring or filtered water	3/4 cup whole-wheat pastry flour
1 cup diced green cabbage	1/4 cup yellow cornmeal
1 small carrot, diced	Pinch of sea salt
1 small parsnip, diced	Pinch of dried rosemary
1 turnip, diced	2 tablespoons corn oil
1 onion, diced	1/4 cup cold spring or filtered water
1 cup bite-size chunks seitan	
1 tablespoon soy sauce	
1 teaspoon corn oil	
1/3 cup whole-wheat pastry flour mixed with a little cold water	

Bring water to a boil in a large pot and cook each vegetable separately (in the order listed above) until almost done. Reserve cooking water in pot. Combine vegetables with seitan in a bowl and set aside.

Add soy sauce and corn oil to vegetable cooking water and cook over low heat 5 minutes. Stirring constantly, slowly add flour mixture. Cook, stirring, until thickened, about 3 minutes. Pour mixture over vegetables and seitan and stir well. Spoon this mixture into a lightly oiled deep-dish pie pan.

Preheat oven to 350F (175C). Prepare the crust by combining flour, cornmeal, salt, and rosemary in a small bowl. Stir in oil and water with a fork and mix well. Knead briefly to form a ball. Roll out dough, between waxed paper, into a thin round. Cut crust into thin strips and arrange over top of vegetables in a lattice pattern, tucking edges of strips into the filling. Bake until filling is bubbling and top of pie is golden brown and firm. Serve hot. ✐ M a k e s 5 o r 6 s e r v i n g s

Seitan in Rainbow Sauce
I like to serve this really pretty simple-to-make dish during the summer months when vegetables are the most plentiful, not to mention flavorful. The vegetables cook only long enough to tenderize them

slightly. Combining the wonderful textures of golden-fried seitan and crispy, summer veggies is perfect. Seitan is a heavier protein and the light veggies lift the energy of the dish, so you feel strong and steady, not heavy or stuffed.

Safflower oil for deep-frying

1 pound seitan, cut into thin strips

About 1/4 cup yellow cornmeal

2 to 3 cups Vegetable Stock (page 96)

1/2 red bell pepper, roasted over a flame, peeled, seeded and cut into thin strips

2 green onions, cut into long, thin diagonal slices

1 red onion, cut lengthwise into thin slices

1 lemon, peeled and cut into thin slices

2 teaspoons kuzu, dissolved in small amount cold water

Makes 4 servings

Heat 3 inches of oil in a deep pot over medium heat. While oil is heating, dredge seitan strips in cornmeal. Add seitan to oil and deep-fry until golden and crispy. Drain on paper towels and set aside.

Bring stock to a boil over medium heat. Stir in vegetables and lemon and simmer 1 or 2 minutes. Stir in dissolved kuzu and cook, stirring, until mixture is thickened, about 3 minutes. Arrange seitan on a serving platter and spoon sauce over top. Serve immediately with cooked whole grains or pasta and some freshly cooked vegetables.

Seitan-Barley Stew

When barley cooks for a long time, it takes on a delightful creamy texture and its natural, uplifting, dispersing energy makes it a complement to the heavier protein of seitan. I serve big, steaming bowls of this stew in the winter, with a side of lightly steamed green vegetables and crusty whole-grain bread for a hearty lunch or simple, casual supper.

1 cup bite-size chunks seitan

Spring or filtered water

2 tablespoons barley miso

3 or 4 green onions, thinly sliced,
   for garnish

1 onion, diced

2 or 3 celery stalks, diced

2 cups cubed winter squash

1 cup cubed cabbage

1/2 cup whole barley, rinsed and
   soaked 6 to 8 hours

In a soup pot, layer onion, celery, squash, cabbage, barley, and seitan. Add water to just cover ingredients and bring to a boil. Reduce heat, cover, and cook over low heat until barley is very creamy, 1 to 1 1/2 hours. Remove about 1 tablespoon cooking broth and mix with miso until dissolved. Stir mixture into stew and simmer 3 to 4 minutes. Serve hot, garnished with green onions. ✆ Makes 4 servings

Chinese Orange Seitan

Seitan is a very common meat substitute in Oriental cuisine. Meaty in texture and savory in flavor, it is a perfect catalyst for sauces and the perfect companion for crisply cooked Oriental-style vegetables, which provide a lightness to balance its more dense nature. Serve over rice or pasta. ✆

1/2 cup fresh orange juice

Dash of soy sauce

1/4 cup spring or filtered water

2 teaspoons arrowroot

Generous pinch of powdered ginger

Dash of umeboshi vinegar

1 teaspoon brown rice syrup

2 tablespoons light sesame oil

1 pound seitan, cut into strips

2 tablespoons toasted sesame oil

4 or 5 slices gingerroot, minced

2 cloves garlic, minced

4 or 5 green onions, cut into 1-inch
   pieces

1 carrot, cut into thin matchsticks

1 or 2 stalks broccoli, broken into
   flowerets

1 red bell pepper roasted, cut into
   thin strips

4 or 5 button mushrooms, brushed
   clean and thinly sliced

1/4 pound fresh snow peas, trimmed
   and left whole

For sauce, combine orange juice, soy sauce, water, arrowroot, powdered ginger, vinegar, and rice syrup in a bowl and set aside.

Heat 1 tablespoon of the oil in a wok over medium heat. Add seitan strips and stir-fry 3 to 4 minutes or until browned. Remove from wok and set aside.

In the same wok, heat remaining oil. Add minced ginger, garlic, and green onions and stir-fry 1 to 2 minutes. Add carrot and broccoli and stir-fry 2 to 3 minutes. Add bell pepper and mushrooms and stir-fry 2 to 3 minutes. Add snow peas and cooked seitan. Stir the sauce mixture and add to wok. Cook, stirring, until clear and thickened, about 3 minutes. Serve hot. ✐ Makes 4 servings

Seitan with Roasted Pears & Wild Rice

This dish has an interesting combination of sweet and tart fruits with cinnamon and the smoky flavor of wild rice. I love to serve this dish at dinner parties, especially when there are guests present who think that healthy cuisine tastes like mildly seasoned cardboard. ✐

1 cup wild rice, rinsed well
2 cups unsweetened apple juice
1/2 cup water
Pinch of sea salt
1 pound seitan, cut into bite-size pieces

1/2 cup unsweetened dried cherries
2 teaspoons brown rice syrup
Generous pinch of ground cinnamon
2 small pears, cored and sliced lengthwise into 1/2-inch pieces

Combine wild rice, juice, water, and salt in a heavy pot over medium heat and bring to a boil. Reduce heat, cover, and cook over low heat until liquid is absorbed and rice is tender, about 1 hour.

Preheat oven to 450F (220C). Lightly oil a baking sheet. Lightly oil a deep casserole dish. Combine cooked rice, seitan, cherries, rice syrup, and cinnamon. Spoon mixture into prepared casserole dish. Set aside.

Arrange pear slices on prepared baking sheet in a single layer. Bake, uncovered, about 10 minutes or until tender. Reduce oven to 400F (205C). Arrange roasted pear slices over seitan and rice mixture. Cover and bake until seitan is tender, about 30 minutes. Serve warm. ✐ Makes 4 servings

Fu & Daikon Stew

This very clean-tasting simple stew combines vegetables with fu, a wheat gluten product. Fu is very high in protein and is very satisfying when fried and stewed in this manner. Combining fried foods with daikon is ideal, since the daikon will help the body assimilate the oil from the frying process. A very warming winter centerpiece dish. ✐

Safflower oil for deep-frying

2 to 3 round disks fu, soaked until
  soft, then quartered

About 1/2 cup arrowroot

2 onions, cut into thick wedges

2 to 3 cups 1/4-inch rounds daikon

About 1 cup spring or filtered water

Soy sauce

Fresh ginger juice (page 242)

1 teaspoon kuzu, dissolved in
  1/4 cup cold water

Heat 2 to 3 inches of oil in a deep saucepan over medium heat. Coat softened fu in arrowroot until completely covered. Add fu to oil and deep-fry until crispy, less than 1 minute per piece. Drain well on paper towels and set aside.

In a heavy pot, layer onions, daikon and, finally, fried fu pieces. Add about 1/2 cup water and cover. Bring to a boil, reduce heat, and cook over low heat about 20 to 25 minutes. Season lightly with soy sauce and ginger juice to taste and simmer 5 to 7 minutes. Remove cover and slowly add dissolved kuzu. Cook, stirring gently, until a thin glaze forms over stew, about 3 minutes. Transfer to a bowl and serve hot. ✐ M a k e s   4   s e r v i n g s

Sweet Vegetable Pie with Fu Crown

Fu is most frequently marketed in two forms—round disks or flat sheets. Both are very versatile protein sources and very easy to use. In this dish, flat fu creates a unique vegetable pot pie. Pretty and delicious, it is chock-full of vegetables and is nicely complemented by a simple soup and lightly steamed greens. ✒

1 to 2 onions, cut lengthwise into thin
    slices
2 cups diced winter squash
2 to 3 parsnips, cut into large dice
4 or 5 dried chestnuts, soaked 6 to
    8 hours and pressure-cooked
    15 minutes

3 to 4 dried shiitake mushrooms,
    soaked until soft, then diced
Spring or filtered water
1 to 2 teaspoons barley miso
1 to 2 teaspoons kuzu, dissolved in
    1/4 cup cold water
2 to 3 sheets flat fu, soaked until soft

Preheat oven to 350F (175C). Lightly oil a casserole dish; set aside. Layer onions, squash, parsnips, chestnuts and mushrooms in a deep skillet. Add about 1 cup of water and bring to a boil over medium heat. Reduce heat, cover, and cook over low heat about 10 minutes. Remove 2 or 3 tablespoons cooking water and use to dissolve miso. Stir miso mixture into vegetable mixture and simmer 3 to 4 minutes. Stir in dissolved kuzu and cook, stirring, until vegetables are covered with a thin glaze, about 3 minutes. Spoon vegetables into oiled casserole dish.

Slice soaked fu sheets into thin strips. Arrange, net-like, over casserole, tucking the edges of the strips down the sides of the dish. Cover loosely and bake 30 minutes. Remove cover and return to oven to brown the fu topping and set the filling, about 5 minutes. Allow to stand about 10 minutes before serving. ✒

Makes 5 or 6 servings

A FISH TALE

L ike the land, the sea contains both a vast plant and animal kingdom. Our bountiful oceans have long provided humankind not only with sea plants, but also with edible animal life. The sea's nutritious abundance has nourished us throughout the history of the world.

Interestingly, while the land provides the lion's share of our nutrition, Earth is composed primarily of bodies of water—approximately 70 percent of the surface of our planet is covered by fresh or salt water. These sources of water are intimately connected to our own biology. It seems that many of the chemical and biological properties of the sea correspond directly to chemical and biological properties of our blood, not the least of which is the salty, alkaline condition of both.

Just as the sea represents the lifeblood of Earth, the many varieties of foods available to us from the sea have a profound effect on human existence and well-being. Many of the sea's microorganisms, algae, and animal life correspond to the structures contained in our bloodstream—white and red blood cells and other components that help our body maintain its health in our own internal sea.

The Earth's water systems consist of both freshwater and saltwater bodies. While our oceans provide quite a large portion of the world's food supply, we are also nourished by plant and animal life from freshwater sources, although differently. Food sources from salt water would, energetically, have a more profound effect on our naturally salty bloodstream, while our lymph system would be influenced more strongly by foods taken from freshwater sources.

FISH IN MACROBIOTIC COOKING

So what about fish? To eat fish or not to eat fish—that seems to be the ever-present question in the minds of many people making healthier food choices. It is a question for me, as well. So in the process of creating this book, I was faced with the importance of my own ethics, which exclude any animal food from my diet, and the task of presenting macrobiotics in as true a light as my understanding will allow. And the truth of the matter is that macrobiotics is not necessarily a vegetarian diet, although it can be, by choice. Herein lies the greatest difference, in my opinion, between macrobiotics and vegetarianism.

The difference between the macrobiotic philosophy of life and vegetarianism is the understanding that everything is connected and has a unique energetic effect on us. By understanding that, you can then make appropriate choices for your own health and well-being—and it may be that animal food plays a part in your health.

In general, in macrobiotic cooking, our meals do not center around the protein source—fish, beans, tofu, tempeh—rather, these foods are considered supplemental to whole grains and vegetables. So even those who choose to include fish in their diet, do so in small quantities. Since fish is, on some level, an animal source of protein, humans should take caution with how much they actually consume; most people add fish to their largely vegetarian diets about once a week, with vegetable proteins, like beans and tofu, providing any other protein desired.

Earth's waters contain many forms of animal life, with as many energetic effects on us. In general, fish, as we know, can not breathe on land. We, as humans, live on land, unable to breathe in a water environment. What that means for us is that energetically, eating fish affects our respiratory system. Algae (water plants), which are consumed by the fish, produce an incredibly high concentration of chlorophyll, which turns to oxygen in the blood, giving them the ability to enhance respiratory function.

Considering that there are over 30,000 species of fish, with that many types of energies, you will need to set some parameters for your choices. And you can do that by understanding more about the various energies of the fish available to you. Then you can choose wisely, instead of blindly. In general, fish have poor vision and rely on their senses of hearing and taste as well as their body sensitivity to survive. Having four sets of gills, fish extract their needed oxygen from the water as it passes through. As more oxygen exists in colder water, those fish requiring more oxygen, like salmon and trout, thrive in the colder waters of the planet, while those fish requiring less oxygen will inhabit warmer waters.

Saltwater fish generally have more flavor than freshwater, while cold-water fish, fattier because of the colder climate, contain higher concentrations of omega-3 fatty acids (reputed to affect development of disease at the cellular level as well as boost the immune system).

The energetics of fish and the understanding you will need to choose appropriately for yourself can be obtained by observing their environment. Freshwater fish can live anywhere from lakes to streams, to rivers, to ponds, to marshes. Ocean, or saltwater, fish may be bottom dwellers, inhabit reefs, live close to shore or far out to sea. All of these aspects play a part in the energetics of the fish.

Just a couple more fish facts before we talk about the types of fish most commonly used in macrobiotic cooking. Fish adjust their body temperature in response to the temperature of their surrounding waters. Fish have a naturally low blood pressure because their blood is thicker than ours and their hearts have only two chambers, as opposed to our four-chamber heart. And last, while mammals and birds cease to grow when they reach maturity, fish will continue to grow as long as they live, as long as they have adequate food sources.

In general, eating fish has a very interesting effect on us, as humans. While fish can be supportive in maintaining our health, any effects are determined by the quantity and quality of fish being consumed. Obviously, the larger the quantity of fish eaten, the more frequent the consumption, the more intense the effects. The cleaner the environment of the fish, the more easily we process the effects of these foods.

What Fish Do We Choose?

Fish tend to create a cooling effect in the body over a long period of time, although initially, they produce a warming effect because of their high protein content. Fattier fish, like tuna and salmon, of course, will produce a more intense warming than lighter, white-meat fish, like cod, sole, flounder, halibut. The lighter fish also seem to affect the body more mildly and slowly, and are more easily assimilated and processed after consumption.

The general energetic effects of fish, as with any foods, are twofold—the positive and negative—the results of eating the appropriate amount for you or overconsuming. For instance, fish provide us with quick, short-term bursts of energy, ideal when you are fatigued or weakened. The downside of overeating fish is a sense of nervousness. Fish can provide us with a sharp mental clarity, with the downside tending toward paranoia. Fish can also provide us with physical speed—or with tightening in the chest from stress. Eating fish can increase our lung capacity—or make us feel the need for more and more oxygen. And finally, fish can help adjust the body temperature from warm to cool, but overconsumption can lead to a lack of emotional warmth as well. So, you see, the effects of this strong food can be quite dramatic.

In macrobiotic cooking, we tend to stay within the species of fish that produce a light, white, mild-tasting flesh. These types of fish have a less dramatic effect on the body, in general, while providing the nutrition and energetics we may desire, because their flesh is more delicate. Our most common fare would include cod, scrod, flounder, sole, halibut, the currently popular orange roughy, mahimahi, and red snapper. What you are looking for is a pale, delicate flesh with a mild flavor.

This is not to say, however, that other fish are not incorporated into the diet. It's just that you want to reserve stronger fish for when you might need that extra burst of energy. So fish like salmon, carp, trout, pike, dolphin, mackerel, tuna, bass, or bluefish are used infrequently in macrobiotic cooking. These fleshier, fattier fish have a tremendously strong energetic effect on us—they possess great ability to sustain us in a struggle, to help us really fight—great energy to create when we need it, but excessive when we don't.

One family of sea animals minimized in macrobiotic cooking is the shellfish family. Our reasoning for minimizing the use of shellfish is based on energy. On the one hand, shellfish stimulate mental performance, since they are almost pure protein, which in this case provides the brain with abundant supplies of an amino acid, tyrosine, which energizes brain chemistry. On the other hand, most of these animals are carnivorous, eating any flesh they find, including each other. Nice, huh? They also create a hard, protective outer covering, securely encasing their sweet flesh. This produces a stern, stubborn character, with just a touch of self-righteousness thrown in for charm. Inwardly, however, this same character will be shy and rather insecure, well-protected by his or her shell. This kind of hard, outer coating will create a slower circulation of blood through the body, resulting in emotional insensitivity and the inability to let go of the past and move on. And finally, since these animals are scavengers by nature, eating anything in sight, eating these foods can create a tightness in the stomach and pancreas from overwork.

COOKING FISH

You will be happy to note that cooking fish, in macrobiotic thinking, is not complicated. Since the energy of fish is so strong, we usually choose simple, mild forms of cooking to create balance. In general, it is advised to cook fish in one of several simple ways—poaching, boiling, broiling, or steaming, with an occasional grilling or baking. Fried fish is reserved as a rare treat. Sound boring? I can assure you that there are myriad sauces and marinades to help you create some of the most delicious, delicate fish dishes you can imagine.

One last note before we begin cooking. Normally, a macrobiotic meal contains a whole-grain dish. However, when cooking fish as your protein dish, it will be easier on the digestive system to include either a cracked-grain dish or pasta rather than heavier whole grains. Since fish is a heartier protein source, the lighter grains lend themselves to better digestion.

Please note that any recipe in this section calling for a particular white-fleshed fish will work well with any substitution you may desire. And on that thought, let's cook.

Carp Soup

In Japanese cooking the carp is revered for its ability to impart strength, since its nature is to move along the bottom of the sea, slowly and steadily. This very traditional soup is used in the case of weakness and to strengthen the blood as well as to help strengthen a new mother's milk when nursing. My experience has been that people find it so delicious, they line up for a bowl when I prepare it for others. It's a bit of work, so I have no concern that you might overdo it . . . . 🌿

1 (about 2-lb.) carp
Spring or filtered water
1 cup kukicha tea twigs
1 tablespoon light sesame oil
1 pound burdock, cut into thin
    matchsticks
Sea salt

1 pound carrots, cut into thin
    matchsticks
1/2 teaspoon barley miso for each cup
    of soup
2 or 3 green onions, thinly sliced, for
    garnish

When purchasing the carp, request that the fishmonger keep the fish intact, removing only the thyroid and yellow bone. Do not scale the fish or remove any other part; they contribute to this soup's ability to give strength.

Cut the carp into 2-inch pieces, again discarding nothing. Wash well and place in a large pressure cooker or heavy pot. Add enough water to just cover. Next, wrap tea twigs in a piece of cheesecloth or thin cotton, securing it to form a bag, and place in pot with fish. This will soften the bones. Cover and bring pressure cooker to full pressure over medium heat. Reduce heat to low to maintain pressure and cook 1 hour. If cooking in a pot, simmer 2 hours or until fish is tender.

Heat oil in a large soup pot over medium heat. Add burdock and a pinch of salt and cook 2 to 3 minutes. Add carrot and a pinch of salt and cook, stirring, 2 to 3 minutes. When carp has cooked as needed, transfer it, the tea twigs, and the cooking water to the soup pot with the vegetables. Add enough water to create the soup consistency you desire. Cover and cook over low heat until fish falls apart, bones and all, usually 1 to 2 hours.

Finally, remove a small amount of hot broth, stir in miso until dissolved, and stir mixture into the soup. Simmer 3 to 4 minutes and serve garnished with green onions.

🌿 M a k e s 4 s e r v i n g s

VARIATION You may create a quicker version of this soup by using whole trout with sautéed carrots and onions, cooking the fish by itself 1 hour, then adding the vegetables and cooking for another 35 minutes.

Haddock Stew

Served with crusty bread and a fresh salad, this hearty fish stew is a great one-dish meal. ✐

2 teaspoons extra-virgin olive oil

1 or 2 small leeks, rinsed well and thinly sliced

Sea salt

1 or 2 tablespoons dried basil

3 or 4 small turnips, cut into 1/2-inch pieces

1 or 2 small rutabagas, cut into 1/2-inch pieces

1 or 2 medium carrots, cut into 1/2-inch pieces

3 cups soy milk or rice milk

1/2 pound haddock or other firm, white-fleshed fish, cut into 1-inch pieces

Minced fresh parsley, for garnish

Heat oil in a soup pot over medium heat. Add leek, a pinch of salt, and the basil and cook, stirring, until they begin to soften, about 3 minutes. Add turnips, rutabagas, carrots, and a generous pinch of salt and cook about 1 minute, just enough to coat with oil. Add soy milk and bring to a boil, covered. Reduce heat and cook until vegetables are just tender, about 10 minutes. Add fish and simmer, uncovered, until vegetables are soft and fish is opaque in the center, about 10 minutes. Season to taste with salt and simmer 5 to 7 minutes. Serve garnished with parsley. ✐ M a k e s 4 s e r v i n g s

Poached Salmon with Lemon-Chive Sauce

If you choose to eat salmon, poaching is the way to go. It gentles the strong flavor and energetic effect, making it an ideal base for a myriad of sauces. This is just one . . . .

1 (1-lb.) salmon fillet (about 1 1/2
     inches thick), skinned

Juice and grated zest of 1 orange

Juice and grated zest of 1 lemon

3 to 4 tablespoons mirin

2 teaspoons soy sauce

2 teaspoons fresh ginger juice
     (page 242)

Lemon Sauce (opposite)

Spring or filtered water

Whole chives, for garnish

LEMON SAUCE

3/4 cup Vegetable Stock (page 96)

1/3 cup mirin

4 or 5 shallots, minced

Generous pinch of sea salt

1 tablespoon balsamic vinegar

1/2 cup rice milk or soy milk

Juice of 1 lemon

1 or 2 tablespoons minced fresh
     chives

Place salmon in a shallow baking dish. For marinade, combine orange juice and zest, lemon juice and zest, mirin, soy sauce, and ginger juice in a small bowl. Pour marinade over salmon. Marinate at room temperature 30 minutes or refrigerate several hours.

To make the sauce, combine stock, mirin, shallots, salt and vinegar in a saucepan over medium heat. Boil until mixture is reduced to about 1/3 cup, about 10 minutes. Add rice milk and boil 2 to 3 minutes. The sauce will thicken slightly. Remove from heat and stir in lemon juice and chives. Set aside.

Poach the salmon by placing it in a deep skillet along with the marinade. Slowly add enough water to cover the salmon by one-quarter its thickness. Cover and bring to a boil over medium heat. Reduce heat and cook salmon just below a simmer until just opaque in the center, about 10 to 12 minutes.

Pool sauce on individual serving plates and place servings of poached salmon on top. Serve garnished with whole chives. Makes 4 servings

Red Snapper with Watercress Sauce

The mild taste of this delicate white-meat fish is a lovely complement to the natural peppery flavor of the watercress. This sauce is also lovely over salmon. Serve with sides of pasta and lightly cooked vegetables to round out the meal. ✐

2 to 3 tablespoons extra-virgin olive oil	**1 1/2 cups rice milk or soy milk**
1 small onion, minced	**2 or 3 large Chinese cabbage leaves**
Sea salt	**4 small red snapper fillets (about**
2 bunches watercress, rinsed well and left whole	**1 pound)**

Heat oil in a heavy skillet over medium heat. Add onion and a pinch of salt and cook, stirring, until onion begins to soften, about 3 minutes. Add watercress, reserving a few stems for garnish, and a pinch of salt and cook until it begins to wilt, but remains bright green, about 5 minutes. Add rice milk, bring to a full boil, and remove from heat. Transfer sauce to a blender or food processor and puree until almost smooth. Transfer to a saucepan.

Line a bamboo steamer with cabbage leaves. Place snapper on leaves and sprinkle lightly with salt. Place steamer over a pot of simmering water and steam, covered, until snapper is just opaque in the center, about 10 minutes.

Reheat sauce over low heat, whisking gently to keep it smooth. Transfer snapper to serving plates and spoon watercress sauce over each piece. Serve immediately, garnished with fresh watercress sprigs. ✐ M a k e s   4   s e r v i n g s

Gray Sole with Basil Sauce

Gray sole, with its delicate flavor and flaky texture, is the perfect fish to complement a strongly flavored sauce. It just melts in your mouth as the fragrant basil delights your senses. ✑

8 ounces silken tofu

2 or 3 cloves garlic, peeled

1/2 cup tightly packed basil leaves

Sea salt

2 tablespoons plus 1 teaspoon extra-virgin olive oil

4 (5-oz.) gray sole fillets

Several leaves leafy greens, like kale or collards, thinly sliced

Line a bamboo steamer or a steamer basket with cheesecloth or a coffee filter. Place tofu and whole garlic cloves in steamer and place over a pot of simmering water for about 5 minutes, just to cook slightly. Transfer to a food processor, add basil, season lightly with salt, and puree until smooth. Set aside.

Heat 2 tablespoons oil in a skillet over medium heat. Add fish and pan-fry until lightly browned on the bottoms, about 2 minutes. Turn fish and brown the other sides, about 3 minutes. Fish should be just opaque in the center. Transfer to a plate.

Wipe out the skillet and heat the remaining teaspoon olive oil. Add greens and a pinch of salt and cook, stirring, until limp, but still bright green, about 5 minutes.

Arrange greens on a serving platter and top with fish. Spoon sauce generously over the fish and serve immediately. ✑ M a k e s   4   s e r v i n g s

Manly Marinated Grilled Salmon

This hearty, tangy marinade is not for the faint of heart. Just delicious over a meatier fish like salmon or tuna, served with grilled summer vegetables, corn on the cob, and a fresh salad. ✑

1 (1-lb.) salmon fillet, cut into 4 equal
pieces
3/4 cup extra-virgin olive oil
1/2 cup fresh orange juice
Grated zest of 1 orange
Juice and grated zest of 1 lemon
4 to 5 tablespoons soy sauce

1 red onion, cut lengthwise into thin
slices
4 or 5 cloves garlic, thinly sliced
1 (1-inch) piece gingerroot, thinly
sliced
1/2 teaspoon shi-chi-mi spice (see
Note below) or chili powder

Place salmon in a shallow baking dish. For marinade, combine remaining ingredients in a medium bowl. Pour marinade over salmon. Marinate in the refrigerator 2 to 3 hours, occasionally spooning marinade over salmon.

Lightly oil grill rack and preheat grill. Drain salmon, reserving marinade. Place salmon on rack over medium heat. Cook, brushing frequently with marinade, until browned on the bottom side, about 3 minutes. Turn and grill until the salmon is just opaque in the center, about 3 minutes. Transfer to a serving platter and serve immediately. ✇ Makes 4 servings

NOTE Shi-chi-mi is a combination of chiles, sesame seeds, orange peel, and other spices. It is available in Japanese markets.

Grilled Cod Fillets with Spicy Blueberry Sauce

I can hear you now—fish with blueberries? Trust me, this spicy fruit sauce is intensely flavored, making it a lovely complement to the mild taste of the cod. A great summer barbecue entree. ✇

4 (4-oz.) cod fillets

5 to 6 tablespoons mirin

3 to 4 tablespoons soy sauce

1/4 cup spring or filtered water

BLUEBERRY SAUCE

2 teaspoons safflower oil

1 small onion, finely minced

Sea salt

1 small jalapeño chile, seeded and
    minced (about 1 tablespoon)

1/4 cup brown rice vinegar

1 tablespoon brown rice syrup

4 to 5 tablespoons prepared spicy
    mustard

1 cup fresh blueberries, picked over
    and rinsed

Place cod in a shallow baking dish. For marinade, combine mirin, soy sauce, and water in a small bowl. Pour marinade over cod and marinate at room temperature 30 minutes.

Prepare sauce by heating oil in a small saucepan over medium heat. Add onion and a pinch of salt and cook, stirring, until translucent, about 2 minutes. Add chile and cook, stirring, 2 minutes. Add rice vinegar, rice syrup, and mustard and simmer over low heat about 5 minutes. Stir in blueberries and simmer 10 minutes. Sauce will thicken slightly. Transfer sauce to a food processor and puree until smooth. Set aside while grilling fish.

Lightly oil grill rack and preheat grill. Drain cod and discard marinade. Place cod on rack over medium heat and grill until browned on the bottom side, about 3 minutes. Turn and grill other side until browned, 3 to 4 minutes. Fish should be just opaque in the center. Transfer cod to a serving platter. Dollop 2 to 3 tablespoons sauce over each piece of fish and serve immediately. ✐ M a k e s   4   s e r v i n g s

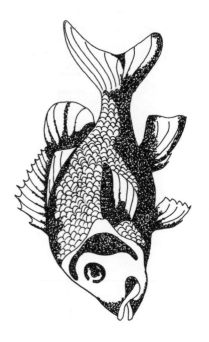

Smoked Salmon Pâté

The interesting blend of flavors and smooth, rich texture of this pâté make it a wonderful starter for any meal, served with toast points or bread rounds. I mold this pâté as individual servings, lining small ramekins with plastic wrap and oiling it to ensure ease in unmolding. Lightly oiling the molds will also work.

2 tablespoons whole hazelnuts

6 to 8 ounces smoked salmon

8 ounces firm tofu, steamed or boiled

5 minutes

4 ounces soy margarine, very cold or frozen

2 teaspoons minced fresh chives

2 teaspoons dried basil

2 tablespoons mirin

Toast points

Parsley sprigs, for garnish

Preheat oven to 350F (175C). Line 4 ramekins with plastic wrap, oil wrap and set aside.

Arrange hazelnuts on a baking sheet and oven-roast until lightly browned and fragrant, about 10 minutes. Transfer nuts to a paper sack, seal tightly, and allow to cool about 10 minutes. Then gently rub nuts in a towel to remove skins. Mince coarsely and set aside.

Place salmon, tofu, margarine, chives, basil, and mirin in a food processor and pulse until smooth. Pack mixture tightly into prepared ramekins and chill completely, about 2 hours.

Release pâtés by inverting ramekins on serving plates and pulling gently at the plastic wrap. Serve with toast points, garnished with minced hazelnuts and parsley sprigs.

Makes 6 to 8 servings

Orange Roughy & Corn Chowder

This chowder is at its best when the corn is fresh, but its velvety texture makes it a hit any time of year.

3 cups Vegetable Stock (page 96) or spring or filtered water

2 cups rice milk or soy milk

2 cups fresh corn kernels

4 or 5 green onions, finely diced

1 red bell pepper, roasted, finely diced

Sea salt

2 tablespoons kuzu, dissolved in

4 tablespoons cold water

1/2 pound orange roughy, coarsely diced

1/4 cup minced fresh parsley

Place stock and rice milk in a soup pot and bring to a boil, uncovered. Add corn, green onions and bell pepper, cover, and simmer over low heat 5 minutes. Season lightly with salt and simmer another 5 minutes.

Stir in dissolved kuzu and cook, stirring, until soup thickens, about 3 minutes. Partially puree soup to create a velvety texture, but retain some of the corn and pepper bits.

Return soup to pot. Add fish and simmer, covered, until fish is cooked, about 5 to 7 minutes. Fish should be opaque when done. Stir in minced parsley and serve immediately. ✐ Makes 5 or 6 servings

Spicy Mahimahi Salad

This salad, served warm or chilled, has just the right touch of Asian spices to get your attention. ✐

Spicy Asian Dressing (opposite)

1 carrot, cut into thin matchstick pieces

2 celery stalks, cut crosswise into thin slices

4 or 5 snow peas, trimmed

1 (6-oz.) piece mahimahi

8 ounces whole-wheat somen noodles, cooked and rinsed

Lettuce leaves (Romaine or red leaf)

SPICY ASIAN DRESSING

1/4 cup brown rice vinegar

1 teaspoon powdered ginger

5 to 6 teaspoons brown rice syrup

1 tablespoon spicy sesame oil

1 tablespoon dark sesame oil

2 or 3 cloves garlic, finely minced

1 small onion, finely minced

1 tablespoon soy sauce

Prepare dressing: Combine vinegar, ginger and rice syrup in a small bowl and set aside. Heat sesame oils in a small skillet over medium heat. Add garlic, onion and soy sauce and sauté 2 to 3 minutes. Stir in vinegar mixture and simmer 1 to 2 minutes. Set aside.

Bring a saucepan of water to a boil. Add carrot and cook just until crisp-tender, about 2 minutes. Remove and add celery. Cook just until crisp-tender, about 2 minutes. Remove and add snow peas. Cook just until crisp-tender, about 30 seconds, drain, and set vegetables aside.

Steam fish in a bamboo steamer over boiling water until opaque in the center, about 10 minutes. Flake fish into chunky pieces.

Combine noodles, vegetables, and fish with dressing, mixing with your hands to avoid breaking up the fish. Line individual serving plates with lettuce leaves and top with salad. ✍ Makes 2 or 3 servings

VARIATION To serve salad warm, dip noodles in hot water and drain before mixing into salad. Roll the salad in the lettuce leaves, like egg rolls, instead of serving on plates.

Italian-Style Baccala

Baccala—dried, salted cod fish—is quite a traditional food in most of Italy. Stiffly dried, it requires 2 days of soaking, changing the water every 8 hours, before cooking. A bit of work, I know, but the resulting fish, when cooked, has a rich flavor and texture. This recipe is adapted from my Sicilian husband's family version. ✒

1 pound baccala

1 tablespoon extra-virgin olive oil

3 or 4 cloves garlic, finely minced

1 red onion, cut lengthwise into thin
slices

Soy sauce

1 red bell pepper, roasted over a
flame, peeled, seeded and cut into
thin strips

2 to 3 teaspoons capers, drained and
lightly rinsed

10 to 12 oil-cured ripe olives, pitted
and coarsely minced

Spring or filtered water

Parsley sprigs and lemon wedges, for
garnish

Soak the baccala 48 hours, changing the water every 8 hours to remove the excess salt left from the curing process.

Heat oil in a deep skillet over medium heat. Add garlic, onion and a dash of soy sauce and sauté 2 to 3 minutes. Add bell pepper, capers and olives and cook 2 to 3 minutes. Spread vegetables evenly over the bottom of the skillet.

Cut baccala into 4 equal portions. Place on top of the vegetables and add about 1/8 inch of water. Cover and steam over medium heat about 10 minutes, until baccala is tender and flakes easily and liquid has evaporated. Gently transfer fish to a serving platter and top with cooked vegetables. Serve immediately, garnished with parsley and lemon wedges. ✒ M a k e s   4   s e r v i n g s

Poached Flounder with Citrus-Leek Vinaigrette

The light, refreshing citrus tang of this sauce is nicely supported by the delicate flavor of the flounder—not overpowering nor overpowered. I love to serve this dish on warm, summer nights, with a light grain dish and steamed vegetables or a fresh salad on the side. ✒

1 tablespoon extra-virgin olive oil	**Juice and grated zest of 1 lime**
1 leek, rinsed well and sliced into	**1 tablespoon sweet brown rice vinegar**
thin rounds	**1 tablespoon brown rice syrup**
Generous pinch of crushed red pepper	**4 (5-oz.) flounder fillets**
Soy sauce	**Soy sauce**
Juice and grated zest of 1 lemon	**Spring or filtered water**

Heat oil in a skillet over medium heat. Add leek, crushed pepper and a dash of soy sauce and sauté until leek is limp, but still bright green, about 2 minutes. Stir in lemon juice and zest, lime juice and zest, vinegar, and rice syrup and simmer 1 to 2 minutes over medium heat. Set aside.

Place flounder fillets in a skillet and add enough water to cover by one-fourth of the thickness of the fillets. Season lightly with soy sauce and cover. Bring to a gentle boil over medium heat, reduce heat to low and simmer until fish is just opaque in the center.

Transfer fish to a serving platter and spoon sauce over top. Serve immediately. ✒

Makes 4 servings

Broiled Halibut in Lemony Hazelnut Sauce

Halibut is one of Robert's favorites because, he says, it's got some real meat to it . . . a bit much for my taste, but I do love the rich, lemony sauce that bathes it. I love it on broccoli. ✑

1/4 cup extra-virgin olive oil

2 to 3 shallots, finely minced

Soy sauce

1/4 cup prepared stone-ground mustard

4 (6-oz.) halibut fillets

Juice and grated zest of 1 lemon

1/4 cup hazelnuts, oven-toasted, skins rubbed away, then minced (see page 323)

Preheat broiler. Lightly oil a broiler pan. Heat oil in a small skillet over medium heat. Add shallots and a dash of soy sauce and cook about 2 minutes. Add mustard and stir well. Simmer over low heat, uncovered, 5 to 7 minutes to reduce the sauce slightly.

Place halibut on prepared broiler pan. Broil 6 to 8 minutes, until just opaque in the center.

Remove sauce from heat and stir in lemon juice, lemon zest, and hazelnuts. Arrange halibut on individual plates and spoon sauce over top. Serve with a light grain dish and cooked vegetables. ✑ Makes 4 servings

Baked Rainbow Trout with Tart Apples

One of the heartier ways to serve fish. The breading process can be a bit tricky, since we don't use cream or eggs to bind, but my method has proved quite effective in giving this dish that lovely crunchy coating associated with breaded, baked fish. ✎

4 (8-oz.) boneless trout	1/2 cup whole-wheat pastry flour
1 teaspoon corn oil	1/2 cup yellow cornmeal
2 tart apples, cored and thinly sliced	1/4 cup whole-wheat bread crumbs
into wedges	1 cup rice milk or soy milk
Sea salt	2 tablespoons arrowroot
1 tablespoon mirin	1/4 cup extra-virgin olive oil

Rinse trout well under cold water and set aside.

Heat corn oil in a small skillet over medium heat. Add apple slices and a pinch of salt and cook, stirring, 1 minute. Add mirin and cook until apples are quite soft and beginning to brown, about 7 minutes. Set aside.

Combine flour, cornmeal and bread crumbs in a bowl. Combine rice milk and arrowroot, blending well, in another bowl. Coat each trout in rice milk mixture (arrowroot will help bind as an egg would) and then place quickly into the flour mixture, pressing the breading onto both sides of the trout. Place on a plate and refrigerate about 1 hour. This will help the breading to adhere to the fish.

Preheat oven to 350F (175C). Lightly oil a shallow baking dish. Heat olive oil in a deep skillet and quickly pan-fry breaded trout about 3 minutes per side, until coating is golden brown. Transfer to the baking dish and bake, uncovered, 7 to 10 minutes, until cooked through.

Remove from oven and arrange trout on a serving platter. Spoon apples over trout and serve immediately. ✎ M a k e s 4 s e r v i n g s

Gray Sole Roll-Ups with Shiitake Sauce

This is a really pretty dish to serve. The delicate, almost translucent flesh of the sole is gently rolled around bright-colored julienned vegetables and served in a pool of rich shiitake sauce. It's important to cut vegetables into pieces no bigger than a matchstick. 🍃

4 (6-oz.) gray sole fillets
1 small carrot, cut into thin
   matchstick pieces
1/2 cup thin matchstick pieces fresh
   daikon
1 small yellow summer squash, cut
   into thin matchstick pieces

SHIITAKE SAUCE
1 teaspoon light sesame oil

6 to 8 dried shiitake mushrooms,
   soaked until soft and thinly sliced
2 tablespoons mirin
Soy sauce
1 cup spring or filtered water
2 teaspoons kuzu, dissolved in
   1/4 cup cold water
Lemon slices, for garnish

Split fillets lengthwise and lay flat on a dry work surface. Place a fillet with a short end closest to you. Arrange a small amount of each of the vegetables crosswise across the end closest to you. Gently roll the fish around the filling and secure it with a wooden pick at the end. Repeat with remaining fillet pieces and vegetables. Arrange roll-ups in a small skillet, cut side up. Arrange any leftover vegetables around the roll-ups. Add enough spring water to come one-quarter of the way up the fish. Cover and bring to a boil over medium heat. Reduce heat and simmer 5 to 7 minutes, until fish is just opaque.

While fish cooks, prepare the shiitake sauce. Heat oil in a skillet over medium heat. Add mushrooms, mirin and a dash of soy sauce and cook, stirring, 3 to 4 minutes. Add water and bring to a boil. Cover, reduce heat and simmer 5 to 7 minutes or until mushrooms are tender. Season lightly with soy sauce, stir in kuzu mixture, and simmer, stirring, 2 to 3 minutes.

Pool shiitake sauce in individual serving plates and arrange two roll-ups in the center, surrounded by some of the extra vegetables. Serve garnished with fresh lemon slices. 🍃 M a k e s 4 s e r v i n g s

Poached Cod with Lemon and Capers

A satisfyingly light way to serve fish, nicely balanced with the richness of capers and the tartness of fresh lemon juice.

1 tablespoon extra-virgin olive oil

1 red onion, cut lengthwise into thin slices

Soy sauce

2 tablespoons capers, drained well

1 carrot, cut into thin matchstick pieces

2 or 3 green onions, cut into 2-inch-long pieces

4 (4-oz.) cod fillets

Whole-wheat pastry flour for dusting

Spring or filtered water

2 lemons

Heat oil in a deep skillet over medium heat. Add onion and a dash of soy sauce and sauté 2 minutes. Add capers and sauté 1 minute. Add carrot, a dash of soy sauce and cook 2 minutes. Stir in green onions. Spread vegetables evenly over the bottom of the skillet.

Lightly dust the cod with flour. Lay cod on vegetables in skillet. Add a small amount of water to just cover the bottom of the skillet. Cover and cook until fish is just opaque in the center, about 10 minutes.

Gently transfer fish to a serving platter. Top with vegetables and capers. Just before serving, squeeze the lemons over the entire dish. ✐ Makes 4 servings

Braised Haddock with Balsamic Vinaigrette

A mild-tasting fish like haddock is the perfect foil for a more intensely flavored sauce like this one. Any mild white-fleshed fish will work well here.

4 (6-oz.) haddock fillets

Whole-wheat pastry flour for dusting

2 tablespoons extra-virgin olive oil

2 tablespoons minced carrot

2 tablespoons minced celery

2 tablespoons minced green onion

2 tablespoons minced red bell pepper

1/4 cup mirin

Sea salt

1/4 cup balsamic vinegar

2 or 3 tablespoons prepared stone-ground mustard

8 to 10 fresh basil leaves, shredded, or generous pinch of dried basil

1 tablespoon extra-virgin olive oil

Green onions, sliced, for garnish

Rinse fish and, while still wet, dust with flour to cover. Heat oil in a skillet over medium-low heat. Add fish and cook about 2 minutes each side or until browned. Add minced vegetables and mirin, season lightly with salt and cover. Cook over low heat 2 to 3 minutes.

Whisk together vinegar and mustard and pour over cooking fish. Sprinkle with basil leaves, cover pan and simmer until fish is cooked through and vegetables are soft, 4 to 5 minutes.

Remove fish to a serving platter. Remove cooked vegetables from heat, quickly add olive oil and swirl into the sauce. Spoon sauce over fish and serve immediately, garnished with sliced green onions. ✐ Make 4 servings

White Fish Nishime

Any mild white fish will do well in this hearty, strengthening fish and vegetable stew. Combined with strong root vegetables, this dish will create energy and vitality. Accompanied by crusty bread and a light vegetable salad, it makes a meal to be remembered. ✒

1 (2-inch) piece kombu

2 onions, cut into 8 wedges each

2 carrots, cut into 1/2-inch chunks

1 burdock, cut into 1/2-inch chunks

1 cup spring or filtered water

Soy sauce

3/4 pound white-fleshed fish, such as
    cod, haddock, or sole, cut into
    1-inch pieces

1 teaspoon fresh ginger juice
    (page 242)

2 teaspoons kuzu, dissolved in
    1/4 cup cold water

Grated daikon, for garnish

Place kombu in the center of a heavy pot. Arrange vegetables so that each is in its own section. Add water and a sprinkle of soy sauce. Cover and bring to a slow boil over medium-low heat. Reduce heat to low and simmer until vegetables are almost done, about 15 minutes.

Add fish pieces, season lightly with soy sauce, add ginger juice, and cook, covered, until fish chunks are cooked through and vegetables are soft, about 10 minutes. Gently stir in dissolved kuzu, taking care not to break fish too much, and cook, stirring occasionally, until stew is slightly thickened, about 3 minutes. Serve in individual bowls, garnished with about 1 tablespoon grated daikon mounded on top. ✒

Makes 4 to 6 servings

Steamed Orange Roughy with Orange-Ginger Sauce

This sauce is fabulous on any fish—light, fresh, with just enough sweet and spice to satisfy everyone. Over orange roughy, however, it's pure heaven, according to my husband. 🌿

3 tablespoons thin matchstick pieces gingerroot

1 cup fresh orange juice

1 tablespoon brown rice syrup

1/4 teaspoon sea salt

4 (6-oz.) orange roughy fillets

Juice of 1 lime

1 teaspoon brown rice vinegar

1 orange, peeled and sliced

Combine ginger, orange juice, rice syrup and salt in a small saucepan over low heat and simmer about 10 minutes to blend flavors.

Place fish in a deep skillet. Add enough water to half-cover fish, cover and bring to a slow boil over medium-low heat. Reduce heat to low and simmer until fish is just opaque in the center, about 10 minutes.

Transfer fish to a serving platter. Place sauce over high heat, causing it to foam. Remove from heat and stir in lime juice and vinegar. Spoon sauce immediately over fish and serve, garnished with orange slices. 🌿 M a k e s 4 s e r v i n g s

Grilled Mahimahi with Shiitake Sauce

Mahimahi is one of Robert's favorite fish—are you getting the idea here that my husband loves fish? This dish is particularly lovely for a couple of reasons: The rich shiitake mushroom glaze makes for a most satisfying taste, and the fact that shiitake's energy helps the body assimilate protein is an added plus—in my book, anyway . . . ✑

10 to 12 dried shiitake mushrooms, soaked until tender and thinly sliced

2 cups spring or filtered water

4 to 5 tablespoons soy sauce

2 or 3 cloves garlic, minced

2 teaspoons kuzu, dissolved in 1/4 cup cold water

4 (6-oz.) mahimahi fillets

2 teaspoons light sesame oil

1 bunch green onions, cut into 1/2-inch pieces

Place mushrooms in a small saucepan with water, soy sauce, and garlic. Cover and bring to a boil over medium heat. Reduce heat to low and simmer until mushrooms are tender, about 10 minutes. Stir in dissolved kuzu and cook, stirring, until sauce thickens and is clear, about 3 minutes.

Preheat grill or broiler. Cook fish on grill or under broiler until opaque in center, about 4 minutes per side, depending on the thickness of the fillet.

Heat oil in a small skillet over medium heat. Add green onions and cook, stirring, about 1 minute, until bright green. Transfer fish to a serving platter and spoon sauce over top. Garnish with green onions and serve immediately. ✑ M a k e s   4   s e r v i n g s

Poached Salmon on Broccoli Rapini with Lima Beans

My Italian relatives loved the combination of bitter broccoli rapini cooked with sweet, tender lima beans. Top that combination with lightly poached salmon and the result is breathtaking. ✎

1 (1-inch) piece kombu
1 cup dried lima beans, sorted, soaked
  in lightly salted water 4 to 6 hours
  and drained
5 cups spring or filtered water
1 small onion, diced
1 celery stalk, diced
1 carrot, diced

4 to 6 cloves garlic, minced
4 (4-oz.) salmon fillets or 1 (1-lb.)
  salmon
2 teaspoons extra-virgin olive oil
1 bunch broccoli rapini, thinly sliced
Soy sauce
1/4 cup minced fresh parsley
Lemon slices or freshly grated daikon

Place kombu in a medium saucepan. Add lima beans and 3 cups of the water. Bring to a boil, uncovered, and boil on high heat 5 to 7 minutes. Reduce heat, cover, and cook on low heat until just tender, but not mushy, 45 to 50 minutes. Drain away any remaining cooking liquid and set beans aside.

Place onion, celery, carrot, and 2 or 3 garlic cloves in a deep skillet and add remaining 2 cups water. Bring to a boil and simmer, uncovered, over low heat 5 minutes. Add fish, cover, and cook over medium heat 5 to 7 minutes or until fish is opaque in the center. Gently remove fish and set aside. Either discard vegetables or use in another dish.

Heat olive oil in a skillet over medium heat. Add remaining garlic and cook 1 minute. Add rapini, season lightly with soy sauce, and cook, stirring, until rapini begins to wilt, about 5 minutes. Add cooked lima beans, season lightly with soy sauce and cook, stirring carefully not to break the beans, until rapini is deep green and limp and beans are incorporated all through, about 2 minutes.

Arrange rapini and lima beans on a serving platter and serve, garnished with lemon slices or grated daikon. ✎
Makes 4 servings

Pan-Seared Cod Fillets in Orange-Ginger Broth

For this dish, I prefer thicker cod fillets, as they hold up really well while pan-searing and do not fall apart in the broth when served. I love to serve this fish on a bed of steamed white basmati rice with a fresh green salad on the side. ❧

1 onion, cut lengthwise into thin slices

1 carrot, cut into thin matchstick pieces

2 celery stalks, cut into thin diagonal slices

1 (2-inch) piece gingerroot, cut into thin matchstick pieces

Grated zest of 1 orange

1/4 cup mirin

2 cups spring or filtered water

Soy sauce

1 tablespoon extra-virgin olive oil

4 (6-oz.) cod fillets

Sea salt

Basmati rice, cooked, to serve

3 or 4 green onions, thinly sliced, for garnish

4 tablespoons freshly grated daikon, for garnish

Place vegetables, ginger, orange zest, and mirin in a saucepan over medium heat and bring to a slow boil. Reduce heat and simmer 5 minutes. Add water and soy sauce and simmer, uncovered, 10 minutes. The broth will reduce slightly.

While the broth simmers, heat the olive oil in a deep skillet over high heat. Season the fish lightly with salt. Add fish to skillet and cook until the bottom sides are nicely browned, about 5 minutes. Gently turn fish and add vegetables and broth to skillet. Cook over high heat until fish is opaque in the center and the broth is reduced, about 6 minutes. Serve over a bed of white basmati rice, garnished with green onions and 1 tablespoon grated daikon per serving. ❧ M a k e s   4   s e r v i n g s

Steamed Haddock over Warm Lentil Salad

The rich, peppery flavor of lentils shines in this recipe, which is nicely balanced by the mild flavor of the lightly marinated, steamed haddock.

1 (1-inch) piece kombu
1 cup green lentils, preferably baby duPuy, sorted and rinsed
3 cups spring or filtered water
2 cloves garlic, minced
1 carrot, diced
2 celery stalks, diced
1/2 red bell pepper, roasted, diced
2 teaspoons fresh ginger juice (page 242)
Soy sauce
Generous dash of umeboshi vinegar

4 (6-oz.) haddock fillets
Marinade (below)
1/4 cup minced fresh parsley, for garnish
Lemon slices, for garnish

MARINADE

2 cups spring or filtered water
Grated zest of 1 orange
1 tablespoon soy sauce
2 or 3 shallots, minced

Place kombu in a heavy pot and add lentils and water. Bring to a boil and cook, uncovered, over high heat 10 minutes. Reduce heat, cover, and cook 30 to 35 minutes. Add garlic, vegetables, and ginger juice and simmer, covered, 10 minutes. Season lightly with soy sauce and simmer 5 to 7 minutes, until any remaining cooking liquid has been absorbed. Remove from heat and stir in umeboshi vinegar.

While lentils cook, place fish in a shallow dish. Combine marinade ingredients, pour marinade over fish and marinate 30 minutes.

When the lentils are ready, drain the fish and place in a bamboo steamer. Steam over simmering water until the fish is opaque in the center, about 10 minutes.

Spoon individual servings of lentils onto plates, top with steamed fish and serve garnished with minced fresh parsley and lemon slices. ☞ Makes 4 servings

Red Snapper Teriyaki with Stir-Fried Vegetables

No time to get a decent meal on the table? This entrée is for you. In about 30 minutes, you can be serving this deliciously unique fish dish over a bed of whole-wheat noodles, accompanied by a fresh vegetable salad. ✐

Teriyaki Sauce (opposite)

4 (6-oz.) red snapper fillets

1 teaspoon light sesame oil

1 onion, cut lengthwise into thin slices

Soy sauce

2 carrots, cut into thin matchstick pieces

1 yellow summer squash, cut into thin matchstick pieces

1 or 2 stalks broccoli, cut into small flowerets

Freshly grated daikon

TERIYAKI SAUCE

1/4 cup soy sauce

2 to 3 tablespoons mirin

2 to 3 tablespoons umeboshi or brown rice vinegar

2 tablespoons brown rice syrup

1 to 2 tablespoons fresh ginger juice (page 242)

Combine sauce ingredients in a small saucepan over low heat and simmer until reduced to half its original amount. Transfer sauce to a shallow baking dish and cool to room temperature. Add fish and marinate 15 minutes, turning several times.

While fish marinates, heat oil in a wok over medium heat. Add onion and a dash of soy sauce and stir-fry 2 minutes. Add carrots and a dash of soy sauce and stir-fry 2 minutes. Add squash and a dash of soy sauce and stir-fry 1 minute. Add broccoli and a little water, cover the wok and steam until the broccoli is bright green, about 3 minutes.

Transfer fish and marinade to a deep skillet, add a little water, and simmer over medium-low heat, covered, until fish is opaque in the center, about 10 minutes.

Arrange fish on a serving platter. Spoon stir-fried vegetables over top and serve immediately, with a garnish of grated daikon on the side. ✐ Makes 4 servings

Poached Halibut with Marinated Artichoke Hearts

I love artichoke hearts so much, I could almost eat this dish myself—okay, so I would really only eat the veggies, but you get the picture.

2 teaspoons extra-virgin olive oil

2 or 3 cloves garlic, minced

1 small leek, rinsed well and thinly sliced

Soy sauce

2 cups button mushrooms, brushed clean and thinly sliced

1/2 cup marinated artichoke hearts, drained and quartered

1/4 cup mirin

2 cups Vegetable Stock (page 96)

2 bay leaves

2 teaspoons kuzu, dissolved in 1/4 cup cold water

2 teaspoons balsamic vinegar

4 (6-oz.) halibut steaks

Sea salt

Spring or filtered water

Lemon slices, for garnish

Heat oil in saucepan over medium heat. Add garlic, leek and a dash of soy sauce and cook, stirring, 2 to 3 minutes. Add mushrooms and a dash of soy sauce and cook until mushrooms are limp, about 3 minutes. Add artichoke hearts and cook 1 minute. Stir in mirin and simmer over medium heat 5 minutes. Gently add stock and bay leaves, season lightly with soy sauce and simmer, covered, 10 minutes. Stir in dissolved kuzu and cook, stirring, until mixture thickens slightly, about 3 minutes. Remove from heat and stir in vinegar.

Place fish in a deep skillet with enough water to half-cover. Season lightly with salt and bring to a slow boil, covered, over medium heat. Reduce heat to low and cook until fish is opaque in the center, about 10 minutes. Transfer fish to a serving platter and spoon sauce and vegetables over top. Serve immediately, garnished with lemon slices.

Makes 4 servings

Fettuccine with Red Snapper & Sun-Dried Tomatoes

This dish has an Italian influence from my stay in Italy.

2 tablespoons extra-virgin olive oil

1 cup button mushrooms, brushed clean and thinly sliced

Sea salt

4 (6-oz.) snapper fillets, cut into small pieces

1 cup sun-dried tomatoes, soaked until soft and thinly sliced

2 to 3 cloves garlic, finely minced

10 to 12 fresh basil leaves, thinly sliced

2 or 3 green onions, minced

1/4 cup spring or filtered water

3/4 cup rice milk or soy milk

1 pound fettuccine

Basil sprigs, for garnish

Heat oil in a skillet over medium heat. Add mushrooms and a pinch of salt and sauté until limp, about 5 minutes. Add sun-dried tomatoes and garlic and cook, stirring, 2 minutes. Add basil leaves, onions, water and rice milk; season with salt to taste. Top with fish. Cook, covered, over low heat 5 minutes.

While the fish simmers, cook the fettuccine in a large pot of boiling water until just tender to the bite. Drain well, but do not rinse. Return fettuccine to cooking pot and add snapper and sauce. Stir well to coat fettuccine and transfer to a serving bowl. Serve immediately, garnished with basil sprigs. M a k e s 4 t o 6 s e r v i n g s

Steamed Tilapia Spring Rolls

Tilapia is a delicate, mild fish that lends itself to strong sauces and sharp-flavored vegetables. ✎

3/4 pound tilapia

1 to 2 cups mung bean sprouts

4 or 5 green onions, diced

1/2 red bell pepper roasted over an open flame, peeled, seeded, and cut into thin strips

2 or 3 teaspoons minced fresh mint leaves

Juice of 1 lime

18 (8-inch) rice paper wrappers

DIPPING SAUCE

1 cup spring or filtered water

2 to 3 tablespoons soy sauce

1 tablespoon brown rice vinegar

1 teaspoon brown rice syrup

Steam tilapia over boiling water until opaque in center, about 10 minutes. Mince coarsely. Combine tilapia with sprouts, green onions, bell pepper, mint, and lime juice.

On a dry work surface, moisten 1 rice paper wrapper with a clean, wet sponge until wrapper is soft. Place a heaping tablespoon of filling in the center and fold over all 4 corners to form a small, square, flat pocket. Repeat with remaining filling and wrappers. Arrange spring rolls in a bamboo steamer and steam over simmering water 5 to 7 minutes.

Whisk sauce ingredients together in a small pan and warm 3 to 4 minutes over very low heat. Serve spring rolls with dipping sauce. ✎ Makes 4 servings

VARIATION You may also deep-fry these spring rolls for a richer dish.

EAT YOUR VEGGIES!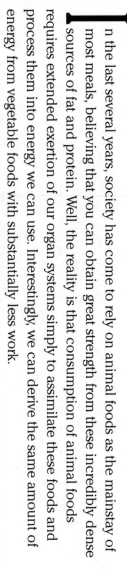

I n the last several years, society has come to rely on animal foods as the mainstay of most meals, believing that you can obtain great strength from these incredibly dense sources of fat and protein. Well, the reality is that consumption of animal foods requires extended exertion of our organ systems simply to assimilate these foods and process them into energy we can use. Interestingly, we can derive the same amount of energy from vegetable foods with substantially less work.

Which brings us to vegetables. Having long suffered under the myth that anything good for you must taste just awful, I am here to tell you that veggies not only are delicious and beautiful to serve, but they are some of the most nutritionally sound foods we can consume, chock-full of all the vitamins, minerals and other nutrients we need to maintain good health.

Vegetables are never boring. If you let the seasons dictate which vegetables to eat, you will find that variety is rarely a problem and that vegetables taste best when grown as nature intended, picked at the height of ripeness and cooked as soon as possible after picking.

CHOOSING VEGETABLES

So now that you've committed to at least trying to eat more vegetables, what do you buy? What do you look for? How do you know you are choosing good quality? Let's start with what to buy. Always try to choose seasonal and, whenever possible, locally grown organic produce. You reduce, substantially, your intake of harmful pesticides by doing so, but you won't believe the difference in the taste of foods allowed to grow unhampered by chemicals. "Organic" means food grown free of chemical intervention of any kind— pesticides, fungicides, hormones, antibiotics, etc. "Certified organic" means food that has been pesticide-free for at least three years.

Choose a good variety of vegetables, combining root vegetables (carrots, turnips, parsnips, burdock, rutabaga), round and ground vegetables (squash, onion, broccoli, cabbage, Brussels sprouts, cauliflower, Chinese cabbage), lots of hearty and delicate leafy greens (kale, collards, mustards, watercress, rapini) and some mild herbs and grasses. To maintain optimum health, there are some vegetables that you may choose to minimize, including spinach, asparagus, some of the nightshade family, including tomato, potato, bell peppers and eggplant, and some fruits and vegetables of tropical origin. Simply stated, these particular vegetables can cause the blood to become acidic, resulting in all sorts of ailments that modern people have come to accept as "normal" afflictions.

In the case of tropical foods, you must remember that these foods are cultivated in extreme conditions of weather. That kind of intense energy is needed in that weather, and should be consumed by people who live in tropical areas of the world. But for those of us living in temperate zones, these kinds of foods are a bit too extreme. For example, tropical fruits and vegetables are extremely high in moisture, to provide the cooling energy needed in the intense heat of the tropics. That kind of cooling energy, when consumed in great quantities in temperate zones, results in discomfort during our cooler weather, like air-conditioning in February.

Nightshade vegetables have been linked to the aggravation of arthritic conditions, and minimizing them may relieve those same symptoms. What I'm saying is that vegetables with extreme energy should be used prudently in our cooking, but remember that there isn't a vegetable that is "bad" for you. There are simply vegetables that support our health better than others.

With a better understanding, it is easy to choose good quality. Especially when picking through organic produce, don't let appearance blind you in your choices. Organic produce doesn't always look picture perfect. Those arrow-straight carrots and perfectly shiny apples are the result of chemical additives. When choosing from naturally grown produce, of course, avoid limp, yellow greens, vegetables and fruits with blemishes and bruises or produce with a woody, stringy appearance. Remember that organic produce has not been preserved in any way and will spoil or wilt sooner than nonorganic produce. Simply use common sense and choose the freshest, perkiest vegetables and you will do all right. If your schedule permits, buy produce fresh a couple of times each week, buying just what you will use in a few days. You will lose much less to spoilage that way. One last point: while I am almost militant in my support of using organic produce, variety in your choices is equally important. So try not to let cost or availability inhibit getting the variety you need. Supplement your organic purchases with regular produce where necessary to get variety in your diet, ensuring that you and your family get a proper balance of nutrients.

STORING VEGETABLES

Okay, so you've just returned home from shopping and now you need to store your vegetables in a way that will support their freshness. I don't recommend washing vegetables before storing them, unless of course you are certain to dry them very well before refrigerating. If they are wet, you are inviting rot. Vegetables store best in cotton or plastic bags; paper sacks sap the moisture from your vegetables very quickly. Remove all ties and bands from the vegetables, especially greens, so that air can circulate around them. If your kitchen is cool, or you have a cool, dry basement, root vegetables like carrots, rutabaga, turnips, winter squash, and even onions do not need to be refrigerated at all. It just takes a bit of common sense to keep produce fresh for as long as possible.

COOKING VEGETABLES

Now the real dilemma. You have bought wonderful, fresh, organic produce. You have unpacked it and stored it properly. The most frequent comment I hear from my cooking students is that besides steaming and boiling and stir-frying, they are not quite sure what to do. And other students have told me that their vegetable experiences have consisted of overcooked asparagus, mushy, brown broccoli and soggy carrots.

Don't let yourself fall into this trap. Just a few basic principles of cooking can open up new avenues of culinary expression. You can develop a style all your own and begin to create delicious vegetable dishes by learning just a few basics and by stocking your pantry with a few staple ingredients to enhance the natural flavors of vegetables.

Your ingredients, including your produce as well as your staples, need not be fancy, but they should always be of the best quality. Stocking your pantry with some good oils—light and dark sesame, extra-virgin olive oil and corn oil for creating buttery taste; various vinegars—umeboshi, brown rice and balsamic; dried vegetables—daikon, lotus root and mushrooms; nuts, seeds and pine nuts; olives and capers; natural soy sauce and miso—will enable you to easily enhance the flavor of your cooking.

Vegetable cooking turns each meal into a seasonal celebration, but the main reason we cook vegetables is to render them more digestible, so that, in turn, we can assimilate them completely and benefit fully from their nourishment. Regardless of the techniques used, cooking vegetables softens their tough outer coating of cellulose, while the energy of cooking makes the vegetables more alkaline as opposed to acidic, a much healthier nourishment for our blood.

Overcooking and undercooking are the two biggest pitfalls to overcome. Practice and vigilance are the keys to mastering cooking techniques. Vegetables are considered done when a fork easily pierces them or when you taste them and they have achieved the tenderness you like. It's that easy. Cooking times in even the best recipes are only estimates, since everything hinges on the cutting style used as well as the size and freshness of the vegetable.

There are several basic cooking techniques that, once familiar to you, will become the springboards for many delicious dishes. Combining more than one technique to achieve a certain texture in a dish, using oil or water in a sauté, steaming and then baking—all can be used to enhance your cooking.

Boiling & Blanching

If you think of bland, limp, boring vegetables when you think of boiling, well, think again. Boiling is a quick and efficient method of cooking that produces firm, full-bodied flavors with vibrant colors and most of the nutrients intact. Boiling vegetables also employs a good bit of moisture and, as a result, nourishes the skin, making it soft and pliable.

To properly boil vegetables, use a deep pot with plenty of water. Cook the vegetables in small amounts so as not to lose the boil. (You can also add a pinch of salt to the water; this will help return the water to a boil very quickly.) Cooking times will vary, depending on the vegetable, its freshness, cutting style, and size, but what you are looking for is a just-tender vegetable—not mushy, not crunchy, just done.

Blanching is simply a shorter version of boiling and is usually reserved for more delicate vegetables like watercress, red radish and green onions, and for very thinly sliced vegetables when you want a firmer, crispier texture.

Boiled and blanched vegetables continue to cook after being removed from the boiling water, so to keep them from becoming overcooked, simply plunge them briefly into cold water and drain well or undercook them slightly.

Steaming

Steamed vegetables cook in the hot steam produced by boiling a small amount of water. Unlike boiling, the vegetables are cooked on racks above the water. Collapsible stainless-steel racks or bamboo steamers are most commonly used in this cooking style.

Bring the water to a high boil before adding the vegetables and cover the pot tightly while cooking. The best results occur when the vegetables are arranged in a single layer and the rack is not overfilled.

Most vegetables steam very well, retaining their full flavor and vibrant color, but they are less moist than boiled vegetables because they do not come in contact with the water. It is said that they retain more nutrients as a result. Steaming imparts great vitality since the vegetables are cooked over high heat, very quickly, with little moisture. Be careful, though, using only steam to cook vegetables can contribute to dry skin.

Stewing & Braising

Braising is slow simmering in a small amount of stock or some other liquid. Braising is generally employed to cook only one vegetable, whereas stewing usually consists of a combination of several complementary vegetables simmering in their own juices with just a small bit of added liquid to ensure thorough cooking.

Braising and stewing result in incredibly tender, sweet vegetables. The flavors of the vegetables, broth, and seasoning blend together as the liquid is reduced, forming a rich sauce. Firm vegetables, especially sweet root vegetables, are very well suited to this style of cooking. Cutting the vegetables into large pieces, bringing them to a boil gently over medium heat, and cooking them slowly over low heat prevents the vegetables from turning to mush as they cook.

This style of cooking creates great strengthening energy for us, especially if the vegetables are layered in specific ways to enhance the blending of all of their energies.

For example, the grounding, centering energy of carrots on top of the sweet, dispersing energy of onions will make us feel grounded but very relaxed. Vegetables like carrots, turnips, rutabaga, onion, cabbage, winter squash, Brussels sprouts, parsnips, celery, and even fennel lend themselves very well to this style of cooking.

Sautéing

The French word for "jump" is *sauté*, which perfectly describes what sautéing veggies seem to be doing in the hot skillet as they cook to perfection.

To sauté, heat a small amount of oil in a skillet; the hot oil sears the skin of the vegetable, allowing it to cook, but sealing in valuable nutrients and flavor. Add vegetables gradually to prevent the heat from reducing too much, which would steam the veggies instead of sautéing them, and stir frequently or shake the pan to prevent sticking and burning. You may also sauté with water instead of oil, but you will not achieve the rich, full-bodied flavors that you get when sautéing with oil.

Most vegetables adapt well to this style of cooking, if you remember a few basic tips. To avoid limp results make sure the vegetables are dry before cooking. Cut the vegetables uniformly in thickness to ensure even cooking, keeping in mind that the thinner and more delicate the cut, the quicker the vegetables will cook. Diagonal cutting styles expose more surface area to the heat as well as the seasonings, giving a fuller flavor to the finished product. Begin the process of cooking with the vegetables that require the longest cooking time and try not to overfill the skillet. Sautéing requires room to move the vegetables around for even, thorough cooking. Finally, remove the veggies immediately when cooking is complete to maintain the crispness and vitality of the finished sauté.

Frying

I can hear your horrified gasps already. Frying? All that fat? All that oil? Yes, that's what I'm referring to here. Remember that if you are eating in a true vegetarian manner, your daily diet is very low in fat compared to the average modern diet. That gives you a bit of extra freedom when it comes to eating a small amount of fried foods. So, while frying isn't a cooking method to be used daily or several times a week, a few times a month, fried foods add a rich, satisfying flavor to meals.

The most common styles of frying are shallow pan-frying and the ever-popular deep-frying. Shallow frying is done by heating a small amount of oil, about 1/2 inch, in a skillet and cooking the vegetables until golden and crispy. Drain well on paper towels to soak up any excess oil.

Deep-frying is a method that paradoxically uses more oil in cooking, but imparts very little oil to the food, that is, if you deep-fry properly. Deep-frying should be done in a deep pot with at least 2 to 3 inches of oil. I usually use safflower oil because it won't foam as you cook, plus it has a very light flavor. Heat the oil over medium heat so that the oil warms slowly and thoroughly. To test the readiness, simply drop a small piece of what you will be cooking into the oil. If it sinks and returns quickly to the top, your oil is hot enough to fry. When the oil is ready, increase the heat to high and drop a few vegetables into the hot oil. Do not overfill the pot, as this will lower the oil temperature too much to fry well. As soon as the vegetables rise to the top of the oil and are golden, remove them from the oil and drain well on paper towels. Deep-fried foods are best when served hot.

Now, if you fried properly, you will notice that when returning the oil to its container, very little is missing. That is the point. Deep-fried foods should not taste oily but should have a rich, satisfying flavor. Understand that proper deep-frying has the food in the oil for only a brief period, not long enough for it to take on a lot of oil. Also, after deep-frying, filter the oil through paper or cheesecloth, store in a tightly sealed container in the refrigerator and you may reuse it two or three times before discarding it.

Baking & Roasting

While it may take a bit longer than other methods of cooking, baking or roasting requires no work during the cooking process. And the results—rich, succulent, concentrated flavors that melt in your mouth! Baked vegetables take on a sweetness like no other form of cooking can produce. A little dressing up at the beginning of cooking results in a delectable finished product.

Winter squash, Brussels sprouts, onions, carrots, parsnips, leeks, celery and cauliflower are all perfect candidates for baking and roasting. Their firm texture and thicker skins help to preserve their own inner moisture. To prepare vegetables for baking, simply cut them into medium-size wedges or chunks and place in a casserole dish. Sprinkle lightly with sea salt or soy sauce to help seal in moisture and bring out the natural sweet taste, add a tiny amount of water to create steam, cover and bake. Most vegetables give the tastiest results when baked at 350F (175C) for about 1 hour. The slow cooking brings out the natural sweetness in the veggies. You can vary this dish and add richness without the fuss of complicated sauces and gravies, with just a little creativity. Lightly drizzle the vegetables with oil before baking, and, for savory flavor, sprinkle with dried or fresh herbs—a most delicious way to induce people to eat their veggies as well as impart the comforting, warming energy created by baking them. This method of cooking creates a calm, centered feeling and helps keep us warm during the extreme cold weather of winter.

Broiling & Grilling

Most people associate these styles of cooking with meat, poultry and fish but not with vegetables. Well, that thinking is about to change. Grain dishes like polenta or pasta, served with a side dish of grilled summer vegetables, and fresh summer salads composed of crisp greens with broiled vegetables tossed in are heavenly combinations. Top a whole-wheat pizza crust with perfectly grilled or broiled vegetables and a simple sauce to create a pizza that will not miss the cheese. With backyard grills and broilers in every oven, these increasingly popular styles of cooking can be employed any time.

Broiling and grilling consist of cooking vegetables, usually thinly sliced and marinated, over high heat until the outside areas are lightly seared and the insides are tender. Grilling is especially nice with widely cut, thin slices of vegetables that are lightly marinated and then grilled on both sides until limp. These vegetables are even better when the marinade is brushed over them while cooking. Broiling is very quick and at its best when the vegetables are cut like thin strands of ribbon and marinated before cooking under high heat, with occasional bastings of marinade. Both cooking styles are very quick and will require your attention so that the vegetables do not burn.

Lots of vegetables lend themselves well to grilling and broiling: summer squash, carrots, zucchini, parsnips, leeks, onions, corn on the cob (still in thin layers of husk), shallots, red onions, asparagus, celery root and green onions are only a few. Firm, hard vegetables do not take as well to these quick styles of cooking, as they need time over fire to soften and release their flavors.

Marinades can (and should) be very simple. Their job is to enhance the vegetables' flavors, not overpower them. A bit of olive oil, vinegar, mustard, garlic, lemon juice, salt or soy sauce and some herbs are all good choices. Combine ingredients that will support the character of the vegetables you will be cooking.

Pickling

This much-ignored style of preparing vegetables is very simple and yields delicious results. As a chef, I have always delighted in, and used extensively, marinated and pickled fruits and vegetables in my cooking. For me, it is a taste I acquired as a child. My mother would harvest her small vegetable garden at the end of summer, gather up her bounty and prepare pickled fruits and vegetables for use throughout the winter months—pickled tomatoes, peppers, cucumbers and cauliflower filled the jars that lined the shelves in our basement canning room, alongside the lush canned peaches and pickled melon for use in other winter dishes.

As I began my study of macrobiotic and vegetarian cooking, I began to realize that pickles are more than just delightfully tasty; they are also very beneficial to our health. Pickles are reputed to have originated thousands of years ago in the Orient, where ancient cultures developed pickling methods as a way to store vegetables without spoilage.

Pickled foods are also an aid to digestion. The fermentation that is part of the pickling process uses bacteria that change the natural sweetness of vegetables and fruits into lactic acid, an enzyme that aids in digestion, strengthening the stomach and intestines. Pickles are also rich sources of vitamins like B and C. Pickles can be simply and quickly prepared and should become an integral part of any healthy diet.

SEA VEGETABLES

I can almost hear you already. Seaweed? She really expects us to eat seaweed? Well, before you turn the page, let me dispel a few myths. Let's start by not calling it seaweed. I prefer "sea vegetables." "Weed" implies a plant that grows where it isn't wanted and has no practical use; neither description applies here.

Since ancient times, sea vegetables have been prized by many cultures. In sixth-century China, sea vegetables were considered delicacies fit for the most honored guests. And in most traditional cultures, sea vegetables were prized for their medicinal value.

Throughout the South Pacific, sea vegetables have a long history of use. Hawaiian royalty cultivated over seventy varieties, while Maori soldiers sustained themselves on a type of nori during long marches through the arid deserts of the Middle East.

Northern and western Europe also have a long recorded history as well. Ancient Celts and Vikings chewed on dulse during long trips, and nori or laver has been in use since ancient Rome. In fact, laverbread is still sold in markets today.

However, it is the Japanese, with their extensive coastline, who more than those of any other culture developed the culinary art of cooking sea vegetables. They have raised the art of preparation of sea plants to the highest form. In fact, sea vegetables are "farmed" almost as heavily as land vegetables.

The sea is the beginning of all life. For millions of years, land erosion has enriched the sea with a wealth of all the minerals necessary to support life. Sea plants contain between ten and twenty times the minerals of land vegetables, like calcium, iron, potassium, iodine and magnesium, not to mention the trace minerals so necessary for body functions. What this translates to for us is that we need to consume only small amounts of these nutrition-packed foods to benefit—generally about 5 percent of our daily food intake.

With the environment in the condition it is, just how safe is it to eat sea vegetables? Interestingly, sea plants do not absorb pollutants as fish do. Where pollution levels are high, sea plants simply do not grow. In fact, one of the characteristics of sea vegetables is their ability to remove radioactive and metallic poisons from the body. It seems that alginic acid, which sea vegetables contain in abundance, bind toxins in the body, allowing for easy elimination. High in vitamins A, B, C, D, E, K and B-12, sea vegetables can help the body dissolve fat in the organ systems of the body. Sea plants contain chlorophyll, which turns to hemoglobin, strengthening the blood.

Sea plants are among the oldest forms of life that exist. These simple foods reproduce by producing spores and have changed very little over hundreds of thousands of years of evolution. In spite of their simple nature, sea plants vary widely in species. Many, though not all, are edible, but there are several species that are commonly used in cooking today. We have at our disposal today about twelve varieties varying widely in taste, texture and nutritional value.

Sea vegetables are usually sold packaged in dried form, making them ideal for long-term storage. Because they are dried, sea vegetables require brief soaking before preparation. They expand during soaking, so always soak less than you want to cook. Soaking times will vary with each sea vegetable: a rule of thumb is to simply soak them until they are tender, usually between 5 and 10 minutes is sufficient. When they are tender, discard the soaking water and slice the sea vegetables into bite-size pieces for cooking.

Cooking sea vegetables is like cooking any other vegetables. Some may be eaten directly from the package; some require light cooking; and some need stronger cooking techniques, like sautéing or stewing. Seasoning is an important aspect of cooking sea vegetables. Coming from the ocean, they naturally have a mildly salty taste. As a result, seasoning should be delicate and light, so that the natural flavor of the vegetables comes through, not the salty taste.

In this section, I would like to simply introduce you to sea vegetables, with just a small sampling of the vast amount of recipes that exist. I'll introduce you to the most commonly used sea plants and describe some of the most basic cooking techniques that will result in delicious sea vegetable dishes for you to try.

Baked Brussels Sprouts & Shallots

This crowd-pleaser is succulent, so make a good bit of it. They will come back for seconds every time. A rich and tasty dish like this warms the body and makes us feel nourished and satisfied. ✑

2 to 3 cups fresh Brussels sprouts, trimmed and left whole

3 or 4 shallots, halved

2 or 3 cloves garlic, minced

Preheat oven to 375F (190C). Cut a shallow cross in the base of each Brussels sprout—this promotes thorough cooking. In a casserole dish, arrange Brussels sprouts and shallot halves. Sprinkle generously with garlic. Drizzle lightly with soy sauce and olive oil. Finally, add just enough water to cover the bottom of the baking dish, so that the vegetables can steam and become tender. The goal is to cook the vegetables in their own juices, causing them to contract, reduce, and secrete their own sweet tastes.

Cover the casserole dish and bake 40 minutes. Remove the cover and bake until any remaining fluid is reduced and absorbed into the vegetables. Serve warm. ✑

Soy sauce

1 tablespoon extra-virgin olive oil

Spring or filtered water

Makes 4 servings

Brussels Sprouts with Ginger-Plum Sauce

A simple, yet elegant glazed stew that makes a lovely side dish. Very pretty when complete, it is a unique addition to a holiday meal, but you won't want to restrict yourself to once a year with this one. ✑

4 to 5 cups fresh Brussels sprouts, trimmed and left whole

1 to 2 sweet onions, cut into thick wedges

Soy sauce

1 cup spring or filtered water

2 to 3 teaspoons fresh ginger juice (page 242)

2 teaspoons kuzu, dissolved in

1 tablespoon cold water

2 teaspoons umeboshi vinegar

Cut a shallow cross in the base of each Brussels sprout. Layer onion wedges and then the sprouts in a heavy pot. Sprinkle lightly with soy sauce. Add water, cover, and bring to a slow boil, not a rolling boil, over medium-low heat. Simmer 25 to 30 minutes. Season to taste with soy sauce and add ginger juice. Simmer 5 to 7 minutes. Gently stir in dissolved kuzu and cook, stirring without breaking vegetables, until a thin glaze forms over the vegetables, about 3 minutes. Remove from heat and sprinkle lightly with umeboshi vinegar. Transfer to a bowl and serve warm. *Makes 4 servings*

Glazed Carrots

This sweet, sticky carrot dish is delicious served as a side dish, especially when the rest of your meal is simple and you'd like to add a little zip to it.

Sea salt

2 carrots, cut into small irregular pieces

1 (3-inch) piece kombu, soaked until tender and sliced into 1-inch pieces

1/2 teaspoon light sesame oil

2 tablespoons barley malt

2 tablespoons brown rice syrup

Slivered almonds, pan-toasted (page 65), for garnish

Bring a large pot of water to a boil with a pinch of sea salt. Add carrots and cook until just tender, about 5 minutes. Remove with a strainer and cook kombu pieces in the same water 5 to 7 minutes. Drain and toss with carrots. Set aside while preparing the glaze.

Bring oil, barley malt and rice syrup to a boil in a small saucepan over medium heat, cooking until foamy. Stir glaze into carrots and kombu until well-coated. Transfer to a serving bowl and garnish generously with slivered almonds. ✍

M a k e s   4   s e r v i n g s

Savory Roasted Vegetables

This incredibly delicious dish is so simple to make, yet you will be asked for the recipe time and again. Its rich, satisfying taste is balanced nicely with the tang of reduced balsamic vinegar. The combination of vegetables offered here is but one option. Any firm, hearty vegetables will serve nicely, so let your taste guide you. ✍

1-inch piece kombu	**2 leeks, rinsed well and cut into**
2 cups button mushrooms, brushed	**2-inch pieces**
clean and left whole	**2 cups fresh daikon chunks**
2 cups Brussels sprouts, trimmed and	**Soy sauce**
left whole	**Spring or filtered water**
2 parsnips, cut into large, irregular	**Reduced balsamic vinegar (see Note,**
chunks	**page 234)**

Preheat oven to 375F (190C). Place kombu on the bottom of a shallow baking dish to help tenderize and sweeten the vegetables. Arrange the vegetable pieces on top and sprinkle lightly with soy sauce and water. Cover the casserole and bake about 1 hour or until vegetables are tender. Remove the cover and return dish to oven to allow any remaining liquid to be absorbed. Stir in a small amount of reduced balsamic vinegar and transfer to a serving platter. ✍   M a k e s   4   s e r v i n g s

NOTE To reduce balsamic vinegar, place 1 cup balsamic vinegar in a nonreactive saucepan. Simmer, uncovered, over low heat until volume is reduced to 1/2 cup. Store in a tightly sealed glass jar.

The flavor of the vinegar becomes very sweet and concentrated when reduced, so a small amount will go a long way. For instance, a full casserole that will feed four people will need only about 2 to 3 tablespoons of reduced vinegar to achieve the full-bodied flavor you are looking for.

Sesame Daikon

A simple clean-tasting dish that nicely complements a rich, hearty meal. It provides a light taste and aids in the digestion of richer, heavier foods. &

2 cups 1/4-inch rounds fresh daikon
Spring or filtered water
Sea salt
2 tablespoons black sesame seeds

Juice of 2 lemons
Umeboshi vinegar
Lemon slices, for garnish

Place daikon rounds in a saucepan and add just enough water to half-cover. Add a pinch of salt and bring to a boil. Cover and simmer over low heat, until daikon is tender but not mushy, 10 to 15 minutes.

Lightly pan-toast the seeds in a hot, dry skillet over medium heat until fragrant, 3 or 4 minutes, stirring.

Remove daikon from pan and arrange on a serving platter. Drizzle with lemon juice and a little umeboshi vinegar. Sprinkle with toasted sesame seeds and serve garnished with fresh lemon slices. & M a k e s 4 s e r v i n g s

Spicy Daikon & Kombu

A spicy-hot side dish that not only is delicious but aids in digestion and helps get stagnant energy moving. Great for kick-starting weight loss and improving your assimilation of food. 🌿

1 (3-inch) piece kombu, soaked until tender and diced

2 cups 1/4-inch rounds fresh daikon

Generous pinch of chili powder or shi-chi-mi (an Oriental hot pepper condiment)

Spring or filtered water

2 cups packed leafy green vegetables, like mustards or watercress, diced

Juice of 1 orange

Place kombu pieces on the bottom of a deep skillet. Arrange daikon slices on top. Sprinkle with chili powder and add a small amount of water to just cover bottom of pan. Cover and bring to a boil. Reduce heat and simmer about 5 minutes, until daikon is just tender. Add diced greens to pan, re-cover and steam until the greens are bright green, about 5 minutes. Remove vegetables from skillet and transfer to a serving bowl. Drizzle with orange juice and toss to mix ingredients. 🌿 Makes 4 servings

Watercress & Tangy Tangerine Dressing

This "light as a spring breeze" blanched salad is a wonderful dish to add a bit of lightness to a hearty meal or to simply cool off in hot weather. To keep the dressing on the sweet side, you need more tangerine juice than lemon juice. 🌿

1 bunch fresh watercress, rinsed well and left whole

Spring or filtered water

TANGY TANGERINE DRESSING

Juice from 2 to 3 tangerines

Generous dash of umeboshi vinegar

Juice of 1 lemon

Bring a pot of water to a rolling boil. Add watercress and cook about 30 seconds. Plunge into cold water to stop the cooking process and slice into bite-size pieces. For the dressing, whisk together the tangerine juice, umeboshi vinegar, and lemon juice. Chill watercress and dressing separately, tossing together just before serving. 🌿

Makes 4 servings

Vegetable Crepes

Nothing is quite so elegant to serve at a brunch or a light supper as crepes. Impressive to guests and intimidating to most cooks, crepes are a spectacular dish. In reality, they are very easy to make—just give yourself a little practice time to get the hang of them and they will become a standard in your cooking repertoire. 🍃

2 cups whole-wheat pastry flour,
    sifted

Pinch of sea salt

About 2 cups water

Filling (opposite)

Corn oil for cooking crepes

Creamy Mushroom Sauce (page 420),
Roasted Pepper Sauce (page 424),
Parsleyed Nut Sauce (page 423) or
    other sauce

FILLING

1 teaspoon light sesame oil

1 onion, finely diced

Soy sauce

2 cups button mushrooms, brushed
    clean and thinly sliced

1 to 2 carrots, diced

2 cups finely shredded cabbage

1 cup thin matchstick pieces yellow
    summer squash

Sift flour and salt together. Slowly stir in cold water to form a batter similar to pancake batter—thin but not watery. Whisk the batter very well to incorporate air into the crepes to ensure the lightness of the finished product. Set batter aside 15 minutes before proceeding. Prepare the filling while the batter rests.

For the filling, heat sesame oil in a skillet over medium heat. Add onion and a dash of soy sauce and cook, stirring, until onion is wilted, about 5 minutes. Add mushrooms and a dash of soy sauce and cook, stirring, until soft, about 5 minutes. Stir in carrots, cabbage and a dash of soy sauce and cook, stirring, until cabbage begins to wilt, 5 to 7 minutes. Add yellow squash, season lightly with soy sauce and cook, stirring, until vegetables are soft, 2 to 3 minutes. If any liquid has accumulated in the skillet, simmer until completely absorbed. Transfer filling mixture to a bowl and set aside to cool while preparing the crepes.

Lightly oil a 6- to 8-inch skillet or crepe pan over medium heat. Pour in about 1/4 cup of batter and quickly turn the skillet in a circular motion, evenly distributing the batter over the bottom. The crepe should be on the thin side, so adjust the amount of batter as needed. As soon as bubbles appear on the surface of the crepe and it begins to pull away from the pan, turn the finished crepe out of the pan onto a tea towel or parchment paper to cool. Cover with a dampened towel to keep the crepes moist. Do not let the crepes get too cold and stiff before assembling (but if that happens, simply steam them before proceeding).

To assemble the crepes, place a hearty spoonful of filling on the side of the crepe closest to you. Roll, jelly-roll style, to form a cylinder, with the closing edge underneath the crepe to hold it closed. Arrange crepes on a platter and serve with a gravy or sauce either pooled under each crepe or lightly spooned over them. ✺

Makes 4 to 6 servings

Green Beans Vinaigrette

A classic vegetable dish prepared in a deliciously healthful way. Adjust the ingredient amounts in the vinaigrette to achieve the taste you like best. The amounts here are only guidelines to give you a starting point. ✺

1 pound green beans
Spring or filtered water
1 tablespoon extra-virgin olive oil
2 cloves garlic, thinly sliced
Juice of 1 lemon
2 to 3 tablespoons prepared
stone-ground mustard

Soy sauce
1 tablespoon brown rice vinegar
2 tablespoons umeboshi vinegar
Generous pinch of dried rosemary
Slivered almonds, pan-toasted
(page 65), for garnish

Remove bean tips and thinly slice beans on the diagonal, making long, thin slivers. Bring water to a boil in a pot. Add beans and cook until tender and bright green, about 3 minutes. Do not overcook or the dressing will make the beans limp and mushy. Drain beans and plunge into cold water to stop the cooking process. Set aside and prepare the vinaigrette.

Heat olive oil in a small skillet over medium heat. Add garlic and cook until brown, about 3 minutes. Skim garlic from oil and discard. Whisk together lemon juice, mustard, a little soy sauce, vinegars, rosemary to taste and the garlic-flavored oil.

Toss the dressing with the cooked beans and serve warm or chilled, garnished with slivered almonds. ☙ M a k e s 5 o r 6 s e r v i n g s

Carrot Aspic

This unique and delicious approach to serving vegetables can be used with just about any sweet vegetable. This version, using carrots, is especially nice, with its sweet, satisfying taste. ☙

2 cups spring or filtered water
2 to 3 cups small carrot chunks
2 tablespoons agar-agar flakes
1 tablespoon sweet white miso
Juice of 1 lemon

2 tablespoons black sesame seeds,
lightly pan-toasted (page 414)
Several lemon slices, for garnish
Parsley sprigs, for garnish

Bring water to a boil in a pot over medium heat. Add carrots and agar-agar flakes, cover, and simmer over low heat 10 to 15 minutes, until agar-agar dissolves and carrots are soft. Remove a small amount of cooking liquid and use to dissolve miso. Stir mixture into cooked carrots and simmer 3 to 4 minutes. Remove from heat and stir in lemon juice. Puree carrots and liquid in a food processor until smooth. Pour into a cool, wet, shallow casserole and allow to stand 30 minutes at room temperature before chilling. Chill until firm, about 1 hour. Cut aspic into squares and serve garnished with sesame seeds, lemon slices, and parsley sprigs. 🌿 Makes 4 to 6 servings

Stuffed Lotus Root

A unique-looking vegetable, with a potatolike taste, lotus root comes equipped with many tubelike chambers ideal for stuffing. Famous in the Orient for its restorative effect on the lungs, lotus root can be used in many ways, but none quite so unique—or as tasty—as this. 🌿

1 lotus root, cleaned and tips
removed from either end,
exposing tubes
Spring or filtered water

FILLING
2 tablespoons almond butter
2 tablespoons barley miso
Spring or filtered water

Place whole lotus root in a pressure cooker with about 1/2 inch of water. Seal and bring to full pressure. Reduce heat and cook over low heat 7 minutes. Remove from heat and force pressure down according to manufacturer's directions. Remove lotus root to prevent overcooking and set aside to cool while preparing the filling.

For the filling, mix together almond butter and miso with enough water to create a thick, creamy paste. When the lotus is cool enough to handle, press one end into the filling and turn. Continue pressing and turning while the filling travels upward, eventually filling the tubes completely. When all the chambers are filled, slice the lotus root into thin rounds and serve. 🌿 Makes 4 to 6 servings

VARIATION To add a real party flair to this dish, quickly deep-fry the stuffed lotus slices before serving.

Sweet Chinese Cabbage

Pressure-cook a tender Chinese cabbage? Before you have me committed for insanity, hear me out. Quickly pressure-cooking the whole cabbage head brings out its delicate sweetness and creates a warm, strengthening energy without the dish becoming heavy. Try it and see. This dish is so sweet and delicate in taste that no dressings or garnishes are necessary, although some toasted black sesame seeds would be a nice touch. 🌿

1 head Chinese cabbage
Spring or filtered water

Sea salt

Rinse cabbage and leave whole. Do not drain it after rinsing. Place cabbage in a pressure cooker and add 1/2 inch of water and several pinches of sea salt. Seal the lid and bring to full pressure. Reduce heat and cook over low heat 5 minutes. Remove from heat and allow pressure to reduce naturally. Remove cabbage and slice into bite-size pieces. 🌿 Makes 4 to 6 servings

Lemony Chinese Cabbage

This light, refreshing side dish is naturally sweet, with just a little tart zip. 🌿

2 to 3 cups finely shredded Chinese cabbage
Spring or filtered water

Juice of 1 lemon
Soy sauce

Bring a pot of water to a boil over medium heat. Add cabbage and cook until just tender, 2 to 3 minutes. Drain cabbage and place in a bowl. Whisk together lemon juice and a dash of soy sauce. Toss with hot cabbage and set aside to marinate 30 minutes. Serve warm or chill it completely for a real summer cooler. 🌿 Makes 4 servings

Red & Green Cabbage Medley

This marinated, savory cabbage is a delicious side dish, rounding out any hearty autumn or winter meal. And it is gorgeous!

2 cups 1-inch pieces green cabbage
2 cups 1-inch pieces red cabbage
Spring or filtered water

MARINADE
2 tablespoons extra-virgin olive oil

3 tablespoons sweet white miso, dissolved in 1/4 cup water
3 teaspoons brown rice syrup
3 tablespoons umeboshi vinegar
3 tablespoons brown rice vinegar

Place cabbage in a deep skillet. Add 1/4 inch of water and simmer over low heat 4 to 5 minutes, until wilted and just tender. Drain cabbage and transfer to a bowl.

For marinade, warm oil, miso mixture, and rice syrup in a small saucepan over low heat. Remove pan from heat and stir in vinegars. Toss with hot cabbage and allow to stand 30 minutes before serving. Toss well just prior to serving. ⌇

Makes 4 to 6 servings

Hearty Sautéed Greens with Ginger

A different take on leafy greens. The pungent, hot taste of ginger makes this a side dish with a kick. ✒

1 teaspoon dark or light sesame oil

6 or 7 slices gingerroot, cut into fine matchsticks

1 bunch leafy greens (kale or collards), cleaned and finely sliced

Soy sauce

1 to 2 teaspoons fresh ginger juice (optional) (see Note, below)

Heat oil in a deep skillet over medium heat. Add ginger and cook 1 to 2 minutes. Add greens and sprinkle lightly with soy sauce. Cook until bright green and tender, but not mushy, 2 to 3 minutes. If a more intense ginger taste is desired, add a small amount of ginger juice at the end of cooking. Transfer to a serving bowl and serve immediately.

✒ M a k e s   4   s e r v i n g s

NOTE Ginger juice is obtained by finely grating gingerroot and squeezing the juice from the pulp.

Watercress & Summer Vegetables

This light, colorful summer side dish showcases the peppery taste of watercress against a background of bright, fresh seasonal vegetables. Cooking the vegetables beginning with the sweetest or mildest and ending with the strongest taste allows each vegetable to retain its own character and flavor. ✒

1 to 2 yellow summer squash, cut into
thin matchsticks

1 to 2 cups fresh corn kernels

4 to 5 red radishes, thinly sliced

1 bunch watercress, rinsed well and
left whole

1 red bell pepper, roasted over a
flame, peeled, seeded, and cut into
thin strips

Juice of 1 lemon

Balsamic vinegar

Bring a pot of water to a boil and quickly blanch the summer squash, corn, radishes, and watercress separately in the order listed above. Cook each vegetable until just tender, about 2 to 4 minutes. Toss cooked vegetables together. Gently mix in bell pepper strips. Whisk together equal amounts of lemon juice and vinegar. Lightly dress the vegetables just before serving. ✒ M a k e s   4   s e r v i n g s

Mochi-Stuffed Chinese Cabbage

Soft, creamy and oh, so satisfying, this delicious breakfast dish will help keep you warm on chilly winter mornings. ✒

4 ounces brown rice mochi, cut into
4 or 5 (3 × 2-inch) pieces

4 or 5 large Chinese cabbage leaves,
rinsed and left whole

Spring or filtered water

Sea salt or soy sauce

Wrap a piece of mochi in each cabbage leaf and arrange, tightly packed, in a skillet. Pour in 1/2 inch of water and add a generous pinch of salt or a little soy sauce. Cover and cook over medium-low heat until mochi has melted slightly and cabbage is tender, about 7 minutes. Arrange on a serving platter and serve immediately. ✒ M a k e s   4   o r   5   s e r v i n g s

VARIATION If any cooking liquid remains, you can turn it into a delicious sauce by simply stirring in a small amount of dissolved kuzu or arrowroot and cooking until the sauce thickens into a glaze. Spoon over stuffed cabbage and serve.

Marinated Lotus Root

A quick and delicious pickle that you can prepare with very little effort. The slightly sweet taste of the mirin makes this a real winner. 🌿

4 or 5 pieces fresh lotus root, cut into paper-thin slices

Umeboshi vinegar

Spring or filtered water

Mirin

Place lotus slices in a shallow bowl. Completely cover with equal amounts of the vinegar, water, and mirin. Allow to stand at room temperature 1 to 2 hours before serving. This pickle will keep, refrigerated, about 1 week. 🌿 M a k e s 2 s e r v i n g s

Green Rolls

A unique and beautiful way to serve leafy green vegetables. Chilled, these make a most refreshing summer snack, although you will find yourself whipping them up year-round as a delicious accompaniment to any meal. 🌿

3 or 4 carrot sticks

7 or 8 leaves Chinese cabbage, rinsed and left whole

1 bunch collard greens, rinsed and stems removed

1 bunch watercress, rinsed and left whole

Black sesame seeds, toasted (page 414), for garnish

Bring a pot of water to a boil and separately boil each vegetable in the order listed above. Cook each until just tender, not too soft. Plunge each into cold water to stop the cooking process and drain well.

To assemble the rolls, place 2 or 3 collard leaves on a bamboo sushi mat or dish towel. Top with 2 or 3 cabbage leaves. Then place a thick strip of watercress and 1 carrot stick on the edge closest to you. Roll, jelly-roll style, using the mat or towel as a guide.

When completely rolled, squeeze gently to remove excess water and seal the roll. Then simply slice into 1-inch-thick rounds, arrange on a serving platter and sprinkle the tops of the rolls with toasted black sesame seeds for garnish. ✒ Makes 4 servings

NORI ROLLS WITH GREENS

Omit watercress and cabbage. Lay a sheet of nori on a dry surface and cover with 2 to 3 collard leaves. Continue as above with carrot sticks. Serve garnished with a dash of umeboshi paste or a sprinkle of sesame seeds.

Pickled Red Cabbage
The color of this pickle is almost as delicious as its delicate sweet and sour taste. ✒

1 cup finely shredded red cabbage	About 1 tablespoon sweet brown rice vinegar
About 1 tablespoon umeboshi vinegar	About 1 tablespoon mirin

Place shredded cabbage in a bowl and sprinkle generously with equal amounts of the vinegars and mirin. Place a plate on top with a 5-pound weight on top of that. Press for several hours or up to 24 hours. Just prior to serving, taste the pickle; if too salty, rinse gently and serve. This pickle will keep, refrigerated, for several days. ✒

Makes 4 servings

Sukiyaki Vegetables
In this traditional style of cooking, vegetables are lightly simmered with a delicate vinegar-based glaze—a delicious complement or finishing touch to round out any healthy meal. Use as many or as few

vegetables as you desire. This recipe calls for lots of variety, but sukiyaki may be simple as well as abundant. 🌿

1 teaspoon dark sesame oil

2 or 3 cloves garlic, minced

1 leek, rinsed well and thinly sliced

Soy sauce

1 or 2 carrots, cut into thin matchsticks

2 stalks broccoli, cut into small flowerets, with stems peeled and thinly sliced

2 celery stalks, cut into thin diagonal slices

2 to 3 leaves Chinese cabbage, cut into 1-inch pieces

4 or 5 fresh snow peas (in season), trimmed and left whole

1 to 2 cups spring or filtered water

Brown rice vinegar

Umeboshi vinegar

1 to 2 teaspoons kuzu, dissolved in 2 tablespoons cold water

Heat oil in a wok over medium heat. Add garlic, leek, and a dash soy sauce and cook, stirring, 2 to 3 minutes or until leek is bright green and softened. Add carrots and a dash soy sauce and cook, stirring, 2 or 3 minutes. Repeat with broccoli, celery, cabbage and snow peas, adding each in the order listed above with a dash of soy sauce; the most delicate are cooked last, so that none of the vegetables overcook. Sprinkle lightly with soy sauce. Add about 1 cup water. Simmer over low heat, covered, until the vegetables are crisp-tender, about 5 minutes. Season to taste with vinegars. Stir in dissolved kuzu and cook, stirring, until liquid is thickened, about 3 minutes. Transfer to a serving platter and serve warm. 🌿 M a k e s 4 s e r v i n g s

NOTE Do not cook the vinegars too long, as they will turn quite bitter.

Italian-Style Stuffed Mushrooms

This delicious, traditional Italian dish was adapted for a nondairy, low-fat version; just a few ingredient substitutions and you have a tasty alternative to the original. My mother would be pleased . . . Try the Arame Stuffing as a variation. 🌿

About 8 large button mushrooms, brushed clean
1 teaspoon extra-virgin olive oil
2 or 3 cloves garlic, minced
1 onion, minced
Sea salt
Generous pinch of dried basil or 3 or 4 leaves fresh basil, minced
1/4 cup minced fresh parsley
Small piece dried hot chile, minced (optional)
About 1/2 cup fresh whole-wheat bread crumbs
Juice of 1 fresh lemon
Spring or filtered water

Remove mushroom stems and mince. Set caps aside.

Heat oil in a skillet over medium heat. Add garlic, onion, and a pinch of salt and cook, stirring, until onion is translucent, about 4 minutes. Add herbs, mushroom stems, and chile, if using, and mix well. Stir in bread crumbs (the amount will depend on how many and how large the mushrooms) and cook, stirring, until all ingredients are combined. Season lightly with salt, remove from heat, and stir in lemon juice. The stuffing should have the consistency of a thick paste. (Add a small amount of water if stuffing is too dry.)

Preheat oven to 350F (175C). Lightly oil a shallow baking dish. Spoon stuffing into each mushroom cap until full and arrange in a shallow baking dish. Pour 1/16 inch of water into the pan to steam the mushrooms, cover tightly and bake about 20 minutes. Remove cover and return to oven for a few minutes to brown the stuffing. Arrange on a serving platter and serve hot or at room temperature. ᓂ M a k e s 4 s e r v i n g s

ARAME STUFFING
2 teaspoons light sesame oil
1 small onion, minced
1/4 cup dried arame, rinsed, soaked until soft and minced
Soy sauce
Mirin
Juice of 1 fresh lime

Heat oil in a skillet over medium heat. Add onion and minced mushroom stems. Cook, stirring, until onion is translucent, about 4 minutes. Stir in arame. Add water to half-cover ingredients and season lightly with soy sauce and mirin. Simmer, uncovered, until all liquid has been absorbed. Remove from heat and add lime juice. Stir well, use to stuff mushroom caps and bake as directed in Italian-Style Stuffed Mushrooms. ᓂ M a k e s 4 s e r v i n g s

Onion Tartlets

A healthy take on a traditional French onion tartlet recipe.

Pastry (opposite)

1 teaspoon light sesame oil

2 to 3 onions, finely diced

Soy sauce

PASTRY

1 cup whole-wheat pastry flour

Pinch of sea salt

Cold spring water

Prepare pastry: To make the crust, sift the flour and salt together into a bowl. Slowly add water, while stirring with a wooden spoon, until the dough gathers, creating a soft consistency. Gather the dough in a ball and set aside to rest, covered with a damp towel.

Heat oil in a skillet over low heat. Add onions and a dash of soy sauce and cook until soft, sweet, and caramelized, about 1 hour, stirring frequently to avoid sticking.

When the onions are almost done, finish the crusts: Preheat oven to 350F (175C). Lightly oil a muffin pan. On a lightly floured surface, thinly roll out the dough. Cut the dough into about 3-inch rounds and press each one into a muffin cup. Prick each crust in several places and fill each with cooked onions. Bake about 20 minutes, until the crusts are golden and the filling begins to set.

Cool slightly before carefully removing from the muffin cups. Arrange on a platter and serve warm with a fresh salad and a hearty soup for a light, satisfying supper.

Makes 4 servings

Blanched Cole Slaw in Plum-Mustard Dressing

A different take on the usual mayonnaise-laden cole slaw we have come to expect at barbecues. This zesty version will surprise and delight you. A crisp and delicious summer picnic dish. ∽

1 carrot, cut into very fine matchsticks
1 cup finely shredded green cabbage
1 cup finely shredded red cabbage
4 to 6 red radishes, cut into very fine matchsticks
Fresh parsley, minced (optional)

PLUM-MUSTARD DRESSING
2 tablespoons finely minced onion

1 tablespoon umeboshi paste
3 to 4 tablespoons prepared stone-ground mustard
4 ounces tofu, boiled 5 minutes and drained, then finely crumbled
Juice of 1 lemon
2 to 3 teaspoons brown rice syrup
Sea salt

Bring a large pot of water to a boil and quickly blanch carrot, green cabbage, radishes, and finally red cabbage until crisp-tender. Plunge the vegetables into cold water to stop the cooking process, so they retain their crisp texture. Mix vegetables together and set aside while preparing the dressing.

Place all dressing ingredients in a food processor, seasoning lightly with salt. Process until very smooth, adding a little water if needed to achieve a mayonnaiselike consistency. Toss with vegetables and chill thoroughly. Stir in minced parsley just before serving, if desired. ∽ M a k e s 4 s e r v i n g s

Sweet Glazed Onions

These delicate stuffed onions, filled to capacity with fresh corn and vegetables and then smothered with a sweet and spicy glaze, are so delicious. Who says vegetables are boring? ∽

4 medium onions
Corn kernels cut from 1 ear of corn
1/2 cup finely diced winter squash
1 carrot, finely diced
About 1/2 cup fresh whole-wheat bread crumbs
Spring or filtered water

2 tablespoons brown rice syrup
3 to 4 tablespoons prepared stone-ground mustard
Generous dash of balsamic vinegar
Generous pinch of powdered ginger
Sea salt

Preheat oven to 375F (175C). Peel the onions and cut each onion crosswise through the center into 2 equal halves. Remove the centers, leaving a bowl. Dice the centers finely for the filling.

Mix together the diced onion centers, corn, squash, carrot and enough bread crumbs and water to make a stuffing that holds together. Press the stuffing firmly into each onion bowl and arrange in a shallow baking dish so that they fit together snugly. Pour 1/16 inch of water into dish.

Whisk together the rice syrup, mustard, vinegar, ginger and a generous pinch of salt. Spoon a little mustard sauce over each onion, reserving remaining sauce. Sprinkle each onion lightly with bread crumbs, cover and bake 20 to 25 minutes. Remove cover, drizzle onions with remaining mustard mixture and bake about 5 minutes to brown the bread crumbs and glaze the onions. Serve warm. 🍃 M a k e s   4   s e r v i n g s

Winter Greens with Marinated Mushrooms & Walnuts

Although there are several steps in this recipe, the delicious results are worth the extra effort. And trust me, it takes only minutes. Easy and sinfully delicious—don't you just love it? 🍃

2 to 3 tablespoons balsamic vinegar
Pinch of sea salt
2 cloves garlic, finely minced
1/4 cup extra-virgin olive oil

4 or 5 button mushrooms, brushed clean and quartered
3 to 4 tablespoons walnut pieces
1 bunch hearty greens (kale, collards, broccoli rapini), large stems removed

Whisk together vinegar, salt, garlic, and olive oil in a bowl. Add mushrooms and stir to coat. Allow to marinate 1 hour.

Meanwhile, lightly pan-toast the walnuts over medium heat until fragrant, about 3 minutes. Finely mince and set aside to cool. Leaving the greens whole, quickly steam them until they are a dark, rich green, about 5 minutes. Slice the greens into bite-size pieces. Just before serving, toss the greens, walnuts, mushrooms and remaining marinade together. Serve immediately. ✑ M a k e s 4 s e r v i n g s

Sesame Acorn Squash Rings

Simple, steamed winter squash is transformed by the addition of a rich sesame sauce. Fabulous! You will want to make this a meal all by itself, but restrain yourself. The rest of the family has to eat, after all . . . ✑

4 (1-inch-thick) acorn squash rings, seeds removed but not peeled

Spring or filtered water

Pinch of sea salt

SESAME-PARSLEY SAUCE
2 or 3 green onions, cut into thin diagonal slices

1/4 cup spring or filtered water

1/4 cup sesame tahini

2 to 3 teaspoons brown rice syrup

Soy sauce

1/4 cup minced fresh parsley

Place squash rings in a deep skillet with enough water to half-cover. Add salt and bring to a boil over medium heat. Cover and simmer over low heat about 10 minutes, until squash pierces easily with a fork but remains firm. If overcooked, the rings will break apart. Transfer carefully to a serving platter and prepare the sauce.

To prepare the sauce, simmer the green onions in the water until bright green, about 3 minutes. Add sesame tahini and rice syrup and season lightly with soy sauce. Simmer 4 to 5 minutes, stirring frequently, until the sauce thickens slightly. Remove from heat and stir in parsley. Spoon sauce over each squash ring and serve immediately while sauce is hot. ✑ M a k e s 4 s e r v i n g s

Chinese-Style Vegetables

No need to send out for Chinese anymore. Now you can create your own Chinese-style feast, smothered in a rich, savory sauce, without the monosodium glutamate, heavy salt, and oil—so easy to do.

2 or 3 shiitake mushrooms, soaked until tender in warm water

1 teaspoon dark sesame oil

2 or 3 cloves garlic, minced

1 onion, cut lengthwise into thin slices

Sea salt

1 or 2 carrots, cut into thin matchsticks

2 to 3 celery stalks, cut into thick diagonal slices

1 cup thin matchstick pieces daikon

2 or 3 stalks broccoli, cut into small flowerets

1 cup cauliflower, cut into small flowerets

4 or 5 snow peas, trimmed and left whole

CHINESE SAUCE

1 to 2 cups spring or filtered water

Soy sauce

1 to 2 teaspoons kuzu, dissolved in 1/4 cup cold water

Generous dash brown rice vinegar

Cut soaked mushrooms into thin slices and simmer in soaking water 10 minutes to tenderize them. Set aside.

Heat oil in a skillet or wok over medium heat. Add garlic, onion, and a pinch of salt and cook, stirring, 2 to 3 minutes. Drain and add mushrooms and a pinch of salt and cook, stirring, 3 to 4 minutes. Add carrots and a pinch of salt and cook, stirring, 2 to 3 minutes. Stir in remaining vegetables, except snow peas, and cook, stirring, until all are crisp-tender, about 3 minutes. Add snow peas and sprinkle lightly with water. Cover and steam 2 to 3 minutes, until snow peas are bright green. Remove from heat.

Prepare the sauce: Heat water and soy sauce in a saucepan over medium heat. Stir in dissolved kuzu and cook, stirring, until sauce is thick and clear, 3 to 4 minutes. Remove from heat and season with vinegar. Stir well and toss gently with cooked vegetables. Serve hot. ✒ M a k e s 4 s e r v i n g s

Cabbage Wedges with Shiso Condiment

Lightly steamed cabbage wedges tossed with crunchy pumpkin seed–shiso condiment ignite an explosion of flavors sure to please. Shiso powder and dried shiso leaves are easily obtained by mail order or in Asian or natural foods stores. ❧

Spring or filtered water
1 head green cabbage, cut into
2-inch-thick wedges

PUMPKIN SEED–SHISO
CONDIMENT

1 cup pumpkin seeds, rinsed and
well drained

4 to 5 teaspoons shiso powder

Bring 1/4 inch of water to a boil in a pot over high heat. Carefully add cabbage wedges and steam over high heat until tender, about 10 minutes. Transfer to a serving bowl.

Prepare condiment: Pan-toast the pumpkin seeds in a skillet over medium heat until golden, fragrant, and slightly puffy, like pillows, about 5 minutes. Pour seeds into a suribachi (grinding bowl) and grind into a coarse meal. Add shiso powder and continue to grind until ingredients are combined and a coarse powder forms. Toss 1/2 of condiment gently with cooked cabbage and serve warm. (Reserve remaining condiment for serving with whole-grain dishes.) ❧ M a k e s   4   s e r v i n g s

Quick Daikon Pickle

I really don't know of an easier vegetable dish. And pretty, too. 🍃

1 cup thin matchstick pieces fresh daikon	**Umeboshi vinegar**
Spring or filtered water	**Mirin**

Place daikon in a small shallow bowl. Add water to half-cover and add equal amounts of vinegar and mirin until the daikon is submerged. Allow to stand 30 minutes before draining and serving. This pickle will keep, refrigerated, 2 to 3 days. 🍃

M a k e s   4   s e r v i n g s

Lemony Daikon Pickle

This sour-pungent pickle goes quite well with fish or rich-tasting foods, providing a very clean, refreshing taste to balance a heavy meal. ✒

1 cup paper-thin half-slices fresh daikon	**1 lemon, peeled and cut into paper-thin half-slices**
	Umeboshi vinegar

Place daikon and lemon slices in a small bowl and sprinkle lightly with umeboshi vinegar. Toss well. Place a small plate on top with a weight on top of that and press for 30 minutes. Squeeze excess liquid from vegetables before serving. This pickle will keep, refrigerated, for several days. ✒ Makes 4 servings

Daikon Canapés with Walnut Dressing

These simple and delicious canapés combine the clean, peppery flavor of steamed daikon with a rich walnut-miso paste for a unique party appetizer or side dish. ✒

10 to 12 slices fresh daikon	**Spring or filtered water**
1/4 cup walnut pieces	**1 to 2 green onions, thinly sliced, for garnish**
1/4 teaspoon barley miso	

Steam daikon pieces over boiling water until tender, but not too soft. Plunge into cold water to stop the cooking process. Arrange on a serving platter and prepare the chutney.

Lightly pan-toast the walnuts in a skillet over medium heat until fragrant, about 4 minutes. Process walnuts and miso in a blender or food processor until pureed, slowly adding water to create a thick, spoonable paste. Dot each daikon piece generously with dressing and garnish with green onions. Serve at room temperature or chilled. ✒

Makes 4 servings

Wilted Greens with Lemon

A delicious way to serve hearty leafy greens that is commonly seen in Italian restaurants. The zesty tang of fresh lemon juice softens the greens, wilting them and imparting a light citrus essence. But the best part is that the lemon helps the body assimilate the olive oil, making the dish more digestible. Nothing is arbitrary in cooking. ✺

1 teaspoon extra-virgin olive oil

2 to 3 cloves garlic, minced

1 bunch leafy greens (kale, collards, broccoli rapini), cleaned well and sliced into bite-size pieces

Soy sauce

Grated zest of 1 lemon

Juice of 1 lemon

Heat oil in a skillet over medium heat. Add garlic and cook 1 minute. Add greens and a dash of soy sauce and cook until greens are tender and begin to wilt, about 5 minutes. Stir in lemon zest and cook 1 to 2 minutes. Remove from heat and toss greens with lemon juice. Serve immediately. ✺ Makes 4 servings

Wilted Green Beans with Summer Herbs

This dish is like an ode to summer. It is especially fine cooked a bit ahead of time and chilled before serving. ✺

1 pound fresh green beans, trimmed

2 tablespoons extra-virgin olive oil

2 tablespoons balsamic vinegar

6 to 8 leaves fresh basil, minced

1 to 2 sprigs fresh rosemary, minced

1/4 cup minced fresh parsley

Sea salt

Juice of 1 lemon

Lemon slices or red pepper rings and fresh herb sprigs, for garnish

Preheat oven to 500F (260C). Toss whole beans with oil and vinegar, a sprinkling of herbs and a pinch of salt. Spread on a baking sheet without overlapping beans too much. Oven-roast, uncovered, about 10 minutes or until beans are tender, tossing once or twice during the cooking. Remove from oven, toss with fresh lemon juice, and transfer to a serving bowl. Serve garnished with fresh lemon slices or red pepper rings and fresh herb sprigs. ✎ Makes 4 or 5 servings

Braised Leeks with Mushrooms

A rich and savory combination, this tasty dish makes a great appetizer served on crusty whole-grain bread. A great energizer as well, what with the strong upward energy of leeks coupled with the vitality of sautéing. ✎

1/4 cup mirin

1/4 cup spring or filtered water

1 teaspoon light sesame oil

2 or 3 cloves garlic, minced

2 or 3 leeks, cut lengthwise, rinsed well and thinly sliced

1 portobello mushroom, brushed clean and thinly sliced

Soy sauce

Juice and grated peel of 1 orange

Minced fresh parsley, for garnish

Heat mirin, water, and oil in a deep skillet over medium heat. Add garlic and leeks and cook, stirring, about 3 minutes. Add mushroom and cook, stirring, until mushroom is softened. Season lightly with soy sauce, cover, and cook over medium heat about 15 minutes. Remove cover and allow any remaining liquid to be absorbed into the dish. Remove from heat and stir in orange juice and peel. Transfer to a serving bowl and serve garnished with minced parsley. ✎ Makes 4 servings

Onion "Butter"

This smooth, sweet vegetable butter has the dairy version beat hands down. Delicious on bread, as a topping for pizza, dolloped on grains, or even tossed with noodles, this spread is a real winner. It takes a long time to prepare but will keep, refrigerated, for about two weeks, plus, the long cooking time creates a warm, strengthening energy that is hard to beat. ✑

1/2 teaspoon light sesame or corn oil

10 to 12 sweet onions (Vidalia or Walla Walla are best), cut lengthwise into slices

Sea salt

About 2 teaspoons spring or filtered water

Heat oil in a deep, heavy skillet over low heat. Add onions and several pinches of salt to help reduce them quickly. Cook onions until wilted, stirring occasionally, about 20 minutes. Sprinkle lightly with water and cook, covered, over very low heat at least 5 to 6 hours or as long as 9 hours. (Do not add too much water, just a sprinkle from wet fingers, or the mixture will become runny.) The onions will become very creamy and turn a dark, caramel color.

Remove the cover and allow any remaining liquid to absorb into the dish before stirring. The resulting "butter" should be thick and creamy, not watery. ✑

Makes 5 or 6 servings

VARIATION A shorter version of this spread (although not nearly as sweet) can be made by sautéing the onions as above, then baking them, covered, at 400F (205C) for 1 1/2 to 2 hours, then removing the cover and baking until the onions reduce and become creamy.

"Candied" Onions

Sweet and savory, these oven-roasted onions make a great, warming side dish to complement a winter feast. We, however, enjoy them most heaped on toasted bread or pizza . . . These onions will keep, refrigerated, about 1 week. ✑

6 to 8 onions, cut into thick wedges

2 or 3 cloves garlic, finely minced

1 tablespoon extra-virgin olive oil

About 2 teaspoons spring or filtered water

Soy sauce

Reduced balsamic vinegar (see Note, page 234)

Makes 4 servings

Preheat oven to 375F (190C). Arrange onion wedges snugly in a baking dish and sprinkle with minced garlic. Drizzle with oil, water and a little soy sauce. Cover and bake about 45 minutes. Remove cover and bake about 30 minutes or until onions are very soft. Season lightly with balsamic vinegar, stir gently, and transfer to a serving bowl. Serve hot.

Makes 4 servings

Mushroom Pâté

Pâtés are truly lovely, serving as rich spreads, stuffings for vegetable boats or canapés—even dolloped in soups just before serving.

1 teaspoon extra-virgin olive oil

4 or 5 shallots, minced

2 or 3 cloves garlic, minced

1 pound button mushrooms, brushed clean and diced

2 tablespoons pecans, lightly pan-toasted (page 417) and minced

Juice of 1 lemon

Soy sauce

1 teaspoon fresh ginger juice (page 242) (optional)

Fresh parsley sprigs, for garnish

Heat oil in a skillet over medium heat. Add shallots, garlic, and a dash of soy sauce and cook until fragrant, about 3 minutes. Add mushrooms and a dash of soy sauce and cook, stirring, 10 to 15 minutes, until mushroom liquid has been re-absorbed into the vegetables. Transfer cooked mushroom mixture to a food processor and puree until smooth. Spoon into a bowl and gently fold in pecans, lemon juice, a light seasoning of soy sauce and ginger juice to taste, if desired. Transfer to a small serving bowl, cover and refrigerate to cool completely before serving. Garnish with fresh parsley sprigs.

Makes 4 servings

Jim's Sunchoke Salad

Sunchokes, or Jerusalem artichokes, are very versatile tubers with crisp, white flesh and a slightly sweet, nutty flavor. They may be served raw, sautéed, steamed, baked, fried, even pickled. Try them in soups, salads, casseroles or in any recipe calling for potatoes.

This delicious salad comes to me from a dear friend, Jim Caola, one of the finest cooks I have ever met. His delicate choices of seasonings and flavor combinations have earned him quite a reputation as a chef with a unique approach to food. This salad is a real crowd pleaser, especially when smothered in Jim's Tofu-Dill Dressing—a real summer treat. ✒

3 to 4 white turnips, cut into small cubes

4 to 6 Jerusalem artichokes, cut into small cubes

1 onion, cut lengthwise into thin slices

8 ounces green beans, cut into 1-inch lengths

Tofu-Dill Dressing (opposite)

Black sesame seeds, toasted (page 414), and parsley sprigs, for garnish

TOFU-DILL DRESSING

1 pound extra-firm tofu, simmered in water 5 minutes and drained

2 tablespoons sweet white miso

2 tablespoons brown rice vinegar

3 to 4 tablespoons minced fresh dill

Spring or filtered water

Bring a pot of water to a boil and boil turnips until just tender, about 10 minutes. Plunge into cold water to cool. Drain and set aside.

Next, boil the artichokes until you can easily pierce them with a fork, about 10 minutes. Plunge into cold water to cool. Toss with turnips and set aside.

Boil onions until translucent, about 5 minutes, and drain. Cook green beans in boiling water until crisp-tender, about 10 minutes. Drain and toss vegetables together. Cover and chill.

Prepare dressing: Puree all dressing ingredients in a food processor or blender until smooth, adding dill to taste and enough water to make a creamy consistency. This dressing will keep, refrigerated, up to 2 days only.

Toss vegetables with dressing 1 hour before serving and chill until serving time. Serve garnished with black sesame seeds and parsley sprigs. ✒ Makes 4 servings

Sunchokes Vinaigrette

This delicious sweet-and-sour side salad closely resembles the German version of potato salad. ✎

1 to 2 pounds Jerusalem artichokes

3 to 4 tablespoons extra-virgin olive oil

2 tablespoons balsamic vinegar

Pinch of sea salt

Pinch of dried rosemary

Gently scrub artichokes to clean the skin and boil until just tender, about 20 minutes. Plunge into cold water and cut into bite-size pieces. Whisk together the remaining ingredients, adding salt and rosemary to taste. Add dressing to artichokes, toss to combine, and chill 1 hour before serving. Toss again just prior to serving. ✎

Makes 4 to 6 servings

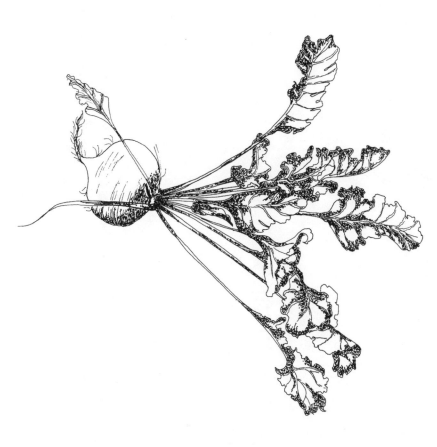

Autumn Greens in Tangy Vinaigrette

Peppery autumn greens serve best in this recipe. Watercress, endive, radicchio and even romaine lettuce have the strong taste needed to stand up to this unusual, cider-based vinaigrette dressing. ✑

4 to 5 cups watercress, endive, radicchio, romaine or a combination thereof
1 shallot, finely minced
2 tablespoons apple cider

2 tablespoons sweet brown rice vinegar
1/4 cup light sesame oil
Soy sauce

Rinse the greens and drain well. Slice into bite-sized pieces and set aside. Whisk together remaining ingredients, seasoning lightly to taste with soy sauce. Toss with greens and allow to marinate 15 to 20 minutes. Toss again just prior to serving. The dressing should have caused a bit of wilting and the flavors will have developed. ✑

M a k e s 4 s e r v i n g s

Lemon Amasake Pickle

This sweet and zesty pickle is a delicious way to wrap up a meal. ✑

1 cup amasake
Juice of 1 lemon
Sea salt

1/2 cup thin matchstick pieces fresh daikon, cut into thin oblong pieces

Combine amasake, lemon juice, and a generous sprinkling of salt in a bowl. Add daikon and press down to cover with liquid. Place a plate on top with a 5-pound weight on top of that. Press at least 1 hour to create a light, crispy pickle. It can be pressed up to 3 days in a cool, dry place but not refrigerated. After pickling, store in a tightly sealed glass jar, refrigerated, for freshness. ✑ M a k e s 2 s e r v i n g s

Winter Vegetable Pâté

This brightly colored pâté heralds the autumn, showcasing the abundance of the harvest. Its sweet taste and rich texture make it a festive way to serve the strengthening, warming ground vegetables we need to get through the cold winter months. ✺

Spring or filtered water	1 cup 1-inch cubes butternut squash
1 onion, diced	Soy sauce
1 garnet yam, cut into 1-inch cubes	2 to 3 tablespoons sesame tahini

Heat a dry skillet over medium heat. Add about 1 tablespoon water and water-sauté the onion until translucent, about 5 minutes. Add yam, squash, a dash of soy sauce, and about 1/4 inch of water and bring to a boil. Cover, reduce heat, and simmer over low heat about 25 minutes, until yam and squash are very tender. Season lightly with soy sauce and allow to simmer, uncovered, until any remaining liquid has been absorbed.

Transfer vegetables to a food processor, add sesame tahini, and process until smooth, thick and creamy, adding water only if the consistency appears too stiff. Transfer to a serving bowl and serve as a spread with crusty, whole-grain bread or crackers. ✺

Makes 4 servings

Mushroom-Leek Strudel

This delicate pastry strudel couldn't be easier. Reduced vegetables wrapped in flaky phyllo dough create a rich, satisfying side course, especially when accompanied by a hearty bean soup and lightly cooked vegetables. ✺

1 teaspoon extra-virgin olive oil	Soy sauce
2 or 3 cloves garlic, finely minced	3 phyllo pastry sheets (see Note, below)
1 or 2 leeks, cut lengthwise, rinsed well and thinly sliced	Corn oil
2 to 3 cups button mushrooms, brushed clean and thinly sliced	Whole-wheat bread crumbs

Heat oil in a skillet over medium heat. Add garlic and cook 1 minute. Add leeks and a dash of soy sauce and cook, stirring, until bright green and just wilted, about 5 minutes. Stir in mushrooms, season lightly with soy sauce, and cook until wilted and beginning to reduce, 5 to 7 minutes. Reduce heat to medium-low, cover, and cook 20 minutes, stirring frequently. The vegetables will get very soft, becoming rather dark in color. Remove the cover and allow any remaining liquid to be absorbed into the vegetables. Transfer to a bowl and set aside to cool.

Preheat oven to 375F (190C). Lightly oil a baking sheet. Lay a sheet of phyllo pastry on a dry, flat work surface. Brush lightly with corn oil and sprinkle with bread crumbs. (This makes the pastry flaky and gives the strudel body.) Repeat with remaining phyllo sheets.

Spread the cooled filling along a short side of the layered phyllo pastry. Quickly and gently roll up the strudel, jelly-roll style, turn under the ends, and transfer to baking sheet, seam side down. With a sharp knife, make deep slits, marking the slices. Brush lightly with oil. Bake about 30 minutes, until the pastry is golden and flaky.

Remove pastry from oven and allow to cool about 5 minutes before slicing completely through on marked lines. Transfer to a serving platter and serve warm. ✒

Makes 4 servings

NOTE The best choice for phyllo pastry is the packaged variety, sold in the freezer department at most supermarkets. Before use, simply thaw in the refrigerator about 6 hours, storing any unused phyllo in the refrigerator or freezer until you need it again. It is very important that you thaw the phyllo in the refrigerator, not at room temperature, to prevent it from getting too soft and sticking together.

Whole-wheat phyllo is available at some gourmet and natural foods stores. I prefer to use it when possible.

Winter Veggie & Bean Stew

A hearty vegetable and bean casserole sure to warm you up on cold winter nights. 🍃

1 teaspoon extra-virgin olive oil

1 onion, cut into large dice

Soy sauce

1 cup large dice winter squash

1 cup large dice white turnips

1 or 2 carrots, cut into large dice

1 or 2 parsnips, cut into large dice

About 2 tablespoons whole-wheat
    pastry flour

1 cup cooked kidney beans, drained

2 to 3 tablespoons prepared
    stone-ground mustard

Fresh ginger juice (page 242)

2 or 3 stalks broccoli, cut into small
    flowerets, for garnish

Preheat oven to 375F (175C). Lightly oil a deep casserole dish.

Heat oil in a skillet over medium heat. Add onion and a dash of soy sauce and cook until wilted. Add squash, turnips, carrots and parsnips and cook, stirring, to combine. Sprinkle lightly with flour and cook, stirring, until flour sticks to vegetable pieces. Season lightly with soy sauce and cook a few minutes more. Set aside.

Mix together kidney beans, mustard and ginger juice to taste in a large bowl. Fold in cooked vegetables. Spoon into prepared casserole dish and sprinkle lightly with water. Cover and bake 45 minutes or until vegetables are tender and have a stewlike consistency. Remove cover and bake about 10 minutes, until stew begins to firm up a bit; it will not set up, but it will thicken.

While the stew is baking, steam broccoli over boiling water until crisp-tender, 5 minutes. When the casserole is done, remove from oven and arrange broccoli around the edges of the casserole. Serve immediately. 🍃 M a k e s 4 s e r v i n g s

Herb-Scented Vegetable Tart

This elegantly beautiful tart makes a lovely centerpiece on any table. Ideal for the holidays or any days . . . . 🌿

8 ounces firm tofu

1 onion, minced

2 to 3 fresh garlic cloves, minced

2 tablespoons dried rosemary

1/4 cup minced fresh parsley

Sea salt

Spring or filtered water

1 teaspoon extra-virgin olive oil

1 onion, cut lengthwise into thin slices

3 or 4 small zucchini, cut into thin matchsticks

2 cups button mushrooms, brushed clean and thinly sliced

4 or 5 sheets phyllo dough

2 or 3 red bell peppers, roasted over a flame, peeled, seeded and cut into thin strips

4 or 5 fresh basil leaves, finely minced, or 2 tablespoons dried basil

2 to 3 tablespoons slivered almonds, pan-toasted (page 65), for garnish

Preheat oven to 375F (175C). Line a 15 × 10-inch jelly-roll pan or deep baking sheet with foil and brush lightly with oil.

Process tofu, minced onion, garlic, rosemary, parsley, a little salt and enough water to make a smooth, spreadable paste in a food processor. Set aside.

Heat oil in a skillet over medium heat. Add sliced onion and a pinch of salt and cook until wilted, about 5 minutes. Add zucchini and a pinch of salt and cook 2 or 3 minutes. Add mushrooms, season lightly with salt and cook about 5 minutes. Simmer, uncovered, until any remaining liquid has been absorbed into the vegetables.

Meanwhile, place a sheet of phyllo pastry in prepared pan so that the edges extend beyond the edges of the pan. Crinkle these edges to form the outer edge of the tart. Brush with oil and add another sheet of pastry. Repeat with remaining pastry sheets, brushing with oil and crinkling the edges of the pastry.

Gently spoon the tofu mixture over the phyllo pastry, spreading evenly. Arrange cooked vegetables over the top of the tofu mixture. Arrange the bell peppers in an attractive pattern on top of the vegetables. Bake, uncovered, about 15 minutes, until the crust is golden brown and flaky. Remove pan from oven and sprinkle the top of the tart with minced basil leaves and slivered almonds. Serve warm. ✎

Makes 4 to 6 servings

Zesty Brussels Sprouts

The naturally sweet taste of Brussels sprouts, cooked until just tender, is balanced by a gently tangy lemon glaze. ✎

2 to 3 cups Brussels sprouts, trimmed	**1/4 cup minced fresh parsley**
and left whole	**Sea salt**
Spring or filtered water	**Brown rice syrup**
Juice and grated zest of 1 lemon	

Bring a pot of water to a rolling boil. Add Brussels sprouts and cook until tender, about 15 minutes.

While the sprouts are cooking, whisk together lemon juice and zest, parsley, a pinch of salt and a generous dash of rice syrup. Drain Brussels sprouts and transfer to a serving bowl. Toss well with lemon mixture and serve hot. ✎ Makes 4 servings

Russian Cabbage Pie

French galette. Called a "pirog," this free-form pie is filled with savory vegetables and makes a great entree, set off by a light soup and a lightly boiled vegetable medley. The Eastern European version of the

2 recipes Basic Sourdough
  Bread (page 435)
Generous pinch of dried rosemary
Spring or filtered water
1/2 head green cabbage, finely
  shredded

1 teaspoon extra-virgin olive oil, plus
  extra for brushing
3 or 4 cloves garlic, minced
1 onion, diced
Soy sauce
1 or 2 carrots, cut into thin matchsticks

Prepare dough as directed in recipe. Quickly knead in rosemary to distribute it evenly through the dough. Shape into a ball and set aside, covered, while preparing the filling.

Bring a pot of water to a boil and cook cabbage 3 to 4 minutes, until it begins to wilt. Drain and set aside.

Heat 1 teaspoon oil in a skillet over medium heat. Add garlic, onion and a dash of soy sauce and cook, stirring, until the onion is translucent, 5 minutes. Add carrots and cook, stirring, to combine. Stir in cabbage and sprinkle lightly with soy sauce. Drizzle with a little water, cover and cook over medium heat 15 minutes, stirring frequently. Remove from heat and allow to cool to room temperature before proceeding.

Preheat oven to 375F (190C). Lightly oil and flour a large baking sheet. On a floured surface, roll out half the dough into a 10 × 14-inch rectangle. Transfer carefully to the baking sheet. Spread cabbage filling over the dough, leaving a 1-inch border all around. Roll out second piece of dough slightly smaller than the first and gently lay on top of the cabbage filling. Seal the pie by pulling up the bottom edges of the pastry, joining with the top dough and crimping to form crust edges. Brush lightly with olive oil. With a sharp knife, cut several vents to allow steam to escape during baking.

Bake on the center oven rack about 40 minutes, until the crust is golden brown and the pie is firm when tapped lightly. Remove from oven and allow to stand 10 minutes before slicing. ✑ Makes 5 or 6 servings

Ragout Provençal

Nothing is more welcoming on a biting cold winter day than coming home to a hearty stew: the aroma tantalizes your senses with anticipation of the delicious food that awaits you. This French-inspired ragout enhances the rich flavors of the vegetables with an aromatic blend of herbs. ∽

1 large onion, cut into medium-thick
   wedges

3 or 4 tomatoes, quartered (optional)

1 cup large chunks white turnip

2 cups button mushrooms, brushed
   clean and quartered

2 red bell peppers, cut into large
   chunks

2 medium zucchini, cut into medium
   chunks

2 to 3 cups cubed winter squash

3 to 4 celery stalks, cut into
   1/2-inch-thick diagonal pieces

8 to 10 ripe olives, pitted

3 or 4 garlic cloves, minced

Generous pinch *each* of dried
   rosemary and basil

About 1 tablespoon extra-virgin
   olive oil

Soy sauce

Mirin

Spring or filtered water

Preheat oven to 300F (150C). Lightly oil a deep casserole dish.

Toss together the vegetables, olives, garlic, rosemary and basil and arrange them so they are evenly distributed in the casserole dish. Drizzle with oil and soy sauce and mirin to taste. Add enough water to barely half-cover ingredients.

Bake, uncovered, about 4 hours, stirring about every 30 minutes, until vegetables are creamy and soft, and adding water as needed to keep the casserole moist. Remove dish from oven and serve over grain or noodles for a hearty winter main course. ∽

Makes 4 servings

Savory Cassoulet

Stewed vegetables in a thick gravy make a great centerpiece for a hearty winter meal. ✿

1/2 head of red cabbage, shredded
1 head cauliflower, cut into medium flowerets
1 head broccoli, cut into medium flowerets
2 or 3 tart apples (Granny Smith or other), cut into large dice
1 cup dried white beans, cooked without seasoning until tender

2 or 3 shallots, diced
2 cloves garlic, minced
3 cups dark beer, water or stock
About 2 tablespoons caraway seeds
Soy sauce
3 to 4 tablespoons whole-wheat pastry flour

Preheat oven to 400F (205C). Combine all ingredients, except flour, in a roasting pan, sprinkling lightly with caraway seeds and seasoning to taste with soy sauce. Sprinkle the top generously with flour.

Bake, uncovered, 30 minutes. Reduce heat to 300F (150C), cover, and bake 2 hours, stirring occasionally. The vegetables will become very tender and the sauce will thicken slightly. Serve hot. ✿ M a k e s 4 o r 5 s e r v i n g s

Italian-Style Sautéed Broccoli

My mother had a knack of making the simplest foods taste delicious. She had a way of cooking the broccoli until just bright green and crisp-tender, and laced through it were lightly sautéed mushrooms and tomatoes. It was rich and delicate at the same time. I hope you enjoy this elegant dish as much as I have over the years. ✿

Spring or filtered water

1 head broccoli, cut into small flowerets, with stems peeled and thinly sliced

1 teaspoon extra-virgin olive oil

2 or 3 cloves garlic, minced

1 onion, diced

Sea salt

4 or 5 button mushrooms, brushed clean and thinly sliced

1 to 2 tomatoes, diced

Bring a large pot of water to a boil over high heat. Add broccoli and cook until bright green but not completely tender, about 3 minutes. Plunge into cold water to stop the cooking process and preserve the bright color.

Heat oil in a skillet over medium heat. Add garlic, onion and a pinch of salt and cook, stirring, until onion is wilted and translucent, 5 minutes. Add mushrooms and a pinch of salt and cook, stirring, 2 or 3 minutes. Add tomatoes, season lightly with salt and stir well. Cover and simmer 10 to 15 minutes. Remove cover and stir in broccoli. Simmer, uncovered, 2 to 3 minutes. Serve hot. ✍ M a k e s 4 s e r v i n g s

Sweet & Sour Cabbage with Tart Apples

My version of this Eastern European dish is savory with caraway seeds and sweetened lightly with red currant jam—great for autumn or winter. ✍

Spring or filtered water

1/2 head red cabbage, shredded

2 tart apples (Granny Smith or other), unpeeled, cored and diced

2 teaspoons brown rice syrup

2 tablespoons brown rice vinegar

2 tablespoons umeboshi vinegar

1/4 cup natural red currant or raspberry jam

About 2 tablespoons caraway seeds

Bring a pot of water to a boil over high heat. Add cabbage and cook until crisp-tender, about 5 minutes. Drain and transfer to a bowl. Toss apples into hot cabbage and set aside.

Whisk together rice syrup, vinegars, jam and caraway seeds to taste. Toss with hot cabbage until combined. Allow to stand about 15 minutes so flavors can develop. Serve warm. ✍ M a k e s 4 s e r v i n g s

Nut-Stuffed Winter Squash

This tantalizing entree combines sweet squash, savory nut meats and aromatic spices—a delicious centerpiece dish, especially when served with a light soup, crusty whole-grain bread and a crisp, fresh salad. 🌿

1/2 cup white rice
Spring or filtered water
Sea salt
2 acorn squash, halved and seeded
1/2 cup minced pecans
1 onion, finely diced

About 2 teaspoons light sesame oil
1/4 cup minced fresh parsley
Pinch *each* of cinnamon and nutmeg
About 1/2 cup fresh whole-wheat
    bread crumbs

Rinse rice several times until water runs clear to help remove excess starch. Bring rice, 1 cup water and a pinch of salt to a boil in a saucepan over medium heat. Reduce heat and cook, covered, over low heat until rice is tender and water is completely absorbed, about 25 minutes.

Preheat oven to 350F (175C). Lightly oil a baking dish large enough to hold squash. Cut the sides off the acorn squash just enough so that each half sits squarely, cut side up. Arrange the squash halves in prepared baking dish.

Combine cooked rice, pecans, onion, a light drizzle of oil, parsley, spices, a little salt and enough bread crumbs to make a stuffing that holds together. Divide stuffing among squash halves, filling them abundantly.

Add a little water to the baking dish. Cover tightly with foil and bake 1 hour, until the squash pierces easily with a fork. Remove cover and bake about 5 minutes to firm the filling. Serve warm. 🌿 M a k e s   4   s e r v i n g s

VARIATION Serve with Creamy Mushroom Sauce (page 420) spooned over top just before serving.

Colorful Squash Medley

A dash of color to brighten up any meal. ✒

1 teaspoon extra-virgin olive oil

2 or 3 cloves garlic, minced

3 or 4 green onions, cut into thin diagonal slices

2 yellow summer squash, cut into thick matchsticks

2 zucchini, cut into thick matchsticks

3 or 4 fresh basil leaves or a generous pinch of dried basil

Sea salt

1 red bell pepper, roasted over an open flame, peeled, seeded, and finely diced

Juice of 1 lemon

Heat oil in a skillet over medium heat. Add garlic and green onions and cook 1 to 2 minutes. Add summer squash, zucchini and basil and cook 5 minutes, stirring frequently. Season lightly with salt and stir in bell pepper. Cook 3 to 4 minutes or until vegetables are tender. Remove from heat and stir in lemon juice. Transfer to a serving bowl and serve immediately. ✒ M a k e s 4 s e r v i n g s

Cauliflower in Creamy Caper Sauce

When I lived in Italy, one of my favorite dishes was boiled cauliflower smothered in a creamy caper sauce. I would travel to Venice on weekends just to have lunch! Here's a slightly altered version, with a lighter, but equally delicious sauce. ✒

Spring or filtered water

1 head cauliflower, cut into bite-size
flowerets

CAPER SAUCE

1 cup soy or rice milk

3 to 4 tablespoons capers, drained well

Extra-virgin olive oil

1 to 2 teaspoons kuzu, dissolved in
2 teaspoons cold water

1/4 cup minced fresh parsley

Juice of 1 lemon

Bring a pot of water to a boil over high heat. Add cauliflower and cook until just tender, about 5 minutes. Drain and arrange flowerets on a serving platter.

To prepare the sauce, combine soy or rice milk, capers and a dash of oil in a small saucepan over low heat. When warmed through, stir in dissolved kuzu and cook, stirring, until the sauce is thick and creamy, about 3 minutes. Remove from heat and stir in parsley. Whisk in lemon juice, spoon over cauliflower, and serve warm.

M a k e s   4   s e r v i n g s

Broccoli with Artichoke Hearts This brightly

colored vegetable dish has a light, fresh taste that goes well with heartier fare.

1 head broccoli, cut into flowerets

1/2 teaspoon extra-virgin olive oil

Pinch of minced dried hot chile or to
taste

2 or 3 cloves garlic, minced

1 (6-oz.) jar marinated artichoke
hearts, drained and halved

Juice of 1 lime

Bring a small amount of water to a boil and steam broccoli flowerets until bright green and crisp-tender, about 5 minutes. Plunge into cold water to stop cooking process, drain and set aside.

Heat oil in a skillet over medium heat. Add hot chile and garlic. Cook 1 minute. Stir in artichoke hearts and cook about 3 minutes. Remove from heat and stir in broccoli and lemon juice. Transfer to a serving bowl and serve immediately.

M a k e s   4   s e r v i n g s

Spicy Mushroom Turnovers

These little treats are a great addition to any autumn party buffet or served as a side dish accompanying a hearty soup and lightly cooked vegetables for a simple but delicious meal. ⬅

1 teaspoon light sesame oil

3 1/2 cups button mushrooms, brushed clean and minced

Sea salt

1/2 cup minced green onions

About 2 tablespoons whole-wheat pastry flour

1/4 teaspoon ground cumin or to taste

1/2 cup firm tofu, crumbled

1/4 cup minced fresh parsley

14 sheets phyllo pastry

Extra-virgin olive oil for brushing

Heat sesame oil in a skillet over medium heat. Add mushrooms and a pinch of salt and cook, stirring, about 8 minutes, stirring frequently. Add green onions and cook, stirring, 3 minutes. Slowly sprinkle in flour, stirring until vegetables are coated. Season lightly with salt and cumin.

Process tofu with enough water to make a smooth paste in a food processor. Stir into vegetable mixture, remove from heat and fold in parsley. Set aside.

Preheat oven to 375F (190C). Lightly oil a large baking sheet. Cut each sheet of pastry in half, lengthwise. Working with 1 sheet at a time, lightly brush the pastry with oil. Spoon about 1 tablespoon of filling onto one end of the pastry piece and begin folding from the bottom left corner. Fold again from the bottom forming a triangle. Continue folding over and over, wrapping pastry around the filling, creating layers of pastry around the mushroom mixture. Place finished turnovers on prepared baking sheet and repeat the process with the remaining pastry and filling.

Just before placing pastries in the oven, lightly brush the surface of each with olive oil. Bake 25 to 30 minutes or until the pastry is flaky and golden brown. Transfer to a platter and serve warm. ⬅ M a k e s 4 t o 6 s e r v i n g s

Golden Squash Rings

Acorn squash is one of the most beautiful autumn vegetables. Cut into rings and baked to perfect, delicate sweetness, it makes this side dish a beautiful homage to the bounty of the harvest.

About 1/4 cup *each* dried whole-wheat
    bread crumbs and cornmeal
Pinch of sea salt
Generous pinch of pumpkin pie spice
    (allspice, cinnamon and nutmeg)
3 tablespoons brown rice syrup
3 tablespoons barley malt

3 tablespoons amasake
1 large acorn squash, cut crosswise
    into 1/2-inch-thick rings, unpeeled
    and seeds removed
Corn oil
Parsley sprigs, for garnish

Preheat oven to 400F (205C). Lightly oil a baking sheet. Combine bread crumbs and cornmeal with a pinch of salt and pumpkin pie spices in a shallow bowl. Whisk together rice syrup, barley malt and amasake in another bowl. Dip each squash ring into syrup mixture, then coat with cornmeal mixture.

Place each ring on prepared baking sheet and drizzle lightly with corn oil. Bake 25 minutes, until squash is tender and coating is crispy. Arrange on a platter and serve garnished with parsley sprigs. Makes 4 to 6 servings

Ume-Radish Pickles

The peppery radishes turn a beautiful, rich pink. Keep about 2 weeks in a tightly sealed jar in the refrigerator. ✑

5 or 6 red radishes, cleaned and left whole

2 or 3 umeboshi plums, pitted

Spring or filtered water

Place radishes, plums, and enough water to cover them in a saucepan over medium heat. Bring to a boil, reduce heat and simmer, uncovered, about 15 minutes, until pale pink and slightly crisp. Remove from heat and allow radishes to stand in the cooking liquid 15 minutes before transferring radishes and cooking brine to a jar. Serve pickles whole, halved or thinly sliced. ✑ M a k e s 2 o r 3 s e r v i n g s

Vegetable-Grain Patties

Another great recipe for leftover grain, these "burgers" make great lunches, snacks or barbecue treats. ✑

1/4 cup *each* finely diced carrot, onion, red bell pepper and celery

2 tablespoons extra-virgin olive oil

2 or 3 cloves garlic, minced

About 1/4 cup rolled oats

1 to 2 cups cooked brown rice

About 1/4 cup dried whole-wheat bread crumbs

Sea salt

Generous pinch dried basil

Combine carrot, onion, bell pepper and celery in a bowl. Heat 1 teaspoon of the oil in a skillet over medium heat. Add garlic and cook, stirring, 2 to 3 minutes. Add combined vegetables and cook about 10 minutes, stirring occasionally. Transfer mixture to a bowl, add rolled oats, rice and bread crumbs and season to taste with salt and basil. Stir well to form a soft, sticky mixture. Shape into 1/4-inch-thick patties.

Heat remaining teaspoon oil in a skillet over medium heat. Add patties and cook until lightly browned on each side, about 4 minutes per side. Arrange the patties on a platter and serve with whole-grain rolls and standard burger toppings or serve without bread, topped with your favorite sauce or gravy. ✑ M a k e s 4 s e r v i n g s

Summer Zucchini with Italian Lemon Relish

This zesty summer dish is a great way to use up some of those zucchini that seem to take over the entire garden. 🌿

5 or 6 zucchini, cut into 1/4-inch-thick diagonal slices

3 or 4 green onions, diced

Juice and grated zest of 1 lemon

1/4 cup minced fresh parsley

2 to 3 tablespoons capers, drained, rinsed and minced

Lemon slices, for garnish

Steam zucchini over boiling water until just tender, about 5 minutes. Transfer to a serving platter.

To prepare the lemon relish, puree together the green onions, lemon juice and zest, parsley and minced capers into a coarse paste. Spoon a small bit of relish over each piece of zucchini and serve garnished with lemon slices. 🌿 M a k e s 4 s e r v i n g s

Cauliflower in Broccoli Sauce

A wintry vegetable dish—inspired by a recipe found in a Williams-Sonoma catalog—that combines simple steamed cauliflower flowerets smothered in a creamy lemon sauce dotted with tiny broccoli buds. 🌿

1 head cauliflower, cut into small flowerets

BROCCOLI SAUCE

1 head broccoli

1/4 cup Vegetable Stock (page 96)

1/4 cup corn oil, plus 2 teaspoons

Juice and grated zest of 1 lemon

Sea salt

Bring a pot of water to a boil and cook cauliflower until just crisp-tender, 5 to 7 minutes. Transfer to a serving bowl and set aside to cool.

To prepare the sauce, trim the flowerets from the broccoli stalks, saving the stems for another recipe. Cut the flowerets into tiny buds. Set aside. Bring stock, 2 teaspoons corn oil, lemon zest and a pinch of salt to a boil over high heat and boil until reduced and syrupy. Remove from heat, stir in lemon juice, and set aside.

Heat the 1/4 cup of oil in a skillet over medium heat. Add broccoli and fry until bright green and crisp-tender, about 3 minutes. Drain broccoli on paper towels. Fold the cooked broccoli into the lemon sauce. Arrange the cauliflower on a serving platter and spoon the broccoli sauce over top. ✑ M a k e s 4 s e r v i n g s

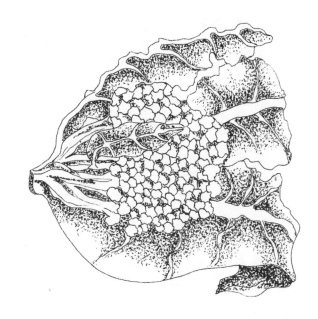

Chestnuts & Greens Medley with Walnuts

Fresh chestnuts can be cooked and peeled ahead of time and kept refrigerated for this recipe. The sweet chestnuts, rich fried tempeh, winter greens, and savory walnuts create a symphony of flavors in this hearty mix of leafy greens—a wonderful dish to grace any holiday table. ✑

8 ounces fresh chestnuts

Spring or filtered water

2 teaspoons corn oil

4 slices whole-grain bread, crusts removed and cut into 1/2-inch cubes

1 or 2 celery stalks, diced

2 or 3 cloves garlic, minced

Sea salt

1 bunch hearty winter greens (kale, collards), thinly sliced

Balsamic vinegar

4 ounces tempeh, cut into 1/4-inch cubes and lightly pan-fried (page 176) until golden

1/2 cup walnut pieces, pan-toasted (page 417) and coarsely minced

Make a slit in the flat side of each chestnut. Cook in boiling water over high heat 15 minutes. Drain the chestnuts, wrap in a towel to keep them warm and set aside 10 minutes. Peel off both the hard outer shell and the inner papery layer. Set chestnuts aside while preparing the rest of the dish.

Heat 1 teaspoon of the corn oil in a skillet over medium heat. Add bread cubes and cook, stirring constantly, until crispy, a few minutes only. Transfer to a bowl and add remaining teaspoon oil to the same skillet. Add celery, garlic and a pinch of salt and cook 2 minutes. Add greens, sprinkle lightly with salt and cook, stirring, until deep green and shiny with oil, about 8 minutes. Remove from heat and stir in a little vinegar. Transfer to a bowl and toss with chestnuts, bread cubes, tempeh, and walnuts until ingredients are well-incorporated. Arrange on a platter and serve immediately. ✐ M a k e s 4 s e r v i n g s

Galettes

You may call them pies, tarts or free-form quiches, but you will always call them delicious. These vegetable-filled pastries—*galettes*—are French in origin and can be filled with any manner of braised vegetables, purees, even vegetable and bean combinations. Their crusts are heartier and their fillings more substantial than pizzas; they are flat and free-form shaped, unlike their more sophisticated tart counterparts. Ragged edges and slightly lopsided shapes create the charm of this peasant fare. (But for those cooks who love symmetry, the dough can be trimmed and shaped to please your eye as well.)

Note that each recipe will make 1 large galette or 4 individual galettes.

1/2 recipe Basic Sourdough Bread
(page 435)

Filling of choice (recipes follow)

Extra-virgin olive oil

Prepare bread dough as directed. Prepare filling.

Preheat oven to 400F (205C). On a floured baking sheet or baking stone, roll out dough into a round, about 14 inches in diameter. Spread filling evenly over surface, leaving a 2-inch border. Fold up edges, pinching between your fingers to create pleats, exposing the filling in the center. Brush crust lightly with oil. Bake about 40 minutes, until the dough rises slightly and turns a deep golden brown. Remove from oven and serve hot. ✎ M a k e s 4 t o 6 s e r v i n g s

Winter Squash & Tofu Cheese Galette Filling ✎

1 medium winter squash (butternut or buttercup)

Corn oil

Sea salt

1 onion, diced

Generous pinch of dried basil

1/2 cup Tofu Cheese (page 162) crumbled coarsely

Preheat oven to 375F (175C). Halve the squash and remove the seeds. Lightly brush the cut sides with oil and sprinkle lightly with salt. Arrange in a baking pan. Bake until squash is tender, about 1 hour. Scoop out flesh and mash until smooth.

Heat 1 teaspoon corn oil in a skillet over low heat. Add the onion and basil and cook, stirring, about 5 minutes. Season lightly with salt and stir into mashed squash. Gently fold in half the tofu cheese.

Use to fill galette. Sprinkle the remaining tofu cheese on top of the exposed filling. ✎ M a k e s   e n o u g h   f i l l i n g   f o r   1   g a l e t t e

Mushroom-Leek Galette Filling ✑

1 teaspoon extra-virgin olive oil

3 or 4 cloves garlic, minced

2 leeks, cut lengthwise, rinsed well,
    and thinly sliced

Generous pinch of dried rosemary

Soy sauce

1 1/2 pounds button mushrooms,
    brushed clean and thinly sliced

Juice of 1 lemon

Heat oil in a skillet over medium heat. Add garlic, leeks, rosemary and a dash of soy sauce and cook, stirring, 2 to 3 minutes. Add mushrooms and a dash of soy sauce and cook until they begin to exude liquid and darken in color, stirring frequently. Season lightly with soy sauce, cover and cook over low heat until vegetables are soft, about 30 minutes. Remove from heat and stir in lemon juice. Cool to room temperature before using to fill galette. ✑ M a k e s   e n o u g h   f i l l i n g   f o r   1   g a l e t t e

Italian Vegetable Galette Filling ✑

1 teaspoon extra-virgin olive oil

2 or 3 cloves garlic, minced

2 or 3 shallots, minced

Sea salt

1 or 2 zucchini, cut into large dice

2 or 3 celery stalks, cut into large dice

1 cup button mushrooms, brushed
    clean and diced

2 to 3 plum tomatoes, cut into
    large dice

About 2 tablespoons sweet white miso

Spring or filtered water

Heat oil in a skillet over medium heat. Add garlic, shallots and a pinch of salt and cook, stirring, 2 to 3 minutes. Add zucchini, celery, mushrooms and a pinch of salt and sauté 5 minutes, stirring only occasionally. Add tomatoes and a pinch of salt and stir well. Dissolve miso in about 1/4 cup warm water and pour over vegetables. Cover and cook over low heat about 40 minutes until vegetables are soft. Remove cover and allow any remaining liquid to be absorbed. Cool to room temperature before using to fill galette. ✑ M a k e s   e n o u g h   f i l l i n g   f o r   1   g a l e t t e

Holiday Parsnips

This rich, oven-roasted dish is so meltingly sweet it will have sugar plums dancing in your head. And if the sweet taste, as rich as it is, isn't enough for you, it is also incredibly low in fat. ✒

1 cup fresh chestnuts	**Sea salt**
Spring or filtered water	**About 2 teaspoons extra-virgin**
5 or 6 shallots, peeled and halved	**olive oil**
2 to 3 cups parsnips, cut into 1/2-inch	**1/2 cup Vegetable Stock (page 96)**
pieces	**1/4 cup minced fresh parsley**

Make a slit in the flat side of each chestnut. Cook in boiling water over high heat 15 minutes. Drain the chestnuts, wrap in a towel to keep them warm and set aside 10 minutes. Peel off both the hard outer shell and the inner papery layer. Break chestnuts into halves. Set aside while preparing the rest of the dish.

Preheat oven to 425F (220C) and lightly oil a casserole dish. Arrange shallots and parsnips evenly in the dish and season lightly with salt and olive oil. Bake about 25 minutes, uncovered, until vegetables are tender and lightly browned.

Meanwhile, combine chestnuts and stock and bring to a boil. Cook over high heat until the stock has reduced by two-thirds, about 5 minutes. Remove roasted vegetables from oven and stir in chestnuts along with any remaining reduced stock. Toss with parsley and serve hot. ✒ M a k e s   4   s e r v i n g s

Wilted Cabbage with Caraway

This dish is inspired by Eastern European cuisine. The beauty of the dish is that it traverses the seasons beautifully. I serve it chilled in the summer and piping hot to warm up winter meals.

1 to 2 cups Vegetable Stock (page 96)

1 leek, cut lengthwise, rinsed well and sliced into 1-inch pieces

2 or 3 cloves garlic, minced

1/2 head green cabbage, finely shredded

Balsamic vinegar

2 to 3 teaspoons barley malt

About 2 tablespoons caraway seeds

Heat about 1/2 inch of stock in a deep skillet over medium heat. Add leek and garlic and simmer about 3 minutes. Add cabbage, cover and cook until almost all the broth has been absorbed, about 10 minutes.

Whisk together a few teaspoons vinegar and the barley malt. Stir mixture into cabbage with caraway seeds and simmer, uncovered, 2 to 3 minutes. Transfer to a serving bowl and serve warm or chilled.   Makes 2 or 3 servings

Scalloped Vegetables

I remember loving the creamy sauce my mother concocted to create the most delicious scalloped vegetables. When I changed my approach to food, I began experimenting with healthier, low-fat ingredients, still trying to achieve rich, satisfying dishes. Here is one success. ✧

Spring or filtered water

2 onions, cut into thick wedges

2 cups cauliflower, cut into small flowerets

1/2 head green cabbage, cut into 2-inch wedges

2 cups Brussels sprouts, trimmed and halved

White Sauce (opposite)

4 ounces brown rice mochi, grated

About 1/4 cup fresh whole-wheat bread crumbs

WHITE SAUCE

1/4 cup Onion Stock (page 98)

2 tablespoons whole-wheat pastry flour

1 1/2 cups soy milk or rice milk

Sea salt

Heat 1/4 inch water in a skillet over medium heat. Add onions and simmer 2 minutes. Top with other vegetables, cover, and lightly steam until crisp-tender, about 5 minutes. Transfer to a bowl and set aside while preparing the sauce.

Preheat oven to 350F (175C). Lightly oil a deep casserole dish. Combine stock and flour in a saucepan over medium heat. Cook until bubbly, stirring. Whisk in soy milk and simmer until the sauce thickens, about 10 minutes, stirring frequently to prevent scorching. Season lightly with salt and remove from heat.

Layer vegetables and sauce in casserole dish, finishing up with sauce on top. Spread a thin layer of grated mochi over sauce and top with bread crumbs. Cover and bake about 25 minutes, until mochi melts. Remove cover and return to oven to brown the top. Serve hot. ✧ Makes 4 to 6 servings

Tender Spring Vegetables

Nothing heralds the coming of spring quite like fresh, tender vegetables, delicately cooked and tossed with a light chive dressing.

6 to 8 baby carrots, cut into 2-inch pieces

4 or 5 snow peas, trimmed and left whole

6 to 8 red radishes, halved lengthwise

4 or 5 green onions, cut into 3-inch lengths

3 or 4 small turnips, cut into thin half-rounds

1 bunch watercress

1 teaspoon corn oil

Sea salt

Juice and grated zest of 1 lemon

Small handful fresh chives, minced

Bring a pot of water to a boil and separately cook each vegetable, in order listed, until crisp-tender, not soft. Plunge each vegetable into cold water to stop the cooking process and preserve its fresh, light energy. Toss together in a bowl.

Heat oil in a skillet over medium heat. Add all the vegetables, stirring only until coated with oil. Season lightly with salt and remove from heat. Gently stir in lemon juice and zest and chives. Arrange on a platter and serve immediately.

Makes 4 servings

Grilled Summer Squash

Grilling is a most wonderful way to prepare vegetables. Quick and easy, it is an ideal cooking technique for summer, when vegetables are at their peak. Grilling cooks the vegetables over direct heat, one side at a time, browning the outside. The delicious, smoky exterior gives way to a tender and juicy interior. Marinating the vegetables before cooking adds a bit of extra zip.

2 tablespoons balsamic vinegar

2 teaspoons prepared stone-ground mustard

1 clove garlic, thinly sliced

2 to 3 tablespoons extra-virgin olive oil

Pinch of sea salt

4 or 5 fresh basil leaves, finely minced

4 or 5 summer squash, cut lengthwise into about 1/4-inch-thick slices

In a small bowl, whisk together all ingredients except squash. Place squash in a shallow baking dish and spoon marinade over top to cover. Allow to marinate about 30 minutes. Remove garlic slices from marinade before grilling.

Preheat grill. Lightly oil grill rack. Arrange squash slices on rack and grill over medium heat until lightly browned on each side, basting occasionally with marinade. Cooking time may vary, but usually 2 to 5 minutes per side is sufficient. Arrange on a platter and serve immediately by itself or as part of a salad. ✒

Makes 4 servings

Italian-Style Marinated Carrots

My mother used to make this dish every summer. She usually served them as part of a cold antipasto, but I have discovered that they make a great summer side dish on their own.

4 or 5 carrots, cut into 1/2-inch-thick rounds

1/2 cup umeboshi vinegar

1 clove garlic, minced

1/4 cup extra-virgin olive oil

Pinch of sea salt

Generous pinch of fresh or dried rosemary

Bring a small amount of water to a boil over high heat. Add carrots, cover and cook over medium heat 10 to 15 minutes, until just tender. Drain and transfer to a bowl.

Combine remaining ingredients in a small bowl and toss with cooked carrots until well-mixed. Cover and refrigerate several hours. When ready to serve, stir well and allow carrots to stand, unrefrigerated, 30 minutes. ✒ Makes 4 to 6 servings

Stuffed Winter Squash

This is a lovely centerpiece dish to serve at holiday feasts or buffets. Along with the basic recipe are several variations on stuffings, one more delicious than the next, so choosing the one you want to make could be the toughest part of the recipe. In each recipe, you will notice the directions call for cooling the stuffing before filling the squash. Placing hot stuffing in a naturally sweet squash can cause it to sour, so take the time to cool it down before proceeding. ✐

1 large winter squash (buttercup, hokkaido or hubbard)

Light sesame oil

Spring or filtered water

Stuffing of choice (recipes follow)

Preheat oven to 325F (165C). To begin, remove the top of the squash, jack-o-lantern style, so that you can scoop out the seeds and pulp. Replace the top and lightly oil the outer skin. Place in a baking dish with about 1/2 inch of water. Bake, uncovered, about 25 minutes. Remove from oven and allow to cool while preparing the stuffing.

To stuff squash, pack filling firmly into the opening, until stuffed. Replace the squash top and place in a baking dish with a small amount of water. Increase oven temperature to 350F (175C). Cover squash and bake until squash pierces easily with a fork and filling is hot. The exact baking time will vary, depending on the size of the squash, anywhere from 1 to 3 hours. ✐ Makes 4 to 6 servings

NOTE Any filling that doesn't fit in the squash can be baked separately in a casserole dish for about 35 minutes.

Sourdough Stuffing

1 large sourdough loaf, crusts
  removed and cubed
1 teaspoon light sesame oil
1 clove garlic, minced
1 onion, diced
2 cups diced celery
1 cup button mushrooms, brushed
  clean and diced

1 cup tempeh cubes, pan-fried
  (page 172) until golden
1/2 cup pine nuts, lightly pan-toasted
  (page 417)
Soy sauce
Fresh ginger juice (page 242)
1/4 cup minced fresh parsley
Spring or filtered water

Preheat oven to 300F (150C). Arrange bread cubes on a baking sheet. Bake until bread
dries slightly, about 10 minutes.

Meanwhile, heat oil in a skillet over medium heat. Add garlic and onion and cook
2 to 3 minutes. Add celery and mushrooms and cook, stirring, until tender, about 7
minutes. Combine bread cubes, vegetables, fried tempeh, pine nuts, soy sauce, ginger
juice to taste and parsley. Slowly add enough water, while mixing, to make a soft stuffing.
Allow to cool completely before using. ✎

Makes enough stuffing for 1 large winter squash

Bulgur-Pecan Stuffing ✎

1/2 cup currants or raisins
Mirin
Spring or filtered water
1 cup pecans
Sea salt
2 1/2 cups bulgur

1 teaspoon extra-virgin olive oil
3 onions, diced
2 to 3 celery stalks, diced
Generous pinch dried basil
2 pears (Bosc or other), halved, cored
  and cubed

Preheat oven to 400F (205C). Soak currants in a mixture of half mirin and half water until tender, about 30 minutes. Spread pecans evenly on a baking sheet and toast them lightly in oven, about 8 minutes. Coarsely dice pecans and set aside.

In a medium saucepan, bring 5 cups of water to a boil with a pinch of salt. Stir in bulgur, cover and cook over low heat about 15 minutes, until all liquid has been absorbed and bulgur is tender.

While the bulgur cooks, heat oil in a skillet over medium heat. Add onions and cook until translucent, 5 minutes. Add celery and cook over medium heat until tender, about 10 minutes. Add basil, stir in pears and cook 2 to 3 minutes. Transfer mixture to a large bowl and add bulgur and pecans. Drain currants and gently fold into mixture. Allow to cool completely before using.

Makes enough stuffing for 1 large winter squash

Mushroom-Rice Stuffing

2 to 3 dried shiitake mushrooms
1 to 2 dried porcini mushrooms
Spring or filtered water
2 cups polished white rice, rinsed well
1 cup wild rice, rinsed well
6 cups Mushroom Stock (page 97)
Sea salt

Bay leaves
2 cloves garlic, minced
1 onion, diced
2 to 3 celery ribs, diced
1 pound button mushrooms, brushed
    clean and diced
1/4 cup minced fresh parsley

Soak dried mushrooms in hot water until tender. Combine both rices and stock, 3 pinches of salt and bay leaves in a pressure cooker over medium heat. Seal and bring to full pressure. Reduce heat to low and cook 30 minutes. Remove from heat and allow pressure to reduce naturally. Transfer rice to a bowl, discard bay leaves and set aside.

Heat 2 tablespoons water in a skillet over medium heat. Add garlic, onion and a pinch of salt and water sauté 3 to 4 minutes. Add celery, button mushrooms and a pinch of salt and cook until very soft, about 8 minutes. Drain porcini and shiitake mushrooms, remove stems and dice. Stir into vegetables and simmer 3 to 4 minutes. Add the mushroom mixture to cooked rice, season to taste with salt and mix well. Fold in parsley and allow to cool completely before using. ✒

Makes enough stuffing for 1 large winter squash

Cornbread & Chestnut Stuffing ✒

Cornbread with Fresh Corn (page 440), cubed

1 loaf sourdough bread, crusts removed and cubed

1 pound fresh chestnuts

1 teaspoon extra-virgin olive oil

1 onion, finely minced

Generous pinch of dried rosemary

1/4 cup minced fresh parsley

Soy sauce

2 or 3 celery stalks, minced

1 cup firm tofu, cut into tiny cubes and deep-fried (page 161) until golden

2 cups Vegetable Stock (page 96)

Preheat oven to 300F (175C). Spread bread and cornbread cubes evenly on a baking sheet. Bake 20 to 30 minutes to dry. Set aside.

Make a slit in the flat side of each chestnut. Cook in boiling water over high heat 15 minutes. Drain the chestnuts, wrap in a towel to keep them warm and set aside 10 minutes. Peel off both the hard outer shell and the inner papery layer. Set chestnuts aside.

Heat oil in a skillet over medium heat. Add onion, rosemary, parsley and a dash of soy sauce and cook, stirring, 2 or 3 minutes. Add celery and a dash of soy sauce and cook until tender, about 8 minutes. Season lightly with soy sauce and remove from heat. Stir in chestnuts and fried tofu cubes and transfer to a large bowl.

Add bread cubes and mix well, slowly adding stock until stuffing forms a soft ball. Taste and adjust seasoning. Allow to cool completely before using. ✒

Makes enough stuffing for 1 large winter squash

Twice-Stuffed Squash

We love squash. I mean we really love squash, to the point that, by the end of winter, the palms of our hands have turned a lovely orange. This delightful centerpiece dish can be made with any flavorful winter squash: hokkaido, buttercup, even acorn. ✑

1 small winter squash (about 2 lbs.)
Spring or filtered water
1/2 teaspoon corn oil
1 onion, diced
Sea salt

1 cup firm tofu, crumbled
1/4 cup minced fresh parsley
1/2 cup hazelnuts, pan-toasted
    (page 323) and minced
Parsley sprigs, for garnish

Preheat oven to 375F (190C). Lightly oil a baking dish. Halve the squash lengthwise and place, cut side down (seeds and all), in prepared baking dish. Add a little water to dish and bake about 40 minutes, until you can just pierce the skin with a fork.

Heat corn oil in a skillet over medium heat. Add the onion and a pinch of salt and cook, stirring, until translucent, 5 minutes. Stir in crumbled tofu and cook about 5 minutes. Set aside.

Scoop out the seeds and stringy pulp from the squash halves. Remove the flesh, reserving one half for stuffing. Place squash flesh and tofu mixture in a food processor. Season lightly with a pinch or two of salt. Process until smooth, adding only a little water if needed to produce a creamy texture. Stir in parsley.

Spoon squash mixture into the reserved squash shells and place in a lightly oiled baking dish. Sprinkle with hazelnuts and bake, uncovered, until the top is golden, about 20 minutes. Transfer to a platter and serve hot, garnished with parsley sprigs. ✑

Makes 2 large servings

Olive Broccoli

My mother really had a challenge cooking for me as a kid. I hated everything. This was one of her favorites—and one that I would actually eat! ✑

1 head broccoli

Spring or filtered water

1 teaspoon extra-virgin olive oil

Umeboshi vinegar

Juice and grated zest of 1 lemon

1 red bell pepper, roasted over an open flame, peeled, seeded, and diced

1/2 cup oil-cured ripe olives, pitted and minced

Split broccoli lengthwise into spears, trimming off any coarse stems and leaves. Bring a small amount of water to a boil over high heat. Add broccoli and steam until bright green and crisp-tender, about 4 minutes. Drain and transfer to a bowl. Immediately drizzle lightly with oil and vinegar and toss gently. Stir in lemon juice and zest, bell pepper and minced olives and turn the ingredients gently to combine. Arrange on a platter and serve warm. ✍ M a k e s   4   s e r v i n g s

Baked Herbed Onions

Baking onions whole and unpeeled helps keep their full-bodied, sweet flavor. ✍

5 or 6 red or Vidalia onions, unpeeled

3 to 4 fresh basil sprigs, slivered

1 to 2 fresh rosemary sprigs

1/4 cup extra-virgin olive oil

2 tablespoons brown rice syrup

1 tablespoon brown rice vinegar

2 tablespoons balsamic vinegar

1 cup Onion Stock (page 98)

Soy sauce

Preheat oven to 375F (190C). Lightly oil a baking dish. Slice the base off each onion, retaining the root, to make a flat surface so the onions stand upright. Make a small slit in the top of each onion and insert some basil and rosemary into each one. Arrange the onions in prepared baking dish.

Whisk together the oil, rice syrup, vinegars, stock and a dash of soy sauce. Pour mixture over the onions and bake, uncovered, basting occasionally, until the onions are soft when pierced with a knife, about 1 to 1 1/2 hours. Before serving, split the skins and remove; they should pull away very easily. Transfer onions to a platter and serve hot.

✍ M a k e s   5   o r   6   s e r v i n g s

Rutabaga & Carrot Puree

Rutabagas are a wonderful autumn vegetable and create a delicious, mild base for this simple, yet elegant dish. The sweet carrots and tart apples are complementary flavors. Other vegetables can be substituted in this dish, depending on what flavor and color you are looking for. The bright orange of this version symbolizes autumn deliciously. 🍃

1 teaspoon extra-virgin olive oil

1 clove garlic, minced

1 onion, diced

3 rutabagas, diced (and peeled if commercially waxed)

2 cups Vegetable Stock (page 96)

4 or 5 carrots, diced

2 tart apples (such as Granny Smith), peeled, cored and diced

Sea salt

1 cup soy milk or rice milk

Thin apple slices tossed in lemon juice, for garnish

Heat oil in a skillet over medium heat. Add garlic and onion and cook, stirring, until translucent, 5 minutes. Add the rutabagas and stock and simmer, uncovered, about 15 minutes. Add the carrots and apples, season lightly with salt and simmer until tender, about 15 minutes.

Drain and puree mixture until smooth, either with a masher or a food mill. Stir in the soy milk and transfer to a saucepan. Cook over medium heat until the soy milk is absorbed and the mixture thickens slightly, about 8 minutes. Spoon into a bowl and serve garnished with fresh apple slices. 🍃 M a k e s 5 o r 6 s e r v i n g s

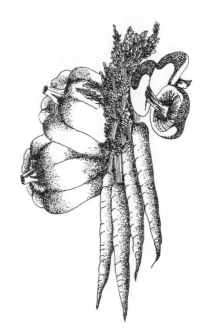

Sesame Cabbage

Chinese cabbage is a mild Asian vegetable with a delicate taste and versatile nature. More hearty than lettuce, it can be used in a variety of ways: shredded in slaws, blanched, pressed, sautéed or steamed. In this dish, it is lightly simmered and gently flavored. ✐

1/2 cup tan sesame seeds, rinsed and
    well drained

1 cup Vegetable Stock (page 96)

4 or 5 green onions, cut into thin
    diagonal slices

1 small head Chinese cabbage,
    shredded

1 teaspoon light sesame oil

Pinch of minced dried hot chile or
    to taste

Sea salt

Brown rice vinegar

In a hot, dry skillet, lightly pan-toast the seeds over medium heat until fragrant, about 4 minutes. Place in a bowl and set aside.

Bring the stock to a boil over high heat and boil 3 to 4 minutes to reduce and concentrate the flavors. Add the green onions and cabbage, reduce the heat to medium and cook until vegetables are tender, 3 to 4 minutes. Drizzle with oil and stir in the chile. Season lightly with salt and stir well. Remove from heat and stir in vinegar. Toss with seeds and transfer to a serving bowl. Serve hot or, in warm weather, chilled. ✐

Makes 4 to 6 servings

Braised Onions, Shallots & Leeks

Love onions? Then this recipe is for you. 🌿

1 teaspoon extra-virgin olive oil

3 red onions, cut into thick wedges

3 Vidalia (or yellow) onions, cut into thick wedges

Sea salt

4 or 5 shallots, halved

3 leeks, cut lengthwise, rinsed well and sliced into 2-inch lengths

Spring or filtered water

Fresh basil, minced, or dried basil

Juice of 1 lime

Reduced balsamic vinegar (see Note, page 234)

Heat oil in a deep skillet over low heat. Add onions and a pinch of salt and cook, stirring, until they begin to soften, about 10 minutes. Add shallots and a pinch of salt and cook, stirring, 4 to 5 minutes. Add leeks and a pinch of salt and cook, stirring, until bright green and tender, 5 minutes. Add a little water and a sprinkling of herbs. Cover and cook over medium heat until tender, about 30 minutes. Season lightly with salt and simmer until any remaining liquid has been absorbed. Remove from heat and stir in lime juice and reduced vinegar. Transfer to a platter and serve. 🌿 M a k e s 4 t o 6 s e r v i n g s

Chestnuts & Brussels Sprouts

When I lived in Italy and the winter arrived, the cold air brought with it an abundance of fresh chestnuts or *castagne*. And we used them in everything, from desserts to stuffings to snacks. In this dish, the sweet taste and chewy texture of the chestnuts harmonize beautifully with the crisp, fresh taste of Brussels sprouts. (If fresh chestnuts are unavailable, you may use canned or frozen ones.) 🌿

12 to 15 fresh chestnuts
Spring or filtered water
1 teaspoon extra-virgin olive oil
2 cloves garlic, minced
2 pounds Brussels sprouts, trimmed
Sea salt
2 cups Vegetable Stock (page 96)
Juice and grated zest of 1 lemon

Make a slit in the flat side of each chestnut. Cook in boiling water over high heat 15 minutes. Drain the chestnuts, wrap in a towel to keep them warm and set aside 10 minutes. Peel off both the hard outer shell and the inner papery layer. Set chestnuts aside.

Heat oil in a deep skillet over medium heat. Add garlic and cook 1 to 2 minutes. Add sprouts and a pinch of salt and cook, stirring to combine. Add chestnuts and stock, cover and simmer over low heat until sprouts are just tender, 10 to 12 minutes. Season lightly with salt and simmer 3 to 4 minutes. Remove from heat and drain well if any liquid remains. Stir in lemon juice and zest and transfer to a serving bowl. Serve warm.

 M a k e s   4   t o   6   s e r v i n g s

Ginger-Glazed Acorn Squash

The sweet and spicy glaze makes this side dish better than dessert! 🌿

2 acorn squash, halved lengthwise
  and seeds removed
Spring or filtered water
3 tablespoons corn oil
3 tablespoons brown rice syrup
2 teaspoons powdered ginger

Dash of grated nutmeg
Dash of ground cinnamon
Sea salt
5 tablespoons unsweetened or
  fruit-sweetened apricot preserves

Preheat oven to 350F (175C). Lightly oil a baking dish. Place squash halves, cut side down, in prepared baking dish. Add a little water and bake about 20 minutes.

Whisk together the corn oil, syrup, spices, a dash of salt and preserves. Remove the squash from the oven and turn them cut side up. Brush insides of the squash with syrup mixture and spoon the remaining mixture equally into each hollow. Cover loosely with foil or oiled parchment paper and return squash to the oven. Bake until tender, about 35 minutes. Arrange on a platter and serve hot. 🌿 M a k e s   4   s e r v i n g s

Parrot Fritters

No, no, I'm not suggesting you sauté your pet. It's just a name that I gave to these fritters made of parsnips and carrots. The creamy, sweet taste of the vegetables is complemented deliciously by the crispy outer coating achieved by pan-frying—a great starter dish or party food.

3 parsnips, cut into 2-inch pieces

3 carrots, cut into 2-inch pieces

Spring or filtered water

Sea salt

Pinch of baking powder

About 1/4 cup whole-wheat pastry flour

1/2 cup coarsely minced walnut pieces

1/4 cup minced fresh parsley

About 1/2 cup yellow cornmeal

Safflower oil, for frying

Parsley sprigs, for garnish

Place carrots, parsnips and a small amount of water in a saucepan over medium heat and bring to a boil. Cover, reduce heat and simmer until tender, about 25 minutes. Drain and spoon vegetables into a food processor. Season lightly with salt and a pinch of baking powder. Process, slowly adding flour, until mixture begins to firm up. Transfer to a bowl and fold in walnuts and parsley.

With moist hands, shape batter into 2-inch ovals or discs. Pour cornmeal into a bowl and coat each fritter, covering the entire surface.

Heat about 1/2 inch of oil in a deep skillet over medium heat. Fry several fritters at a time until golden, about 3 minutes per side. Try not to overfill the skillet as it will reduce the temperature of the oil, resulting in oily fritters, not crispy treats. Drain well on paper towels before arranging on a serving platter. Serve garnished with fresh parsley sprigs.

Makes 4 to 6 servings

Ray's Brussels Sprouts & Corn

One of the greatest inspirations for me is sharing recipes and seeing how people interpret and make them their own. I gave this simple vegetable stew recipe to a good friend. The only change he made was to add bay leaves during the cooking. The result was fabulous. ✎

2 onions, cut into thick wedges

2 pounds Brussels sprouts, trimmed and left whole

2 ears of corn, cut into 1 1/2-inch rounds

Spring or filtered water

2 to 3 bay leaves

Sea salt

In a heavy pot, layer onions, Brussels sprouts and corn rounds. Add about 1/16 inch of water and bring to a boil over medium heat. Add bay leaves. Reduce heat, cover and cook over low heat 15 minutes. Season lightly with salt and simmer 10 minutes. Remove the lid and allow any remaining liquid to be absorbed. Remove bay leaves and discard. Transfer vegetables to a bowl and serve warm. ✎ M a k e s 4 t o 6 s e r v i n g s

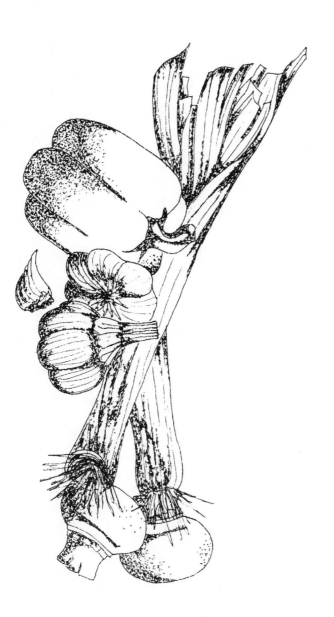

Parsnip Slaw

A unique take on cole slaw. Served warm, this sweet side dish has become a standard on my Thanksgiving table.

Spring or filtered water
5 to 6 parsnips, cut into thin matchsticks
1 red onion, cut lengthwise into thin slices

1/4 cup minced fresh parsley
1 recipe Tofu Mayo (page 415)

Bring a pot of water to a boil, add parsnips and boil 2 to 3 minutes, until crisp-tender. Remove from pot with a strainer, drain and place in a bowl. In same water, quickly blanch onion, about 30 seconds, and add to parsnips. Toss vegetables with parsley and Tofu Mayo and serve warm. Makes 4 servings

Christmas Parsnips

This wonder dish came to be when I had to create a quick and colorful dish for a fund-raiser televised by our local public broadcasting station affiliate. The task was quick and easy holiday cooking. I think you'll agree, this dish fits the category.

1 teaspoon extra-virgin olive oil
2 or 3 cloves garlic, minced
1 cup fresh cranberries, sorted and rinsed
Soy sauce
2 cups thin matchstick pieces parsnips

3 or 4 green onions, cut into 1-inch pieces
1/2 cup fresh orange juice
1 to 2 teaspoons kuzu, dissolved in 3 tablespoons cold water

Heat oil in a wok or skillet over medium heat. Add garlic and cook 1 minute. Add cranberries and a dash of soy sauce and cook until cranberries begin to pop. Add parsnips and a dash of soy sauce and cook until parsnips are just tender, about 4 minutes. Stir in green onions and cook 1 minute. Stir in orange juice and dissolved kuzu and cook until a thin glaze forms over the vegetables, about 3 minutes. Transfer to a platter and serve hot. Makes 4 servings

Nori Condiment

Delicious as an accompaniment for whole grains.

7 or 8 sheets of nori
Spring or filtered water

Soy sauce

Shred nori into small pieces and place in a small saucepan. Add enough water to just cover and season lightly with soy sauce. Bring to a boil over low heat and cook, uncovered, until all liquid has been absorbed and the nori has become very creamy, about 20 minutes. Transfer to a small bowl and serve warm or at room temperature. ✒

Makes 4 servings

Fresh Daikon & Kombu in Orange Sauce

A refreshingly clean-tasting dish. ✒

Spring or filtered water
1 (6-inch) piece kombu, soaked about
    5 minutes or until tender and cut
    into thin pieces
1 medium daikon, cut into 1/2-inch
    rounds

ORANGE SAUCE
Juice and grated zest of 1 orange
1 teaspoon umeboshi vinegar
1 teaspoon balsamic vinegar

Bring about 1 inch of water to a boil in a small saucepan. Add kombu and cook over low heat, about 10 minutes. Remove with a strainer and cook daikon rounds in the same water until just tender, about 10 minutes. Drain and combine with kombu. Arrange on a serving platter and make the sauce.

Whisk together all sauce ingredients in a small bowl and spoon over the hot daikon and kombu. Allow to marinate 15 to 20 minutes. Chill completely before serving. ✒

Makes 4 servings

Carrot & Kombu Rolls

A lovely combination of flavors presented in a unique and beautiful way. Use small to medium carrots for this recipe.

4 (8-inch) pieces kombu, soaked about 5 minutes or until tender

Spring or filtered water

12 (3-inch) carrot pieces

Soy sauce

Cut 3 pieces of kombu into 2-inch pieces, reserving the fourth piece. Wrap each piece of kombu around a carrot piece. Cut the remaining piece of kombu in half and into thin strips. Tie each strip around a carrot, holding the wrapped kombu in place with a knot.

Place the carrots in a pot and add enough water to half-cover. Bring to a boil over medium heat, cover, and cook over low heat about 40 minutes. Season lightly with soy sauce and simmer 7 to 10 minutes. Transfer to a platter and serve warm.

Makes 4 servings

Wakame Casserole

This casserole resembles a quiche with its light texture and rich taste.

1 teaspoon dark sesame oil

1 cup diced onion

1 pound tofu, crumbled

1/2 cup toasted sesame tahini

2 cups wakame, soaked 5 minutes and diced

Soy sauce

Black sesame seeds, for garnish

Heat oil in a skillet over medium heat. Add onion and cook, stirring, until translucent, 5 minutes. Set aside.

Preheat oven to 350F (175C). Lightly oil a casserole dish. Process tofu and sesame tahini in a food processor until smooth. Transfer to a bowl and mix in onion, wakame and soy sauce to taste. Spread evenly in the casserole dish and sprinkle generously with sesame seeds as a garnish. Cover and bake 35 minutes. Remove cover and bake until the top browns and the casserole sets, about 10 minutes. Serve hot. ✑

Makes 4 to 6 servings

Marinated Wakame & Vegetables A quick and

easy vegetable dish with a zesty marinated taste. ✑

Spring or filtered water

1/2 cup thin matchstick pieces carrot

1 head cauliflower, cut into small
flowerets

4 or 5 snow peas, trimmed and
left whole

1/2 cup wakame, soaked 3 minutes
and diced

MARINADE

Juice of 1 lime

1/4 cup brown rice vinegar

1 teaspoon soy sauce

1 tablespoon balsamic vinegar

Spring or filtered water

Bring a pot of water to a boil. Separately cook each vegetable until crisp-tender: carrots about 30 seconds, cauliflower about 4 minutes, and snow peas about 30 seconds. Drain well and mix with diced wakame.

Mix together marinade ingredients, adding only enough water to gentle the flavor of the marinade but not make it watery. Toss the vegetables with the marinade and allow to stand about 30 minutes to allow the flavors to develop. Toss gently just before serving.

✑ Makes 4 to 6 servings

Dulse with Corn & Broccoli
A colorful and delicious summer sea vegetable dish. 🌿

Spring or filtered water
Corn kernels cut from 3 ears of corn
2 stalks broccoli, cut into flowerets, with stems diced
1 cup dulse, rinsed, soaked to soften, and diced

1 green onion, cut into thin diagonal slices
Brown rice vinegar
Balsamic vinegar

Bring a pot of water to a boil and separately blanch the corn, broccoli stems and broccoli flowerets until crisp-tender. Toss with dulse and green onion. Drizzle with equal amounts of each vinegar and toss gently to incorporate all ingredients. Transfer to a bowl and serve warm or, in hot weather, chilled. 🌿 M a k e s 4 s e r v i n g s

Jim's Hiziki Strudel
Cooking for people who are not necessarily attracted to sea vegetables can be quite a challenge. A friend of mine came up with this dish and, so far, no one has been able to resist the rich sautéed vegetables and hiziki wrapped in a flaky pastry crust. 🌿

1 teaspoon light sesame oil
1 cup hiziki, soaked until tender (about 10 minutes), and drained
1/2 teaspoon mirin
Spring or filtered water
1 onion, cut lengthwise into thin slices
1 cup thin matchstick pieces carrots
Soy sauce

Strudel Dough
Tan sesame seeds

STRUDEL DOUGH
1 cup whole-wheat pastry flour
1/2 cup yellow cornmeal
Pinch of sea salt
1/4 cup corn oil
About 2 tablespoons spring or filtered water

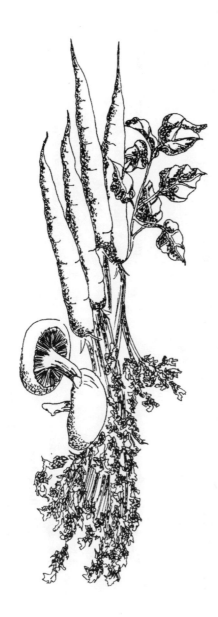

heat. Add hiziki and cook, stirring, about 4

half-cover and simmer over low heat 20

ghtly with soy sauce, cover and simmer 10

cook until any remaining liquid has been

e to cool while preparing the strudel dough.

salt into a bowl. Stir in corn oil with a fork until

ugh just holds together. Gather into a ball and

oil a baking sheet. Roll out dough between

le. Remove 1 sheet of paper and spread hiziki

filling over pastry, leaving about 1 inch of dough exposed all around. Roll, jelly-roll style, using paper to help roll, and seal the ends of the strudel with a fork. Gently transfer to prepared baking sheet. Cut several slits in the top of the strudel so it will not split during baking. Sprinkle with sesame seeds.

Bake about 35 minutes, until golden and the strudel sounds hollow when tapped. Cool about 10 minutes before slicing. Cut into 1-inch-thick slices, arrange on a platter, and serve warm. ✎ Makes 6 to 8 servings

Vinegared Hiziki ✐ A small amount of this zesty strong dish will go a

long way.

1/2 cup hiziki, soaked 10 minutes

Spring or filtered water

Soy sauce

1/2 red pepper, roasted over an open
    flame, peeled, seeded, and diced

1 cup diced watercress

2 tablespoons brown rice vinegar

Juice of 1 lemon

Place soaked hiziki in a saucepan with enough water to half-cover, season lightly with soy sauce and bring to a boil. Reduce heat and simmer, uncovered, 5 minutes. Cover and cook 30 minutes more. Add bell pepper, cover and simmer 5 minutes. Remove cover and cook away any remaining liquid. Remove pan from heat. Toss diced watercress into the hot hiziki and then stir in vinegar and lemon juice. Transfer to a bowl and serve warm. ✐ M a k e s   4   s e r v i n g s

Arame Sauté ✐ A quick and delicious dish chock-full of lightly cooked

vegetables, accented with arame. ✐

1/2 cup arame

Spring or filtered water

Soy sauce

1 teaspoon mirin

1 teaspoon dark sesame oil

2 or 3 shallots, diced

2 cups button mushrooms, brushed
    clean and thinly sliced

1 cup thin matchstick pieces carrots

2 or 3 stalks broccoli, flowerets and
    stems diced

2 tablespoons sunflower kernels,
    lightly pan-toasted (page 404)

Rinse arame well and set aside. It will soften in a few minutes without soaking.

Place arame in a small saucepan with enough water to half-cover. Bring to a boil, cover and cook over low heat 15 minutes. Season lightly with soy sauce and mirin and cook until all liquid has been absorbed.

Heat oil in a skillet over medium heat. Add shallots and cook, stirring, until translucent, 5 minutes. Add mushrooms and cook, stirring, until wilted. Add carrots and cook, stirring, 1 to 2 minutes. Finally, stir in broccoli, and season lightly with soy sauce. Cover and cook over low heat until broccoli is bright green and crisp-tender, about 4 minutes. Stir in arame and sunflower kernels. Transfer to a bowl and serve warm.

Makes 2 or 3 servings

Dulse Croquettes

An exceptional way to serve dulse.

1/2 cup dulse, soaked briefly and diced
1/2 cup rolled oats
3 or 4 green onions, diced
1/2 cup grated carrot
Spring or filtered water
About 1/2 cup yellow cornmeal
Dipping Sauce (opposite)
Safflower oil for deep-frying

DIPPING SAUCE
1/2 cup spring or filtered water
1 teaspoon soy sauce
2 teaspoons grated daikon
1 teaspoon fresh ginger juice
(page 242)

Whisk sauce ingredients together in a small bowl. Set aside.

Combine the dulse, oats, green onions, and carrot with enough water to make a stiff batter. Shape into 2-inch rounds or ovals. Pour cornmeal into a shallow bowl. Coat each croquette in cornmeal and place on a plate.

Heat about 2 inches of oil in a deep skillet over medium heat. Add the croquettes, in batches, and deep-fry until golden, 2 to 3 minutes per side. Drain on paper towels, arrange on a platter, and serve immediately with sauce. Makes 4 servings

PASTABILITIES

There is nothing on earth I would rather eat than a bowl of pasta. Growing up in an Italian household, pasta was a staple of our diet. I can remember my mother asking what we would like for dinner and all of us piping up "macaroni" (it hadn't yet been dubbed "pasta"). As I grew, and my love affair with cooking developed, I began experimenting with pasta and sauces from every cookbook, magazine, and booklet I could get my hands on. Later, as I traveled around the Mediterranean, I came across the most amazing chefs creating a wide variety of pasta dishes—delicious combinations of simple, fresh ingredients resulting in stunning sauces and accompaniments to this remarkable food.

Pasta is undeniably the most popular food in our diet today. Surrounded by folklore and stereotypical images, it is nonetheless true that pasta is a serious and very important food. It is an extraordinary dietary staple that has remained a constant throughout culinary history and has achieved worldwide popularity.

Today, thanks to our increasing knowledge of calories and excess fat, pasta has become the victorious queen of the table. Simple to prepare and completely delicious, pasta is being touted as a central food in today's new low-fat, low-cholesterol diet. And easy? With today's hectic pace, it is nice to know that there is a healthful and delicious food choice that can become the centerpiece dish in everything from a quick weekday supper to an elegant dinner party designed to impress.

Pasta seems to have threaded its way through just about every culture recorded, but I will concentrate on the use of noodles in Asian and Italian cuisine, since these are the cultures that use pasta on a grand scale. Although present in many other cultures, noodles have not been embraced so completely as by Asians and Italians.

While I will include recipes for making pasta from scratch, the purpose of these recipes is to show you how to use ready-made, good-quality pastas. I will admit that although I love to make noodles from scratch on occasion, my schedule usually doesn't allow me the luxury too often. But, with all the great pasta products available to us today, you can have great quality anytime. However, I will tell you that pasta-making is a great art and a wonderful way to relax in your kitchen when you have spare time. And nothing tastes quite like it.

Pasta is a general term for a wide variety of noodle shapes on the market today. Traditionally, pasta was made simply of wheat flour, water, and salt. As modern people craved richer and richer foods, chefs created pastas made with eggs and even cheese, unnecessary ingredients for delicious pastas. I recommend that you read labels and make your choices. Most pasta is composed of durum or semolina flour, a hard wheat. This particular grain gives the pasta a lovely texture and light flavor with a light yellow color. Asian pastas are composed of everything from whole-wheat flour to buckwheat flour. And domestic pastas are made from wheat, rice, corn, and even more exotic grains, like quinoa and amaranth. In addition, of course, there are available many flavors and styles of pasta made from organic ingredients, which I prefer to the "enriched" flour products used in many domestic commercial brands. Like everything else I prepare, I always want the best-quality ingredients available to me.

In this section, I will discuss a variety of pasta types, shapes and styles as well as sauces and styles of cooking. Pasta loves sauce, everything from oil and garlic to rich savory gravies. And we will discuss many of the ways we enjoy pasta today: salads, appetizers, main courses and side dishes. An impressive array of creative recipes awaits you—colorful dishes made with the finest-quality pastas and combined with fresh vegetables, herbs and spices, light dressings and rich sauces. Use these recipes as a stepping stone to creating your own pasta repertoire.

COOKING TIPS

A few tips on cooking pasta before we begin. *Al dente* means "chewy" ("to the tooth," to be exact); pasta should still retain some body after cooking. It should be firm, but not undercooked, and certainly not mushy. To test noodles for doneness, simply taste one and cook until the texture you like is achieved or remove a noodle from the water and cut it with your fingernail. If the noodle is cooked through and cuts easily, the pasta is ready to drain. And there is always the method of throwing pasta against the wall. If it sticks, it's done. Kind of a drag when cleanup time rolls around, though . . .

Also, remember to cook pasta in a large pot with lots of water so it can cook thoroughly and evenly and not stick together. Salting the water is optional. It returns the water to a boil quicker than unsalted water and, some say, prevents the noodles from becoming too soft and mushy.

TO RINSE OR NOT TO RINSE

Rinsing helps remove excess starch from the pasta and prevents the noodles from clumping together in one large lump. When you rinse pasta, use an amply sized colander with plenty of room for the noodles to be moved. Rinse until no warmth remains to ensure that they will not stick. If you want the noodles to be hot when you serve them, simply plunge them into hot water just before serving time. This method is great when making pasta salads or when you want to serve the sauce ladled over the pasta and not incorporated throughout the dish. However, most Italian cooks will tell you, and I concur, that rinsing pasta is unnecessary; that unrinsed pasta holds the sauce better, which is true. In this case, cook the pasta, drain it and immediately toss it with the desired sauce and serve. Personally, the only noodles I rinse before serving are those from Japan. My experience has been that they are a bit more salty than other noodles and rinsing helps remove some of that excess salt from their surface.

Pasta e Fagioli

I can remember my mother making *pasta e fagioli* just about every Friday for dinner. My father loved this thick pasta and bean soup. I, on the other hand, hated it. It would take me hours to eat because I had to pick every bean out of my bowl. Luckily, I grew out of this obsession and have grown to love this hearty dish.

1 cup white beans or chick-peas, rinsed and soaked 6 to 8 hours

Spring or filtered water

1 (1-inch) piece kombu

2 bay leaves

4 cloves garlic, 2 left whole and 2 minced

4 teaspoons extra-virgin olive oil

Generous pinch of dried sage

1/4 cup *each* diced onion, celery and carrot

Sea salt

Generous pinch of dried rosemary, ground

1 1/2 cups small pasta (elbows, orzo or acini), cooked

1/4 cup minced fresh parsley

Preheat oven to 325F (165C). Place soaked beans in a baking dish with enough water to cover plus 1 inch more. Add kombu, bay leaves, 2 whole cloves garlic, 2 teaspoons olive oil, and sage. Cover and bake 1 hour.

Meanwhile, in a soup pot, heat remaining 2 teaspoons olive oil over medium heat. Add minced garlic and onion and cook, stirring, until fragrant, about 2 minutes. Add celery and carrot and cook, stirring, until softened, about 5 minutes. Add 5 cups water and bring to a boil, uncovered. Take the beans from the oven and remove bay leaves and kombu. Puree half the beans in a food processor. Add pureed and whole beans to the soup. Reduce heat, cover, and simmer 35 minutes. Season lightly with salt and sprinkle with rosemary. Simmer 7 to 10 minutes and stir in cooked pasta. Serve garnished with fresh parsley. Makes 5 or 6 servings

Gnocchi

I thought that I invented this gnocchi recipe. I was so excited that I called an Italian friend to break this groundbreaking culinary news. Much to my dismay, he informed me that chefs in Northern Italy have been making gnocchi with rice for many years; that, in fact, gnocchi made with potatoes is a relatively recent development. So much for my invention. Oh, well, they are truly delicious anyway, so enjoy. ✎

1/2 cup white rice	1 cup unbleached white flour
1 cup plus 1/4 cup spring or	Sea salt
filtered water	Extra-virgin olive oil
1 1/2 cups semolina flour	

Cook rice in 1 cup water over low heat until soft, about 30 minutes. Puree cooked rice in a food processor until creamy. Combine with semolina and unbleached flours and pinch of sea salt, mixing until a stiff dough forms, slowly adding remaining water if necessary. Knead dough about 10 minutes until flexible, ear-lobe consistency. Next, take a fork or a gnocchi comb and coat it with flour. Pull off a small piece, about a 2-inch ball of dough, and roll, by hand, on a floured surface, into a long, thin cylinder, about 1/4 inch thick. Cut crosswise into bite-size pieces of dough and push the fork or comb along the piece so that a roll forms with ridges. Place each gnocchi on a floured baking sheet while preparing the rest of the pasta.

You may either cook the pasta immediately or allow them to dry for a few days, on the baking sheet, covered lightly with a cloth. Store dried gnocchi in an airtight container until cooked.

To cook gnocchi, bring a large amount of water to a boil with a pinch of sea salt and a dash of olive oil. Drop in gnocchi and stir. When they rise to the top of the pot, taste one. Continue to cook until the tenderness you desire is achieved. They should be chewy, but not hard or undercooked or mushy. ✎ M a k e s 4 t o 6 s e r v i n g s

Cauliflower Sauce

This simple sauce is deliciously reminiscent of conventional white sauces, without the dairy fat and high caloric content.

1 teaspoon extra-virgin olive oil

2 cloves garlic, sliced

Several leaves fresh basil, minced, or generous pinch of dried basil

1/2 cup diced onion

1 head cauliflower, cut into small flowerets with stem diced

Rice or soy milk

Sea salt

1 recipe Gnocchi (page 313) or other pasta, cooked

1/4 cup minced fresh parsley

Heat oil in a skillet over medium heat. Add garlic and cook until brown. Remove garlic from oil and discard. Add basil and onion and cook, stirring, until translucent, about 5 minutes. Add cauliflower and stir well. Add enough rice milk to just half-cover ingredients, season lightly with salt, and cover. Reduce heat and simmer, uncovered, until cauliflower is soft, about 10 to 15 minutes. Puree until smooth, adding water if necessary to achieve a creamy sauce. Toss with hot gnocchi and parsley and serve immediately. Makes 4 to 6 servings

Soba Noodles with Ginger & Green Onions

This noodle dish, quickly sautéed with ginger and garlic, makes a delicious supper served with lightly cooked green vegetables and a soup.

1 (8-oz.) package soba noodles

1 teaspoon light sesame oil

2 cloves garlic, minced

2 or 3 dried shiitake mushrooms, soaked until tender and sliced

1 to 2 teaspoons freshly grated gingerroot and juice (page 242)

2 or 3 green onions, thinly sliced

1 teaspoon mirin

Soy sauce

1/4 cup sesame seeds, toasted (page 414)

1/4 cup minced fresh parsley or mint

Parsley or mint sprigs, for garnish

Cook noodles as directed on the package, 8 to 10 minutes or until tender. Drain, rinse well, and set aside. Heat oil in a skillet over medium heat. Add garlic and cook, stirring, until fragrant, about 2 minutes. Add mushrooms and cook, stirring, 3 to 4 minutes. Add ginger juice and pulp to taste, green onions, mirin, a dash of soy sauce and sesame seeds and cook, stirring, 2 to 3 minutes. Toss mixture with noodles and stir in minced parsley or mint. Serve in individual noodle bowls garnished with parsley or mint sprigs. ❧

Makes 2 or 3 servings

Capellini with Olives & Walnuts

This variation of *pasta Puttanesca* eliminates the tomatoes from the classic recipe but does retain the rich, pungent flavors of olives, capers, and garlic, beautifully enhanced by nut meats. ❧

1 tablespoon extra-virgin olive oil
2 or 3 cloves garlic, minced
2 to 3 tablespoons capers, drained and lightly rinsed
1/2 cup walnut pieces, pan-toasted (page 417)

Spring or filtered water
1 (8-oz.) package capellini
10 to 12 pitted olives, minced
1/4 cup minced fresh parsley

Heat oil in a skillet over medium heat. Add garlic and cook, stirring, until fragrant, about 2 minutes. Add capers and cook, stirring, 3 to 4 minutes. Add walnut pieces and a small amount of water. Cover and simmer 7 to 8 minutes over medium-low heat. Puree the sauce in a food processor until walnuts are about half broken. The sauce should be coarse, not smooth. While the sauce simmers, cook pasta according to package directions until just tender to the bite. Drain pasta; do not rinse. Toss immediately with the hot sauce, olives, and parsley and serve. ❧ Makes 2 or 3 servings

Chinese Noodle Salad

A quick and easy salad, jam-packed with fresh, crisply cooked vegetables and a spicy, sweet and sour sauce. 🍃

1/4 cup diced carrot

10 to 12 snow peas, cut into thin matchsticks

1/4 cup thin matchstick pieces daikon

2 or 3 green onions, cut into thin diagonal pieces

3 or 4 slices gingerroot, cut into thin matchsticks

Marinade (opposite)

1 (8-oz.) package thin lo mein noodles or somen, cooked until just tender

1/2 cup shelled peanuts

Orange zest strips

2 tablespoons minced fresh cilantro or mint (optional)

MARINADE

1/2 cup fresh orange juice

2 tablespoons fresh ginger juice (page 242)

1 teaspoon sweet rice vinegar

1/4 teaspoon soy sauce

1 teaspoon dark sesame oil

Generous dash of umeboshi vinegar

Quickly add the carrot, snow peas, and daikon separately, in that order, to boiling water and boil until crisp-tender. Rinse under cold water, drain, and place in a bowl. Add green onions and ginger and set aside.

Mix the marinade ingredients together in a small bowl. Pour over the vegetable mixture. Allow to marinate 30 minutes.

Toss the noodles with the marinated vegetables, peanuts, orange zest, and cilantro, if using. Chill before serving. 🍃 M a k e s 2 o r 3 s e r v i n g s

Linguine with Summer Vegetables in Orange Sauce

I lived in Florida for several years and fell completely in love with the flavor of fresh orange juice in cooking. This unique pasta dish, tossed with fresh vegetables and dressed in a surprisingly sweet orange oil, is ideal in the summer months.

1 cup fresh green peas
Corn kernels cut from 2 ears of corn
1 (8-oz.) package linguine
1 teaspoon corn oil
1/4 cup minced onion
Sea salt

1/2 red bell pepper (optional), roasted
    over an open flame, peeled, seeded
    and thinly sliced
Generous dash of mirin
Juice and grated zest of 1 orange
2 or 3 fresh chives, minced

Bring a large pot of water to a boil and add the peas and corn kernels. Bring back to a boil and remove vegetables with a slotted spoon. Return water to a boil and cook linguine according to package directions until just tender to the bite.

Meanwhile, heat corn oil in a deep skillet over medium heat. Add onion and a pinch of salt and cook, stirring, until onion is wilted, about 5 minutes. Add bell pepper, if using, and cook, stirring, 3 to 4 minutes. Sprinkle with mirin and add juice. Cover and simmer 1 to 2 minutes; not too long, as the juice can change from sweet to bitter if overcooked.

Drain linguine; do not rinse. Stir linguine into skillet along with peas and corn. Toss with orange zest and chives, transfer to a bowl, and serve warm. ✐

Makes 2 or 3 servings

Udon Kanten

I was taught this wonderful dish by one of my dearest friends and wisest cooking instructors, Diane Avoli. This noodle entree is so cool, you will love it. Who would have imagined a pasta dish cut into squares and served in chunks that isn't lasagne? It goes great with a lightly pressed or raw salad, or with your favorite sauce spooned over the top. ✐

1 teaspoon light sesame oil

1/2 cup diced leek

Soy sauce

Corn kernels cut from 1 ear of corn

1 medium carrot, diced

1 (4-oz.) package brown rice mochi

Spring or filtered water

1 to 2 tablespoons agar-agar flakes

1 (8-oz.) package udon, cooked, drained and rinsed well

Heat oil in a skillet over medium heat. Add leek and a dash of soy sauce and cook, stirring, until leek is wilted, about 5 minutes. Add corn, carrot and a dash of soy sauce and cook, stirring, until vegetables are tender, 2 to 3 minutes. Set aside.

Grate mochi into a saucepan and add enough water to cover. Bring to a boil and cook to melt mochi, about 5 minutes. Add about 2 cups water and agar-agar flakes (1 tablespoon flakes to each cup of water), sprinkle lightly with soy sauce and simmer 10 minutes.

Toss noodles and vegetables together and spread evenly in a shallow casserole dish. Pour mochi mixture over noodles to cover and set aside until firmly set. Serve by cutting into squares or scoops. ✐ M a k e s   4   s e r v i n g s

Penne with Broccoli & Raisins

This recipe is a different take on pasta with oil and garlic that is quite common in Italy. The delicately sweet taste of the raisins gives this dish a unique little surprise with every bite. ✐

1/4 cup raisins

1/4 cup extra-virgin olive oil

2 or 3 cloves garlic, minced

1 large onion, minced

Sea salt

1/2 cup pine nuts or walnuts

1 head broccoli, cut into small
    flowerets, with stems cut into fine
    matchsticks

8 ounces penne

Fresh parsley or basil (optional),
    minced

Soak the raisins in warm water to cover for 10 minutes and drain.

Heat the oil in a skillet over medium heat. Add the garlic, onion, and a pinch of salt and cook, stirring occasionally, until the onion is translucent, about 3 minutes. Add pine nuts and sprinkle lightly with salt. Cover, reduce heat and allow to simmer while pasta cooks.

Bring a large pan of water to a boil and cook pasta 4 to 5 minutes. Add broccoli to the pot and cook until pasta is just tender to the bite and broccoli is bright green. Drain well; do not rinse. Toss pasta and broccoli with onion mixture and raisins and serve garnished with fresh parsley or basil, if desired. ✒ M a k e s 3 o r 4 s e r v i n g s

Cialsons with Leafy Green Pesto

Cialson is the Sicilian name for ravioli. This recipe is part of my husband's rich Sicilian heritage. My version eliminates a few undesirable ingredients but retains the classic spicy, herb-scented flavor. I especially love to serve these pasta pockets filled with aromatic pesto lightly dressed with a light olive oil sauce. ✑

1 recipe Basic Pasta Dough (page 355)
1/4 cup whole-wheat bread crumbs
2 tablespoons spring or filtered water
1 small bunch kale, boiled until deep
    green, then finely minced
Generous pinch of cinnamon
Generous pinch of nutmeg
1 teaspoon dried rosemary

1 tablespoon minced fresh parsley
1/4 cup extra-virgin olive oil
2 cloves garlic, minced
1 onion, minced
Sea salt
Fresh parsley or rosemary, minced,
    for garnish

Prepare dough. Cover and set aside.

Place bread crumbs in a bowl and add water, mixing until water is absorbed and bread crumbs are soft. Combine cooked greens with bread crumbs, cinnamon, nutmeg, rosemary and parsley.

On a floured surface, thinly roll out dough. Using a round cutter or a glass, cut out 3-inch circles, using as much of the dough surface as possible. Place about 1 teaspoon of kale mixture on each circle, fold in half, and seal edges with a fork.

Bring a large pot of water to a boil and cook cialsons 3 to 5 minutes or until just tender to the bite. They should be chewy and not too soft. They will rise to the top of the boiling water when they are done.

Heat olive oil in a skillet over medium heat. Add garlic, onion, and a pinch of salt and cook until garlic is fragrant, about 2 minutes. Drain cialsons; do not rinse. Toss immediately with garlic mixture. Garnish with minced parsley or rosemary. ✑

M a k e s   4   s e r v i n g s

VARIATION Substitute 1 recipe Fresh Basil Pesto (page 426) for the kale filling above.

320   ✑   Cooking the Whole Foods Way

Spaghetti with Walnut Sauce

The rich taste of walnuts is nicely balanced by the peppery taste of the bitter greens, which interestingly, also serve to aid the body in digesting the rich sauce.

1 bunch dandelion, broccoli rapini
   or watercress
1 (16-oz.) package spaghetti
1 cup walnut pieces, blanched
2 to 3 cloves garlic, minced
8 to 10 leaves fresh basil or generous
   pinch of dried

3 tablespoons white miso
2 to 3 teaspoons extra-virgin olive oil
1 cup rice milk
Soy sauce
1 teaspoon kuzu, dissolved in
   3 tablespoons cold water
Fresh basil, for garnish

Bring a large pot of water to a boil. Add greens and boil until bright green, about 5 minutes. Remove with a strainer, cool, and mince. Return water to a boil and cook pasta while preparing sauce.

Process walnuts, garlic, basil, miso, olive oil, rice milk and a dash of soy sauce in a food processor until coarsely pureed. Transfer puree to a saucepan and cook, stirring, over low heat until hot. This helps render the ingredients more digestible as well as develops the flavors. Stir in dissolved kuzu and cook, stirring, until creamy and thickened, 3 to 4 minutes.

Drain pasta; do not rinse. Toss immediately with sauce and serve garnished with fresh basil. ✒ M a k e s   4   o r   5   s e r v i n g s

Fettuccine Alfredo

This classic dish has been called a heart attack on a plate by nutritionists. This version gets its rich flavor from pine nuts, without the high fat and calorie contents. 🌿

1 cup pine nuts

1 tablespoon sweet white miso

2 cloves garlic, minced

2 teaspoons umeboshi vinegar

1 teaspoon brown rice syrup

1/4 cup extra-virgin olive oil

Spring or filtered water

1 (8-oz.) package fettuccine, cooked

Place nuts, miso, and garlic in a food processor. With motor running, slowly add all the liquid ingredients, except water, and process until blended. Add water in small amounts to adjust the consistency, keeping the sauce fairly thick. Transfer to a saucepan and cook, stirring, over low heat just enough to warm the miso and oil but not enough to turn the vinegar bitter, about 1 minute.

Cook fettuccine according to package directions just until tender. Drain fettuccine; do not rinse. Toss immediately with sauce and serve. 🌿

Makes 2 or 3 servings

VARIATION Sometimes, I finish off this sauce by squeezing a lemon over the whole dish just prior to putting it on the table. It adds zip and helps the body digest the rich sauce.

Linguine with Hazelnuts

Hazelnuts play a large role in Italian cooking. Their slightly sweet taste has helped create many a delicious sauce or condiment. People have said that I should buy stock in a hazelnut farm to cut my expenses. I think that may be a hint of some kind.

1 head garlic, unpeeled

1/4 cup plus 2 teaspoons extra-virgin olive oil

Soy sauce

1 cup hazelnuts

1 pound whole-wheat or semolina linguine

1 onion, diced

Sea salt

1/4 cup minced fresh parsley

1/4 cup reduced balsamic vinegar (see Note, page 234)

Parsley sprigs, for garnish

Preheat oven to 350F (175C). Slice the top (about 1/4 inch) off the garlic head and place in a small ovenproof dish. Sprinkle lightly with 2 teaspoons oil and a little soy sauce, cover and bake until soft, about 1 hour. Remove garlic from oven and allow to cool enough so it can be handled. Squeeze the garlic pulp from each clove and mash thoroughly.

Spread hazelnuts on a baking sheet and roast in the oven until fragrant, about 15 minutes. Transfer to a paper sack and seal for 10 minutes. Roll roasted nuts in a towel to remove most of the thin outer skins. They will not all come off. Grind the nuts into a coarse meal and set aside.

Cook linguine according to package directions until just tender.

While the linguine cooks, heat the remaining 1/4 cup olive oil, roasted garlic pulp, onion, and a generous pinch of salt over low heat until heated through; this will develop the flavors and render the oil and onion more digestible. Remove from heat and stir in parsley, reduced vinegar, and most of the hazelnuts, reserving a few for garnish.

Drain linguine; do not rinse. Toss sauce with the hot linguine and transfer to a serving platter. Garnish with remaining nuts and parsley sprigs. Serve hot. ✑

Makes 4 to 6 servings

Angel Hair with Red Peppers

The smoky taste of roasted red bell peppers is nicely offset by the crisp, fresh taste of snow peas. Sparklingly beautiful colors make this dish a terrific centerpiece for any meal. ✐

1 teaspoon corn oil
2 or 3 shallots, diced
Sea salt
Small piece of dried hot chile, diced
2 red bell peppers, roasted over a flame, peeled, seeded and cut into thin strips
1 green bell pepper, roasted over a flame, peeled, seeded and cut into thin strips

15 to 20 snow peas, trimmed
1 pound angel hair pasta
10 or 12 leaves fresh basil or generous pinch of dried basil
Spring or filtered water
Red bell pepper rings or parsley sprigs, for garnish

Heat oil in a skillet over medium heat. Add shallots and a pinch of salt and cook until shallot is translucent, about 5 minutes. Add chile, roasted bell peppers, and a pinch of salt and cook, stirring, 2 to 3 minutes. Add snow peas and cook, stirring, until crisp-tender, about 2 minutes. Set aside.

Cook pasta according to package directions until just tender to the bite. Drain pasta, reserving 1 cup cooking water; do not rinse. Return pasta and water to the pot. Add the cooked vegetables and basil and salt to taste. Toss well and transfer to a platter. Serve immediately garnished with red pepper rings or parsley sprigs. ✐

Makes 4 to 6 servings

Udon Noodles in Squash & Black Bean Sauce

Udon are a wide whole-wheat or rice-based noodle available in most natural foods stores and Asian markets. This hearty noodle is the perfect complement to this rich thick sauce. The savory taste of the sauce is nicely contrasted with fresh, lightly cooked broccoli.

1/2 cup black turtle beans

2 cups spring or filtered water

1/4 cup mirin

1 (1-inch) piece kombu

1 teaspoon light sesame oil

2 cloves garlic, minced

**1 medium leek, cut lengthwise and
rinsed well, then thinly sliced**

1 cup diced winter squash

Soy sauce

Small piece of dried hot chile, minced

1/2 cup Onion Stock (page 98)

**2 to 3 stalks broccoli, cut into
small flowerets**

Generous dash of umeboshi vinegar

**1 (16-oz.) package udon, cooked,
drained and rinsed**

Soak beans in 1/2 cup water and mirin 6 to 8 hours. Drain and discard soaking liquid. Place kombu and beans in a small saucepan with 1 1/2 cups water. Bring to a boil and cook, uncovered, 10 minutes. Reduce heat, cover, and cook over low heat until tender, about 45 minutes. (This step can be done ahead of time so that the dish comes together quickly.)

Heat oil in a deep skillet over medium heat. Add garlic, leek, squash and a dash of soy sauce and cook, stirring, about 3 minutes. Stir in chile and sprinkle lightly with soy sauce. Mash the beans until half broken and stir into leek mixture. Add stock, cover, and simmer 10 minutes over low heat. Add broccoli and cook over low heat until broccoli is bright green and crisp-tender, about 4 minutes. Liquid should have cooked away. Remove sauce from heat, sprinkle lightly with umeboshi vinegar, and mix gently.

Arrange pasta on a serving platter and top with sauce. Serve immediately. ✒

Makes 4 to 6 servings

Noodle Sushi

This is a great dish. I mean it. Making maki rolls sushi is easy. Your tool investment involves an inexpensive (about 99 cents—I told you it was inexpensive!) bamboo mat, available at most natural and Asian food stores. There's a trick to this dish that makes it a snap to make: the noodles are tied into bundles. You'll have to trust me on the filling. It may sound strange, but it is a wonderful study in contrasting tastes. Try it and see.

1 (8-oz.) package soba noodles
3 sheets of toasted nori
Peanut butter

Dill pickles, cut lengthwise into spears
Pickled ginger, for garnish

Cut several pieces of cotton string about 4 inches long. Remove noodles from the package and tie them into small bundles with several pieces of string, about 1 inch from the ends of each bundle.

Bring a large pot of water to a boil and cook noodle bundles until just tender to the bite. Gently drain, and rinse, without pulling bunches apart. Lay out a cotton towel and gently spread the noodle bunches flat on the towel. By bundling them, you eliminate the time it would take to straighten all the noodles out after cooking. With a sharp knife, trim away the short tied ends of the bunches and discard, because those parts did not cook thoroughly. Wrap the noodles carefully in the towel to absorb any excess water. I usually leave the noodles wrapped for about 1 hour before proceeding.

Next, lay a sheet of nori on the bamboo mat, shiny side against the mat. Place one-third of noodles flat against the nori, leaving 1 inch of nori exposed on the side away from you. Spread a thin line of peanut butter along the noodles on the edge close to you. Place pickle spears on top of the peanut butter to cover the length of the noodles. Using the mat as a guide, roll the nori around the noodles and filling, jelly-roll style, gently pressing as you roll. Wet the edge of the nori with moist fingers to seal the roll and press gently. With a sharp knife, slice the nori roll into 1-inch pieces and arrange on a serving platter, cut side up, and repeat with remaining noodles, filling, and nori. Serve garnished with pickled ginger. *Makes 4 or 5 servings*

Curried Lentils & Udon

Lentils are easy to cook because they do not require soaking and cook relatively quickly, in about 40 minutes. Combined with curried, sautéed veggies, this dish is infused with flavor. I love to serve it as a hearty stew in cold weather, complemented by some lightly cooked green vegetables on the side and a loaf of crusty whole-grain bread. ◎

1 (1-inch) piece kombu

1 cup green or brown lentils, rinsed
   and drained

3 cups Onion Stock (page 98) or
   spring or filtered water

Soy sauce

1 teaspoon extra-virgin olive oil

2 medium red onions, cut into
   thin rings

2 teaspoons curry powder, briefly
   pan-toasted to bring out flavor

1 cup fresh or frozen green peas

1 (16-oz.) package whole-wheat or
   rice udon

2 to 3 green onions, cut into thin
   diagonal slices, for garnish

Place kombu in a pot, top with lentils, and add stock. Bring to a boil and cook, uncovered, 10 minutes. Reduce heat, cover, and cook until tender, 40 to 45 minutes. Season to taste with soy sauce and simmer 5 minutes. Set aside, retaining any cooking liquid that remains.

Heat olive oil in a skillet over medium heat. Add onions and a dash of soy sauce and cook, stirring, until onions are translucent and slightly browned, 10 to 12 minutes. Sprinkle in curry powder, stirring to coat the onions, and cook about 5 minutes. Add lentils and a small amount of their cooking liquid and simmer, uncovered, 5 to 7 minutes. The mixture will thicken slightly. Stir in peas and simmer 1 to 2 minutes.

Place udon noodles in individual serving bowls. Top generously with curried lentils and broth and serve garnished with green onions. ◎ Makes 4 to 6 servings

Chilled Soba Noodles

A summer dish in traditional Japanese cooking, it serves us just as well in warm weather. Refreshingly chilled and served with spicy condiments and a rich dipping sauce, this simple noodle dish is appealing for lunch or dinner. I round out this meal with steamed vegetables or a fresh salad and lightly pressed pickles. ✒

Spring or filtered water
1 (8-oz.) package soba noodles
Dipping Sauce (opposite)
Condiments: thinly sliced green
    onions, fresh wasabi or hot chiles
    and very thin strips of nori

DIPPING SAUCE

2 cups Onion Stock (page 98)
1/2 teaspoon soy sauce
2 teaspoons brown rice syrup
2 tablespoons fresh ginger juice
    (page 242)
1 tablespoon brown rice vinegar

Bring a large pot of water to a boil and add noodles. Return the water to a boil and add 1 cup cold water. Return the water to a boil and add 1 cup cold water. Return the water to a boil for a third time. The noodles should be done. Drain and rinse well and drain again. Chill cooked noodles completely before serving. If they stick together, simply run cold water over them and drain well just prior to serving.

Prepare dipping sauce: Season stock with soy sauce and simmer over low heat. Stir in the rice syrup and ginger juice and warm 3 to 4 minutes. Remove from heat and stir in vinegar. Pour dipping sauce into small individual bowls. Place chilled noodles in individual serving bowls as well.

This dish is traditionally served accompanied by a condiment tray consisting of green onions, fresh wasabi or hot chiles, and very thin strips of nori. After each person dips noodles into the sauce, they eat them garnished with an item or two from the condiment tray. ✒ M a k e s 2 o r 3 s e r v i n g s

Pasta Primavera

Usually, this very traditional Italian dish is served smothered in a heavy cream sauce complemented by lightly cooked vegetables. My version creates a rich, white sauce without dairy, using slowly cooked onions to give the sauce a sweet, smoky flavor. Tossed with freshly cooked, crisp vegetables, it is a taste sensation. ✐

1 teaspoon extra-virgin olive oil

4 cloves garlic, minced

2 onions, diced

10 tablespoons whole-wheat
    pastry flour

Sea salt

2 cups rice milk

1/2 cup green beans, rinsed and
    cut into 1-inch pieces

1/2 cup thin half-moon slices
    yellow summer squash

1 medium carrot, cut into thin
    matchsticks

2 stalks broccoli, cut into small
    flowerets, with stems trimmed
    and sliced

1 (16-oz.) package fettuccine

Parsley sprigs, for garnish

Heat oil in a skillet over low heat. Add garlic and cook until fragrant, about 2 minutes. Add onions and a pinch of salt and cook, stirring, until onions are wilted and lightly browned, about 10 minutes. Slowly stir in flour to coat the onions and season lightly with salt. Slowly whisk in rice milk, stirring constantly to avoid lumps. Cook, stirring frequently, until the sauce thickens, about 5 minutes.

While the sauce is cooking, bring a large pan of water to a boil and separately cook each vegetable until crisp-tender: 2 to 3 minutes for the green beans; 1 to 2 minutes for summer squash; 1 to 2 minutes for the carrot; and 2 to 3 minutes for broccoli. Drain each vegetable and toss them together. Set aside.

Return the water to a boil. Cook the fettuccine in the vegetable cooking water until just tender to the bite, about 8 minutes. Drain well; do not rinse. Toss the hot fettuccine with the cooked vegetables and white sauce until all ingredients are combined. Serve immediately, garnished with parsley sprigs. ✐ M a k e s 4 t o 6 s e r v i n g s

Pesto-Filled Ravioli

This very rich-tasting dish is at its best when served in a simple sauce of warmed olive oil and minced fresh parsley—a bit of effort, but worth it for a special occasion.

Ravioli Dough
Pesto Filling
Extra-virgin olive oil and minced
   parsley or seasoned broth to serve

RAVIOLI DOUGH

2 cups semolina flour
1/2 cup unbleached white flour
Pinch of sea salt
About 1 cup cold water

PESTO FILLING

1 cup pumpkin seeds, lightly
   pan-toasted (page 404)
2 to 3 teaspoons sweet white miso
1/2 cup extra-virgin olive oil
2 cloves garlic, minced
1 cup tightly packed fresh parsley,
   coarsely minced
2 teaspoons umeboshi vinegar
1/2 teaspoon brown rice syrup

To make dough, combine the flours and salt thoroughly in a bowl. Slowly add water, mixing until a spongy dough forms. Knead on a lightly floured surface about 20 minutes, until the dough takes on a silky, firm texture. Wrap the dough in a damp cotton towel and allow to rest 30 minutes before proceeding.

Prepare filling: To make the filling, process all filling ingredients together in a food processor until a thick, smooth paste forms. Do not add any extra water. This paste needs to be very thick to work as a filling in ravioli that will be boiled.

On a floured surface, roll the dough as thinly as possible. Cut into 4-inch squares. Place 1 teaspoon of filling on 1 corner of dough square and fold into a triangle shape. Seal with fingers, crimping the edges or use a fork to seal the ravioli to create a decorative edge. Repeat until dough and filling are used up.

Bring a large pot of water to a boil and cook ravioli until tender; the time will depend on the thickness of your dough and size of your ravioli. They should be chewy, but not doughy or sticky. Drain ravioli, rinse gently, and serve tossed lightly with warm olive oil and freshly minced parsley. These ravioli are also delicious served in a lightly seasoned broth. Makes 4 servings

Tofu-Noodle Bake

This hearty casserole is an easy one-dish meal. I simply round out dinner with a fresh salad or lightly steamed vegetables. With all the rich flavors in the casserole, you really don't need much else. ✍

8 ounces firm tofu, crumbled

1 teaspoon white miso

1 teaspoon umeboshi paste

3 tablespoons roasted sesame tahini

1 teaspoon brown rice syrup

1/2 teaspoon soy sauce

4 to 6 tablespoons spring or filtered water

2 cups cooked small noodles (elbows, shells, bows, spirals, etc)

2 shallots, diced

1 carrot, diced

1 stalk broccoli (including stem), diced

1 (4-oz.) package brown rice mochi, very thinly sliced

Preheat oven to 400F (205C). Lightly oil a casserole dish. In a food processor, process tofu, miso, umeboshi paste, tahini, rice syrup, and soy sauce with enough water to make a creamy, spoonable paste.

Toss noodles and vegetables together and gently fold in the sauce. Spoon the noodle mixture into the prepared casserole dish, spreading evenly. Cover the top of the noodles with the thinly sliced mochi and sprinkle very lightly with water, so the mochi will melt. Make a loose foil tent over the casserole, without touching the mochi, as it will stick. Bake about 40 minutes or until mochi has melted. If mochi has not melted, sprinkle with a little more water and return to the oven for about 5 minutes.

When the mochi has completely melted, remove the cover and return casserole to the oven to brown the top, about 5 minutes. Serve hot. ✍

Makes 4 to 6 servings

Noodles with Pickled Ginger

The pickled ginger not only adds a unique flavor to this dish but also aids the body in assimilating the oil from the sautéing. ✿

1 (8-oz.) package udon noodles

1 teaspoon toasted sesame oil

1 clove garlic, cut into matchsticks

3 or 4 green onions, cut into thin diagonal slices

Soy sauce

1 cup button mushrooms, brushed clean and thinly sliced

1 carrot, cut into thin matchsticks

1/2 cup green cabbage, shredded

1/4 cup pickled ginger, diced (see Note, below)

Spring or filtered water

2 tablespoons sliced green onions or slivered nori strips, for garnish

Bring a large pot of water to a boil and cook the udon until three-quarters done, 4 to 5 minutes. Cooking will be completed when they are added to the wok to steam with the vegetables.

Heat sesame oil in a wok or deep skillet. Add the garlic, green onions, and a dash of soy sauce and cook 1 to 2 minutes. Add mushrooms and a dash of soy sauce and cook until mushrooms are wilted, about 3 minutes. Add carrot, cabbage, and a dash of soy sauce and cook until cabbage begins to wilt, about 3 minutes. Add ginger and stir in well. Spread the vegetables evenly over the bottom of the wok and top with noodles. Season lightly with soy sauce and add a small amount of water so that everything can steam. Cover and cook over medium heat about 7 minutes or until vegetables are tender.

Remove the cover and allow any remaining liquid to be absorbed. Stir well and transfer to a serving bowl. Serve garnished with sliced green onions or slivered nori strips. ✿ M a k e s 2 o r 3 s e r v i n g s

NOTE When purchasing pickled ginger, your best bet is a natural foods store. While available in Asian markets, most of the brands available there will have added sugar. So you must read labels before buying.

Cellophane Noodles with Sea Palm

This unique and quite beautiful dish was taught to me by my first macrobiotic cooking mentor, Geraldine Walker. The relatively strong taste of sea palm is nicely gentled by the neutral flavor of cellophane noodles. Dotted with colorful vegetables, this dish is an interesting presentation. ✒

4 ounces sea palm, soaked until tender (about 10 minutes) and sliced
1 teaspoon mirin
Spring or filtered water
8 ounces cellophane noodles
Soy sauce
Umeboshi vinegar

1 teaspoon light sesame oil
2 or 3 green onions, diced
1/2 red bell pepper roasted over an open flame, peeled, seeded, and diced
Corn kernels cut from 2 ears of corn
Sweet brown rice vinegar

Place sea palm, mirin, and 1/4 inch of water in a pressure cooker. Seal and bring to full pressure. Reduce heat to low, and cook 5 minutes. Allow pressure to reduce naturally and transfer cooked sea palm to a bowl, draining away any remaining liquid.

Bring a pot of water to a boil and cook cellophane noodles according to package directions until tender. Drain and rinse lightly. Place cooked noodles in a small bowl and season lightly with soy sauce and umeboshi vinegar. Toss well and allow to marinate 30 minutes.

Meanwhile, heat oil in a skillet over medium heat. Add green onions and a dash of soy sauce and cook, stirring, until onions are bright green, about 2 minutes. Add bell pepper, corn, and a dash of soy sauce and cook 4 to 5 minutes. Season lightly with soy sauce, stir in sea palm and cook, stirring, 5 minutes over medium-low heat. Remove from pan and toss gently with noodles and a generous dash of rice vinegar. Transfer to a bowl and serve immediately. ✒ M a k e s 4 s e r v i n g s

Crispy Chinese Noodles & Vegetables

A delicious tradition that you can serve at home, too. 🖋

1 (16-oz.) package udon noodles

3 teaspoons dark sesame oil

1/2 leek, cut lengthwise, rinsed well,
and thinly sliced

Sea salt

1 carrot, cut into small 1/2-inch chunks

1 cup small 1/2-inch chunks daikon

2 stalks broccoli, cut into small
flowerets, with stem trimmed
and diced

1 cup 1-inch pieces seitan

Soy sauce

1 to 2 teaspoons fresh ginger juice
(page 242)

Spring or filtered water

1 tablespoon kuzu, dissolved in
2 tablespoons cold water

Juice and grated zest of 1 lemon

Green onions, sliced, or parsley
sprigs, for garnish

Bring a large pot of water to a boil and add noodles. Return the water to a boil and add 1 cup cold water. Return the water to a boil and add 1 cup cold water. Return the water to a boil for a third time. The noodles should be done. Drain and rinse well and drain again.

Heat 2 teaspoons of the oil in a skillet over medium heat. Add noodles and cook, tossing, until they are coated with oil. Cook until the edges of some noodles get crispy. Transfer to a serving platter and cover while preparing the vegetables.

Heat remaining 1 teaspoon oil in the same skillet. Add the leek and a pinch of salt and cook 2 minutes. Add carrot, daikon, broccoli stems and another pinch of salt and cook 3 to 4 minutes, stirring frequently. Add seitan and broccoli flowerets and season lightly with soy sauce and ginger juice to taste. Add about 1/8 inch of water and cook until vegetables are crisp-tender, 3 to 5 minutes. Stir in dissolved kuzu and cook, stirring, until a thin glaze forms over vegetables, about 3 minutes. Remove from heat and stir in lemon juice and zest. Spoon mixture over crispy fried noodles and serve immediately, garnished with sliced green onions or parsley sprigs. 🖋 M a k e s 4 t o 6 s e r v i n g s

Spaghetti Pancakes

My mom used to make these from leftover spaghetti, fresh vegetables, ricotta, and mozzarella cheese. We thought they were the greatest thing. I have made a few changes in the recipe, like using mochi instead of cheese, but the essence of this dish remains intact. I hope your kids enjoy it as much as we did . . . and still do as grown-up kids . . .

3 to 4 teaspoons extra-virgin olive oil

1 small onion, diced

Sea salt

1/2 red bell pepper, roasted, diced

1/2 cup button mushrooms, brushed clean and diced

1 small carrot, diced

Soy sauce

8 ounces firm tofu

1 green onion, diced

Umeboshi vinegar

Spring or filtered water

1 (4-oz.) package brown rice mochi, grated

6 to 8 ounces leftover whole-wheat spaghetti

Heat 1 teaspoon of the oil in a skillet over medium heat. Add onion and cook, stirring, until translucent, about 5 minutes. Add bell pepper, mushrooms and a pinch of salt and cook until mushrooms are wilted, about 5 minutes. Add carrot, season lightly with soy sauce and cook, stirring, until carrots are crisp-tender, about 4 minutes. Set aside.

Crumble tofu into a food processor or blender. Add green onion and a dash of umeboshi vinegar. Process, slowly adding a small amount of water, until a coarse consistency, somewhat like ricotta cheese. Set aside.

To make the pancakes, heat remaining oil in a skillet over medium heat. Place about 4 tablespoons of mochi in the center of the skillet, forming a small circle. Top with a small bit of spaghetti, cooked vegetables, and tofu mixture. Cover with another 4 tablespoons of mochi. Fry on one side until crispy and golden brown and then turn the pancake over and cook the other side. Remove to a serving platter and repeat until ingredients are used up. Serve immediately. ❧ Makes 4 or 5 servings

White Lasagne

I am really not into "mock" dishes. You know the ones: vegetarian versions of conventional meat or poultry recipes—those disappointing copycat foods that never really taste like the real thing. If you continue to cook these kinds of dishes, even vegetarian versions, you will never really change your thinking about food or your way of being. ✎

2 recipes Béchamel Sauce (page 418)

3 tablespoons roasted sesame tahini

Soy sauce

Spring or filtered water

6 to 8 ounces whole-wheat lasagne noodles, cooked until almost done

1 onion, cut lengthwise into thin slices

1 cup button mushrooms, brushed clean and thinly sliced

2 or 3 stalks broccoli, cut into tiny flowerets

1 (4-oz.) package brown rice mochi, very thinly sliced

Preheat oven to 400F (205C). Lightly oil a 13 × 9-inch baking dish. Combine the sauce with the tahini and season lightly with soy sauce. You may need to thin it slightly with water to maintain the slightly loose, creamy consistency desired. Spread a thin layer of sauce over the bottom of the baking dish and add a single layer of noodles, taking care to completely cover the bottom of the dish. Top the noodles with a generous layer of sauce and then one-third of the vegetables, evenly distributed over the sauce. Arrange a few slices of mochi over the vegetables. Repeat until all ingredients are used up, making sure to end with noodles, then mochi on the top. Sprinkle lightly with water so the mochi will melt and cover loosely with foil, making a tent over the casserole. Bake 35 minutes or until mochi melts.

Remove cover and return dish to oven to brown the top, about 5 minutes. Allow the lasagne to stand about 15 minutes before cutting to allow the ingredients to firm up a bit. ✎ Makes 4 to 6 servings

Macro Chow Mein

A traditional crowd pleaser, this version has lots of fresh veggies served over homemade, crunchy chow mein noodles. I learned this version from Wendy Esko. ✎

Pasta with Tofu Cheese & Mushrooms

The original version of this recipe uses crumbled feta cheese. My nondairy version substitutes tofu cheese—a rich, cheeselike product lightly fermented in miso. The result is so much like the real thing (not to mention easy to make), you won't even miss the feta.

Safflower oil for deep-frying

1 (8-oz.) package whole-wheat spaghetti, cooked and drained

1 (1-inch) piece kombu

Spring or filtered water

1 onion, cut lengthwise into thin slices

1 carrot, cut into thick matchsticks

2 celery stalks, cut into thick diagonal slices

1 cup button mushrooms, brushed clean and thickly sliced

1 cup sliced water chestnuts, drained well

10 to 12 snow peas, trimmed

1 cup shredded Chinese cabbage

8 ounces firm tofu, cubed

Soy sauce

1 tablespoon kuzu, dissolved in 1/4 cup cold water

Green onion, sliced, for garnish

Heat about 3 inches of oil in a deep pot over medium heat. Add small batches of the spaghetti and deep-fry until golden brown and crispy. Drain well and set aside.

In a medium saucepan, place kombu and about 2 inches of water. Simmer the kombu 5 minutes and remove. Add onion, carrot, celery, mushrooms and water chestnuts to the pot and cook over low heat until just tender, about 5 minutes. Add snow peas, Chinese cabbage and tofu, season lightly with soy sauce, and simmer until cabbage is wilted, about 5 minutes. Stir in dissolved kuzu, and cook, stirring, until a thin glaze forms over vegetables, about 3 minutes.

Arrange fried spaghetti on a serving platter and spoon vegetables and sauce over top. Serve immediately, garnished with sliced green onions. &

Makes 4 servings

1 teaspoon extra-virgin olive oil

1 cup button mushrooms, brushed clean and thinly sliced

Sea salt

1 bunch watercress

1 pound small pasta (spirals, rotini, twists, etc.), cooked and drained

1 recipe Fresh Basil Pesto (page 426), substituting parsley for basil

4 ounces Tofu Cheese (page 162), crumbled coarsely

Heat olive oil in a skillet over medium heat. Add mushrooms and a pinch of salt and cook, stirring, until mushrooms are wilted, about 5 minutes. Set aside.

Bring a pot of water to a boil, blanch watercress for about 30 seconds, then plunge into cold water to stop the cooking process. Cut into small pieces and mix with mushrooms.

Finally, toss together pasta, pesto and vegetables. Gently fold in the crumbled tofu cheese just before serving. Arrange in a bowl and serve warm.

Makes 4 servings

Fettuccine with Broccoli

This is a colorful, full-bodied pasta entree sure to please even the most fussy eaters. It combines the smoky taste of roasted peppers with pungent olives, all nicely offset by fresh, crisp broccoli.

1 teaspoon extra-virgin olive oil

2 cloves garlic, minced

10 to 12 oil-cured olives, pitted and halved

1 red bell pepper, roasted over a flame, peeled, seeded and cut into thin strips

1 green bell pepper, roasted over a flame, peeled, seeded and cut into thin strips

Juice and grated zest of 1 orange

Balsamic vinegar

1 (8-oz.) package fettuccine

2 stalks broccoli, cut into small flowerets

1/4 cup minced fresh parsley

Parsley sprigs, for garnish

Heat oil in a skillet over medium heat. Add the garlic and cook until fragrant, about 2 minutes. Add olives and cook 1 to 2 minutes. Add bell peppers and cook, stirring, 3 to 4 minutes. Stir in juice and zest and simmer 2 to 3 minutes. Remove from heat and sprinkle lightly with balsamic vinegar. Set aside.

Bring a large pot of water to a boil, add fettuccine, and cook 3 to 4 minutes. Add broccoli and cook until broccoli is bright green and fettuccine is just tender to the bite, about 5 minutes. Drain pasta and broccoli and immediately toss with olive and bell pepper mixture. Gently fold in parsley and arrange on a platter. Serve warm, garnished with parsley sprigs. ⌇ Makes 2 or 3 servings

Linguine Rustica

A fresh vegetable sauce creates a kaleidoscope of colors and a symphony of tastes—the perfect topping for pasta. This makes a great meal rounded out with crusty whole-grain bread and a fresh salad. ⌇

1 (8-oz.) package linguine

1 teaspoon extra-virgin olive oil

3 cloves garlic, minced

3 to 4 shiitake mushrooms, thinly sliced

1 small leek, cut lengthwise, rinsed well and thinly sliced

Sea salt

2 carrots, diced

2 small zucchini, diced

1 1/2 cups Mushroom Stock (page 97)

2 teaspoons kuzu, dissolved in 1 tablespoon cold water

10 to 12 leaves fresh basil, minced, or generous pinch of dried basil

1/2 cup walnuts, lightly pan-toasted (page 417)

Minced fresh parsley

Parsley or basil sprigs, for garnish

Bring a large pot of water to a boil. Add linguine and cook according to package directions until just tender to the bite.

While linguine is cooking, heat olive oil in a skillet over medium heat. Add garlic and cook, stirring, until fragrant, about 2 minutes. Add mushrooms, leek, and a pinch of salt and cook until mushrooms are wilted. Stir in carrots and zucchini. Gently add stock and bring to a boil. Reduce heat and simmer, uncovered, until vegetables are tender, about 5 minutes. Stir in dissolved kuzu and cook, stirring, until the sauce thickens slightly and is clear, about 3 minutes.

Drain linguine; do not rinse. Stir linguine into the vegetables and season lightly with salt. Stir in basil, walnuts and parsley and simmer 1 to 2 minutes before transferring to a pasta platter. Serve immediately, garnished with parsley or basil sprigs. ✍

Makes 2 or 3 servings

Fusilli with Basil & Kale

This fun-shaped pasta with long spiraling curls makes a festive dish. Dotted with vegetables and tossed in a garlicky sauce, Roman-style, this recipe is a real attention grabber. ✍

1 pound fusilli

2 teaspoons extra-virgin olive oil

7 or 8 cloves garlic, minced

3 or 4 shallots, minced

Sea salt

1/2 cup sun-dried tomatoes, soaked until tender and diced

1 cup Vegetable Stock (page 96)

1 bunch kale, finely diced

2 teaspoons kuzu, dissolved in

1 tablespoon cold water

12 to 18 fresh basil leaves, minced, or generous pinch of dried basil

Bring a large pot of water to a boil and add fusilli. Cook until just tender to the bite, 8 to 10 minutes.

While fusilli cooks, heat olive oil in a deep skillet over medium heat. Add garlic and cook 1 to 2 minutes. Add shallots and a pinch of salt and cook, stirring, until shallots are translucent. Stir in sun-dried tomatoes and season lightly with salt. Add stock and simmer until tomatoes are soft, 6 to 8 minutes. Add kale and cook until kale is wilted and turns a deep green, about 8 minutes. Stir in dissolved kuzu until a thin sauce forms, about 3 minutes.

Drain fusilli; do not rinse. Add fusilli and sauce to pasta cooking pot and stir until fusilli is well-coated with sauce. Gently fold in basil. Transfer fusilli to a pasta bowl and serve immediately, garnished with fresh basil leaves. ✍ Makes 4 servings

Penne with Black Beans & Mangoes

This dish takes me back to my life in Miami, where the influence of Latin cuisine coupled with abundant tropical fruits made for incredibly creative approaches to food. This pasta entree is just one delicious example. ✹

1 (8-oz.) package penne pasta

1 teaspoon extra-virgin olive oil

2 to 3 cloves garlic

1 small piece dried hot chile, minced

1 onion, diced

Sea salt

1 cup cooked black turtle beans or
    organic canned beans, drained

Spring or filtered water

1 small ripe mango, peeled and cubed

Juice of 1 lemon

Minced fresh parsley

Bring a large pot of water to a boil and cook penne according to package directions until just tender to the bite. Drain, rinse well, and set aside.

Heat olive oil in a skillet over medium heat. Add garlic and chile and cook until fragrant, about 2 minutes. Add onion and a pinch of salt and cook, stirring, until onion is translucent, about 5 minutes. Top with beans, spreading evenly over skillet. Add 1/8 inch of water, cover and cook over low heat, uncovered, 10 to 15 minutes; the bean sauce will naturally thicken. Add mango pieces, season lightly with salt, and simmer 5 minutes or until mangoes are just tender. Remove from heat and stir in lemon juice and parsley. Arrange penne on a platter and spoon black bean sauce over the pasta just before serving. ✹ Makes 2 or 3 servings

Udon with Ginger-Scented Vegetables

This pasta dish is inspired by one of the many cookbooks I have turned to for inspiration over the years. The original dish is from Faye Levy; like most other recipes I have adapted, it has evolved and changed over time and, frankly, never comes out exactly the same way twice. ✐

1 (8-oz.) package udon noodles

3 tablespoons dark sesame oil

2 cloves garlic, minced

4 or 5 green onions, cut into thin diagonal slices

1 carrot, cut into long, thin sticks

Sea salt

1 cup finely shredded Chinese cabbage

1 tablespoon finely minced gingerroot

10 to 12 snow peas, tips and strings removed, left whole

Soy sauce

Bring a large pot of water to a boil and cook noodles until just tender to the bite, 10 to 12 minutes. Rinse noodles well and drain. Set aside.

Heat sesame oil in a wok over medium heat. Add garlic and green onions and sauté 1 to 2 minutes. Add carrot and a pinch of salt and sauté 1 to 2 minutes. Stir in cabbage, a pinch of salt and cook until wilted, about 5 minutes. Add ginger and cook 3 to 4 minutes. Add snow peas and season to taste with soy sauce. Cook until snow peas are bright green and crisp-tender, about 3 minutes. Quickly toss in cooked udon noodles and stir until ingredients are combined. Serve immediately. ✐ Makes 2 or 3 servings

Capellini in Creamy Mushroom Sauce

More delicate, milder sauces are perfect for capellini. Its thin strands easily absorb more gentle flavors. In this dish, mushrooms simmer in a savory broth with soy or rice milk to create a creamy sauce. ✐

1 teaspoon corn oil

1 onion, diced

Sea salt

2 cups button mushrooms, brushed clean and thinly sliced

1 portobello mushroom, thinly sliced

1 1/2 cups Mushroom Stock (page 97)

1/2 cup soy milk or rice milk

1 (8-oz.) package capellini

Fresh chives, minced

Heat corn oil in a medium saucepan over medium heat. Add the onion and a pinch of salt and cook, stirring, until onion is translucent, about 5 minutes. Add button mushrooms and a pinch of salt and cook, stirring, until mushrooms are wilted. Add portobello mushroom and a pinch of salt and cook, stirring, 2 to 3 minutes. Add stock and soy milk, season lightly with salt, and bring to a boil. Reduce heat and cook, uncovered, about 30 minutes or until the mushrooms are very soft and the sauce is flavorful and thickens slightly.

While the sauce is cooking, bring a large pot of water to a boil and cook the capellini according to package directions until just tender to the bite. Drain; do not rinse. Toss pasta immediately with the mushroom sauce and stir in chives. Transfer to a pasta bowl and serve immediately. ∽ Makes 2 or 3 servings

Fettuccine with Pecans

This dish was a challenge to put on paper; you can use just about any vegetables, herbs and even the nuts can vary. This is my favorite combination, but try this dish with yours. ∽

1 (8-oz.) package fettuccine

2 teaspoons corn oil

2/3 cup pecans, coarsely minced

2 cloves garlic, minced

2 or 3 shallots, diced

Sea salt

1 red bell pepper, roasted over an open flame, peeled, seeded, and cut into small strips

1 yellow summer squash, cut into thin matchsticks

4 or 5 Brussels sprouts, thinly sliced

1 parsnip, cut into thin matchsticks

Spring or filtered water

Green onions, cut into thin diagonal slices

Bring a large pot of water to a boil and cook fettuccine according to package directions until just tender to the bite. Drain, rinse well, and set aside.

Heat 1 teaspoon of corn oil in a skillet over medium heat. Add pecans and cook until lightly browned, about 3 minutes. Set aside.

In the same skillet, heat the remaining teaspoon oil. Add garlic, shallots, a pinch of salt and cook 2 minutes. Add bell pepper, summer squash, and a pinch of salt and cook 2 to 3 minutes. Stir in sprouts, parsnip, a pinch of salt, and 1/8 inch of water. Simmer vegetables, uncovered, until tender, about 5 minutes. Season lightly with salt and simmer another 5 to 10 minutes. The cooking liquid should be absorbed.

Toss cooked fettuccine with vegetables, pecans, and green onions. Transfer to a pasta platter and serve immediately. ✺ M a k e s   2   o r   3   s e r v i n g s

Baked Tempura Noodles

This very traditional dish is a real treat. It's not a complicated recipe, but there are several steps involved. Take heart; the finished dish is so rich and satisfying, that you'll completely forget the work as you sit back, completely sated. ✺

Tempura Batter (opposite)
Safflower oil for deep-frying
1 onion, cut into thick wedges
2 carrots, cut into thin diagonal slices
4 or 5 button mushrooms, brushed clean and halved
1 burdock root, cut into thin diagonal slices
1 parsnip, cut into thin diagonal slices
1 (8-oz.) package udon, cooked, rinsed and drained

1 to 1 1/2 cups Vegetable Stock (page 96)

TEMPURA BATTER
1 cup whole-wheat pastry flour
Pinch of sea salt
1 tablespoon powdered kuzu
About 3/4 cup dark beer or sparkling water

To make the batter, combine the flour, salt and powdered kuzu in a bowl. Slowly stir in beer until a thin, pancakelike batter forms. The batter should not be too thin. Set aside 30 minutes before using.

Heat about 3 inches of oil in a deep pot over medium heat. Coat vegetable pieces in batter, letting excess drip off, and add to oil. Increase heat to high. Deep-fry, in small batches, until golden brown and crispy. Do not fry too many pieces at one time or the oil temperature will cool and the vegetables will be oily instead of crispy. Drain the vegetables on paper towels. Repeat until all the vegetables are cooked.

Makes 4 servings

Preheat oven to 350F (175C). Lightly oil a deep casserole dish. Layer noodles and vegetables alternately until ingredients are used up, ending with vegetables on top. Pour 1 to 1 1/2 cups stock over the casserole, cover and bake 1 hour. Remove the cover and return to the oven 5 to 10 minutes to set up the casserole. Serve immediately.

Makes 4 servings

Spicy Peanut Noodles

A wonderful pasta dish flavored with peanuts and lemon. And incredibly easy—you'll have dinner ready in the time it takes to cook the noodles.

1 (8-oz.) package udon noodles	2 teaspoons fresh ginger juice (page 242)
1/2 cup natural peanut butter	1/4 cup minced, shelled, boiled peanuts
1 teaspoon brown rice syrup	Green onions, cut into thin diagonal slices for garnish
Dash of soy sauce	
Juice and grated zest of 1 lemon	

Bring a large pot of water to a boil and add udon. Return water to a boil and add 1 cup cold water. Return water to a boil and add another 1 cup cold water. Return water to a boil a third time. When the water boils the third time, the noodles are done. Drain and rinse well. Set aside.

Process peanut butter, rice syrup, soy sauce, lemon juice and zest, ginger juice, and peanuts in a blender or food processor until smooth. For a thinner sauce, add a small amount of water, but don't make it too runny. If it is too thin it won't stick to the noodles as well. Toss cooked udon with sauce and serve garnished with green onions.

Makes 2 or 3 servings

Deep-Fried Rice Noodles with Raspberry Sauce

This unique pasta dish incorporates a lot of flavors. The raspberry sauce is naturally sweet and tart. Add to that crispy, deep-fried noodles and you have a truly wonderful dish. 🍃

Safflower oil for deep-frying
1 package rice noodles, cooked and drained well (see Note below)

RASPBERRY SAUCE
1 teaspoon corn oil
2 shallots, peeled and minced

Sea salt
Spring or filtered water
1/2 cup soy milk or rice milk
1 to 2 teaspoons kuzu, dissolved in
1 tablespoon cold water
Raspberry vinegar
1 cup fresh raspberries

Heat about 3 inches of oil in a deep pot over medium heat. Add noodles, in batches, and deep-fry until crispy. Drain well on paper towels and set aside.

Heat corn oil in a saucepan over medium heat. Add shallots and a pinch of salt and cook, stirring, until shallots are translucent. Add about 1/4 inch of water and simmer 5 minutes. Stir in soy milk and simmer 5 minutes. Stir in dissolved kuzu and cook, stirring, until the sauce thickens and is clear, about 3 minutes. Remove from heat and stir in a generous dash of raspberry vinegar. Fold in fresh raspberries. Arrange noodles on a platter and spoon raspberry sauce on top. Serve immediately. 🍃

Makes 4 servings

NOTE Rice noodles can be found in Asian and natural foods stores.

Fusilli with Mushrooms, Asparagus & Sun-dried Tomatoes

A curly pasta is ideal for a dish like this one because it stands up well to the vegetables and traps the creamy, rich sauce in all its little nooks and crevices. ✑

2 tablespoons extra-virgin olive oil
2 to 3 cloves garlic, minced
2 to 3 cups mixed wild mushrooms (crimini, shiitake, or button), brushed clean, and thinly sliced
10 to 12 asparagus spears, cut into 1-inch pieces
4 ounces sun-dried tomatoes (not oil-packed), thinly sliced

Sea salt
1/4 cup mirin
4 ounces silken tofu
1/2 cup rice milk
1/4 cup minced fresh parsley
1 pound fusilli

Heat oil in a deep skillet over medium heat. Add garlic and sauté about 1 minute. Add mushrooms, asparagus, sun-dried tomatoes, and a pinch of salt. Cook until vegetables are tender and most of the liquid has evaporated, about 10 minutes. Add mirin and boil until reduced by half, about 3 minutes. Combine tofu and rice milk with parsley until blended. Stir mixture into skillet, season lightly with salt, and simmer until liquid is reduced to sauce consistency, about 8 minutes.

While the sauce simmers, bring a pot of water to a boil. Add fusilli and cook according to package directions just until tender to the bite. Drain well; do not rinse. Transfer to a large bowl. Spoon sauce over pasta and toss to coat. ✑

Makes 4 servings

Rice Noodles with Basil, Fresh Mint & Peanuts

Inspired by Vietnamese cuisine, I have changed this recipe slightly, using basil in place of the traditional cilantro. My dear husband refuses to eat anything remotely associated with cilantro, so I have learned to cook without it. ✍

1/4 cup brown rice vinegar

1/4 teaspoon soy sauce

1 tablespoon brown rice syrup

1 small onion, cut into thin rings

1 cucumber, peeled, seeded and sliced into paper-thin rounds, then halved

1 (8-oz.) package somen noodles

Safflower oil for frying

4 ounces firm tofu, cut into 1/2-inch cubes

Juice of 1 fresh lime

2 tablespoons light sesame oil

1/2 teaspoon dried, crushed red pepper flakes

1/3 cup tightly packed fresh mint leaves, minced

1/3 cup loosely packed fresh basil leaves, minced

4 green onions, cut into thin diagonal slices

3 fresh plum tomatoes (optional), seeded and diced

3 to 4 tablespoons shelled, boiled peanuts

Whisk vinegar, soy sauce and brown rice syrup together in a bowl. Add onion rings and cucumber and toss to coat well. Set aside to marinate at least 30 minutes or up to 4 hours, stirring occasionally.

Bring a pot of water to a boil. Add noodles and cook according to package directions until tender. Drain and rinse under cold water. Drain well. Set aside.

Heat about 1/2 inch safflower oil in a skillet over medium heat. Quickly shallow-fry the tofu cubes until golden brown. Drain on paper towels and set aside.

Whisk together the lime juice, sesame oil and crushed pepper flakes. Stir in mint and basil. Combine cooked noodles with fried tofu cubes, lime juice mixture, onions and cucumbers with marinade, green onions, and tomatoes. Toss gently to combine ingredients. Sprinkle with peanuts and serve. ✍ M a k e s   2   t o   3   s e r v i n g s

Fettuccine with Seitan & Sugar Snap Peas

A lovely, fresh pasta dish that says summer; this simple-to-prepare, one-dish meal is nicely complemented by a crisp summer salad and crusty whole-grain bread. ✑

10 to 12 ounces sugar snap peas, trimmed

1 or 2 carrots, cut into thin matchstick pieces

1 (8-oz.) package fettuccine

2 teaspoons extra-virgin olive oil

1 pound seitan, cut into 1/2-inch pieces

1/4 cup minced fresh parsley

1 to 2 tablespoons whole-wheat pastry flour

1 cup Vegetable Stock (page 96)

1/4 cup mirin

Sea salt

3 or 4 green onions, cut into thin diagonal slices

Generous pinch of paprika

Lemon wedges

Bring a small pot of water to a boil and boil snap peas 1 minute. Remove with a strainer and rinse under cold water. Add carrots, cook 30 seconds and drain. Rinse under cold water and mix with peas. Set aside.

Bring a large pot of water to a boil and cook fettuccine according to package directions just until tender.

While the fettuccine cooks, heat oil in a deep skillet over medium heat. Add seitan pieces and cook until golden brown, about 2 minutes, turning as needed. Transfer to a plate, cover loosely, and set aside.

In the same skillet, stir in parsley and flour and cook 30 seconds. Stir in broth and mirin and season lightly with salt. Simmer until sauce thickens, stirring constantly, about 2 minutes. Add peas and carrots and simmer 1 minute, stirring constantly.

Drain fettuccine; do not rinse. Arrange on a serving platter. Spoon sauce over fettuccine and top with seitan pieces. Sprinkle lightly with green onions and paprika and serve with fresh lemon wedges. ✑ Makes 2 or 3 servings

Capellini with Chile Sauce

A Mexican dish, *sopa seca* (dry soup), is served the same way Italians serve a pasta course. This version makes a great side dish, first course, or complete lunch entree. The lime slices are a must when serving, as they cool the fire of the chiles, and help the body assimilate the oil. ✎

4 fresh ancho chiles, stems, seeds and
  veins removed and minced
2 to 3 cups Vegetable Stock (page 96)
  or spring or filtered water
Generous pinch of cumin

2 cloves garlic, minced
Sea salt
1/4 cup extra-virgin olive oil
4 ounces capellini (packaged in nests)
1 to 2 limes, quartered

Place chiles in a saucepan with enough water to just cover and simmer 5 minutes. Remove from heat and allow to soak 5 minutes. Drain and set aside.

Pour 1/4 cup of the stock into a blender or food processor and add cumin and garlic. Puree into a smooth paste. Season lightly with salt, add 1 cup of stock and the chiles and process until pureed, adding more stock, if needed, to thin the sauce.

Heat oil in a large saucepan over medium heat. Add capellini nests and fry, keeping nests intact, until golden, turning as needed to brown evenly. Drain off any excess oil.

Add sauce to the capellini and simmer over low heat about 3 minutes, stirring occasionally to prevent sticking. Cover and simmer until pasta is tender, 6 to 8 minutes. Transfer to a serving bowl and serve with lime quarters. ✎

Makes 2 or 3 small servings

Penne with Vegetable Sauce

This traditional dish of sun-washed Apulia, Italy, is reflective of the fertile region that makes up the heel of Italy's boot. Apulia's abundant produce finds its way beautifully into a wide variety of pasta dishes. ✑

2 teaspoons extra-virgin olive oil

1 onion, diced

2 or 3 cloves garlic, minced

1 red bell pepper, roasted over an open flame, seeded, peeled, and diced

Sea salt

2 or 3 small zucchini, cut into 1/4-inch pieces

2 or 3 yellow summer squash, cut into 1/4-inch pieces

4 ounces sun-dried tomatoes (not oil-packed), soaked 10 to 15 minutes in warm water, then drained and diced

1/2 cup spring or filtered water

1 (8-oz.) package penne

10 to 12 leaves fresh basil, minced

Basil sprigs, for garnish

Heat oil in a deep skillet over medium heat. Add onion, garlic, and a pinch of salt and cook 10 minutes, until quite soft. Add bell pepper, zucchini and summer squash, season lightly with salt and cook until the vegetables begin to soften, about 3 minutes. Add tomatoes and water, cover skillet and reduce heat to simmer, cooking until the vegetables are soft and a sauce begins to form, about 10 minutes, adding water as needed to achieve a saucelike consistency.

While the sauce cooks, bring a large pot of water to a boil and cook penne according to package directions just until tender. Drain; do not rinse. Toss pasta immediately with sauce and minced basil and serve immediately, garnished with basil sprigs. ✑ Makes 2 or 3 servings

Tagliatelle with Green Beans

Another gem from Apulia. In this unique pasta dish the fresh green beans are simmered a long time so that they become soft. That way, you can twirl them on your fork along with the pasta.

1 tablespoon extra-virgin olive oil

4 cloves garlic, minced

1 red onion, cut lengthwise into thin slices

Generous pinch of crushed red pepper flakes

5 or 6 plum tomatoes, peeled and diced

1 pound long, thin green beans, trimmed and left whole

1/2 cup Vegetable Stock (page 96)

Sea salt

1 (8-oz.) package tagliatelle or linguine

Parsley sprigs, for garnish

Heat oil in a large saucepan over medium heat. Add garlic and sauté about 1 minute. Add onion, red pepper flakes and tomatoes and cook 2 minutes. Add beans, stock and a light seasoning of salt. Cover pan and reduce heat until mixture just simmers. Cook until the beans are very tender, about 1 to 1 1/2 hours, stirring occasionally and adding water as needed. Stir frequently near the end of cooking to prevent scorching.

Bring a large pot of water to a boil and cook tagliatelle according to package directions just until tender. Drain, reserving 1/4 cup cooking water; do not rinse. Return the pasta to the pot. Add the sauce and the pasta water to help sauce coat the noodles. Toss well and transfer to a serving bowl. Serve immediately, garnished with parsley sprigs.

Makes 2 to 3 servings

Orecchiette with Seitan & Broccoli Rapini

The sharp flavor of the rapini is best preserved, along with its vitamins, if you steam it. It is also a lovely complement to the rich taste of the seitan. ◎

2 pounds broccoli rapini, rinsed well
and drained

2 tablespoons extra-virgin olive oil

1 onion, cut lengthwise into thin slices

Sea salt

1 pound seitan, coarsely minced

3 or 4 cloves garlic, minced

Generous pinch of dried crushed red
pepper flakes

1 pound orecchiette

1/4 cup extra-virgin olive oil

Parsley sprigs, for garnish

Add about 1 inch of water to a large pot and bring to a rolling boil over high heat. Add rapini, cover the pot and steam until bright green, about 1 minute. Drain and set aside.

Heat olive oil in a skillet over medium heat. Add onion and a pinch of salt and sauté until onion is translucent, 3 to 4 minutes. Add the seitan and cook, stirring frequently, over low heat until browned, about 10 minutes. Stir in garlic and red pepper flakes and season lightly with salt. Cook until garlic has softened, about 3 minutes.

Slice rapini into small pieces and stir into skillet. Add 1/8 inch of water, cover and cook over low heat 5 to 7 minutes.

While the sauce is cooking, bring a large pot of water to a boil, add orecchiette, and cook until just tender to the bite, 15 to 18 minutes. Drain orecchiette; do not rinse. Transfer pasta to a serving bowl and toss with seitan, rapini sauce and the remaining olive oil. Serve immediately, garnished with parsley sprigs. ◎ M a k e s 4 s e r v i n g s

Penne with Cauliflower & Golden Raisins

Sautéed cauliflower with capers, golden raisins and pine nuts is a classic southern Italian combination. Tossed with penne, the sweet and pungent flavors are simply exquisite. ◎

1/2 cup golden raisins

1/4 cup mirin

1/2 cup pine nuts

1 head cauliflower, cut into small
flowerets

1/4 cup extra-virgin olive oil

3 to 4 tablespoons capers, drained
and lightly rinsed

Generous pinch of dried, crushed
red pepper flakes

Sea salt

1 pound penne

1/4 cup minced fresh parsley

Combine the raisins and mirin in a small bowl and soak 20 minutes.

Pan-toast the pine nuts in a hot, dry skillet over medium-low heat, stirring constantly, until slightly golden and fragrant, about 4 minutes. Set aside.

Bring a pot of water to a boil. Add cauliflower and cook about 5 minutes, until tender. Remove cauliflower with a strainer and return water to a boil for penne.

Heat oil in a skillet over medium heat. Add capers and sauté 1 minute. Add cauliflower and sauté until just beginning to brown, about 3 minutes. Stir in the pine nuts, raisins with mirin, and red pepper flakes. Season with salt. Reduce heat to low and simmer until the liquid is almost gone.

Cook penne in boiling water until just tender to the bite. Drain well, reserving about 1/4 cup cooking water; do not rinse. Transfer penne to a bowl. Toss with cauliflower sauce, cooking water, and minced parsley. Serve immediately. ✍

Makes 4 servings

Fettuccine with Leeks & Butternut Squash

This is a great winter pasta entree. Wide fettuccine is ideal for holding the hearty, creamy squash sauce. Served with lightly cooked greens and crusty bread, this dish is the stuff of dreams. ✍

2 tablespoons extra-virgin olive oil
2 or 3 medium leeks, cut lengthwise, rinsed well and thinly sliced
Sea salt
1 medium butternut squash, halved, seeded, peeled and diced
1/4 cup Vegetable Stock (page 96) or spring or filtered water

1 cup rice milk
1 pound fettuccine
1 teaspoon kuzu, dissolved in 1/4 cup cold water
1/4 cup minced fresh parsley

Heat oil in a skillet over medium heat. Add leeks and a pinch of salt and sauté until wilted, about 5 minutes. Add squash and a pinch of salt and cook, stirring frequently, 5 to 6 minutes. Add stock and rice milk and season lightly with salt. Cover, reduce heat to low and cook until squash is quite soft, about 10 minutes, stirring occasionally.

While sauce is cooking, bring a large pot of water to a boil. Add fettuccine and cook just until tender to the bite, about 10 minutes.

While fettuccine cooks, transfer squash and leek mixture to a food processor and puree until smooth. Return to skillet and simmer over low heat 2 to 3 minutes. Stir in dissolved kuzu and cook, stirring, until mixture thickens, about 3 minutes.

Drain fettuccine; do not rinse. Toss with sauce and minced parsley and serve immediately. ✍ Makes 4 servings

Basic Pasta Dough

To determine whether the dough has been kneaded enough, pinch some between your fingers, it should have the same consistency as your ear lobe. ✍

1 1/2 cups unbleached white flour
1 1/2 cups semolina flour

Pinch of sea salt
About 1 cup cold water

Combine flours and salt thoroughly. Slowly add water to form a spongy dough. On a lightly floured surface, knead the dough for about 20 minutes, until the dough becomes silky and smooth. Wrap the dough in a damp towel and allow to stand for 30 minutes before using. ✍ Makes 4 servings

VARIATIONS To make whole-wheat pasta, simply substitute whole-wheat bread flour for the semolina flour. To make buckwheat pasta, substitute buckwheat flour for the semolina.

Tricolor Spirals with Red Onion & Radicchio

A traditional dish from my mother's native Naples, it literally bursts with a symphony of flavors. A great starter dish or main course. 🌿

1/4 cup extra-virgin olive oil
2 large red onions, cut lengthwise
 into thin slices
3 to 4 tablespoons capers, drained
 and lightly rinsed
10 to 12 oil-cured ripe olives, pitted
 and minced

1/2 cup mirin
1 large head radicchio, shredded
Sea salt
1 pound tricolor spirals
Parsley sprigs, for garnish

Heat oil in a deep skillet over low heat. Add onions and cook, stirring frequently, until soft and just beginning to brown, about 30 minutes.

Add capers and olives to onion mixture and cook, stirring, 4 minutes. Add mirin and cook until liquid is almost gone, 4 to 5 minutes. Add radicchio, season lightly with salt, and cook, stirring constantly, until it turns a dark burgundy color, 3 to 4 minutes.

Bring a large pot of water to a boil. Add pasta and cook just until tender to the bite, about 10 minutes. Drain, reserving about 1/2 cup cooking liquid; do not rinse. Return pasta to the empty pot and toss with sauce and pasta cooking water. Transfer to a bowl and serve garnished with fresh parsley sprigs. 🌿 Makes 4 servings

SENSATIONAL SALADS ✍

Throughout the world, salads stand as a symbol of freshness and lightness. Salads make me appreciate the endless variety of foods available to us in the vegetable kingdom.

To the whole foods cook, salads are so much more than a plate of raw, limp lettuce, tomato and cucumber slices, with a couple of radish slivers thrown in for flair and drenched with a heavy dressing. Salad preparation is simply another way of living and eating in harmony with our surroundings. A wide range of cooking techniques and ingredients make salads a limitless culinary adventure.

John Evelyn, a seventeenth-century horticulturist, noted that a successful salad depended largely on the proper balance of ingredients. In Japan the success of *sunomono* and *aemono*, the traditional equivalents of salads, whose names translate to "vinegared" and "dressed," are centered around composition, harmony, and balance.

Until modern times salads have never been limited to servings of raw vegetables. The word *salad* derives from the Latin *herba salata*, meaning "salted greens," which is exactly what composed the original forms of salads. In traditional cuisine, the edible parts of green herbs and plants were tossed only with salt. It was intuitively known that processing raw vegetables with salt or vinegar was a way to create balance: the contracting energy of salt draws moisture from the expanded nature of raw vegetables, making them softer and easier to digest.

In warmer, traditional cultures, like Greece and Italy, salads were dressed with salt, plus oil and vinegar. The addition of these ingredients serves to balance the salt as well as lubricate the plant fibers, making them much more digestible. An added plus from the use of vinegar is the natural fermentation it causes in vegetables, again, a digestive aid.

Remember too, that human beings are not built to digest large quantities of raw foods. We have great difficulty digesting cellulose, the tough outer fiber that protects plants. Since we lack this ability, we invented methods of cooking, pickling and fermenting to break down foods for easier digestion.

It's interesting how we, as a culture, moved from traditional salads to the consumption of more raw foods. In terms of energy, raw vegetables have an expanded energy and a cooling effect on the body. This type of energy can help balance the contracting, heat-producing effects of meat, cheese, egg and poultry consumption. So the rise in popularity of raw foods can be directly linked to the increase of animal foods that we have seen in modern times. It is nature's way of attempting to restore balance under extreme conditions.

In whole foods cooking, salads resemble their traditional predecessors. I use a wide variety of cooked, marinated, pickled, and even raw ingredients to compose salads. I serve them, year-round, in various forms, as a means of adding light and fresh energy to my meals. I use just about anything to make a base for a salad. In this section, I would like to introduce you to a wide cross section of my favorites, including whole-grain salads, pasta salads, vegetable salads, bean and bean-product salads, sea vegetable salads (oh, be daring!) and the ever-glorious fruit salads.

Cooking methods for salads encompass just about anything in addition to and including not cooking. Typical salads from my kitchen might be boiled, blanched, pressure-cooked (yes, you read right, pressure-cooked), steamed, pressed, pickled, deep-fried, roasted, grilled and sautéed. Using one or combining several of these techniques has resulted in some wonderfully unique and satisfying salad dishes on our table.

VEGETABLE SALADS

Cucumber Dill Salad

Salads don't come easier than this one. Simply cut the vegetables, blanch the greens and toss with dressing for a dish that is so refreshing, you'll make it a regular on your summer dinner table. ◎

7 or 8 leaves of leafy greens, such as kale, collards and Chinese cabbage

Spring or filtered water

1 cucumber, thinly sliced into rounds, then cut into halves

1 recipe Lemon-Parsley Dressing (page 413)

Use one or more greens and cook in a pot of boiling water until bright green and just tender, about 5 minutes. Drain and cool in iced water to stop the cooking process. Drain well and cut into bite-size pieces. Toss the cooked greens and cucumber with the dressing. Chill several hours before serving. ◎ M a k e s   4   s e r v i n g s

Marinated Root Vegetable Salad

This is a simple, yet elegant winter salad. It has a robust taste, so I usually serve it in small amounts as a side dish. The white miso imparts a distinctly "cheesy" taste, which is nicely complemented by the sweet mirin. ◎

1/3 cup *each* thin matchsticks carrot, daikon, rutabaga, and turnip

2 teaspoons white miso

1 teaspoon mirin

1 teaspoon soy sauce

2 tablespoons spring or filtered water

Place vegetables in a medium bowl. Mix miso, mirin, soy sauce and water until smooth, pour mixture over vegetables and toss. Marinate at least 30 to 45 minutes before serving, tossing occasionally while marinating. ◎ M a k e s   4   o r   5   s e r v i n g s

Vegetable Aspic

Aspics are an unusual way to serve chilled vegetables. Cut into squares and served on a bed of lightly dressed wild greens, aspics are a unique approach to serving salads. This recipe is a particularly pretty version. ✎

1/2 cup *each* corn kernels, diced carrot, diced celery and tiny cauliflower flowerets

4 cups Vegetable Stock (page 96)

5 to 6 tablespoons agar-agar flakes

Soy sauce

4 or 5 cups torn salad greens

Lemon-Parsley Dressing (page 413)

Cook corn, peas, carrot, celery and cauliflower separately in the order listed by adding to boiling water, bringing back to a boil, removing with a slotted spoon, then cooling in iced water. Drain vegetables well and mix together in a shallow 1 1/2-quart casserole.

Place stock and agar-agar in a pan over medium-low heat and cook, uncovered, until flakes dissolve, about 10 minutes, stirring occasionally. Season lightly with soy sauce and simmer 7 minutes more.

Pour hot liquid over vegetables and allow to stand in a cool place until just beginning to gel, about 30 minutes. Chill thoroughly before cutting into squares. Serve on a bed of greens drizzled with Lemon-Parsley Dressing. ✎

Makes 5 or 6 servings

French Carrot Salad

This recipe was given to me by one of my dearest friends, Liliane Papin, a delightfully creative French cook. The naturally sweet salad is deliciously balanced by the delicate tart flavors of vinegar and lemon. ✎

2 cups grated carrots

3 tablespoons umeboshi vinegar

2 tablespoons extra-virgin olive oil

Juice of 1 lemon

Toss the carrots with the vinegar, oil and lemon juice. Allow to marinate at least 30 minutes in the refrigerator before serving. Toss occasionally while marinating to be sure the flavors blend evenly. Serve chilled or at room temperature. ꩜

Makes 4 servings

Warm Salad with Cranberry Dressing
The unique dressing makes this salad truly deluxe. I love to serve this as the final course at my holiday feasts. ꩜

Several leaves *each* of bok choy, kale and collards

1/2 bunch watercress

CRANBERRY DRESSING

2 cups fresh cranberries, picked over and rinsed

Juice and zest of 1 orange

....

2 or 3 tablespoons brown rice syrup

2 tablespoons extra-virgin olive oil

Sea salt

1 teaspoon powdered ginger

1/8 cup soy sauce

1/8 cup umeboshi vinegar

1/4 cup pecans (optional), minced and pan-toasted (page 417)

Lightly steam the greens separately in the order listed until bright green and just tender. Cool in iced water to stop the cooking, drain and cut into bite-size pieces. Place in a bowl and toss together. Set aside while preparing the dressing.

Prepare the dressing: place cranberries, orange juice and zest and rice syrup in a food processor and pulse until finely minced. Combine olive oil, a pinch of salt, ginger and soy sauce in a small saucepan over low heat and warm. Stir in cranberry mixture and simmer until warmed through, 5 to 7 minutes. Remove from heat and stir in vinegar. Toss with cooked greens just before serving. Top with pecans, if desired. ꩜

Makes 4 servings

Yellow Squash Salad

Bright colors blend wonderfully with the delicate flavors of these tender summer vegetables. I love to serve this salad at weekend brunches simply because of its cheery colors. 🍃

1 to 2 teaspoons extra-virgin olive oil
1 pint cherry tomatoes, quartered
2 or 3 yellow summer squash, cut into
　　about 1/2-inch cubes
2 or 3 fresh green onions, cut into
　　1/2-inch lengths
2 small Kirby cucumbers, cut into
　　1/2-inch pieces

1 to 2 tablespoons balsamic vinegar
1 tablespoon brown rice vinegar
Soy sauce, warmed over low heat,
　　3 to 4 minutes
Juice of 1 lemon
Juice of 1 lime
Several fresh basil leaves, minced

Heat olive oil in a skillet over medium heat. Add tomatoes, yellow squash and green onions and cook, stirring, until just tender, about 4 minutes. Stir in cucumbers and cook, stirring, 1 minute more. Transfer to a bowl.

Prepare the dressing: whisk together the vinegars, soy sauce, lemon juice, lime juice and basil. Pour dressing over vegetables and toss gently. This salad is best served warm, but it can be made ahead and served chilled. 🍃 M a k e s 5 o r 6 s e r v i n g s

Roasted Zucchini Salad

By the end of the summer, the zucchini that has taken over the garden has been used in just about every way I can imagine, everything from soups to breads to quiches to muffins to stirfries . . . well, you get the picture. This warm salad is a real end-of-summer treat. ✑

1/4 cup pine nuts or walnuts

2 or 3 fresh zucchini, cut into 1/2-inch sticks

2 or 3 yellow summer squash, cut into 1/2-inch sticks

About 2 tablespoons extra-virgin olive oil

Sea salt

About 1 teaspoon dried basil

Juice of 1 lemon

2 or 3 tablespoons balsamic vinegar

1 bunch bitter greens, like watercress or arugula, rinsed well and diced

In a dry skillet, lightly toast the nuts until lightly browned and fragrant, about 5 minutes, stirring. Set aside.

Preheat oven to 375F (190C) and lightly oil a baking sheet. In a medium bowl, toss the zucchini and summer squash with a small amount of oil and a sprinkling of salt and basil. Spread evenly on prepared baking sheet and roast, uncovered, until lightly browned, 15 to 20 minutes. Set aside to cool slightly.

Whisk together the lemon juice and balsamic vinegar, pour over cooked squash and nuts and toss. Serve warm over greens. ✑ M a k e s 5 o r 6 s e r v i n g s

Gazpacho Salad

I discovered this recipe in my favorite food magazine, *Food & Wine*. I must tell you that I have had great fun over the years adapting recipes from this publication. Some adaptations have been major overhauls and some, like this one, have only needed a bit of tinkering here and there. ✑

TOMATO VINAIGRETTE

2 or 3 tomatoes, peeled

1/2 red onion, diced

2 or 3 cloves garlic, minced

1/4 cup extra-virgin olive oil

Sea salt

6 tablespoons balsamic vinegar

3 tablespoons umeboshi vinegar

Tomato Vinaigrette (opposite)

6 cups diced whole-grain sourdough bread, crusts removed

2 or 3 ripe tomatoes, diced

1 cucumber, peeled, seeded and diced

1 red bell pepper, roasted over an open flame, peeled, seeded and diced

3 or 4 green onions, diced

2 tablespoons minced fresh parsley

Prepare the vinaigrette: puree the tomatoes, onion and garlic in a blender or food processor. In a small saucepan, warm the oil with a pinch of salt. Whisk in the vinegars and mix with the tomato puree.

In a medium bowl, toss the bread with half the vinaigrette and marinate about 30 minutes. Just before serving, mix together the vegetables, marinated bread, and remaining vinaigrette. Serve immediately. ✐ Makes 6 servings

Red & Green Cabbage Salad

A simple marinated salad that is delicious served warm or chilled. The easy miso marinade is complemented by the nutty flavor of the caraway seeds. ✐

MARINADE

3 tablespoons light sesame oil

3 tablespoons spring or filtered water

3 tablespoons white miso

2 teaspoons brown rice vinegar

2 tablespoons brown rice syrup

1/2 head green cabbage, finely shredded

1/4 head red cabbage, finely shredded

About 2 tablespoons caraway seeds

Bring a pot of water to a rolling boil. Add green cabbage and cook until just tender, about 5 minutes. Remove with a slotted spoon and place in a bowl. Add red cabbage to boiling water and cook until just tender, about 5 minutes. Drain, add to green cabbage, and toss with caraway seeds.

Whisk together the marinade ingredients until blended. Toss with warm cabbage and allow to marinate, tossing occasionally, about 15 minutes before serving.

Makes 6 servings

Italian Antipasto

Antipasto is one of the most delightful parts of an Italian feast. Simple or complex, these salads can be the starter for your meal or the meal itself! When I was in Italy, I learned that the only constraints on composing a great antipasto were the limits of the imagination. This is one of my favorite variations.

Marinade (opposite)

1 teaspoon extra-virgin olive oil

1 red onion, cut into thin rings

1 carrot, cut into thin matchsticks

1 cup thin matchsticks rutabaga

1 small turnip, cut into thin matchsticks

2 or 3 celery stalks, thinly sliced

1 cup button mushrooms, brushed clean and quartered

1 red bell pepper, roasted over an open flame, peeled, seeded and sliced into thin strips

About 1/4 cup ripe olives, pitted and left whole

Lettuce leaves

Whole-wheat crackers or toast points (optional)

MARINADE

2 teaspoons sweet rice vinegar

Juice of 1 lemon

2 teaspoons balsamic vinegar

1 tablespoon mirin

3 tablespoons extra-virgin olive oil

1/2 cup spring or filtered water

Pinch *each* of dried basil and rosemary

2 cloves garlic, minced

1 teaspoon dry mustard

Sea salt

Whisk together marinade ingredients, seasoning lightly with sea salt. Set aside.

Heat olive oil in a skillet over medium heat. Add onion and cook, stirring, until limp, 2 to 3 minutes. Add carrot, rutabaga and turnip and cook, stirring, 2 to 3 minutes. Add remaining vegetables and cook, stirring, until tender, 4 to 5 minutes more. Stir in marinade and simmer, uncovered, until liquid is mostly absorbed, about 10 minutes. Remove from heat and allow to cool completely before serving. Arrange on a serving platter over a bed of crisp lettuce. Garnish with olives. Serve accompanied by crackers or toast points, if desired. Makes 6 servings

Marinated Vegetable & Tofu Salad

Similar to antipasto, this marinated salad combines fresh crisp vegetables with lightly sautéed tofu cubes—a salad version of East meets West. This salad takes several hours to make, so it is probably best to put it together the day before you will be serving it. 🌿

Marinade (opposite)

1 carrot, cut into thin matchsticks

1 onion, cut in half through stem end, then thinly sliced crosswise

1/2 red bell pepper, cut into thin strips

1/2 yellow bell pepper, cut into thin strips

1 or 2 zucchini, cut into thin matchsticks

1-pound brick tofu

3 or 4 tablespoons dark sesame oil

1 clove garlic, minced

Soy sauce

MARINADE

1/2 cup barley malt

1/2 cup brown rice syrup

1/4 cup spring or filtered water

1/4 cup toasted sesame oil

2 cloves garlic, finely minced

Generous dash of soy sauce

Combine marinade ingredients in a small saucepan over low heat and heat 3 to 4 minutes, until warmed through. Toss with carrot, onion, bell peppers and zucchini. Cover and refrigerate about 4 hours, tossing occasionally.

Cut tofu into 16 cubes and pat with paper towels to absorb excess water. Heat sesame oil in a deep skillet over medium heat. Add garlic and cook 2 minutes. Add tofu and cook until golden on all sides, turning carefully. Sprinkle lightly with soy sauce and cook 2 to 3 minutes more.

Stir tofu into vegetables and marinate 3 to 4 hours more in the refrigerator, tossing occasionally. Serve chilled. 🌿 M a k e s   4   s e r v i n g s

Composed Salad Plate

This is a classic salad plate that will conjure up images of warm summer days in an outdoor French café. ✎

Herb Dressing (opposite)

Spring or filtered water

1/2 pound green beans, trimmed and cut into 1-inch pieces

3 or 4 whole red radishes

1 red onion, cut in half through stem end, then thinly sliced crosswise

1 small bunch watercress, rinsed and left whole

1 cup cooked white navy beans, drained

Several ripe olives, pitted and left whole

HERB DRESSING

2 tablespoons prepared mustard

2 tablespoons balsamic vinegar

2 or 3 tablespoons extra-virgin olive oil

2 cloves garlic, finely minced

1/4 cup minced fresh parsley

1/4 cup minced fresh chervil

Pinch of dried basil

Sea salt

Whisk together dressing ingredients, seasoning with just a pinch of sea salt.

Bring water to a boil in a pot over high heat. Add green beans and cook 1 to 2 minutes. Remove with a slotted spoon and cool in iced water. Drain and set aside. Add radishes and boil, whole, 2 to 3 minutes. Remove with a slotted spoon and cool in iced water. Drain and set aside. Add onions and boil 30 seconds. Remove with a slotted spoon and cool in iced water. Drain and set aside. Finally, stir watercress into boiling water and cook 30 seconds. Drain and cool in iced water. Drain and set aside.

Divide vegetables among individual salad plates, arranging the vegetables in an attractive design. I like to ring the plates with watercress, then arrange the onion, navy beans and green beans in the center and top the salad with several radishes and olives. Just before serving, drizzle the salads with the dressing and serve immediately. ✎

Makes 4 servings

Bitter Green Salad

Bitter greens go very well with a sweet-tasting dressing. For this particular combination of flavors, I have found that a raspberry-based dressing creates a delicious and satisfying final course.

Lemon Dressing (see below)

4 cups bitter greens (a combination of arugula, watercress, endive and radicchio)

1/4 cup walnut pieces, lightly toasted (page 417)

LEMON DRESSING

1 tablespoon soy sauce

2 tablespoons balsamic vinegar

Juice and zest of 1 lemon

1 to 2 tablespoons brown rice syrup

Pinch of sea salt

1 cup fresh or thawed frozen raspberries

Whisk together all the dressing ingredients, except the berries, and chill completely.

Rinse the greens very well and pat dry. Tear greens into bite-size pieces. (Do not slice, as the greens can take on an unpleasant flavor.) Arrange room-temperature greens on chilled plates. Stir raspberries into dressing and drizzle over greens. Garnish with nuts and serve immediately. Makes 4 servings

Mesclun Salad

A very nice spring salad. *Mesclun* is a term used to describe a combined assortment of tender baby lettuces and bitter greens, like arugula and radicchio. In this case, a sweet, citrus-laced vinaigrette completes the dish.

Orange Vinaigrette (see below)

4 cups mesclun mix, rinsed well and drained

ORANGE VINAIGRETTE

Juice of 2 oranges

1/4 cup balsamic vinegar

2 tablespoons umeboshi vinegar

1/2 cup extra-virgin olive oil

Several fresh chives, minced

2 or 3 teaspoons prepared mustard

Pinch of powdered ginger

Sea salt

Whisk together vinaigrette ingredients, seasoning lightly with salt to taste. Set aside.

Tear larger greens into bite-size pieces and, just before serving, toss gently with dressing. Divide among individual plates and serve immediately.

Makes 4 servings

Grilled Vegetable & Green Salad

This is a great dish; the smoky flavors of grilled vegetables complement the fresh, earthy tastes of spring greens. I like to use watercress or arugula in this recipe because of their distinct peppery taste. Serve this up with warm, crusty whole-grain bread for a delicious, light repast. ✒

Lemon-Miso Dressing (opposite)

1 red onion, cut into thick wedges

1 or 2 zucchini, cut into 1/4-inch-thick diagonal slices

1 or 2 parsnips, cut into 1/4-inch-thick diagonal slices

1 or 2 celery stalks, cut into 2-inch-thick pieces

1 red bell pepper, cut into thick strips

1 bunch watercress, large stems removed

2 tablespoons pine nuts, toasted (page 417)

LEMON-MISO DRESSING

2 tablespoons balsamic vinegar

Juice and grated zest of 1 lemon

1 tablespoon sweet white miso

1 to 2 tablespoons soy sauce

1/4 cup extra-virgin olive oil

Pinch of dried basil

Sea salt

Preheat grill or broiler. Whisk together dressing ingredients, seasoning lightly with salt to taste.

Toss all the vegetables, except watercress, with dressing. Arrange vegetables on grill and cook, turning, until tender, about 5 minutes.

Bring some water to a boil in a saucepan over high heat. Drop watercress into boiling water, drain, and cool in iced water. Drain and cut into bite-size pieces. Arrange the watercress around the edges of individual salad plates and heap the grilled vegetables in the center. ✒ M a k e s 4 s e r v i n g s

South-of-the-Border Salad

I love this salad, not only for its spicy citrus dressing but also for its beautiful colors. It really dresses up a table. I usually arrange the veggies on one big platter and serve them with the dressing on the side, accompanied by crisp tortilla chips.

Citrus Dressing (opposite)

Romaine, green leaf or red leaf lettuce leaves

1 cucumber, peeled and cut into very thin slices

1 or 2 oranges, peeled and cut into thin slices

1 cup cooked black turtle beans, drained

5 or 6 cherry tomatoes, halved

1 red onion, cut in half through stem end, then thinly sliced crosswise, blanched in boiling water 30 seconds (optional)

2 tablespoons pumpkin seeds, lightly toasted (page 382)

CITRUS DRESSING

Juice of 1 lime

Juice of 1 orange

1 teaspoon dry mustard

1 tablespoon extra-virgin olive oil

Generous pinch *each* of cayenne and cumin

2 or 3 pinches of sea salt

Whisk together dressing ingredients and chill while preparing the salad.

Tear the greens into bite-size pieces and arrange around the rim of a large serving platter. Then arrange the cucumber and orange slices in concentric circles. Heap the beans in the center, arrange the onion around the beans and sprinkle with cherry tomato halves. Sprinkle with pumpkin seeds and serve with the dressing on the side. ⌇

Makes 4 servings

Elegant Boiled Salad

There really isn't a more delightful complement to a hearty meal than a medley of simple boiled vegetables, not drenched in dressing or sauce, just nobly and beautifully served au naturelle. Sound boring to you? Trust me on this one. Served as part of a more complicated meal, this simple medley of fresh, lightly cooked vegetables will shine. 🍃

1 carrot, cut into thin rounds

1 cup finely shredded green head cabbage

1 or 2 yellow summer squash, halved lengthwise, then cut into thin slices

2 cups cauliflowerets

1 bunch hearty leafy greens (kale, collards, watercress or mustard)

1 cup thin matchsticks fresh daikon

1 red onion, cut in half through stem end, then thinly sliced crosswise

Cook carrot, cabbage, summer squash, cauliflower, greens, daikon and onion separately in the order listed by adding to boiling water, bringing back to a boil, removing with a slotted spoon, then cooling in iced water. When you get to the greens, boil them whole and then cut into bite-size pieces after cooling. When all the vegetables are prepared, simply toss together and serve warm or chilled. 🍃 M a k e s 4 s e r v i n g s

Grilled Vidalia Onion Salad

There is nothing sweeter (in my very own opinion) on earth than grilled Vidalia onions. This cooking technique really brings out the naturally sweet taste of these onions. Marinated in a light balsamic vinaigrette, this salad is a real treat. ✎

2 tablespoons extra-virgin olive oil

Juice of 1 lemon

Pinch of dried basil or several fresh basil leaves, minced

2 or 3 tablespoons balsamic vinegar

2 teaspoons umeboshi vinegar

2 large Vidalia onions, cut into 1/8-inch-thick slices

Green or red leaf lettuce

Preheat grill or broiler. Mix together oil, lemon juice, basil, and vinegars in a small bowl. Brush onion slices on both sides with oil mixture and grill until lightly browned on both sides and limp, 3 to 4 minutes per side. Arrange lettuce leaves on a serving platter and top with grilled onion rings. Serve immediately. ✎ M a k e s 4 s e r v i n g s

Italian Onion Antipasto

I am never really sure whether to serve this as a side dish or a warm salad. I lean toward salad, because smaller portions are better. ✎

4 large onions, peeled and ends removed

4 cloves garlic, peeled

4 pinches of dried thyme

Extra-virgin olive oil

Soy sauce

Spring or filtered water

4 to 6 leaves romaine or red leaf lettuce

Preheat oven to 375F (190C). Lightly oil a shallow casserole dish.

Stand the onions on their root ends in the casserole dish. Press a clove of garlic and a pinch of thyme into the center of each onion. Drizzle with a little olive oil and soy sauce. Add just enough water to cover the bottom of the baking dish, cover and bake 40 minutes. Remove cover and return casserole to oven for about 10 minutes or until onions are tender. Remove onions from casserole, slice into thick wedges and serve 2 or 3 hot wedges on lettuce. ✎ M a k e s 4 s e r v i n g s

Artichoke & Olive Salad

This salad has incredible flavor. I use jars of marinated artichoke hearts, which I lightly broil to give the dish a delicate, smoky flavor. ✑

2 (14-oz.) jars of marinated artichoke
    hearts
Extra-virgin olive oil
Generous pinch of dried basil
2 cups green or ripe olives, pitted

About 1/4 cup minced fresh parsley
1/4 cup pine nuts, lightly toasted
    (page 417)
Balsamic vinegar
Several radicchio leaves

Preheat oven to 375F (190C) or preheat broiler. Drain and halve artichoke hearts. Lightly oil a baking sheet and arrange artichokes in a single layer on oiled sheet. Drizzle with a little olive oil and sprinkle with basil. Bake or broil until lightly browned. Remove from oven and cool. Toss with olives, parsley, pine nuts and a light drizzle of balsamic vinegar. Serve warm or chilled on a bed of radicchio. ✑ M a k e s 4 s e r v i n g s

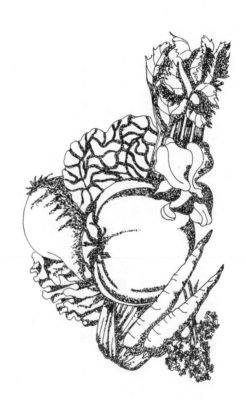

Broccoli-Cauliflower Terrine

This is a beautiful dish. I adapted the recipe from conventional terrines and created a rich, creamy version minus the heavy cream.

1/2 head cauliflower, diced

2 cups spring or filtered water

Sea salt

4 tablespoons agar-agar flakes

1/2 red bell pepper, roasted, diced

Umeboshi vinegar

**Several button mushrooms, brushed
clean and left whole**

2 or 3 stalks broccoli, diced

1/2 cup soy or rice milk

3 to 4 cups salad greens

Place cauliflower, 1 cup of the water, a pinch of sea salt and 2 tablespoons of the agar-agar in a saucepan over medium-low heat. Bring to a boil and simmer until cauliflower is tender and agar-agar has dissolved, about 10 to 12 minutes. Process in a food processor or blender until pureed. Transfer mixture to a small bowl and fold in bell pepper and a light seasoning of umeboshi vinegar.

Lightly oil an 8 × 4-inch loaf pan. Press plastic wrap into the pan and lightly oil plastic wrap. Spoon cauliflower mixture into the pan and spread it evenly. Take the whole mushrooms and slice off 2 sides of the caps, so that each mushroom has 2 flat sides. Press mushrooms vertically into cauliflower mixture, with flat sides touching. Allow to begin to set up while preparing the broccoli portion of the terrine.

Place broccoli, remaining 1 cup water, remaining 2 tablespoons agar-agar, a pinch of sea salt and soy or rice milk in a saucepan over medium-low heat. Bring to a boil and simmer until broccoli is tender and agar-agar has dissolved, about 10 to 12 minutes. Process in a food processor or blender until pureed. Cool to about room temperature before spooning it gently over the almost-set cauliflower mixture, spreading evenly.

Cover the terrine tightly with plastic wrap and chill 2 to 3 hours, until firmly set. Turn the terrine out gently onto a platter and cut into 6 thick slices. Each slice will show a rich green layer on top of the creamy, white bottom with a cross-section of a whole mushroom appearing in the middle. Serve chilled over a bed of delicate greens. ⟩

Makes 6 servings

BEAN SALADS

Navy Bean Salad

Serve this dish as a starter or side dish. It is especially memorable served with warm whole-grain bread and a light soup for a quick and easy summer dinner. 🌿

1 (1-inch) piece kombu
1 cup dried navy beans, sorted, rinsed and soaked overnight
3 cups spring or filtered water
1/4 cup *each* fresh corn kernels, diced carrot, thinly sliced green onion, and diced cucumbers
1 recipe Green Sauce (page 421)
Fresh parsley sprigs, for garnish

Place kombu on the bottom of a pot and top with beans and water. Bring to a boil, uncovered, and boil 10 minutes. Reduce heat, cover and cook until beans are tender, 40 to 45 minutes. Drain and cool.

Drop corn, carrot and, if you like, the green onion into boiling water. Drain, cool in iced water and drain again. Toss bean mixture with a generous amount of Green Sauce and serve garnished with parsley. 🌿 M a k e s 4 t o 6 s e r v i n g s

VARIATION This dish is also delicious if you puree the beans before adding the veggies, creating a most wonderful and unique pâté, dotted with vegetables. Serve in a pool of the sauce with toast points.

Italian Bean & Tomato Salad

With interesting ingredients, salads can become much more than plates of raw lettuce. This hearty salad, accompanied by warm, crusty bread, makes a summer meal all on its own.

About 3 cups shredded green leaf lettuce

4 or 5 cherry tomatoes, diced

2 celery stalks, diced

1 carrot, shredded

1 cup cooked Great Northern beans

2 tablespoons balsamic vinegar

3 tablespoons soy sauce

2 tablespoons extra-virgin olive oil

Generous pinches of dried rosemary and basil

Sea salt

Gently combine shredded lettuce, tomatoes, celery, carrot, and cooked beans in a medium bowl. Whisk together vinegar, soy sauce, herbs, oil, and a pinch of sea salt. Toss dressing with salad. Serve at room temperature or chilled. ❧ M a k e s 4 s e r v i n g s

Kissimmee Orange-Chick-pea Salad

I must confess. This recipe was originally designed to be a chicken salad, but the ingredients screamed "chick-peas!" to me. What do you think? ❧

1 (1-inch) piece kombu

1 cup chick-peas, soaked 6 to 8 hours

3 cups Vegetable Stock (page 96) or spring or filtered water

2 oranges

2 or 3 celery stalks, cut into thin diagonal pieces

3 or 4 fresh green onions, cut into very thin diagonal pieces

Several leaves fresh basil, minced

3/4 cup slivered almonds

Juice and grated zest of 1 lemon

1 tablespoon brown rice syrup

2 tablespoons prepared mustard

1 cup Tofu Mayo (page 415)

Sea salt

2 to 3 cups shredded mesclun mix or other tender greens

Place kombu in a heavy pot, top with chick-peas and water and boil, uncovered, over high heat 10 minutes. Cover, reduce heat and cook until beans are tender, about 1 hour. Drain and set aside.

Peel the oranges and with a sharp knife, removing all the bitter white pith surrounding the flesh of the fruit. Separate the segments and cut into small pieces. Set aside.

Mix together the chick-peas, celery, green onions, basil, almonds and oranges. Whisk together the lemon juice and zest, rice syrup, mustard, Tofu Mayo and a generous pinch of sea salt. Toss dressing gently with the salad and serve on a bed of greens, chilled or at room temperature. ✒ Makes 4 to 6 servings

Black Bean Salad

A very versatile salad. I love serving it chilled at a summer lunch or warm as the centerpiece dish of a hearty autumn or winter meal. Dressed lightly with a zesty citrus vinaigrette, this dish is a real crowd pleaser. ✒

1 (1-inch) piece kombu

1 cup dried black turtle beans, soaked

6 to 8 hours

3 cups spring or filtered water

1 red bell pepper, roasted over an open flame, peeled, seeded, and diced

2 or 3 celery stalks, diced

1 red onion, diced

1/4 cup minced fresh parsley

Zest of 1 lemon, grated

DRESSING

1/3 cup extra-virgin olive oil

Soy sauce

2 teaspoons umeboshi vinegar

3 tablespoons balsamic vinegar

2 teaspoons brown rice syrup

2 cloves garlic, minced

Juice of 1 lemon

Juice of 1 orange

Place kombu in a pot, top with beans and water and boil, uncovered, over high heat about 10 minutes. Cover, reduce heat, and simmer over low heat until beans are tender, about 45 minutes. Drain and transfer to a medium bowl. Stir in bell pepper, celery, onion, parsley and lemon zest.

To prepare the dressing, warm oil and generous dash of soy sauce over low heat 3 to 4 minutes. This makes them more digestible. In a small bowl, whisk together all the dressing ingredients and gently toss with the salad. Serve warm or chilled. ✑

Makes 4 servings

Chickenless Chicken Salad

This amazing salad has fooled some of the biggest chicken salad fans. It has all the ingredients that make a great chicken salad, except the bird! This salad is great on a bed of fresh, crisp greens or served as a hearty sandwich. ✑

1-pound extra-firm brick tofu

Soy sauce

Spring or filtered water

3 celery stalks, diced

1 small red onion, diced

1 red bell pepper, roasted over an open flame, peeled, seeded, and diced

1/2 teaspoon *each* basil, sage, rosemary and oregano

2 teaspoons paprika

1 to 1 1/2 cups Tofu Mayo (page 415)

Preheat oven to 400F (205C). Lightly oil a baking sheet. Cut tofu into 1/4-inch-thick slices. Place slices in a shallow dish and cover with a mixture that is 1 part soy sauce to 4 parts water. Allow tofu to marinate 10 minutes. Place tofu slices on oiled baking sheet and bake 30 to 35 minutes or until deep, golden brown and crispy on the outside.

Remove tofu slices from oven and allow to cool until you can handle them. Then, shred the tofu slices with a sharp knife, creating irregular, angular pieces similar to shredded chicken. Mix with vegetables, spices, and Tofu Mayo until ingredients are coated. Chill thoroughly before serving. ✑ Makes 4 servings

VARIATION Broil tofu for a few minutes rather than baking it.

Walnut-Watercress Salad

A lovely and simple side salad to be served warm or chilled with a smooth creamy dressing.

1 bunch watercress, rinsed well and
   patted dry
2 tablespoons walnut pieces, lightly
   toasted (page 417)

1 recipe Sour Tofu Dressing
   (page 411)

Bring a pot of water to a boil and add watercress. Cook about 1 minute. Drain and place in iced water to stop the cooking process. Slice into bite-size pieces and toss with toasted nuts.

To serve, toss watercress with dressing and serve immediately. Don't dress this salad too early; the heavy texture of the creamy dressing can really destroy the delicate nature of the watercress. Makes 4 servings

Country Bean Pâté

If you make this dish, be sure to have plenty of great bread to spread it on. It will go so fast, your head will spin. I like to lightly oil the bread and broil it until crispy brown before serving it with this creamy, incredibly easy-to-make, low-fat dip. An ideal party dish that actually allows the cook to enjoy as well.

2 cups cooked white navy beans
1 small onion, diced
2 cloves fresh garlic, minced
1/2 cup whole-wheat bread crumbs
2 teaspoons prepared mustard
Juice of 1 lemon

1 teaspoon brown rice syrup
1/2 teaspoon *each* dried basil and
   dill weed
Soy sauce
Lettuce leaves

Place all ingredients except lettuce in a food processor, lightly seasoning with soy sauce, and puree until smooth. Transfer mixture to a serving bowl lined with crisp greens, cover tightly with plastic wrap and chill thoroughly before serving. Makes 4 to 6 servings

Cooking the Whole Foods Way

Basil–White Bean Salad

Crusty whole-grain bread and freshly cooked vegetables are the ideal companions for this pesto-dressed bean salad. ✑

1 (1-inch) piece kombu

1 cup dried white beans

3 cups spring or filtered water

1 bunch watercress, blanched until bright green

2 or 3 celery stalks, diced

1 red bell pepper, roasted over an open flame, peeled, seeded and diced

PESTO

1/2 cup Tofu Mayo (page 415)

2 cloves garlic, minced

1 cup loosely packed fresh basil leaves

1 teaspoon white miso

1/4 cup pine nuts or walnuts

1 tablespoon umeboshi vinegar

1 teaspoon brown rice syrup

Place kombu in a pot, top with beans and water and boil, uncovered, over high heat about 10 minutes. Cover, reduce heat, and simmer over low heat until beans are tender, about 45 minutes. Do not season. Dice blanched watercress and toss together with beans, celery, and bell pepper.

Combine all pesto ingredients in a food processor and process until smooth. Transfer to a small bowl, cover and chill completely.

About 1 hour before serving, whisk pesto to loosen and toss gently into the salad. Transfer to a serving bowl, cover and chill about 30 minutes before serving. ✑

Makes 4 servings

VARIATION I must tell you that I also like to serve this salad warm, lightly warming the dressing and tossing it with freshly cooked beans just before serving, so the choice is yours.

Spicy Kidney Bean Salad

Kidney beans are large red beans that can really hold their own in a strong recipe. The dressing in this salad combines chiles, cilantro and citrus to create an unforgettable, spicy bean salad. ✐

1/2 cup pumpkin seeds (pepitas)

2 small poblano chiles

1 teaspoon extra-virgin olive oil

1 cup cooked kidney beans, drained

Sea salt

1/4 cup mirin (optional)

1 small turnip, cut into thin matchsticks

2 to 3 tablespoons minced cilantro

Juice of 1 lemon

Juice of 1 orange

Juice of 1 lime

1/2 cup Tofu Mayo (page 415)

Mixed lettuce leaves

Lime wedges, for garnish

Lightly pan-toast the pumpkin seeds in a dry skillet over medium heat until lightly golden and puffed, about 5 minutes, stirring. Set aside.

Roast the chiles over a gas flame or under the broiler until charred all over. Transfer to a paper sack, seal tightly and allow to steam several minutes before gently peeling away the outer skin. Remove stems and seeds. Dice the chiles and set aside.

Heat olive oil in a skillet over medium heat. Add beans, sprinkle lightly with salt and drizzle with mirin. Stir in the turnip and simmer until turnip is just tender, about 4 minutes. Remove from heat and stir in chiles, cilantro, citrus juices and Tofu Mayo. Just before serving, toss in pumpkin seeds. Serve on a bed of mixed lettuces, garnished with fresh lime wedges. ✐ M a k e s   4   s e r v i n g s

Tuscan Bean Salad

Any recipe that uses rosemary reminds me of my time in the hills of Tuscany. The aromatic flavor of this herb scented more foods than I can even remember. I especially love it mixed with delicate white beans and fresh vegetables to create this refreshing summer centerpiece dish. ✒

Rosemary Dressing (opposite)

2 cups cooked cannellini beans, drained

1 small red onion, finely diced

2 or 3 red radishes, diced

1 cucumber, seeded and diced

ROSEMARY DRESSING

1/4 cup extra-virgin olive oil

Soy sauce

2 to 3 tablespoons balsamic vinegar

Juice of 1 lemon

1/4 cup minced fresh rosemary

2 or 3 cloves fresh garlic, peeled

Prepare dressing: In a small saucepan, gently warm the oil and a dash of soy sauce. Remove pan from heat and whisk in the vinegar, lemon juice and rosemary. Set aside.

Take the whole garlic cloves and gently rub them around the interior of the salad bowl. This will give you the essence of the garlic with only a hint of flavor, without competing with the strong rosemary infusion.

Place the cooked beans and vegetables in the salad bowl and toss well with the dressing. Cover tightly and refrigerate several hours before serving, allowing the flavors to fully develop. ✒ M a k e s 4 s e r v i n g s

Peppery Chick-pea Salad

One of the most popular and versatile beans, chick-peas are always favorite salad ingredients, since they stand up well in both hot and cold dishes. My only caution is to remember to cook chick-peas very well, so that they are tender but firm, not crunchy. This salad draws upon a lot of Mediterranean dishes, laden with peppers, olives, and marinated artichoke hearts, lightly dressed in a garlic vinaigrette.

2 cups cooked chick-peas

1 *each* yellow, red and green bell peppers, roasted over an open flame, peeled, seeded and diced

1 small red onion, diced

10 to 12 oil-cured ripe olives, pitted and coarsely diced

1 (14-oz.) jar marinated artichoke hearts, drained and quartered

2 celery stalks, diced

Lightly steamed greens

GARLIC VINAIGRETTE

1/4 cup extra-virgin olive oil

3 or 4 cloves garlic, minced

3 to 4 tablespoons balsamic vinegar

Juice and grated zest of 1 lemon

Sea salt

Toss together all the ingredients except the dressing in a large bowl and set aside while preparing the dressing.

Heat oil in a small skillet over medium heat. Add garlic and cook about 1 minute. This infuses the oil with garlic flavor, while mellowing the sometimes sharp taste. Remove from heat and whisk in remaining ingredients. Toss with the salad and serve warm over a bed of steamed greens. Makes 4 servings

Tempeh Salad

Now, before you continue, I have to explain that when I was a kid my idea of fish was tuna salad or the crunchy outer coating of frozen fish sticks. As a grown-up finicky eater, I still didn't like fish, but remembered the taste of tuna salad. This is my vegetarian version of that type of creamy, sandwich-filler salad.

1 (8-oz.) package tempeh, steamed
    10 minutes
1/4 cup *each* diced carrot, red onion
    and celery

2 or 3 tablespoons organic sweet
    relish (from a natural foods store)
Generous pinch of dried dill weed
Tofu Mayo (page 415)

Cool steamed tempeh to room temperature and crumble into a coarse meal. Toss with diced vegetables, relish, dill and Tofu Mayo to form a creamy salad. Serve chilled over a bed of lettuce or in your favorite sandwich. Makes 4 servings

VARIATIONS Some people like to toss in some powdered kelp to create an authentic tuna-salad taste in this recipe. Also remember that if you would like the veggies to be more tender, simply blanch them before using them in the recipe.

Split-Pea Pâté
A pâté, this time featuring split peas, that is truly spectacular and amazingly easy to make.

1 cup split peas, soaked 4 to 6 hours
1 (1-inch) piece wakame, soaked
    briefly until tender and diced
3 cups spring or filtered water
Soy sauce
2 cups whole-wheat elbow noodles,
    cooked, rinsed and drained

1/4 cup *each* fresh corn kernels, diced
    carrot, diced onion and diced celery
Umeboshi vinegar
Lightly steamed greens

Combine peas, wakame and water in a pot and bring to a boil. Boil, uncovered, several minutes or until the foam that forms dissipates. Cover and cook over low heat until creamy, about 45 minutes. Season lightly with soy sauce and cook several minutes more. Turn off heat and stir in noodles, vegetables and a light sprinkling of umeboshi vinegar. Pour into an oiled, shallow 1-1/2-quart casserole dish and refrigerate until set. Slice into squares and serve on a bed of lightly steamed leafy greens.

Makes 4 to 6 servings

GRAIN SALADS

Brown Rice Salad

This is a refreshing way to serve brown rice in warm weather. The light citrus-scented dressing flavors the salad in the most tantalizing way. ✒

1/4 cup *each* corn kernels, green peas, diced carrot and diced celery

Small handful of watercress sprigs

Pinch of sea salt

3 tablespoons brown rice vinegar

3 tablespoons umeboshi vinegar

1/2 cup fresh orange juice

Grated zest of 1 orange

Juice of 1 lemon

1 tablespoon balsamic vinegar (optional)

2 cups cooked brown rice

Cook corn, peas, carrots, celery and watercress separately in the order listed by adding to boiling water, bringing back to a boil, removing with a slotted spoon, then cooling in iced water. Drain vegetables well and mix together in a bowl. Toss vegetables with sea salt and remaining ingredients except rice. Allow to marinate 30 minutes. Toss vegetables with rice just before serving or the rice will be soggy. ✒ Makes 4 servings

VARIATION You may substitute any cooked whole grain or pasta in this recipe, and you may use any combination of vinegars, lemon juice, etc.

Quinoa & Roasted Veggie Salad

A meal in itself. I was inspired by a fine Southwestern restaurant with this recipe. A few tweaks to their dish, and I had an easy-to-assemble salad that makes a great potluck dish—among other things! ✒

1 cup quinoa, rinsed and drained

2 cups Vegetable Stock (page 96) or spring or filtered water

Pinch of sea salt

Light sesame oil

8 slices gingerroot, cut into matchstick pieces

2 or 3 shallots, minced

1 teaspoon *each* dried marjoram and thyme

1 carrot, diced

2 or 3 celery stalks, diced

2 medium zucchini, cut into thin diagonal slices

2 or 3 parsnips, cut into thin diagonal slices

1 red onion, cut in half through stem end, then thinly sliced crosswise

2 red bell peppers, cut into thin strips

Several cherry tomatoes (optional), halved

Juice of 1 lemon

Soy sauce

To prepare the salad, combine quinoa and stock in a saucepan and bring to a boil. Add salt, cover and cook over low heat until all the stock has been absorbed, about 25 minutes. Fluff with a fork, transfer to a medium bowl and set aside.

Heat 1/2 teaspoon sesame oil in a skillet over medium heat. Add ginger, shallots, and herbs and cook, stirring, until shallots are translucent. Add carrot and celery and cook, stirring, until vegetables are just tender, 3 to 4 minutes. Remove from heat and stir in lemon juice. Mix into the quinoa and set aside.

Preheat oven to 400F (205C) and lightly oil a baking pan or shallow casserole dish. Arrange remaining vegetables in the pan and lightly drizzle with sesame oil and soy sauce. Roast, uncovered, until vegetables are tender and lightly browned, 20 to 25 minutes.

To serve, arrange a layer of roasted vegetables on individual plates and top with a generous scoop of quinoa salad. Serve warm. ∽ Makes 4 servings

Curried Rice Salad

A tropical twist on rice salad: aromatic basmati rice laced with shredded coconut and vegetables, scented with curry and complemented by the heady flavors of fruit—a wonderful warm salad. ∽

1 cup unsweetened shredded coconut
1/2 cup cashews
1 teaspoon safflower oil
2 cloves garlic, minced
1 onion, diced
1 tablespoon curry powder
1/2 teaspoon powdered ginger
1 cup brown basmati rice, rinsed

2 cups spring or filtered water
Pinch of salt
2 celery stalks, diced
1/2 cup dried currants
1 Granny Smith apple, cored and diced
3 or 4 green onions, diced
1 recipe Sweet Mustard Vinaigrette
    (page 414)

Preheat oven to 350F (175C). Spread coconut on a baking sheet. Lightly toast in oven until golden, about 3 minutes. Arrange cashews in a baking pan. Lightly toast in oven until lightly browned, about 5 minutes. Set coconut and cashews aside to cool.

Heat oil in a deep skillet over medium heat. Add garlic and onion and cook about 3 minutes. Stir in curry powder and ginger and cook, stirring, 2 minutes more. Stir in the rice. Slowly stir in water and bring to a boil. Add salt, cover, and cook over low heat 20 minutes. Add celery, currants and apples to rice. Do not stir. Cover and cook over low heat until all liquid has been absorbed, about 20 minutes.

Remove from heat and stir in cashews and green onions. Just before serving, stir in toasted coconut and Sweet Mustard Vinaigrette. Serve warm. ✿
Makes 4 servings

Sushi Salad
Don't panic! It's not a raw fish salad. It's a lovely rice salad laced with fresh vegetables, spices and shredded nori. ✿

2 tablespoons fresh ginger juice
    (page 242)
2 tablespoons soy sauce
2 teaspoons brown rice vinegar
1 tablespoon brown rice syrup
1 tablespoon toasted sesame oil
3 tablespoons diced red onion

Kernels from 1 ear of corn
1 cup fresh or frozen green peas
2 cups cooked short-grain brown rice
1/4 cup minced fresh parsley
2 sheets nori, toasted and finely
    shredded

Whisk together ginger juice, soy sauce, vinegar, syrup, and sesame oil in a medium bowl. Add onion, corn and peas and toss gently to coat. Allow to marinate 30 minutes.

Combine cooked rice, marinated vegetables, parsley and nori and serve immediately. ✍ M a k e s 4 s e r v i n g s

Italian Rice Salad

Rice is almost more prevalent than pasta in Italian cuisine. In some regions, it is more important. This recipe was a favorite during the hot summer months I spent in Tuscany, when cooking a lot wasn't a high priority. We served it hot or cold as a satisfying lunch dish. ✍

1 tablespoon prepared mustard

2 tablespoons balsamic vinegar

1 teaspoon brown rice syrup

Pinch of sea salt

1/4 cup extra-virgin olive oil

Juice of 1 lemon

3 cups cooked long-grain brown or white rice

1 red bell pepper, roasted over an open flame, peeled, seeded and cut into thin strips

3 or 4 green onions, cut into thin diagonal slices

1/4 cup capers, drained and rinsed well

1/2 to 2/3 cup oil-cured ripe olives, pitted and coarsely diced

2 or 3 cloves garlic, peeled

1/4 cup minced fresh parsley

Whisk together mustard, vinegar, syrup, sea salt and olive oil in a small saucepan. Warm over low heat 3 to 4 minutes. Remove from heat and set aside to cool. Whisk in lemon juice.

Mix together rice, bell pepper, onions, capers and olives in a large bowl. Add oil mixture and toss to combine. Rub the garlic cloves all around the interior of a salad bowl and discard. Transfer rice salad to the serving bowl and mix in parsley just before serving. Serve warm or chilled. ✍ M a k e s 4 s e r v i n g s

Wild Rice Salad

The rich colors of wild rice create a pretty contrast against the delicate white of polished rice. For this salad, it's okay to cook the rices ahead of time, but I usually toss everything together just before serving because white rice is so soft, it can get mushy if mixed in too soon. ✍

1/2 cup wild rice

3/4 cup white short-grain rice

2 cups spring or filtered water

Pinch of sea salt

Safflower oil for deep-frying

8 ounces extra-firm tofu, drained
    and cubed

2 tart apples, like Granny Smith,
    unpeeled, cored and diced

1/2 cup apple juice

Juice of 1 orange

Dash of umeboshi vinegar

Generous pinch of dried tarragon

1 bunch watercress

3 or 4 green onions, cut into thin
    diagonal slices

2 celery stalks, diced

1/4 cup pecans, lightly toasted
    (page 417) and finely chopped

Rinse rice well to remove excess starch and any dust that has gathered. Place rinsed grains and water in a deep saucepan and bring to a boil, uncovered. Add salt, cover and simmer over low heat until wild rice is tender and all liquid has been absorbed, 35 to 40 minutes. Stir gently to loosen grains and transfer to a bowl to cool.

Heat oil in a deep skillet to 375F (190C). Add tofu and deep-fry until golden and crispy, 3 to 4 minutes.

Whisk together the apples and orange juice, vinegar and tarragon.

Bring a small pan of water to a boil. Add watercress and cook until bright green and just tender, about 30 seconds. Drain and cool in iced water to stop cooking process. Drain again.

Form a ring of cooked watercress around the edge of a serving platter. Toss together the rices, onions, celery, tofu, apples, and juice mixture. Mound salad in the center of the platter and sprinkle with pecans. Serve at room temperature or chilled. ✍

Makes 4 servings

Brown Rice & Black Bean Salad

Inspired by Spanish cuisine, this salad seems to be at its best when made the day before, allowing the flavors plenty of time to fully develop. And what a delicious way to use up leftover cooked rice! ✑

1 teaspoon extra-virgin olive oil

2 cloves garlic, minced

1 onion, minced

Generous pinch of cumin

1 or 2 green chiles, seeded and
   minced

Soy sauce

1 1/2 cups cooked black turtle beans,
   unseasoned

Juice and grated zest of 1 orange

Brown rice vinegar

2 to 3 cups cooked medium-grain
   brown rice

1/4 cup slivered almonds, lightly
   toasted (page 65)

1/4 cup minced fresh parsley

Orange slices and parsley sprigs, for
   garnish

Heat olive oil in a skillet over medium heat. Add garlic and onion and cook, stirring, 2 to 3 minutes. Stir in cumin, chiles and a dash of soy sauce and cook, stirring, 3 to 4 minutes. Add beans and cook, stirring, 3 to 4 minutes, just long enough for ingredients to combine thoroughly. Remove from heat and stir in orange juice and rice vinegar to taste.

Combine bean mixture, rice, almonds and minced parsley and press firmly into a lightly oiled bowl or mold. Chill about 1 hour. Invert salad onto a serving platter just before serving and garnish with orange slices and parsley sprigs. ✑

Makes 5 or 6 servings

PASTA SALADS

Couscous Salad

Combined with chick-peas and vegetables and lightly dressed, this salad makes a deliciously satisfying one-dish meal. ✒

6 cups spring or filtered water
Pinch of sea salt
3 cups couscous
2 or 3 green onions, thinly sliced
2 or 3 red radishes, thinly sliced,
    then halved

1/2 cup cooked chick-peas
2 celery stalks, thinly sliced
2 tablespoons minced fresh parsley
1 recipe Istanbul Sauce (page 422)

Bring water and salt to a boil in a large saucepan over medium heat. Add couscous, reduce heat and simmer 5 minutes. Remove from heat and allow to stand in the pan, covered, 10 minutes. Fluff with a fork before proceeding with the recipe.

For a slightly milder taste, drop green onions and radishes into boiling water 30 seconds, drain, cool in iced water and drain before adding to other ingredients.

Toss all ingredients with sauce and serve. ✒ M a k e s 6 s e r v i n g s

VARIATION Bulgur may be substituted for the couscous in this recipe.

Pesto Noodle Salad

Traditional basil pesto has always been one of my favorite ways to dress pasta. And served chilled as a summer salad, it was hands-down the greatest. When I changed my diet, eliminating animal foods, I took great pains to create a healthy version that was as delicious as the pesto I was used to making. I think I did it. What do you think? ✑

1 (1-lb.) package whole-wheat noodles
1/2 cup extra-virgin olive oil
2 tablespoons white miso
1/2 cup pine nuts or walnuts, lightly
　　pan-toasted (page 417)
1 cup lightly packed fresh basil leaves
2 tablespoons umeboshi vinegar

....

1 teaspoon brown rice syrup
1 or 2 cloves garlic, minced
Spring or filtered water
2 stalks broccoli, cut into tiny flowerets
　　and steamed until bright green
Pine nuts, toasted (page 417) for
　　garnish

Cook noodles according to package directions. Drain and rinse well so that noodles do not stick together. Rinse until no warmth remains when you run your hands through the noodles. Set aside and prepare the pesto.

Place oil and miso in a small saucepan over low heat and warm through for a few minutes. Warming makes these ingredients more digestible. Combine oil mixture, pine nuts, basil, vinegar, syrup and garlic in a food processor or blender and process until smooth. Gradually add a small bit of water to make a thick creamy sauce.

Toss the cooked noodles and broccoli together and chill thoroughly. Separately chill the pesto. When ready to serve, toss together the noodles, broccoli and pesto with some toasted pine nuts for garnish. Serve chilled. ✑ M a k e s 6 s e r v i n g s

VARIATION This dish is also delicious served warm.

Oriental Noodle Salad with Cashews

A zesty, marinated salad with plenty of color and crunch.

8 ounces whole-wheat udon noodles

2 to 3 cups shredded Chinese cabbage
or bok choy

1 yellow summer squash, cut into
matchsticks

1 zucchini, cut into matchsticks

1/2 cup matchstick pieces daikon

1 carrot, cut into matchsticks

3 or 4 green onions, cut into thin
diagonal slices

Marinade (opposite)

1/4 cup cashews, lightly toasted
(page 417)

MARINADE

2 tablespoons dark sesame oil

2 tablespoons soy sauce

Juice of 1 orange

2 tablespoons sweet brown rice vinegar

2 teaspoons mirin

1 clove garlic, minced

Pinch of powdered ginger

3 to 4 tablespoons black sesame seeds,
lightly pan-toasted (page 414) and
partially crushed

Cook noodles, drain, rinse well and set aside. Combine cabbage, summer squash, zucchini, daikon, carrot and green onions in a large bowl.

To prepare marinade, warm oil and soy sauce gently in a small saucepan over low heat 3 to 4 minutes. Whisk remaining marinade ingredients into oil mixture and pour over the vegetables. Allow to marinate 30 minutes, tossing occasionally.

Just before serving, toss marinated vegetables and any remaining marinade with noodles. Stir in cashews and serve at room temperature or chilled.

Makes 2 servings

Warm Pasta Salad with Tofu Cheese

This hearty salad is a great one-dish meal: satisfying pasta smothered in a creamy mushroom sauce and tossed with fresh greens and crumbly, pickled Tofu Cheese. ✑

1 pound rotini, rigatoni, spirals or
    other pasta
2 cups Mushroom Stock (page 97)
1 small leek, sliced lengthwise, rinsed
    well and diced
2 cups button mushrooms, brushed
    clean and thinly sliced

Sea salt
3 or 4 leaves hearty leafy greens, diced
Generous pinch of dried rosemary
2 teaspoons kuzu, dissolved in
    1/4 cup cold water
1 cup crumbled Tofu Cheese
    (page 162)

Cook pasta in a large pot of boiling water until just tender, drain, rinse and set aside.

Bring 1 cup of the stock and leek to a boil in a saucepan and simmer 2 minutes. Add remaining stock, mushrooms and a light seasoning of salt and cook, covered, over low heat until mushrooms are tender, 5 to 10 minutes. Add diced greens, rosemary and dissolved kuzu and cook, stirring constantly, until sauce thickens slightly, about 3 minutes.

To serve, arrange pasta on a platter or in a bowl. Gently stir tofu cheese into sauce and spoon over top of pasta. Serve immediately. ✑ M a k e s 6 s e r v i n g s

Tofu Spaghetti Pancakes

I learned this recipe from Wendy Esko, a fine whole foods cook and instructor—and really fun friend. A unique take on pasta, these crispy, rich pancakes are always a hit at my table.

2 teaspoons corn oil

1 onion, diced

Sea salt

1 1/2 cups button mushrooms, brushed clean and thinly sliced

1 carrot, coarsely grated

Soy sauce

1 1/2 pounds brown rice mochi, coarsely grated

6 ounces spaghetti, cooked, drained and rinsed well

1/2 cup Tofu "Cream Cheese" (page 159)

1/2 cup ripe olives, pitted and sliced into thin rounds

Heat 1 teaspoon of the oil in a skillet over medium heat. Add onion and a pinch of salt and cook, stirring, 2 minutes. Add mushrooms, carrot and a pinch of salt and cook, stirring, 2 to 3 minutes, stirring occasionally. Season lightly with soy sauce and cook 2 minutes or until vegetables are tender. Set aside.

Heat remaining teaspoon of oil in a fresh skillet or on a griddle and tilt to distribute evenly over the pan's surface. Place about 4 tablespoons grated mochi in the center of the skillet and press with back of spoon to form a 4-inch round. Place a small handful of cooked spaghetti on top. Evenly spread about 3 tablespoons cooked vegetables over spaghetti and top with a tablespoon of tofu cream and a few olive slices. Sprinkle another 3 tablespoons grated mochi over top. Cover pan and cook over medium-low heat about 5 minutes. Gently flip the pancake and cook another 5 minutes. Both sides of the pancake should be golden and crisp. (If not brown, turn the heat up to high and cook until browned.) Transfer to a serving platter. Repeat process until all ingredients are used up, making 5 or 6 pancakes. Serve immediately.

Makes 5 or 6 servings

Noodle Watercress Salad

An elegant side salad that makes a great summer lunch or centerpiece dish for a summer brunch buffet. I like to serve this salad chilled and dress it just prior to serving so that the dressing stays smooth and creamy and doesn't get gummy, as can happen when a pasta salad is dressed too far in advance. ✍

1 red bell pepper	**1 bunch watercress**
1 cucumber, halved lengthwise, then sliced crosswise	**1 (8-oz.) package small shell pasta, cooked, rinsed and drained**
1 or 2 celery stalks, cut into thin diagonal slices	**1 recipe Creamy Sesame Dressing (page 413)**
1 or 2 green onions, cut into thin diagonal slices	**Several red pepper rings for garnish**

Roast the pepper by placing over an open gas flame or under a grill and charring outer skin. Transfer to a paper sack, seal tightly and allow to steam several minutes. Then simply rub the skin away gently with your fingers, removing all the black pieces. Halve the pepper, remove the seeds and slice into strips. Toss pepper with cucumber, celery and green onions and set aside.

Bring a saucepan of water to a boil. Add watercress and cook about 30 seconds. Plunge into iced water to stop the cooking process, drain and cut into bite-size pieces. Toss with other vegetables.

In separate bowls, chill the pasta, vegetables and dressing. Just before serving, gently toss all ingredients together, arrange on a platter or in a bowl and serve immediately, garnished with bell pepper rings. ✍ Makes 2 or 3 servings

Herald-of-Spring Salad

Nothing says spring quite like a lightly dressed pasta salad dotted with fresh, tender vegetables, in this case, lightly grilled and blanched. ✎

1 yellow squash, cut into thin
   diagonal slices
1 zucchini, cut into thin diagonal slices
1 red onion, cut in half through stem
   end, then thinly sliced crosswise
1 teaspoon extra-virgin olive oil
1 carrot, cut into thin matchsticks

1 cup fresh green peas
3 or 4 Brussels sprouts, quartered
1 cup matchstick pieces daikon
8 ounces whole-wheat udon noodles,
   cooked, drained and rinsed
1 recipe Green Goddess Dressing
   (page 411)

Preheat grill or broiler. Brush squash, zucchini and onion with oil and grill until tender and lightly browned, about 5 minutes. Set aside.

Bring water to a boil in a pot over high heat. Add carrot and cook 1 minute. Remove with a slotted spoon and cool in iced water. Drain and set aside. Add peas and boil 30 seconds. Remove with a slotted spoon and cool in iced water. Drain and set aside. Add Brussels sprouts and boil 2 to 3 minutes. Remove with a slotted spoon and cool in iced water. Drain and set aside. Finally, add daikon to boiling water and cook 1 minute. Drain and cool in iced water. Drain and set aside.

Just before serving, arrange grilled vegetables around a serving platter. Toss blanched vegetables and pasta with dressing and mound in the center of the platter. Serve immediately. ✎ M a k e s   2   o r   3   s e r v i n g s

SEA VEGETABLE SALADS

Sea Palm Salad
A beautiful and delicious salad that really showcases the delicate flavor of sea palm, nicely complemented by a light vinaigrette-type dressing.

**1 cup dried sea palm, soaked and
    sliced into bite-size pieces**
Spring or filtered water
Soy sauce
1 cup corn kernels

1 carrot, diced
1/2 red onion, diced
1/2 red bell pepper, roasted, diced
1 recipe Italian Dressing (page 412)

Dice soaked sea palm and place in a small saucepan with water to half cover. Sprinkle with soy sauce and bring to a boil. Reduce heat, cover and simmer until tender, about 35 minutes. Remove lid and allow any remaining cooking liquid to cook away.

Cook corn, carrot, and onion separately in the order listed by adding to boiling water, bringing back to a boil, removing with a slotted spoon, then cooling in iced water. Drain vegetables well and mix together in a bowl with bell pepper. Toss cooked sea palm and cooked vegetables with Italian Dressing and marinate 30 minutes, allowing the flavors to fully develop. Serve at room temperature or slightly warm. ✒

Makes 4 servings

Hiziki Ribbon Salad
A strong-tasting salad, nicely balanced with tender vegetables and a light citrus dressing. I serve this one in small amounts as a complementary dish to round out a meal. ✒

1 cup dried hiziki, rinsed well and
soaked until tender (about
10 minutes)
Spring or filtered water
Soy sauce
1 tablespoon mirin

3 or 4 red radishes, thinly sliced
Umeboshi vinegar
1 cup fresh green beans, French cut
1 yellow summer squash, cut into
matchsticks
Juice of 1 lemon

Place hiziki in a small saucepan with just enough water to cover, a dash of soy sauce, and mirin. Simmer, uncovered, until tender, about 25 minutes. If water evaporates too quickly, add a bit more and reduce heat so hiziki can cook thoroughly. Cooking, uncovered, gentles hiziki's strong flavor and brings out its natural sweetness.

While the hiziki is cooking, place radish slices in a small bowl and cover with umeboshi vinegar. Allow to marinate 15 minutes. Bring a small pan of water to a boil and separately boil green beans and squash until just tender, about 10 minutes for beans and 3 to 4 minutes for squash. Cool in iced water, drain and set aside.

When hiziki is tender and cooking liquid has completely evaporated, remove from heat. Add mirin, toss gently and allow to cool to room temperature before stirring in marinated radishes, blanched vegetables and lemon juice. Serve chilled or at room temperature. ✐ Makes 4 servings

Cucumber-Dulse Salad
Simple to make and very refreshing in summer weather, this salad is a must for hot sticky days. Packed with potassium, dulse is an ideal supplement to your diet during the summer months. ✐

2 cucumbers, peeled, seeded and cut
into very thin slices
Umeboshi vinegar
1 cup dulse

Juice of 1 lemon
Juice and grated zest of 1 orange
1/4 cup sunflower seeds, lightly
toasted (page 404) or blanched

Place cucumbers in a small bowl and sprinkle generously with umeboshi vinegar. Rub between your fingers to coat with vinegar and allow to marinate 1 hour.

Rinse and dice dulse. Toss with lemon and orange juice and allow to marinate 1 hour.

Just before serving, squeeze excess liquid from cucumber slices and toss with dulse, orange zest and sunflower seeds. Serve chilled or at room temperature. ◎

Makes 4 to 6 servings

Boiled Salad with Wakame

This simple salad of lightly cooked vegetables is made more interesting by the addition of gently marinated wakame.

1 carrot, cut into thin rounds
1 cup small cauliflowerets
2 stalks broccoli, cut into small flowerets
1 cup sliced fresh daikon
1/2 cup wakame, soaked until tender (3 to 4 minutes)

Brown rice vinegar
Umeboshi vinegar
2 tablespoons balsamic vinegar
2 teaspoons mirin

Bring a pot of water to a boil over high heat. Add carrot and cook 1 minute. Remove with a slotted spoon and cool in iced water. Drain and set aside. Add cauliflower and boil 2 to 3 minutes. Remove with a slotted spoon and cool in iced water. Drain and set aside. Add broccoli and boil 2 to 3 minutes. Remove with a slotted spoon and cool in iced water. Drain and set aside. Finally, add daikon to boiling water and cook 2 minutes. Remove with a slotted spoon and cool in iced water. Drain and set aside.

Slice wakame into thin pieces. Toss with vinegars and mirin and marinate 15 to 20 minutes. Finally, toss vegetables with wakame and marinade and serve. ◎

Makes 4 servings

FRUIT SALADS

Fire & Ice Melon Salad

This is a refreshing summer salad of sweet, tender melon and fiery picante sauce. ✒

1 cup honeydew melon balls

1 cup cantaloupe balls

1 cup watermelon balls

2 tablespoons medium-hot picante sauce

1 tablespoon brown rice syrup

Juice of 1 lime

Lettuce

Combine melon balls in a bowl. Whisk together the picante sauce, rice syrup, and lime juice. Toss gently with melons and serve on a bed of crisp lettuce. Serve at room temperature or nicely chilled. ✒ Makes 4 servings

Winter Pear Salad

A crunchy salad with a symphony of flavors. I like to serve this salad with the dressing lightly warmed. It adds a nice bit of freshness to the usual heartier fare that makes up winter cooking. ✒

1 bunch watercress

2 cups shredded radicchio

6 Bosc or Bartlett pears, cored and
thinly sliced

1 cup crumbled Tofu Cheese
(page 162)

1 cup walnut pieces, lightly
pan-toasted (page 417)

1 cup pecan pieces, lightly pan-toasted
(page 417)

1 cup raspberries, preferably fresh,
but frozen will work

1/4 cup minced fresh parsley

DRESSING

1/4 cup balsamic vinegar

1/4 cup extra-virgin olive oil

3 tablespoons apple juice

Pinch of sea salt

1/2 teaspoon powdered ginger

Bring a saucepan of water to a boil. Add watercress and cook about 30 seconds. Plunge into iced water to stop the cooking process, drain, and cut into bite-size pieces. Toss with shredded radicchio and arrange on a large salad platter. Arrange pear slices decoratively in fan shapes over the greens and sprinkle with tofu cheese, nuts, raspberries and parsley.

Whisk together dressing ingredients in a small saucepan and gently warm over low heat. Just before serving, drizzle over pear salad. Serve at room temperature with warm dressing. Makes 6 to 8 servings

Marinated Strawberry Salad

A wonderfully unique way to serve fresh strawberries. The delicate taste of the sweetened vinegar dressing enhances the natural flavor of the berries but doesn't overpower their natural sweet taste.

1 quart fresh strawberries, hulled
but left whole

1/2 cup balsamic vinegar

Juice of 1 lemon

3 tablespoons maple syrup granules

Arrange berries in a bowl. Whisk together vinegar, lemon juice and maple granules in a small bowl. Toss gently with berries and allow to stand 15 to 30 minutes before serving at room temperature or chilled. Makes 4 to 6 servings

Fruit & Radish Slaw

A perfect side dish for winter, when produce is at its most scarce. This sweet, fresh-tasting salad combines a variety of ingredients for a most delicious result. 🌿

1/4 cup sunflower kernels

2 to 3 cups shredded Chinese cabbage

1 carrot, cut into matchsticks

3 or 4 red radishes, cut into thin half moons

1/2 cup raisins or dried currants

1 tart apple, cored and diced

2 tablespoons sweet brown rice vinegar

2 teaspoons brown rice syrup

Sea salt

Juice and grated zest of 1 orange

Juice of 1 lemon

Lightly toast the kernels in a small, dry skillet over medium heat until golden and fragrant, about 5 minutes, stirring. Set aside.

Bring a pot of water to a boil over high heat. Add cabbage and cook 1 to 2 minutes. Remove with a slotted spoon and cool in iced water. Drain and set aside. Add carrot and boil 1 minute. Remove with a slotted spoon and cool in iced water. Drain and set aside. Finally, add radishes and boil 10 seconds. Drain and cool in iced water. Drain and set aside.

Toss seeds, blanched vegetables, raisins and apple together. Whisk vinegar, rice syrup, a pinch of salt, orange zest and juice, and lemon juice together. Gently toss dressing with salad and serve warm. 🌿 Makes 4 servings

Radicchio & Apple Salad

The creamy poppy seed dressing is a nice addition to this hearty autumn salad. I like to serve this when apples are at their peak. Use only crisp fresh apples. ✎

1 large Granny Smith apple, cored
and cut into thin slices

1 large Golden Delicious apple, cored
and cut into thin slices

1 large Red Delicious apple, cored
and cut into thin slices

2 teaspoons lemon juice

2 teaspoons spring or filtered water

3 or 4 large radicchio leaves, shredded

Creamy Poppy Seed Dressing
(opposite)

1/2 cup pecan pieces, lightly toasted
(page 417)

CREAMY POPPY SEED DRESSING

4 ounces silken tofu

1/2 teaspoon poppy seeds

Juice of 1 lemon

2 teaspoons brown rice syrup

Dash of umeboshi vinegar

2 tablespoons spring or filtered water

Working quickly so the apples do not discolor, toss the slices in lemon juice and water. Arrange shredded radicchio on a salad platter. Decoratively arrange apple slices on top.

To prepare the dressing, bring a small pot of water to a boil over medium heat. Add tofu and cook 5 minutes. Drain well.

Transfer tofu to a food processor or blender, add remaining ingredients, except water, and puree until smooth. Add a small amount of water if needed to make a spoonable dressing.

Spoon dressing over apples and radicchio leaves and sprinkle with pecan pieces just before serving. Serve at room temperature. ✎ M a k e s 4 s e r v i n g s

Fruit & Veggie Platter with Citrus Dressing

A crunchy, refreshing summer treat of a salad, with exotic jicama as the featured ingredient. Tossed with a zippy citrus dressing, it's a sure bet to cool down hot summer days. 🌿

1 tart apple, cored and thinly sliced

1 teaspoon lemon juice

1 to 2 cups matchstick pieces jicama

1 red bell pepper, roasted, cut into thin strips

3 oranges, peeled and thinly sliced

1 small cucumber, peeled and thinly sliced

CITRUS DRESSING

1/2 cup fresh orange juice

Juice of 1 lime

Juice of 1 lemon

1/4 cup minced fresh parsley

1 tablespoon extra-virgin olive oil

Grated zest of 1 orange

Toss apple slices in lemon juice to prevent discoloration. Arrange apple, jicama, bell pepper, oranges and cucumber attractively on a platter.

Whisk together dressing ingredients in a small bowl and spoon over vegetables. Allow to marinate 15 to 20 minutes before serving. 🌿 Makes 4 servings

Apricot-Almond Salad

A unique combination of colors, flavors, and textures compose this creamy salad. Serve this dish when you want your meal to have a distinctive flair. ℐ

4 ounces silken tofu

1 clove garlic, minced

1/4 teaspoon sea salt

Spring or filtered water

1 cup dried apricots, soaked in warm water until soft (about 30 minutes)

1 red onion, diced

1/2 red bell pepper, roasted over an open flame, peeled, seeded, and diced

2 celery stalks, diced

Generous pinch of dried basil

1/4 to 1/2 cup slivered almonds, lightly toasted (page 65)

Romaine lettuce leaves

Bring a small pot of water to a boil over medium heat. Add tofu and cook 5 minutes. Drain well.

Transfer tofu to a food processor or blender. Add garlic and salt and process until smooth, adding a small amount of water to achieve a creamy dressing. Spoon into a small bowl and allow to stand 15 minutes.

Dice softened apricots and gently fold into tofu dressing. Toss with onion, bell pepper, celery, basil and almonds. Serve on a bed of crisp lettuce leaves. ℐ

Makes 4 servings

American Fruit & Red Onion Salad

This salad capitalizes on America's love of fruit. But I balance it with the peppery taste of red onions, all lightly marinated—a unique take on fruit salad. 🍃

1 bunch kale or collards, lightly
  steamed
1 red onion, cut into thin rings
2 oranges, peeled and cut into
  thin rings
10 to 12 fresh strawberries, thinly
  sliced

1/2 cup fresh blueberries

DRESSING

1 tablespoon umeboshi vinegar
2 tablespoons balsamic vinegar
1 teaspoon brown rice syrup
Dash of soy sauce

Arrange steamed greens on a serving platter, top with onion rings, then with oranges. Arrange berry slices and blueberries over onion and oranges.

Whisk together dressing ingredients in a small bowl and drizzle over salad. Allow to marinate 30 minutes to 1 hour before serving. 🍃 M a k e s 4 s e r v i n g s

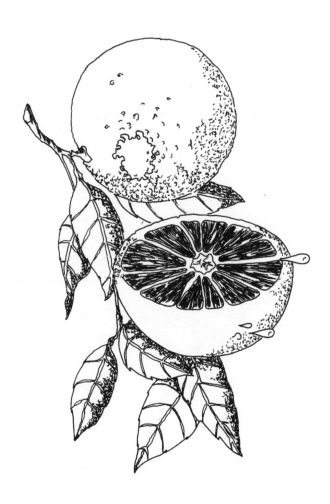

SASSY SAUCES
& DRESSINGS

There is nothing more basic to the preparation of a fine dish than the dressing or sauce that may accompany it. This section includes a wide selection of foundation sauces that I employ regularly, plus traditional and more contemporary approaches to sauces and dressings. It is my sincere hope that these ideas will inspire your own experimentation with creating your own sauces and dressings.

Sometimes a sauce can be the savior of an otherwise pedestrian meal. I can't tell you how many times I have relied on a spectacular dressing to add sparkle to a simple meal of grains and vegetables. A sauce or dressing can make the difference between a ho-hum dinner or one that impresses everyone at the table.

All the ideas herein for dressings and sauces stand on their own. I do not provide many suggestions for uses with these recipes. I leave it to you, the chef, to determine which sauce or dressing goes best on pasta, vegetables, grains, beans, sea vegetables or fruit. Mix and match; experiment and determine what combinations work best for you.

When making your own sauces, anything goes, but, personally, I don't enjoy a whole bunch of conflicting flavors in my recipes. I prefer a predominant taste that is supported by complementary ingredients. I like sauces and dressings that are easy to put together, without a lot of time-consuming steps and procedures.

The only other tip I will give you about sauces and dressings is this: look at your recipe to determine when to dress or sauce the dish. A light salad will wilt and turn limp if dressed too soon with a heavy vinaigrette. However, sometimes you want a soft, wilted salad lightly tossed with a citrus-based dressing. And sometimes you want the flavors to develop all together, in which case you add the dressing well before serving. And then there are the times when a dish is cooked in a sauce or sauced late in the recipe. Look at the dish you are making and decide what texture and taste you want for the final product and follow that lead.

Here are some of my favorite dressing and sauce recipes. I hope that you enjoy them and that they help you to create some of your own delicious signature recipes.

Creamy Tofu Dressing

4 ounces silken tofu	2 teaspoons balsamic vinegar
1/2 small onion, grated	Dash of soy sauce
2 tablespoons toasted sesame tahini	Juice of 1 orange

Bring a small pot of water to a boil over medium heat. Add tofu and cook 5 minutes. Drain well.

Transfer tofu to a food processor or blender. Add remaining ingredients and puree until smooth and creamy. For a thinner dressing, slowly add a small amount of water until desired consistency is achieved. ✒ M a k e s a b o u t 1 c u p

VARIATION Sour Tofu Dressing. Replace orange juice with juice of 1 lemon. Add 2 tablespoons brown rice vinegar.

Green Goddess Dressing ✒

4 ounces tofu
1/4 cup brown rice vinegar

....

Small handful minced fresh parsley
3 or 4 green onions, minced

Bring a small pot of water to a boil over medium heat. Add tofu and cook 5 minutes. Drain well.

Transfer tofu to a food processor or blender. Add remaining ingredients and puree until smooth. Add a small amount of water to make a thinner dressing. ✒ M a k e s a b o u t 3 / 4 c u p

French Dressing ✒

1/2 cup light sesame oil
1/2 cup spring or filtered water
2 tablespoons minced fresh parsley

....

1/2 teaspoon *each* dried basil,
   oregano and dill
Pinch of sea salt

Warm oil gently in a small saucepan over low heat 3 to 4 minutes. Place all ingredients in a glass jar, seal tightly and shake well. ✒ M a k e s a b o u t 1 c u p

NOTE Warming the olive oil makes it more digestible.

French Vinaigrette ✎

1/2 cup extra-virgin olive oil

1 clove garlic, minced

1/4 cup balsamic vinegar

Juice of 1 lemon

....

1 shallot, grated

1 teaspoon stone-ground mustard

Pinch of sea salt

Generous pinch of minced chives

Warm oil and garlic gently in a small saucepan over low heat 3 to 4 minutes. Add remaining ingredients and whisk together until combined. ✎
M a k e s   a b o u t   1   c u p

Italian Dressing ✎

1 clove garlic, peeled

1/4 cup extra-virgin olive oil

Soy sauce

1 onion, grated

....

2 umeboshi plums, pitted

2 to 3 tablespoons balsamic vinegar

Dried basil or rosemary to taste

Rub garlic on the bottom of a suribachi (grinding bowl). Warm olive oil and a dash of soy sauce in a small saucepan over low heat 3 to 4 minutes. Combine oil mixture and remaining ingredients in a grinding bowl and grind until smooth. ✎
M a k e s   a b o u t   1 / 2   c u p

VARIATION If a grinding bowl isn't available, use a mortar and pestle.

Lemon-Parsley Dressing ❧

Juice of 1 lemon

1/2 cup orange juice

1/4 cup minced fresh parsley

Dash of soy sauce

2 tablespoons sweet rice vinegar

Spring or filtered water

Combine all ingredients in a blender and puree until smooth, using only as much water as is needed to make a thin but not runny dressing. ❧ M a k e s   a b o u t   1   c u p

Poppy Seed Dressing ❧

1/4 cup light sesame oil

2 to 3 teaspoons poppy seeds

2 cloves garlic, minced

2 tablespoons brown rice vinegar

2 tablespoons umeboshi vinegar

1 tablespoon stone-ground mustard

1 teaspoon brown rice syrup

Juice and grated zest of 1 orange

M a k e s   a b o u t   3 / 4   c u p

Warm oil gently in a small saucepan over low heat 3 to 4 minutes. Combine oil and remaining ingredients in a bowl and whisk together until blended. ❧

Creamy Sesame Dressing ❧

4 tablespoons toasted sesame tahini

1/2 onion, minced

2 umeboshi plums, pitted

Dash of soy sauce

Juice of 1 lemon

2 teaspoons brown rice syrup

Spring or filtered water

3/4 cup spring or filtered water

Combine all ingredients in a blender and puree until smooth, slowly adding water to achieve a creamy consistency. ❧ M a k e s   a b o u t   1   c u p

Tangy Plum-Mustard Dressing ✑

1 onion, grated

1 tablespoon umeboshi paste

2 tablespoons stone-ground mustard

3 tablespoons toasted sesame oil

2 teaspoons brown rice syrup

Spring or filtered water

Combine all ingredients in a blender and puree until smooth, slowly adding water until desired consistency is achieved. ✑ Makes about 1/2 cup

Thousand Island Dressing ✑

8 ounces firm tofu

2 tablespoons minced fresh parsley

1/2 cup ripe olives, pitted and minced

1/2 onion, grated

2 celery stalks, finely minced

Generous pinch of dill weed

Juice of 1 orange

2 teaspoons brown rice syrup

Pinch of sea salt

Spring or filtered water

Bring a small pot of water to a boil over medium heat. Add tofu and cook 5 minutes. Drain well.

Transfer tofu to a food processor or blender. Add remaining ingredients and puree until smooth, slowly adding water until desired consistency is achieved. ✑ Makes about 2 cups

Umeboshi Vinaigrette ✒

1 teaspoon light sesame oil

1 onion, diced

3 umeboshi plums, pitted

Juice of 1 lemon

Generous dash of umeboshi vinegar

2 tablespoons sesame tahini

Spring or filtered water

Heat oil in a skillet over medium heat. Add onion and cook, stirring, until softened, about 3 minutes. Transfer onion to a food processor or blender. Add remaining ingredients and puree until smooth, slowly adding water until desired consistency is achieved. ✒ Makes about 1 cup

Walnut Raspberry Vinaigrette ✒

1 cup walnut pieces

1/4 cup extra-virgin olive oil

2 teaspoons soy sauce

3 to 4 tablespoons umeboshi vinegar

3 tablespoons no-sugar-added raspberry jam

1 tablespoon brown rice syrup

Lightly dry-roast nut pieces in a skillet over medium heat until fragrant, about 3 minutes. Coarsely mince and set aside.

Warm oil and soy sauce gently in a small saucepan over low heat 3 to 4 minutes. Whisk together all ingredients until combined. ✒ Makes about 1 1/2 cups

Zesty Amasake Dressing 🍃

4 ounces silken tofu

1 cup amasake

2 tablespoons umeboshi vinegar

2 tablespoons balsamic vinegar

1 tablespoon white miso

1 clove garlic, minced

Spring or filtered water

Bring a small pot of water to a boil and cook tofu 5 minutes. Drain well.

Transfer tofu to a food processor or blender and puree with remaining ingredients until smooth, slowly adding water until desired consistency is achieved. You may wish to add water to thin the dressing or to keep it thick, like a sauce. 🍃

Makes about 1 1/2 cups

Béchamel Sauce 🍃

9 tablespoons extra-virgin olive oil

2 or 3 cloves garlic, minced

3 or 4 shallots, minced, or

2 tablespoons minced onion

1/4 cup whole-wheat pastry flour

Pinch of sea salt

1 to 2 cups spring or filtered water

Heat olive oil in a skillet over medium heat. Add garlic and shallots and cook, stirring, 2 to 3 minutes. Stir in flour and sea salt and cook, stirring, until vegetables are coated and a paste begins to form. Add water slowly, while stirring, to avoid lumping. Cook over low heat, stirring constantly, until a thick creamy sauce forms, about 5 minutes. 🍃

Makes about 2 cups

Brown Sauce ❧

1 teaspoon extra-virgin olive oil

1 onion, minced

Sea salt

1 carrot, diced

1 to 2 cups thinly sliced mushrooms,
  brushed free of dirt

2 tablespoons whole-wheat pastry
  flour

1 1/2 cups Vegetable Stock (page 96)

1 tablespoon unsweetened apple
  butter

Soy sauce

Heat olive oil in a skillet over medium heat. Add onion and a pinch of sea salt and cook, stirring, 2 to 3 minutes. Add carrot and mushrooms with another pinch of salt and cook until they all turn brown and caramelize, stirring frequently, 10 to 15 minutes. Stir in flour, then slowly add stock while continuing to stir. Stir in apple butter and simmer 20 minutes, stirring frequently. Add a dash of soy sauce and simmer a few minutes more. ❧ Makes about 2 cups

California Sauce ❧

1/4 cup extra-virgin olive oil

Dash of soy sauce

1 cup orange juice

3 or 4 cloves garlic, minced

1/4 cup minced fresh parsley

Juice of 1 lemon

Warm oil and soy sauce gently in a small saucepan over low heat 3 to 4 minutes. Whisk together all ingredients until combined. ❧ Makes about 1 1/2 cups

Creamy Mushroom Sauce ✑

1 teaspoon extra-virgin olive oil

2 or 3 shallots, minced

4 to 5 dried shiitake mushrooms, soaked 10 minutes, drained and thinly sliced

1 cup button mushrooms, brushed clean and thinly sliced

2 cups Mushroom Stock (page 97)

Soy sauce

1 1/2 tablespoons kuzu, dissolved in 3 tablespoons cold water

Heat oil in a small saucepan over medium heat. Add shallots and cook until translucent. Add shiitake mushrooms and cook 1 minute. Add button mushrooms and cook, stirring, until they begin to release their juices, 5 to 7 minutes. Add stock and bring to a boil. Cover and simmer over low heat 10 minutes. Season lightly with soy sauce and simmer 5 minutes more. Stir in dissolved kuzu and cook, stirring, until sauce thickens slightly and is clear, about 3 minutes. ✑ M a k e s   a b o u t   2   c u p s

Raspberry Barbecue Sauce ✑

1/4 cup raspberry vinegar

2 tablespoons safflower oil

1 tablespoon minced fresh mint leaves

4 ounces silken tofu

1/2 cup no-sugar-added raspberry jam

Pinch of sea salt

Whisk together vinegar, oil and mint. Set aside.

Bring a small pot of water to a boil and cook tofu 5 minutes. Drain well.

Transfer tofu to a food processor or blender. Add vinegar mixture and remaining ingredients and puree until smooth. Refrigerate until ready to use. ✑
M a k e s   a b o u t   1   1 / 4   c u p s

Green Sauce ✎

1/4 cup extra-virgin olive oil
2 umeboshi plums, pitted, or 2 to
   3 tablespoons umeboshi paste
1 bunch green onions, diced

1 bunch fresh parsley, minced
Soy sauce
Spring or filtered water

Warm oil gently in a small saucepan over low heat 3 to 4 minutes. Transfer oil to a food processor or blender. Add plums, green onions, parsley and a dash of soy sauce and process until smooth, slowly adding water to achieve desired consistency. ✎

M a k e s   a b o u t   1   c u p

Gingered-Plum Sauce ✎

1 cup spring water
1 tablespoon umeboshi vinegar
1 teaspoon fresh ginger juice
   (page 242)

1 teaspoon kuzu, dissolved in
   3 tablespoons cold water

Warm water, vinegar and ginger juice gently in a small saucepan over low heat 2 to 3 minutes—not too long or vinegar will become bitter. Stir in dissolved kuzu and cook, stirring, until sauce thickens and is clear, about 3 minutes. ✎

M a k e s   a b o u t   1   c u p

I Can't Believe It's Not Cheese Sauce ✑

2 tablespoons sweet white miso
2 cups spring or filtered water
1/4 cup sesame tahini

2 cloves garlic, minced
Juice of 1 lemon

Dissolve miso in water in a small saucepan over low heat. Add tahini and garlic and warm through. Remove from heat and stir in lemon juice. ✑ M a k e s a b o u t 2 1/2 c u p s

Istanbul Sauce ✑

1 cup tahini
2 tablespoons umeboshi paste
1 onion, grated
Dash of soy sauce

1 to 2 teaspoons fresh ginger juice
(page 242)
Juice of 1 lemon
Spring or filtered water

Combine all ingredients in a blender or food processor and process until smooth, slowly adding water until desired consistency is achieved. ✑ M a k e s a b o u t 1 1/4 c u p s

Lemon-Miso Sauce ✑

1 1/2 tablespoons sweet white miso
1/2 teaspoon soy sauce
1 cup spring or filtered water

Juice and grated zest of 1 lemon
1 tablespoon sesame butter

Warm miso, soy sauce and water in a small saucepan over low heat 3 to 4 minutes. Whisk in remaining ingredients until smooth and creamy. ✑ M a k e s a b o u t 1 c u p

Garlic, Mushroom & Leek Sauce

1/2 teaspoon extra-virgin olive oil	2 cups button mushrooms, brushed
4 to 5 cloves garlic, thinly sliced	clean and thinly sliced
1 leek, sliced lengthwise and rinsed	2 teaspoons white miso, dissolved in
well, then thinly sliced	1/4 cup water
Soy sauce	

Heat olive oil in a skillet over medium heat. Add garlic and cook until dark brown, stirring. Remove garlic from oil and discard. Add leek and a dash of soy sauce and cook, stirring, until bright green. Add mushrooms and a dash of soy sauce and cook until tender, about 5 minutes. Add miso mixture, cover and simmer 4 to 5 minutes. Makes about 2 cups

VARIATION Some freshly squeezed ginger juice is a nice addition to this sauce.

Parsleyed Nut Sauce

1 tablespoon light sesame oil	1 cup spring or filtered water
3 or 4 green onions, finely diced	Soy sauce
1 teaspoon fresh ginger juice with	1 teaspoon kuzu, dissolved in
pulp (page 242)	3 tablespoons cold water
1/4 cup minced fresh parsley	
1 cup walnut pieces, lightly toasted	
(page 417)	

Heat oil in a saucepan over medium heat. Add green onions, ginger and parsley and cook 2 minutes. Add nuts and cook 2 minutes more. Add water and warm through. Season lightly with soy sauce. Stir in kuzu and cook, stirring, until sauce thickens and is clear, about 3 minutes. Makes about 2 cups

Roasted Pepper Sauce ✒

1 cup Vegetable Stock (page 96)
1 tablespoon extra-virgin olive oil
1 onion, diced
2 or 3 cloves garlic, minced
1 carrot, diced

2 celery stalks, diced
4 or 5 red bell peppers
Generous pinch of dried basil
Sea salt

In a deep skillet, bring stock and oil to a boil. Add onion and garlic and simmer over low heat 2 minutes. Add carrot and celery and simmer, covered, 5 to 7 minutes more.

Meanwhile, roast peppers over an open gas flame or under a broiler until outer skin is charred. Transfer to a paper sack, seal tightly and allow them to steam a few minutes. Then simply rub the skin away, remove seeds and dice.

Add diced peppers to skillet along with basil and a light seasoning of salt. Simmer 5 to 7 minutes more or until all vegetables are tender. Transfer mixture to a food processor and pulse a few times to create a slightly chunky sauce. ✒
Makes about 2 cups

Squash Sauce &

1 teaspoon extra-virgin olive oil
2 cloves garlic, minced
1 onion, diced
2 celery stalks, diced
2 to 3 cups peeled and cubed winter squash

1 to 2 carrots, diced
Sea salt
Generous pinch of dried basil
Spring or filtered water
Umeboshi vinegar

Heat oil in a pressure cooker over medium heat. Add garlic and onion and cook, stirring, 2 to 3 minutes. Stir in celery, squash, carrot, a pinch of salt and basil. Add enough water to half cover ingredients and season lightly with sea salt. Seal the lid and bring to full pressure over medium heat. Reduce heat and cook over low heat 25 minutes, maintaining pressure.

Remove pot from stove and allow pressure to reduce naturally. Strain sauce through a food mill and return to pot. If consistency is too thick, add water until desired consistency is achieved. Simmer 2 to 3 minutes. Remove from heat and lightly season with umeboshi vinegar. ✒ M a k e s a b o u t 2 t o 3 c u p s

Roasted Garlic Sauce &

4 heads garlic
3 tablespoons corn oil
1 shallot, minced
1/4 cup mirin or white wine

1/4 cup spring or filtered water
2 tablespoons brown rice vinegar
1/4 cup soy or rice milk
Sea salt

Preheat oven to 350F (175C). Keep garlic heads whole, but remove outer layers of skin. Place in a small baking dish, drizzle lightly with oil and bake about 1 hour, until cloves are very soft. Allow to cool until you can easily handle the cloves. Separate garlic cloves and squeeze soft pulp into a small saucepan. Add shallot, mirin, water and vinegar. Simmer over low heat until liquid evaporates, about 15 minutes. Add soy milk and remaining oil and simmer again until sauce is slightly reduced, about 10 minutes more. Season with salt. ✒ M a k e s a b o u t 1 / 4 c u p

Black Olive Pesto ✎

1/4 cup extra-virgin olive oil
10 to 12 oil-cured ripe olives, pitted
1 cup walnut pieces, lightly toasted
    (page 417)
2 tablespoons umeboshi vinegar

Warm oil in a small saucepan over low heat 3 to 4 minutes. Transfer oil to a food processor or blender. Add olives, walnuts and vinegar and process until smooth. Slowly add water to achieve a thinner consistency, if desired. ✎ Makes about 1 cup

NOTE When making pestos, I usually keep the pesto in a sealed glass jar in the refrigerator. I add water to thin only to the portion I will be using in a particular recipe. A strong pesto like this one will keep in the refrigerator for about 2 weeks. More delicate pestos made with fresh herbs will not keep quite as long.

Fresh Basil Pesto ✎

1/4 cup extra-virgin olive oil
1 cup loosely packed fresh basil leaves
1 cup pine nuts or walnuts, lightly
    toasted (page 417)
2 cloves garlic, minced
2 tablespoons white miso
2 teaspoons umeboshi vinegar
1 teaspoon brown rice syrup
Spring or filtered water

Warm oil in a small saucepan over low heat 3 to 4 minutes. Transfer oil to a food processor or blender. Add basil, walnuts, garlic, miso, vinegar and syrup and process until smooth, adding just enough water to achieve desired consistency. Be careful with water; pestos are best when slightly thicker and creamier. ✎ Makes about 1 1/2 cups

Nori Pesto ✑

1 teaspoon toasted sesame oil
1 onion, diced
1/4 teaspoon hot chili powder

6 or 7 sheets nori, shredded
Soy sauce
Spring or filtered water

Heat oil in a saucepan over medium heat. Add onion and chili powder and cook until translucent, about 5 minutes. Add nori, a dash of soy sauce and enough water to cover. Bring to a boil, reduce heat and cook, uncovered, until all liquid has been absorbed and pesto is creamy, about 20 minutes. You may need to add a bit of water midway through cooking if water evaporates too soon. This is a strong pesto; use just a little. ✑

Makes about 1/2 cup

Apricot Sauce ✑

1 cup apricot halves, dried or fresh
1/4 cup brown rice syrup
2 cups spring or filtered water

Pinch of sea salt
2 teaspoons kuzu, dissolved in
3 tablespoons cold water

If using dried apricots, soak them in warm water 1 hour before making sauce; drain before using. Combine apricots, rice syrup, water and salt in a saucepan over medium heat and bring to a boil. Reduce heat, cover and cook, stirring occasionally, until fruit is soft, about 30 minutes. Stir in kuzu and cook, stirring, until sauce thickens, about 3 minutes. ✑ Makes about 2 cups

Mixed Berry Sauce

2 cups unfiltered apple juice or
   spring or filtered water

Pinch of sea salt

1/4 cup fresh strawberries, quartered

1/4 cup fresh blueberries

1/4 cup fresh raspberries

1/4 cup fresh cherries, pitted
   and halved

1 tablespoon kuzu, dissolved in

4 tablespoons cold water

Dash of pure vanilla extract

Bring juice and salt to a boil in a saucepan over medium heat. Stir in fruit and simmer over low heat 5 to 7 minutes, until fruit softens. Stir in dissolved kuzu and cook, stirring, until mixture thickens slightly, about 3 minutes. Remove from heat and whisk in vanilla. ℐ Makes about 1 cup

Ginger-Kiwi Sauce

1 kiwi fruit, peeled and diced

1 tablespoon brown rice vinegar

Juice of 1 lime

2 teaspoons brown rice syrup

5 or 6 slices gingerroot, cut into
   matchstick pieces

Juice of 1 orange

Combine kiwi fruit with vinegar and lime juice. Lightly mash and set aside.

Simmer rice syrup, ginger and orange juice in a small saucepan over low heat 10 minutes, or until mixture reduces to half of the original amount. Strain out ginger pieces. Combine with kiwi mixture and mix well. ℐ Makes about 1 cup

Mango-Chile Salsa

1 mango, peeled, seeded and diced

1 jalapeño chile, seeded and minced

1 tablespoon minced fresh mint

1/4 red onion, grated

Generous pinch *each* of cumin and chili powder

2 to 3 tablespoons sweet rice vinegar

1 tablespoon extra-virgin olive oil

Mix all ingredients together in a saucepan. Warm gently over low heat 4 to 5 minutes to release flavors. ❧ Makes about 2 cups

BREADS OF LIFE

Is there anything more wonderful in the entire world than fresh bread? One of my favorite lunches is crusty, warm bread with a hot bowl of soup and a fresh salad. I remember traveling around Europe, mostly broke, existing on simple meals of bread (some of the best I have ever tasted), soup and fresh vegetables . . . and being quite content, I might add. It's a winning combination for me to this day.

For me, bread has always symbolized life. Like life, bread baking teaches us about success and failure, perseverance and patience. There is no better feeling than the satisfaction we get as golden, crusty loaves, kneaded by our hands, are pulled from the oven.

Baking bread keeps you humble. We all begin with the same simple ingredients—flour, water and leavening. We all perform the same ritual tasks of baking—mixing, kneading, forming, baking to perfection (hopefully). Bread dough is uncompromising and unpredictable. Whether we realize it or not, we must submit to the influences of our environment: heat, cold, drafts, oven temperature.

Growing up in the home of a great bread baker, I could not help but be influenced by my mother's love for this food. She baked every Saturday morning, always enough bread for the family for the week. While most kids my age were out and about, I was hanging out with my mother, soaking up everything she knew. And my education continues to this day with my husband, Robert, who is the bread master in our house. Many is the night when he emerges from the kitchen, his hands and forearms dusted with flour, lovingly forming a loaf of bread.

As a child, I never remember buying a loaf of bread at a market. And who would want to when the kitchen always held at least two fragrant, crusty loaves for us to feast on? My mother's example gave me the confidence I now possess in the kitchen. She taught me not to be afraid of anything connected to the preparation of good food. She introduced me to the joys of fragrant loaves of raisin bread baking in the warmth of the oven. She taught me to bake with personality. Master the basics, she would say, and then create loaves of bread; don't just bake them. Bread making is a symbol that we possess the ability to nourish not only ourselves, but those we love. My mother used to say that you could always tell homemade loaves of bread because they looked as though they were baked by someone who cared.

INGREDIENTS

First, I use only organic, whole-grain flour for my loaves. These flours produce hearty, nutty loaves with rich, golden interiors and crunchy crusts. I value the nutritive benefits of whole-grain flours, since they retain some of their germ and bran.

I rarely leaven with anything but sourdough starter, although I like to create other naturally leavened breads with cooked sour grain. I don't favor commercial yeasts, not because they don't produce lovely loaves of bread, but because yeast can produce too much expansion in the intestinal tract, weakening our ability to assimilate food. And since sourdough starter creates such incredible breads, why compromise?

Creating your own sourdough starter is easy, and the best part is that starter keeps indefinitely with refrigeration and a bit of attention. And since sourdough is a natural leavening agent, you can omit yeast from any bread recipe, substituting starter in its place. The result will be a nicely leavened loaf, without the negative side effects of yeast. Just bear in mind that rising times for sourdough are longer than for yeasted loaves; sourdough needs 6 to 8 hours, while yeast can do its thing in as little as 1 to 2 hours.

BAKING TIPS

So what's the first rule of bread baking? Take a deep breath and relax. It is not difficult to bake a great loaf of bread. It takes some practice, but with focus, you develop an intuitive sense about your bread. The more you let this sense develop, the better and better your breads will be.

Kneading bread is an art form in itself. Knead too long and bread can become tough; too little, and it won't rise properly. Relax, though; you'll get the hang of it in just a couple of loaves. You know, you really do, when the loaf has been kneaded enough. In the beginning, let your recipes guide you until intuition takes over.

Shaping loaves can include anything from traditional loaf and baguette pans, rising baskets, clay pots or free-form loaves shaped by hand and baked on oven stones. Free-form loaves are my personal favorite because they allow for creativity. Knotting, braiding, making wreath breads or nests of bread—well, you get the idea.

So here we go. I'd like to begin this section with a recipe for sourdough starter and then proceed to some bread recipes that have graced my table, some since I was just a kid learning how to bake in my mother's kitchen.

Basic Sourdough Starter

A starter is simply a leavening agent. A true sourdough starter is made by encouraging the development and growth of wild yeast and benign bacteria in a flour and water atmosphere. It is, in fact, these bacteria that create the acids that sour the starter and create the leavening.

You can make this starter with unbleached white flour or whole-wheat flour. The white starter will create a lighter loaf, but I prefer the heartiness and the stronger flavor of the whole wheat. Keep in mind, however, that any flour can be used to create starters—rye, rice, corn, etc.

The biggest problem people run into with sourdough starter is keeping the starter alive. A little bit of attention will result in your starter lasting a lifetime, literally. Every 10 to 14 days, you will need to "feed" or freshen the starter to maintain it.

Use only filtered or spring water when creating your starter because tap water that contains chemicals can inhibit the activity of the wild yeasts. If your starter develops a brownish liquid on the surface, simply stir it in. If mold appears on the surface, gently scrape it off and freshen the starter with flour and water before using it again. If, however, your starter turns pink, develops an unpleasant sour odor (instead of a fragrant, slightly sour aroma) or doesn't bubble when placed in a warm place for 48 hours, you need to throw it out and begin again. ✦

3 cups warm spring or filtered water

2 cups whole-wheat or unbleached white flour

You will need a crock or container (glass or stoneware is best) that leaves enough room for the starter to double.

Mix the flour and water together well and allow to stand, loosely covered, in a warm place 2 to 5 days. The time will depend partially on the temperature. When you notice that the starter is bubbly and slightly sour-smelling, stir well, cover and refrigerate.

At least once a month, although every other week is best, feed the starter by stirring together 1 part starter, 1 part water and 1 to 2 cups flour and allowing to stand in a warm place 12 to 24 hours before returning it to the refrigerator. If you are not baking bread each week, you will find yourself accumulating starter. What we do in our house, is discard some of the starter (or pass it on to friends with instructions on feeding) before freshening it, so that we don't end up with a refrigerator filled with jars of sourdough starter. When you freshen your starter, wait 2 to 3 days before using it, so that your breads will have a more delicate flavor. ✦ M a k e s a b o u t 4 c u p s o f s t a r t e r

NOTE Some bakers like to begin their sourdough starter by soaking dried organic fruit, like raisins, in the water that will be used for the starter, since the sugars present in these fruits will encourage the growth of the wild yeasts needed. If you choose to begin your starter with fruit, it is important to use organic dried fruits, as they do not have any pesticides or fungicides present on their skins.

Basic Sourdough Bread

From this basic loaf, you can create anything—not only different shapes, of course, but also different loaves. Varying the flour, adding nuts or dried fruits, herbs and spices, garlic and oil or olives are just some of the ways you can create variety.

1 1/4 cups Basic Sourdough Starter
(page 433) (stir before measuring)
2 3/4 cups warm spring or filtered
water (about 110F, 45C)

6 to 7 cups whole-wheat flour
1 to 2 teaspoons sea salt

Combine the starter and water in a large bowl. Add 4 cups of the flour, 1 cup at a time, stirring each one in thoroughly. Add salt and 2 cups of the flour, stirring well, to make a moderately stiff dough.

Turn the dough out onto a floured surface and knead about 10 minutes, adding flour as needed to form a smooth, elastic dough. Place dough in a lightly oiled bowl, turning to coat with oil. Cover tightly with plastic wrap and allow to stand at room temperature 10 to 12 hours.

The dough will be slightly sticky after rising. Turn onto a floured surface and knead briefly, 3 to 5 minutes. Divide into 2 equal pieces.

To create a basic loaf shape, simply take 1 piece of dough and stretch it between your hands until it is about a foot long. Fold each end toward the middle, pressing the ends into the center so that they stick. The dough should be roughly rectangular in shape. Starting with the closest corners of the rectangle, roll them to the center. Continue rolling, forcing the outside to the center until you end up with a loaf resembling a fat football. Find the outside seam and pinch it to seal the loaf. Finally, roll the loaf back and forth on your work surface to smooth, taper and refine your loaf shape. Repeat with remaining dough, creating 2 loaves.

Place loaves on a floured surface (a peel or baking sheet is ideal), cover with a damp kitchen towel and allow to rise at room temperature 2 to 3 hours, until the loaves double in size.

Preheat oven to 450F (230C). Place a shallow pan of water on the lowest rack. Transfer the loaves to a floured baking pan or stone. (If using a stone, remember to heat it in the oven 30 minutes before transferring the bread to it.) With a sharp knife, score each loaf 1/4 inch deep, down the center, along the length of the loaf. Brush each loaf with water and bake 15 minutes. Using a spray bottle, mist the oven with water every 5 minutes during this 15-minute period. This extra effort will result in those delicious outer crusts that we all hold near to our hearts.

At the end of 15 minutes, remove the pan of water, brush the loaves with water and reduce the oven temperature to 375F (190C). Return the bread to the oven and bake about 40 minutes, until the loaves sound hollow when tapped on the bottom. Transfer to a rack and cool. ✍ Makes 2 loaves

SESAME LOAVES Follow the basic recipe, substituting 2 tablespoons toasted sesame oil and 2 tablespoons light sesame oil for 4 tablespoons of the water in the bread. Just before baking, brush the loaves with sesame oil and sprinkle generously with sesame seeds.

POPPY SEED BREAD Follow the basic recipe, sprinkling the loaves generously with poppy seeds just before baking.

LEMON-HERB BREAD Follow the basic recipe, kneading in grated zest of 1 lemon with a generous pinch each of dried oregano, basil and thyme. Follow your instincts with the amount of herbs to add, using just pinches of each; you don't want the taste to overpower the bread or become bitter.

ROSEMARY-OLIVE BREAD Follow the basic recipe, substituting 3 tablespoons extra-virgin olive oil for 3 tablespoons of water and kneading in 1 to 2 tablespoons dried rosemary along with 16 ripe olives that have been pitted and minced.

GARLIC-TOMATO BREAD Follow the basic recipe. Make garlic oil by sautéing 2 cloves of finely minced garlic in 1/4 cup extra-virgin olive oil until deep, golden brown, about 3 minutes. Remove garlic and allow oil to cool before using in bread. Substitute 1/4 cup garlic oil for 1/4 cup water in the recipe. Knead in about 1/3 cup finely minced oil-packed sun-dried tomatoes. (Drain tomatoes well before using.)

OATMEAL RAISIN BREAD Follow the basic recipe, substituting 1 1/2 cups rolled oats for 1 1/2 cups flour. Knead in 2 cups raisins and a generous pinch of cinnamon.

Rye 'n' Raisin Rolls

These lovely little rolls are a wonderful combination of flavors: the hearty, earthy taste of rye is nicely complemented by the delicate sweetness of raisins.

1 cup Basic Sourdough Starter
   (page 433)

3 cups spring or filtered water

4 to 5 cups whole-wheat flour

2 1/2 cups rye flour

2 cups raisins

1 to 2 teaspoons sea salt

Cornmeal for dusting

Combine the starter and water in a large bowl. Add 2 1/2 cups of the whole-wheat flour and 1 1/4 cups of the rye flour, 1 cup at a time, stirring in each one thoroughly. Stir in raisins and salt. Stir in remaining rye flour and enough whole-wheat flour, again 1 cup at a time, to make a moderately stiff dough. Turn out onto a floured work surface and knead about 8 minutes or until smooth but still slightly sticky. Place dough in a lightly oiled bowl and turn to coat with oil. Cover with plastic wrap and allow to rise at room temperature about 3 hours, until doubled in size.

Return the dough to the work surface and knead briefly, about 3 minutes. Divide the dough in half and roll each half into a log, 3 inches in diameter. Cut each log into 12 equal pieces. Roll each piece firmly on the work surface until a round ball forms.

Place the rolls about 2 inches apart on a cornmeal-dusted baking sheet. Cover with a damp kitchen towel and allow to rise until doubled in size, about 45 minutes.

Preheat oven to 450F (230C). Heat a baking stone or tiles 30 minutes. Quickly and carefully transfer the rolls to the stone and bake the rolls 15 minutes, misting the oven with water every 5 minutes.

Reduce the oven temperature to 375F (190C) and continue baking the rolls another 15 minutes, until deep brown and crusty. They should sound hollow when tapped on the bottom. Transfer to a rack and cool. ✒ Makes 24 rolls

VARIATION If a baking stone is not available, bake on an oiled baking sheet.

Juicy Apple Rolls

These sweet little gems are a delight to serve at a brunch or with tea. ✒

1/2 recipe Basic Sourdough Bread (page 435)

1 teaspoon corn oil
1 tablespoon maple syrup granules
Pinch of ground cinnamon

FILLING
4 tart apples (Granny Smith or other)

Prepare the dough through the first rising. When the dough is almost ready, prepare the filling.

Preheat oven to 450F (230C). Halve and core the apples and slice them into 1-inch pieces. Toss the apples with oil, maple granules and cinnamon. Spread evenly on a baking sheet and bake until just tender, about 10 minutes. Set aside to cool and reduce oven temperature to 400F (205C).

Prepare the rolls by turning dough out onto a floured work surface and kneading briefly, about 3 minutes. Roll dough into a log, about 4 inches in diameter. Cut into 9 equal pieces. Roll each piece of dough around on the work surface to smooth the edges. With a rolling pin, roll each piece into an oval, about 7 × 5 inches.

Place a scant 1/2 cup filling in the center of each piece. Beginning with the long side, roll the dough into a cylinder, leaving the short sides open. Place the rolls, seam side down, on a floured surface, cover with a damp kitchen towel and allow to rise at room temperature until doubled in size, about 40 minutes.

Preheat a baking stone in the oven 30 minutes. Just before baking, make 4 to 5 crosswise slits in the tops of the rolls. Transfer rolls to the baking stone and bake 20 to 25 minutes, until they are golden brown. Transfer to a rack and cool. ✑
Makes 9 rolls

VARIATION If a baking stone is not available, bake on an oiled baking sheet.

Focaccia

An Italian tradition, focaccia is fat pizza—or flat bread—with just about any topping you can think of to pile on top of bread. ✑

1/2 recipe Basic Sourdough Bread
(page 435)

TOPPING SUGGESTIONS
Sautéed garlic and onions in olive oil with mushrooms, tomatoes and basil or rosemary

Stir-fried broccoli with carrots, onions and ginger

Follow basic recipe through the first rising. Lightly oil a 13 × 9-inch baking pan. Turn out dough onto a floured work surface and knead briefly, about 3 minutes. Flatten slightly and press into prepared pan. Cover with a damp kitchen towel and allow to rise at room temperature until doubled in thickness, about 40 minutes.

Preheat oven to 450F. Prepare any variety of topping for the focaccia and spread it evenly over surface. Bake 15 to 20 minutes, until golden brown. ✑
Makes 1 focaccia

Cornbread with Fresh Corn

Nothing goes with soup or a hearty bean stew like moist cornbread. This recipe is an adaptation of my mother's family favorite. 🌾

1 1/2 cups whole-wheat pastry flour
1 cup yellow cornmeal
2 to 3 teaspoons baking powder
1/2 teaspoon sea salt
1/4 cup corn oil

2 tablespoons brown rice syrup
1/2 cup rice milk
1/2 to 1 cup spring or filtered water
1/2 cup fresh corn kernels

Preheat oven to 350 F (175C). Lightly oil and flour a 9-inch-square baking dish. Sift together the flour, cornmeal, baking powder and salt into a bowl. In another bowl, whisk together oil, rice syrup, rice milk and 1/2 cup water. Stir into dry ingredients until just blended. Add more water if needed to create a velvety, spoonable batter. Gently fold in corn kernels. Spoon batter into prepared pan and bake 35 to 40 minutes, until golden at the edges and the center springs back to the touch. 🌾 Makes 6 to 8 servings

Rice Kayu Bread

This is a moist, dense loaf that we do not bake. You heard me right. This bread is pressure-cooked or steamed (although you can bake it as well) to create its unique character. The rice for this bread should be cooked to a creamy porridge consistency, by using 5 parts water to 1 part grain. ✣

2 cups soft-cooked brown rice, at
room temperature

2 cups whole-wheat flour

1 teaspoon sea salt

Combine cooked rice with the flour and salt in a bowl. With a wooden spoon, mix the dough as thoroughly as possible before taking over the mixing process with your hands. It will be sticky at this point. Turn the dough onto a floured work surface and begin kneading, adding flour as necessary to create a smooth, elastic dough.

Shape the loaf by placing the dough in the center of a floured work surface and flattening it into a round. Work the dough by turning the edges under toward the center, creating a ball. Be sure to work all the air out of the center when folding. Place the dough in an oiled and floured glass or stoneware container (twice the size of the bread) that will fit comfortably into your pressure cooker. Cover with a damp towel and place in a warm area to rise 6 to 8 hours.

Place container, uncovered, in a pressure cooker with 1 inch of water surrounding the container. Seal the pressure cooker, bring to full pressure, and cook bread over low heat 1 hour. Remove pot from heat and allow pressure to reduce naturally.

Carefully remove bread from pressure cooker and allow to cool slightly before turning out of container. It will come out easiest while still warm, so don't let the bread cool completely. Wrap bread in a damp towel and allow to stand several hours before serving. ✣ M a k e s 1 l o a f

Sour Grain Bread

Any whole grain will make delicious sour grain breads. Again, these loaves will have a more dense, cakelike texture. We use everything from rice to millet, rye, rice with onions, millet with squash and rice with raisins to name a few. ✣

After the grain is cooked, sour it by leaving it at room temperature, lightly covered in a glass bowl, 2 to 3 days. It should have a pleasantly sour aroma when ready. Then, stir in about 1 tablespoon miso and allow the grain to stand one more day. It will begin to bubble lightly and should smell slightly sour. It is then ready to use in bread.

Follow directions as for the Rice Kayu Bread (page 441) in proportions and preparation. The difference between the two is in the slightly stronger taste, and because the grains are lightly fermented in these breads, the loaves are a bit lighter and less dense.

When I bake these loaves, I form the loaves as you would any other, kneading 10 minutes, shaping and placing the loaf in an oiled and floured loaf pan. Allow to rise, covered with a damp towel, 6 to 8 hours in a warm place.

Preheat oven to 250F (120C). Bake loaf 30 minutes. Increase oven temperature to 350F (175C) and bake another 1 to 1 1/4 hours, until the loaf is firm. Remove from pan immediately. Wrap loaf in a damp towel and let rest several hours before serving. ❧

Makes 1 loaf

Fisherman's Bread

Legend has it that Italian sailors took this long-lasting bread on their voyages. I don't know about that; I originally discovered this incredible bread, flavored with anise, pine nuts, raisins and dried fruits, in Genoa. With a few ingredient changes, voilà!—it is a healthy feast. ❧

2 cups whole-wheat pastry flour
1/3 cup maple syrup granules
1 tablespoon anise seeds
2 teaspoons baking powder
1/4 teaspoon sea salt
1 cup golden raisins
1/4 cup diced dried apricots
1/4 cup diced dried apple

2 tablespoons pine nuts, lightly pan-toasted (page 417)
3 to 4 tablespoons grated orange zest
1/4 cup rice milk
1/8 cup mirin
2 tablespoons corn oil
1/8 to 1/4 cup spring or filtered water

Preheat oven to 375F (190C). Lightly oil a baking sheet.

Combine flour, maple granules, anise seeds, baking powder and salt. Add fruits, pine nuts, and orange zest and mix well.

Whisk together rice milk, mirin, corn oil and water. Stir liquids into flour mixture until well-blended and a dough begins to form.

Turn dough out onto a lightly floured surface and knead until smooth, about 2 minutes—the dough will still be slightly sticky. Divide dough in half and shape each half into a flat 6 × 4-inch oval or round. Place loaves, side by side, on the prepared baking sheet. Bake 30 to 35 minutes, until golden brown. Transfer to a cooling rack. ∽

Makes 2 loaves

Herb-Scented Biscuits

These flaky, tender biscuits are so easy to make, it's almost silly. You will love the results—the only problem you will have is making enough. ∽

2 1/2 cups whole-wheat pastry flour

2 teaspoons baking powder

1/4 teaspoon sea salt

1 tablespoon dried rosemary or basil

(not both)

4 tablespoons soy margarine, chilled

2/3 cup rice milk

About 2 tablespoons extra-virgin olive oil

Preheat oven to 350F (175C). Lightly oil a baking sheet.

In a food processor, combine flour, baking powder, salt, herb and margarine. Pulse until the texture of coarse cornmeal. Add rice milk and process until a dough ball forms. Immediately turn off food processor; do not overprocess, or dough will break down. Gather dough into your hands and turn out onto a lightly floured surface.

Roll out dough to a 14 × 12-inch rectangle. Dough will be about 1/8 inch thick. Trim edges evenly. Lightly brush surface of dough with oil. Roll, jelly-roll style, forming a long cylinder. With a sharp knife, slice cylinder into 1-inch-thick rounds. Place, cut side up, on prepared baking sheet. Brush each biscuit with a little oil, if desired.

Bake 20 to 25 minutes on the center rack of the oven, until slightly golden and springy to the touch. Serve warm. ∽ Makes about 12 to 16 biscuits

Sticky Cinnamon Rolls

In under two hours, you can serve up these rolls, jam-packed with raisins, fragrant with cinnamon and dripping with caramel glaze—perfect brunch treats.

3 1/2 to 4 cups whole-wheat pastry
    flour
1 package quick-rising dried yeast
1/2 teaspoon sea salt
1/2 cup rice milk
5 tablespoons brown rice syrup
3 tablespoons corn oil, plus extra
    for brushing

Spring or filtered water
3/4 cup maple syrup granules
1/2 cup coarsely minced pecans
2 teaspoons ground cinnamon
1/2 cup raisins

In a large bowl, mix 2 cups of the flour, yeast and salt. Set aside. In a saucepan, combine rice milk, 2 tablespoons of the rice syrup, 2 tablespoons of the oil and 3/4 cup water. Stir over low heat until very warm.

Add the warm liquid to the dry ingredients and stir until smooth. Stir in remaining flour, 1/2 cup at a time, until the dough is moderately stiff. Turn the dough out onto a lightly floured work surface and knead, gradually incorporating more flour as necessary to prevent sticking, until the dough is smooth and elastic, about 10 minutes.

Place dough in a large, lightly oiled bowl, turning several times to coat with oil. Cover tightly with plastic wrap and let rise in a warm place 30 minutes.

Lightly oil a 13 × 9-inch baking dish. Sprinkle evenly with 1/2 cup of maple granules and the pecans. Drizzle with the remaining 3 tablespoons rice syrup and 1 tablespoon corn oil. In a small bowl, combine cinnamon and remaining 1/4 cup maple granules.

Gently punch down dough and turn onto a lightly floured work surface. Pat and roll the dough into a 15 × 12-inch rectangle. Brush lightly with corn oil. Sprinkle evenly with cinnamon mixture and scatter surface with raisins.

Beginning at a short end, roll the dough, jelly-roll style, into a tight log. Pinch the long edge to seal. With a sharp knife, cut the roll into 12 slices. Place the slices, cut side up, about 1 inch apart, in the prepared baking dish. Cover with plastic wrap and set aside in a warm place to rise about 20 minutes. Preheat oven to 375F (190C).

Bake the sticky buns 25 to 30 minutes, until golden brown. Remove from oven and allow to cool about 30 seconds, then invert onto a tray. Allow to cool a few minutes before serving. ✍ Makes 12 sticky buns

Pecan-Orange Scones

Packed with golden raisins and topped with sticky, rich pecans, these orange-scented, crumbly scones are a most welcome sight on any breakfast table. ✍

1/2 cup golden raisins	8 tablespoons soy margarine, chilled
1/4 cup fresh orange juice	Zest of 1 orange
3 cups whole-wheat pastry flour	1 teaspoon umeboshi vinegar
5 tablespoons maple syrup granules	About 2/3 cup rice milk
1 tablespoon baking powder	1/2 cup brown rice syrup
1/8 teaspoon sea salt	1/4 cup pecans, coarsely minced

Preheat oven to 400F (205C). Line a baking sheet with parchment and place inside another baking sheet to prevent scorching.

Soak the raisins in orange juice to soften and plump.

Sift together the dry ingredients into a bowl. Add the margarine in small pieces and cut into the dry ingredients with a pastry blender, fork or 2 knives until mixture resembles coarse cornmeal. Add raisins and orange juice. Stir the zest and umeboshi vinegar into the rice milk and add to dry ingredients. Stir until the dough is thoroughly moistened and comes together, adding more rice milk if needed, but do not overmix.

Turn the dough out onto a floured work surface and gently form into a round. Slice into 8 wedges, form the wedges into rounds and place on the lined baking sheet, about 1 inch apart. Bake until scones are slightly browned, about 20 minutes.

Remove scones from oven. Heat rice syrup in a small saucepan over high heat until it foams. Stir in pecan pieces. Quickly spoon syrup mixture over each scone. Serve warm. ✍ Makes 8 scones

Oat-Raisin Scones

These hearty scones get just a touch of lightness from a hint of orange zest. Hot from the oven, there is nothing quite like one of these with a cup of tea and lots of strawberry jam.

1/2 cup raisins

5 tablespoons fresh orange juice

1 1/2 cups whole-wheat pastry flour

1/4 cup brown rice syrup

2 teaspoons baking powder

1/4 teaspoon sea salt

4 tablespoons soy margarine, chilled

1 1/2 cups rolled oats

Grated zest of 2 oranges

1/2 cup rice milk, mixed with

1 teaspoon umeboshi vinegar

Preheat oven to 375F (190C). Line a baking sheet with parchment and place inside another baking sheet to prevent scorching.

Soak the raisins in the orange juice to soften and plump. Mix the dry ingredients together in a bowl. Cut the margarine into the dry ingredients with a pastry blender, fork, or 2 knives until mixture resembles coarse cornmeal. Add oats, raisins and juice, mixing to incorporate the ingredients evenly. Add the orange zest to the rice or soy milk mixture and stir into dry ingredients, mixing just until the dough is thoroughly moistened and comes together. Do not overmix.

Turn the dough out onto a floured work surface and gently form into a round about 8 inches in diameter and 1 inch thick. Slice the dough into 8 wedges, shape them into rounds and place on the lined baking sheet about 1 inch apart.

Bake 20 to 25 minutes, until scones are puffy and light golden brown.

Makes 8 scones

Pecan Tea Biscuits

Light, tender and flaky—it's hard to beat the delectable goodness of a biscuit . . . and without all the eggs and milk ✐

2 cups whole-wheat pastry flour
5 tablespoons maple syrup granules
2 teaspoons baking powder
1/4 teaspoon sea salt
1/4 cup soy margarine, chilled

3/4 cup rice milk
1/2 cup pecans, lightly pan-toasted (page 417) and coarsely minced
1/2 teaspoon ground cinnamon

Sift together the flour, 3 tablespoons of the maple granules, baking powder, and salt into a bowl. Cut the margarine into the dry ingredients with a pastry blender, fork or 2 knives until mixture resembles coarse cornmeal. Add rice milk and mix just until dough is thoroughly moistened and comes together. Fold in pecans.

Preheat oven to 425F (220C). Lightly oil a baking sheet.

Gather biscuit dough into a soft ball and turn it out onto a lightly floured work surface. Knead about 30 seconds, just to form the dough. With a floured rolling pin, roll the dough into a 1/2-inch-thick round. Dip a biscuit cutter or a glass in flour. Cut dough into rounds by pushing the cutter straight down into the dough without twisting the cutter, as the biscuits may not be as light. Place biscuits on prepared baking sheet about 1 inch apart.

Combine remaining 2 tablespoons maple granules and cinnamon in a small bowl and sprinkle generously over the biscuit tops. Bake 10 to 12 minutes, until light golden brown. ✐ Makes about 16 biscuits

Onion Biscuits

Nothing complements a hearty bowl of soup quite like a light, flaky biscuit. Adding onions to the batter adds a sweetness you just have to taste for yourself. ℘

1 tablespoon corn oil
1/4 cup finely minced onion
1 1/2 cups whole-wheat pastry flour
1 1/2 teaspoons baking powder

1/8 teaspoon sea salt
1/4 cup soy margarine, chilled
1/2 cup rice milk

In a small skillet, heat the oil over medium heat. Add the onion and cook, stirring, until tender and translucent, about 5 minutes; do not brown. Set aside.

Preheat oven to 425F (220C). Lightly oil a baking sheet. Combine flour, baking powder and salt in a bowl. Cut the margarine into the dry ingredients with a pastry blender, fork or 2 knives until mixture resembles coarse cornmeal. Add onion and rice milk and mix just until dough is thoroughly moistened and comes together.

Turn dough out onto a lightly floured work surface and knead gently about 30 seconds. Roll the dough into a 1/2-inch-thick round. Dip a biscuit cutter or a glass in flour. Cut dough into rounds by pushing the cutter straight down into the dough without twisting the cutter, as the biscuits may not be as light. Place biscuits on prepared baking sheet about 1 inch apart.

Bake 12 to 15 minutes, until light golden brown. ℘

Makes about 12 biscuits

Mincemeat Coffee Ring

For mincemeat lovers only . . . this moist coffee bread laced through with fragrant mincemeat (my version, of course) is a snap to make and partners beautifully with hot tea on Christmas (or any other) morning. ✒

2 cups whole-wheat pastry flour	**1/2 cup rice milk or soy milk**
1 tablespoon baking powder	**3/4 cup No-Meat Mincemeat**
1/4 teaspoon sea salt	**(page 484)**
3/4 cup brown rice syrup	**1 cup brown rice syrup**
1/4 cup corn oil	**2 teaspoons fresh lemon juice**

Preheat oven to 350F (175C). Lightly oil and flour a 9-inch ring pan.

Sift together flour, baking powder and salt into a bowl. Combine rice syrup, oil, rice milk and mincemeat in another bowl. Add wet mixture to dry ingredients and mix until the ingredients are just combined. It will be a dense batter. Spoon the mixture evenly into the prepared baking pan, filling it not more than two-thirds full.

Bake 30 to 35 minutes, until the bread springs back to the touch. Cool in pan 10 minutes before turning out onto a plate. Place the plate over the cake pan and invert so the bread can drop onto the plate.

While the coffee ring is warm, heat rice syrup over high heat until it foams. Remove from heat and stir in lemon juice. Quickly spoon hot syrup over bread and allow to stand 10 minutes or so before slicing. ✒

Makes 1 (9-inch) ring, 10 to 12 servings

Squash Bread

All the goodness of pumpkin pie wrapped up in this moist, slightly sweet snack bread. 🌱

2 cups cubed winter squash or pumpkin

Pinch of sea salt

Spring or filtered water

2 to 3 cups whole-wheat pastry flour

2 teaspoons baking powder

1/4 teaspoon sea salt

1/2 teaspoon ground ginger

1/4 teaspoon ground cloves

1/4 teaspoon ground cinnamon

1/3 cup soy milk or rice milk

1/4 cup corn oil

1/2 cup brown rice syrup

1/2 cup coarsely minced walnut pieces

Place squash and salt in a heavy saucepan with 1/8 inch of water. Cover and bring to a boil. Reduce heat to low and cook until pumpkin is quite soft, about 20 minutes. Transfer to a food processor and process until smooth. Set aside.

Preheat oven to 350F (175C). Lightly oil and flour a 9 × 5-inch loaf pan.

Sift together flour, baking powder, salt and spices into a bowl. Combine cooked pumpkin with rice milk, oil and rice syrup. Stir pumpkin mixture into dry ingredients, mixing just until blended to make a thick, spoonable batter. Fold in walnuts and spoon into prepared pan.

Bake 50 to 55 minutes, until the top of the loaf springs back to the touch. Cool in pan 10 minutes before removing loaf from pan and cooling on a wire rack. 🌱

Makes 1 loaf, 8 to 10 servings

VARIATION Use 1 cup canned pumpkin instead of fresh winter squash or pumpkin.

Cranberry-Almond Bread

The tart sweetness of cranberries perfectly complements the nutty crunch of toasted almonds in this gorgeous loaf, streaked with the rich, red color of the berries. Served warm from the oven, with a hot cup of tea, this bread warms any autumn afternoon. ∽

3/4 cup whole almonds
2 cups whole-wheat pastry flour
2 teaspoons baking powder
1/4 teaspoon sea salt
1/4 teaspoon ground cinnamon
1/4 cup corn oil

3/4 cup maple syrup granules
1 teaspoon almond extract
3/4 cup rice milk or soy milk
2 cups fresh cranberries, sorted, rinsed and towel-dried

Preheat oven to 350F (175C). Lightly oil and flour a 9 × 5-inch loaf pan.

In a hot, dry skillet, lightly pan-toast the almonds over medium heat until fragrant and lightly browned, 5 to 7 minutes. Coarsely mince the almonds by hand or in a nut grinder. Set aside.

Sift together the flour, baking powder, salt and cinnamon into a bowl. Whisk together the oil, maple granules, almond extract, and rice milk. Stir into dry ingredients, mixing just until blended. Gently fold in the cranberries and nuts. Spoon the batter evenly into the prepared loaf pan.

Bake 55 to 60 minutes, until the top of the loaf is golden brown and springs back to the touch or a wooden pick inserted in the center comes out clean. Cool in pan 10 minutes before removing loaf from the pan and cooling on a wire rack. ∽

Makes 1 loaf, 10 to 12 servings

Pancakes

Just like their conventional counterparts, these tender griddle cakes are a great main dish on those lazy weekend mornings when you don't have to rush off and can linger over a leisurely breakfast. Served with any number of conventional or other toppings, these pancakes get their richness from my version of buttermilk—rice or soy milk with just a touch of vinegar to achieve the desired sour taste and leavening needed. ✐

1 tablespoon corn oil, plus extra for cooking

1 cup rice milk or soy milk, mixed with 1 teaspoon umeboshi vinegar

3/4 to 1 cup whole-wheat pastry flour

1/4 teaspoon sea salt

2 teaspoons baking powder

Heat the corn oil in a small saucepan over medium heat. Transfer to a heatproof bowl and quickly whisk in the rice milk. Combine the dry ingredients in a bowl. Stir rice milk mixture into dry ingredients and mix until the batter is just moistened and a bit lumpy.

Heat a skillet or griddle over medium heat. Coat with a little oil. Spoon 1/4 cupfuls of batter onto the hot griddle for each pancake. Cook until bubbles pop through the top of the pancakes, 2 to 3 minutes. Turn the pancakes and cook until lightly browned and cooked through, about 1 minute. ✐ Makes about 12 pancakes

VARIATIONS For an even lighter pancake, use plain amasake in place of the rice milk. Mix the batter the night before you plan to use it and allow it to stand, loosely covered, in a draft-free place until morning. The fermented nature of the amasake will introduce just a bit more leavening to the batter.

BUCKWHEAT PANCAKES Substitute 1/4 cup buckwheat flour for 1/4 cup of the pastry flour.

Iowa Corncakes

These sunny yellow griddle cakes have just the right blend of cornmeal and flour. Lovely for a summer brunch topped with a mound of seasonal fruit or fruit sauce. ✑

1 1/2 cups whole-wheat pastry flour

1/2 cup yellow cornmeal

2 to 3 tablespoons maple syrup granules

1/2 teaspoon sea salt

2 teaspoons baking powder

1 1/2 cups amasake

2 tablespoons corn oil, plus extra for cooking

Combine dry ingredients in a bowl. Whisk together wet ingredients in another bowl. Stir into dry ingredients and mix until the batter is just moistened and a bit lumpy.

Heat a skillet or griddle over medium heat. Coat with a little oil. Spoon batter by 1/4 cupfuls onto hot griddle. Cook over medium heat until bubbles pop through the top of the pancakes, about 3 minutes. Turn and cook until the pancakes are golden and cooked through, about 1 minute. ✑ M a k e s a b o u t 1 2 t o 1 6 p a n c a k e s

Mochi Waffles

These breakfast beauties couldn't be easier to make. Slice the mochi, cook and voilà—puffy, light waffles that make a most delicious, quick breakfast treat. 🍃

1 (8-oz.) package brown rice mochi

Heat a nonstick, Belgian waffle iron.

While the iron warms, slice the mochi into 1/8-inch-thick strips. When the iron is hot, lay the strips, loosely touching, in the waffle iron. You will need to press firmly to close the iron. Cook waffles 1 minute for softer waffles, up to 2 minutes for crispier ones. Remove waffle from iron, top with your favorite sauce, and enjoy. 🍃 Makes 4 or 5 waffles

Lemon-Nut Bread

A not-too-sweet snack bread that serves well in a variety of ways—accompanied by fresh fruit slices, smothered in fruit or nut spreads or, my favorite, cut into thin slices and lightly toasted, with a cup of tea. 🍃

2 1/2 cups whole-wheat pastry flour
2 to 3 teaspoons baking powder
1/4 teaspoon sea salt
3/4 cup rice milk or soy milk
1/4 cup corn oil
1/2 cup brown rice syrup
2 teaspoons grated lemon zest
2 to 3 teaspoons fresh lemon juice
1/2 cup coarsely minced walnut pieces

Preheat oven to 350F (175C). Lightly oil and flour a 9 × 5-inch loaf pan.

Sift together flour, baking powder and salt into a bowl. Whisk rice milk into oil and rice syrup in another bowl. Add lemon zest and juice. Stir into flour mixture and mix until smooth. Fold in nuts. Spoon batter evenly into prepared pan.

Bake 50 to 60 minutes, until the top springs back to the touch and the loaf is golden brown. Cool in pan 10 minutes before removing loaf from the pan and cooling on a wire rack. 🍃 Makes 1 loaf, 10 to 12 servings

Olive-Nut Bread

Olives put a unique twist on this nut bread, creating a savory loaf that beautifully complements any soup, stew or pasta meal.

2 1/2 cups whole-wheat pastry flour
1 tablespoon baking powder
1/4 teaspoon sea salt
1 cup rice milk or soy milk
1/4 cup extra-virgin olive oil

2 teaspoons brown rice syrup
1/2 cup oil-cured ripe olives, pitted
**   and halved**
1 cup coarsely minced walnut pieces

Preheat oven to 350F (175C). Lightly oil and flour a 9 × 5-inch loaf pan.

Sift together flour, baking powder and salt into a bowl. Whisk rice milk into oil and rice syrup in another bowl. Stir into flour mixture and mix until just moistened. Fold in olives and nuts. Spoon batter evenly into prepared pan.

Bake 45 to 50 minutes, until the bread is golden and the top springs back to the touch. Cool in pan 10 minutes before removing loaf from the pan and cooling on a wire rack. Serve sliced in thin pieces. ✦ Makes 1 loaf, 8 to 10 servings

Glazed Orange Bread

Orange marmalade is the star of the show in this loaf, where it flavors both the bread and the glaze—a real showstopper.

3 cups whole-wheat pastry flour

3 teaspoons baking powder

1/2 teaspoon sea salt

1 1/2 cups unsweetened orange marmalade

3/4 cup orange juice

1/4 cup corn oil

1 cup sunflower kernels, lightly pan-toasted (page 404)

1/4 cup brown rice syrup

Preheat oven to 350F (175C). Lightly oil and flour a 9 × 5-inch loaf pan.

Sift together flour, baking powder and salt into a bowl. Reserve 1/2 cup marmalade for the glaze. Combine the remaining marmalade with orange juice and oil. Stir into flour mixture, stirring until just moistened. Fold in the sunflower kernels. Spoon batter evenly into prepared pan.

Bake 55 to 60 minutes, until loaf is golden brown and the top springs back to the touch. Cool in pan 10 minutes before removing loaf from the pan and cooling on a wire rack.

Heat reserved marmalade and rice syrup over high heat until foamy. Immediately spoon over loaf. ✐ M a k e s   1   l o a f ,   1 0   t o   1 2   s e r v i n g s

Stew-Stuffed Loaf

One last recipe. This has become Robert's and my favorite way to eat bread. ✐

Robert makes a loaf of one of his delicious breads. My job is to create a thick, hearty vegetable or chunky vegetable and bean stew. I slice off the top of the loaf and hollow out the interior. (Save all that bread for sopping up the sauce.) Next, I ladle a bit of the sauce from the stew onto a serving platter and place the loaf on top. Then, I fill the loaf to capacity with hot stew and serve. We both then break off bits of the bread for scooping stew into individual soup bowls and feast. ✐

GREAT DESSERT CLASSICS

I love dessert. There, I've said it, openly admitted my love for that food that we have been indoctrinated by society to deny ourselves—or to eat in the closet. So where does dessert fit into a healthy eating plan? Or, more honestly, does it fit in at all?

You can summarize most people's attitudes on healthful eating with an old cliché: we want to have our cake and eat it, too. Of course, we also want to pare fat, cholesterol and excess calories from our diets, but without giving up the pleasure of great-tasting foods. Very few of us can imagine doing without wonderful desserts. While it might make sense to some, from a health viewpoint, to eliminate sweets altogether, only the most determined among us can adhere to such a severe regime. The real question is why should we? Life is meant to be enjoyed, not grimly endured. And I am here to tell you that you can enjoy great-tasting food and desserts and great health at the same time.

I grew up in a family of great chefs, especially in the dessert department. My relatives seemed to have this ongoing, good-natured competition to see who could create the sweetest, richest, most decadent—and beautiful—temptation. It was from these incredible cooks that I cultivated a love of combinations like chocolate, hazelnuts, and raspberries; flaky tortes bursting with rum cream puddings; fudgy brownies smothered in tangy orange sauce; and cherry-topped cheesecake—all common fare among these culinary wizards. I mastered each recipe, each technique, each little tip and trick, developing my skills so that I eventually began to create signature dessert specialties of my very own.

When my health crisis altered my lifestyle, and my approach to and understanding of food completely changed, the thought of being able to enjoy truly luxurious desserts seemed to be a dream just out of my reach. Oh, I tried, believe me. Tofu cheesecakes that were about as creamy as sand, whole-grain cakes and cookies that looked and tasted like hockey pucks, muffins that served double duty as doorstops—you've tried them, too. Dry, unsatisfying, unappealing desserts that tasted terrible but were reportedly good for us: low in fat, high in fiber, low in sugar and cholesterol—and extremely low in taste. After years of failed attempts, I had had enough. I decided that if I was able to make delicious desserts before, I could do it again. So I pulled out all the old rules, tips, wives' tales, techniques and tricks, and gave it a go.

My one rule on dessert creation was that if it didn't look and taste really wonderful, it wasn't worth eating—and certainly wasn't worth all the work to make it. I set out on a quest to create desserts that tasted as irresistible as they looked, without compromising the principles by which I live my life.

Okay, I really have two rules. The second one is simple: dessert isn't medicine. It is to be enjoyed on occasion, not prescribed. Dessert is an indulgence, not a daily staple. Most important, dessert is to be enjoyed; it shouldn't create more anxiety in our lives.

When it comes to dessert creation, I am as unwilling to compromise on health as I am unwilling to compromise on taste and appeal. Particularly in the case of sweet treats, *healthy* and *satisfying* seem to be mutually exclusive terms. So how do we create enjoyable, healthful desserts? How do we bake light, moist cakes and muffins; flaky pie crusts and pastries; rich, chewy cookies? How do we avoid creating those whole foods desserts that have the taste and texture of, well, healthy desserts?

My years of cooking naturally and creating all manner of recipes have taught me that the key is to make healthful desserts seem like indulgences, so that we'll be satisfied and not bypass them for the binge food that will compromise our health. It is possible to balance the demands of healthy foods with the sensual pleasure of eating. We can eat well without giving up one of our most precious indulgences—dessert.

However, is it possible to achieve full, rich flavor; moist, tender crumb; and satisfying sweet taste without eggs, cream, milk and sugar? Yes, very carefully and skillfully. It is all wrapped up in technique and intuition. It is learning, through experimentation and practice, how ingredients react together. For example, conventional cakes are light, moist and springy to the touch due to the combination of eggs, white flour, milk and sugar as well as intense whipping during the mixing process (which imparts air into the batter for that familiar light texture). Whole-grain-based cakes will never, never yield exactly that light, airy texture—no way, never, no how. So forget it. With that in mind, you can create a similar end product—a light, moist cake that has full-bodied taste and texture.

The most important thing to remember when creating desserts is that they are an indulgence—and should taste like one, even if they contain nutritionally superior ingredients. A bit of oil for butteriness, nuts for rich taste, sweetener for satisfaction. All of these minor ingredient indulgences will create the illusion of lush flavor and result in desserts that you will enjoy for a lifetime, not the kind of treats that only desperate dieters would eat.

BAKING TIPS

Assemble all the ingredients you will be needing before you begin to bake. Preheat your oven and prepare your cake pans before you begin. This will allow you to work quickly. You want to mix the batter and get it in the oven. You don't want your batter sitting for several minutes while you prepare your pans and heat your oven. This can result in heavy cakes that will not rise well, for whole-grain flour loves moisture and leaving the batter sitting for several minutes will cause it to saturate itself.

When mixing ingredients, use pastry knives, forks, spoons—anything but your hands. Remember whole grains love moisture, and the oil from your skin is no exception. It can create a tough, spongy dough. Handle the dough only when necessary, or as a recipe requires. Don't knead dough unless the recipe requires it; and when it does, don't overknead or underknead. Inexperienced bakers would do well to follow recipes to the letter until they master certain techniques and develop a "feel" for the doughs and batters they are working with. Whenever I asked my mother how she knew a batter was right (she rarely used recipes), she would say that it "felt right." It has taken me years of trial and error, but I now know what she meant. With practice, you too can develop a "feel" for baking. And, lucky for you, there are currently so many resources available to aid you in whole-grain baking that you can bypass years of practice if you can follow a recipe.

FLOUR

I use only whole-wheat pastry flour when baking cakes, cookies, pie crusts, pastries, muffins, tortes, cupcakes, or other baked treats. A finer grind of flour than regular whole-wheat flour (which is great for breads), it results in a lighter end product. I very rarely use white flour, bleached or unbleached, in my baking. It is highly refined and compromised, nutritionally deficient and really tough on the digestive tract. However, sometimes I combine whole-wheat pastry flour with unbleached white when essential to the final outcome. But that is rarely the case, especially when I can achieve satisfactory results without it.

Always sift flour before mixing with other ingredients to create air in the batter. Mix dry and wet ingredients separately and then simply fold them together until blended. This trick helps you avoid overmixing, which will most assuredly remove air from the batter, leaving you with a heavy, tough dough. Also, remember that whole grain loves moisture, so overmixing will cause the flour to saturate itself. So much for a light, springy cake!

FATS

To create moist textures in your pastries, you need to introduce some kind of fat or fat substitute. Conventional baked goods rely on milk, cream, eggs, butter, margarine, or artificial fat additives. Since I choose not to cook with any of those foods, I needed to find viable alternatives. My experience (and that of many other whole foods chefs) has shown corn oil to be the clear winner. Imparting a buttery flavor unsurpassed by other oils, corn oil creates a tender crumb and flavorful pastry every time. Canola and safflower oil are close runners-up, since they have such a mild taste. However, when adapting recipes, you will need to adjust liquid when using corn oil. Simply cut back equally on other liquids to accommodate the liquid of the oil, but you will see more of that in the following recipes.

And for those of you who wish to eliminate fat altogether in your baking, I have found that applesauce or pureed, poached pears work nicely to create a moist cake. Be careful with that one, though. Other liquids in the recipe will need to be seriously adjusted to accommodate the liquid in the fruit. For instance, in an average cake recipe,

I will use 1 cup of applesauce plus my liquid sweetener and no other fluids to achieve a proper batter. So play with this one a bit. Many low-fat bakers advocate the use of prune puree in the place of oil or fat. That works well in some recipes, but you must remember that pureed prunes will impart a strong taste and dark color to your recipe, so I personally reserve it for heartier items, like spice cakes, fruit cakes or carrot cakes.

Adding citrus zest to a recipe is one of the best ways I have found to add flavor to desserts that may be lacking because of diminished fat content. The zest is the colored part of the outer skin of lemons, oranges and other citrus fruits. Citrus zest adds tangy zip to fruit compotes, sauces, cakes, pastries and puddings. Since zest only has a mild sweet zing to it, you can pretty much use it as you desire.

Egg Substitutes

Eggs are used in desserts for two reasons: to leaven and/or to bind. With that in mind, eliminating them can create leaden pastries and cakes—not good. There are a couple of alternatives to eggs in dessert-making. For leavening, you may simply add 1 teaspoon of baking powder for every egg in the recipe. (You want to look for nonaluminum baking powder when purchasing. The products are clearly marked.) However, you can also whip together, in a blender, equal parts of flax seeds and boiled apple juice, using 1 teaspoon of this mixture for every egg. This leavening is a bit less predictable, so your results may vary. The final and most unpredictable leavener I have used is oatmeal cream. Simply cook oatmeal and spoon the "cream" off the top before stirring. Allow the cream to ferment lightly for a day before using as a leavening agent. My own results with this one have been spotty, but it is worth a try, particularly in pastries like scones, where hearty texture is a good thing.

In recipes where eggs act as binders, I have simply substituted 1 teaspoon kuzu or arrowroot for each egg and have been quite successful. For custards or flan, a combination of agar-agar flakes and kuzu has proved most satisfying in providing a firm, creamy pudding. Usually a teaspoon of each—kuzu and agar-agar—is enough to yield the firmest, creamiest custards.

Nuts are a wonderful addition to healthful desserts for many reasons. Their fat content gives desserts a rich, distinctive flavor and their texture adds an interestingly appealing crunch. To get the best flavor from nuts, simply roast them lightly before use—the lower the oven temperature, the more flavorful the nuts. For instance, I roast pecans at 275F (135C) for about 20 minutes to bring forth their delicate flavor. A too-high roasting temperature will result in bitter flavor. Pan-roasting nuts yields a more delicate flavor and is the method I prefer on most occasions.

SWEETENERS

Now the real issue—sweeteners. The best-quality sweeteners I have found are grain based. Barley malt and brown rice syrup are the sweeteners I choose most often. The beauty of grain sweeteners is that they are complex sugars, not simple sugars, so they are released into the blood slowly, providing fuel for the body instead of the rush and crash we get from simple sugars. They are also not all that refined a product; they are simply whole grains, inoculated with a fermenting agent and then cooked until they reduce to a syrup.

Rice syrup yields a delicate sweetness with no aftertaste that is very satisfying. It is the perfect sweetener for most cakes, pastries, cookies and puddings. Barley malt has a stronger taste, much like molasses, so I reserve its use for desserts that complement that kind of flavor, like spice cakes, carrot cakes, squash custards.

I rarely use honey, maple syrup or fruit sweeteners, again, because they are simple sugars and also because they have such a strong sweet taste. Grain sweeteners yield a lovely sweet taste, so there is no point in compromising for me. However, these are great sweeteners to use if grain sweeteners are unavailable or if you are making the transition from conventional, sugary desserts to healthier treats.

When using grain sweeteners, remember that they are liquid, so you will need to adjust your recipes to accommodate them. In adapting, I have found that substituting 1/2 cup of rice syrup for every 1 cup of sugar in a recipe yields a lovely sweet pastry.

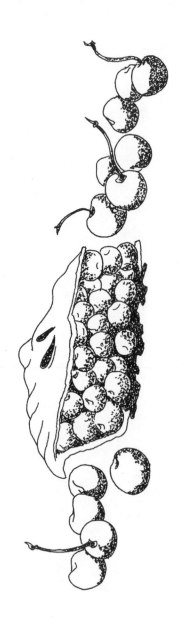

Apricot Pastries

These delicate crescent cookies are a real treat to serve. I love putting a tray out at the close of an autumn brunch or just about any time some friends and I get together for tea. ✑

2 cups whole-wheat pastry flour
Generous pinch of sea salt
3 tablespoons corn oil
1/4 cup spring or filtered water
3/4 cup unsweetened or fruit-sweetened apricot preserves

1/2 cup coarsely chopped walnuts
1/2 cup raisins
2 teaspoons ground cinnamon (optional)

Preheat oven to 350F (175C). Lightly oil a baking sheet. Sift flour and salt together into a large bowl. Add oil and water and stir with a wooden spoon to evenly distribute liquid throughout the flour. Mold dough into 2 balls, adding a small amount of water if dough feels too dry. Dough should be stiff but flexible. Don't overhandle or knead; just gather it into 2 balls.

Roll 1 ball of dough between waxed paper to form a 9-inch circle. Remove top sheet of paper. Spread entire circle with half of the preserves, nuts, raisins, and cinnamon, if using. Cut circle into 8 pie-shaped wedges. From the widest end of each wedge, roll each piece of dough into a crescent shape, pressing the point into the pastry to seal.

Place each pastry on prepared baking sheet, about 1 inch apart. Repeat the process with the other ball of dough.

Bake 12 to 15 minutes or until browned. Immediately remove from baking sheet with a spatula and cool on a wire rack. ✑ Makes 16 pastries

VARIATION While the pastries are still hot, it is a nice touch to glaze them. Simply heat rice syrup over high heat until it foams and pour, while still hot, over pastries. Allow to set about 30 minutes before serving.

NOTE The preserves may run out of the pastry during baking, so remove the pastries immediately from the baking sheet after baking or they will stick to the pan, making removal difficult and breakage of the pastries assured.

Sure-Fire Basic White Cake
This completely whole-grain cake really is a winner. Bake it just once and you will see that desserts can be delicious without compromising your food choices. I also use this great vanilla cake as the base recipe for all my other cakes, building and changing ingredients for each recipe. ✑

2 1/2 cups whole-wheat pastry flour

2 to 3 teaspoons baking powder

1/8 teaspoon sea salt

1/4 cup corn oil

1/2 cup brown rice syrup

1 teaspoon pure vanilla extract

1/2 cup spring or filtered water

1/2 to 2/3 cup rice milk

Preheat oven to 350F (175C). Lightly oil and flour a 9-inch round cake pan or loaf pan.

Sift together flour, baking powder and salt into a bowl. Whisk oil, rice syrup, vanilla, water, and 1/2 cup rice milk together in another bowl. Stir the oil mixture into the flour mixture, mixing until smooth; do not overmix. The batter should be thick and spoonable, not runny. Add more rice milk if needed. Spoon into prepared pan.

Bake on center rack 40 to 45 minutes or until a wooden pick inserted in center comes out clean and cake springs back to the touch; do not open the oven door until cake has baked for 20 minutes or the cake may sink.

Cool cake in pan 10 minutes before turning out of pan and cooling on a wire rack. ✑ Makes 1 cake

NOTE Work carefully with baked cake, realizing that cakes, especially whole-grain-based versions, are delicate.

Lemon Torte with Blackberry Sauce
This sweet and tangy torte is a real crowd pleaser. And the cook gets to take big bows for a beauty of a dessert. Only you and I will know how easy it is to make. The sauce can be used in lots of other ways: it goes great over a fresh fruit salad or spooned over your favorite frozen dessert. ✑

1 recipe Sure-Fire Basic White Cake
  (page 464)
Juice of 1 lemon
2 teaspoons grated lemon zest
3/4 cup unsweetened or
  fruit-sweetened apricot preserves
1/4 cup amasake
2 tablespoons kuzu, dissolved in
  1/4 cup cold water

Preheat oven to 325F (175C). Lightly oil a jelly-roll pan or deep baking sheet.

Make cake batter, adding lemon zest and juice. Spoon batter into pan. Bake 25 to 30 minutes or until center of cake springs back to the touch. Cool in pan 10 minutes before turning out of pan and cooling on a wire rack. Cut cake into 3 equal pieces.

Heat apricot preserves and amasake in a saucepan over medium heat. Stir in dissolved kuzu and cook, stirring, until mixture thickens, 3 minutes. Allow to cool, stirring occasionally so filling doesn't set. Place one of the pieces of cake on a plate and top with filling. Repeat with another cake layer and filling, ending with a thin layer of filling on top. Set aside while preparing the Blackberry Sauce.

Heat berries and rice syrup in a saucepan over medium heat. Stir in dissolved kuzu, and cook, stirring, until thickened, 3 minutes. Stir in lemon juice and remove from heat. Press mixture through a fine strainer to remove seeds. Chill 1 hour.

To serve the torte, pool a small amount of sauce on individual serving plates and place a slice of lemon torte directly on top. ◇ Makes about 10 servings

BLACKBERRY SAUCE

3 cups unsweetened frozen
  blackberries
1/4 cup brown rice syrup
1 tablespoon kuzu, dissolved in
  1/3 cup cold water
2 teaspoons fresh lemon juice

Pear Charlotte

Minus the heavy cream and sugar, this delicious version of a charlotte really showcases the delicate flavors of ripe, succulent pears.

Pastry Dough (opposite)

6 to 7 ripe pears, peeled, cored and thinly sliced

1 tablespoon fresh lemon juice, combined with 1 1/2 cups spring or filtered water

1/4 teaspoon gingerroot, minced

1/2 cup brown rice syrup

3 tablespoons kuzu, dissolved in 1/4 cup cold water

1 teaspoon corn oil

1/3 cup unsweetened or fruit-sweetened apricot preserves, strained

1 tablespoon almonds, pan-roasted (page 451) and minced

PASTRY DOUGH

1 1/2 cups whole-wheat pastry flour

1/4 teaspoon sea salt

1/4 cup corn oil (scant)

1/4 cup cold rice milk or cold water

Preheat oven to 375F (190C). Lightly oil a 9-inch tart pan.

Prepare pastry: Mix flour, salt and oil thoroughly, using a fork to blend ingredients. Slowly add rice milk water and stir to form a stiff but flexible dough. Gather into a ball and knead 1 to 2 minutes. Roll out thinly between sheets of waxed paper to a 10-inch circle. Lay over prepared tart pan, pressing it into the pan without stretching the dough.

Prick pastry all over with a fork. Cover with foil, firmly smoothing over pastry and then folding foil over pan edges so pastry is completely encased. Bake 14 minutes. Remove foil and return to oven 6 minutes or until light brown. Set aside.

Meanwhile, stir pear slices in lemon water to prevent discoloring. Reserve several slices for garnish. Combine pears with ginger and rice syrup in a saucepan and simmer over low heat until a chunky puree forms, 15 to 20 minutes, stirring frequently. Stir in dissolved kuzu and corn oil, and cook, stirring, until mixture thickens, about 3 minutes.

Spread mixture evenly over baked pastry. Arrange reserved sliced pears on top and bake 30 minutes. Remove from oven. Heat apricot preserves over high heat until foamy. Strain and spoon over top of the tart. Allow to stand until cooled before slicing. Sprinkle with almonds before serving. ✑ M a k e s 6 t o 8 s e r v i n g s

NOTE Rice milk makes a much more moist pastry than water.

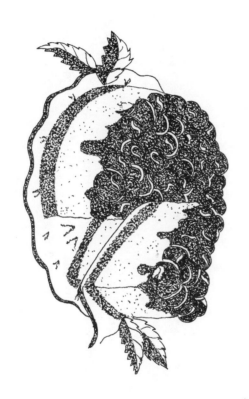

Fruit & Custard Tart
This unusual crust contains rolled oats and almonds instead of flour. ✑

OAT & NUT CRUST
1 cup rolled oats
1/2 cup almonds
1/4 cup corn oil
1/4 cup brown rice syrup

FILLING
1 cup amasake
2 teaspoons kuzu, dissolved in 1/4 cup cold water
1 teaspoon pure vanilla extract

3 to 4 cups fresh fruit: sliced strawberries; halved grapes; sliced peaches, pears or apples (tossed with 1 teaspoon lemon juice to prevent discoloring); blueberries and/or raspberries

GLAZE
1/4 cup unsweetened or fruit-sweetened apricot preserves
1/2 cup brown rice syrup
1/4 cup spring or filtered water
1 teaspoon agar-agar flakes

Preheat oven to 350F (175C).

Prepare crust: Process oats and almonds in a food processor into a fine meal. Add corn oil and rice syrup and process to a stiff dough. With wet hands, press oat mixture firmly into a pie pan. Bake 15 minutes or until set. Set aside.

Prepare the filling: Heat amasake over medium heat. Stir in dissolved kuzu and cook, stirring, until mixture thickens, about 3 minutes. Remove from heat and stir in vanilla. Spoon amasake mixture into pie shell. While still soft and warm, arrange fresh fruit in an attractive pattern, covering the amasake completely.

Prepare the glaze: Heat preserves, rice syrup, water and agar-agar over low heat, stirring constantly, until agar-agar dissolves, about 10 minutes. The mixture will thicken slightly. Brush or spoon mixture over the fruit while very hot. Allow the tart to set up about 1 hour before serving. ✑ Makes 6 to 8 servings

NOTE Pouring the hot glaze over the fruit cooks it just enough to make it slightly tender and brings out the sweetness.

Raspberry Trifle

An impressive, and delicious, dessert that showcases berries when they are at their peak. ✍

1 recipe Sure-Fire Basic White Cake (page 464), baked in a 9-inch-square pan

1 recipe Blackberry Sauce (page 465), substituting raspberries for blackberries

2 recipes Almond Custard (page 472)

2 cups mixed fresh soft fruit: sliced strawberries, halved grapes, whole blueberries or raspberries, thinly sliced peaches, etc.

1 1/2 cups slivered almonds, pan-toasted (page 65)

Cool cake completely; Cut into 1-inch cubes and set aside.

Using a trifle dish or deep clear glass bowl, begin assembling the trifle by drizzling about one-third of the raspberry sauce over the bottom. Arrange half of the cake cubes in a layer, patting them down into the sauce. Spread about one-fourth of the custard over the cake and arrange half of the fruit on top of the custard, pressing some pieces against the glass sides so they show.

Spread half of the remaining custard over the fruit. Sprinkle lightly with slivered almonds. Add another one-third of the raspberry sauce, then the remaining cake, pressing down slightly. Place the remaining fruit on top of the cake. Top with the last of the custard. Cover the top of the custard well with almonds. Using a spoon, create a ring of raspberry sauce around the edge of the bowl. Chill 1 hour, covered, or up to a full day before serving. ✍ Makes 10 to 12 servings

Oatmeal Cookies

These chewy treats are a must in any house that loves cookies. The lightly fermented dough requires no other leavening and the delicate sweet taste makes them a real delight. ✒

1 1/2 cups whole-wheat pastry flour
1 1/2 cups rolled oats
1/8 teaspoon sea salt
1/2 cup raisins
1/2 cup coarsely diced walnuts

1 cup amasake
3 tablespoons corn oil
3/4 cup brown rice syrup
1 teaspoon pure vanilla extract

Combine flour, oats and salt in a large bowl. Mix in raisins and walnuts. Whisk together amasake, oil, rice syrup and vanilla. Fold all ingredients together. Allow to rest, covered with a cloth towel, in a warm place 1 hour or more to allow the dough to ferment slightly so the cookies will rise.

Preheat oven to 375F (190C). Lightly oil a baking sheet. Drop cookie dough by teaspoonfuls onto the prepared baking sheet, leaving about 1 inch between cookies.

Bake 15 to 20 minutes, until golden and firm to the touch. Do not overbake, or the cookies will be tough. It is better to remove the cookies when they feel a bit on the soft side (they'll firm up as they cool), rather than overbake them. ✒

M a k e s   a b o u t   2   d o z e n

Tarte Tatin

I love breaking traditions and making new ones. Yet another delicious, offbeat approach to a very classic dessert.

4 Granny Smith apples, peeled, quartered and cored
2 tablespoons fresh lemon juice, combined with 2 cups water
1/2 cup brown rice syrup
1 tablespoon corn oil
Pinch of sea salt
1 recipe Sure-Fire Basic White Cake (page 464)

Preheat oven to 375F (175C). Stir apples in lemon water to prevent discoloration. Drain fruit well in a colander and set aside.

Combine rice syrup, and corn oil, and salt in a skillet that can be transferred to the oven. Cast iron works well. Stir apples into rice-syrup mixture, taking care to coat the fruit well. Spread mixture evenly over skillet surface. Place over medium heat and warm through. Fruit will begin to release juice. Cook 20 minutes, stirring occasionally. Fruit should become caramelized and pierce easily with a fork. Increase heat if needed so that mixture bubbles vigorously or juices will not brown—but take care not to burn. Remove from heat and allow to cool slightly. Arrange the cooked apple slices attractively in a ring in the same skillet.

Prepare cake batter and immediately spoon over cooked fruit, spreading lightly to evenly coat the surface, but try to not disturb fruit.

Bake on the center rack 30 to 35 minutes. Cake should be nicely browned and a wooden pick inserted in center of cake should come out clean. Remove from oven and allow to cool 4 to 5 minutes. Run a sharp knife around rim of skillet to loosen cake. Center a serving plate over skillet and invert cake onto the plate. If any fruit pieces or juices remain in the skillet, spoon over the top of cake. If fruit is not sufficiently browned, place cake briefly under the broiler until just browned. Do not burn. Let cake stand 5 minutes before slicing. ✒ M a k e s 8 t o 1 0 s e r v i n g s

Coco-Locos

These cookies are decadent! If you love chocolate (Is there anyone not bewitched by it?), then try these. No one will ever know that you have created sinfully delicious treats with healthy ingredients. ✒

1 1/2 cups rolled oats
1 3/4 cups whole-wheat pastry flour
1/8 teaspoon sea salt
1 1/2 teaspoons baking powder
1 cup shredded coconut
1/2 cup minced pecans

1 cup brown rice syrup
1/2 cup corn oil
1 cup nondairy, malt-sweetened chocolate chips (available at natural foods stores)

Preheat oven to 350F (175C). Lightly oil a baking sheet. Combine all ingredients, except chocolate, in a large bowl until blended. Gently fold in chips and drop by spoonfuls onto prepared baking sheet.

Bake 18 to 20 minutes. Cookies should be moist and chewy. Cool on wire racks. ✒

Makes about 2 dozen

Almond Custard Cake Roll

This recipe is a bit tricky and requires some degree of skill in handling whole-grain cakes. But don't be intimidated. It is so beautiful and delicious, it is worth the care and practice to get it right. ✒

1 recipe Sure-Fire Basic White Cake
   (page 464)
Flour
Almond Custard (opposite)
1 cup slivered almonds, pan-toasted
   (page 65)

ALMOND CUSTARD
2 cups amasake
Pinch of sea salt
2 tablespoons kuzu, dissolved in
   1/4 cup cold water
1 teaspoon almond extract

Preheat oven to 350F (175C). Line a jelly-roll pan with parchment paper, allowing it to hang slightly over the edges of the pan. Lightly oil the paper.

Prepare cake recipe: Turn prepared batter into the prepared pan and spread evenly over the surface. Bake on the center rack 7 to 10 minutes. Cake should spring back to the touch. Remove from the oven, drape a damp cloth towel over the cake and set aside.5 minutes. Remove towel and run a knife around the edges of the cake to loosen cake and paper from the pan.

Very lightly dust a long sheet of waxed paper with flour. Lift cake and paper from pan and lay, top side down, on waxed paper. Gently peel off paper. Trim off any dry edges of cake. Cover with a fresh sheet of waxed paper. Let stand 5 to 7 minutes—cake should still be warm.

Turn cake over so original top is facing up. Carefully and firmly roll up cake and paper to form an evenly thick log. Secure in waxed paper by folding or twisting ends. Refrigerate 1 hour before proceeding. (Store in refrigerator up to 2 days or in freezer if not using right away.)

Prepare custard. Heat amasake and salt thoroughly. Stir in dissolved kuzu and cook, stirring, until amasake thickens, about 3 minutes. Remove from heat and stir in almond extract.

To assemble the cake roll, allow cake to come to room temperature. Unroll cake and, if sticky, sprinkle lightly with flour. Reserving some custard to decorate the top of the cake, evenly spread warm custard over surface of cake, leaving about 1 inch all around the edges to avoid squeezing out cream during rolling. Sprinkle with three-quarters of the nuts, reserving the remainder for garnish. Working from a short side, roll the cake up neatly and firmly. Wrap tightly in waxed paper to keep from unrolling. Transfer to a tray and refrigerate at least 2 hours to set.

To serve, remove waxed paper from cake, spread top with remaining custard and sprinkle with nuts. Slice into rounds and serve. ⑤ Makes 8 to 10 servings

Chestnut Cream Pie

This delightfully creamy pie tastes positively sinful, but it's positively not. What fun!

1 1/2 cups dried chestnuts, soaked
    6 to 8 hours
Spring or filtered water
Sea salt
3 cups amasake (almond or plain)
2 tablespoons agar-agar flakes
1 tablespoon kuzu, dissolved in
    3 tablespoons cold water

1/2 cup brown rice syrup
1 teaspoon pure vanilla extract
2 tablespoons sesame tahini
Juice of 1 lemon
1 recipe Pastry Dough (page 466),
    baked until golden brown

Place chestnuts, with enough water to generously cover and a pinch of salt, in a pressure cooker. Seal and bring to full pressure. Reduce heat to low and cook 20 minutes. Remove from heat and allow pressure to reduce naturally.

Heat amasake and agar-agar in a saucepan over low heat 10 to 12 minutes, stirring occasionally, until flakes dissolve completely. Stir in dissolved kuzu and cook, stirring, until mixture begins to thicken, 3 minutes. Add rice syrup and vanilla and remove from heat.

Transfer mixture to a food processor. Add cooked chestnuts, tahini, and lemon juice and blend until smooth. Pour mixture evenly into pie shell and allow to stand 30 minutes before refrigerating 1 hour or until set. Makes 1 pie, 6 to 8 servings

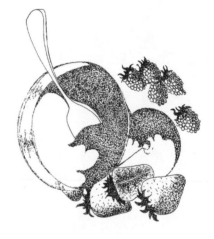

Viennese Vanilla Crescents

My mother was a great baker. She didn't seem to have a specialty; she just went into the kitchen and created heavenly treats. As a kid, I couldn't resist her cookies, especially at Christmas. This recipe is adapted from one of my holiday favorites. ✒

4 cups whole-wheat pastry flour
1/4 teaspoon sea salt
1/4 cup corn oil
1/4 cup brown rice syrup
About 1/2 cup spring or filtered water
1 teaspoon pure vanilla extract

1 teaspoon grated lemon peel
2 cups almonds, ground into a fine meal
2 teaspoons baking powder
About 1/2 cup brown rice syrup, for glaze

Preheat oven to 400F (205C). Lightly oil 2 baking sheets.

Combine all ingredients, except 1/4 cup almond meal, in a large bowl. Mix into a stiff dough. Gather into a ball, wrap in waxed paper and refrigerate 1 hour.

Roll dough into 1/4-inch-thick ropes and cut into 2-inch pieces. Bend into crescent shapes. Arrange on prepared baking sheets, leaving about 1 inch between cookies.

Bake 10 minutes. Heat rice syrup in a saucepan over high heat until foamy. While cookies are still warm, roll in warm rice syrup and remaining almond meal. ✒

Makes 3 to 4 dozen

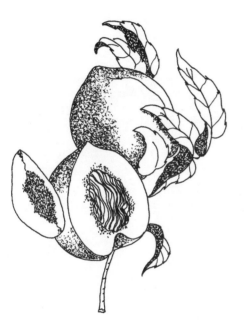

Italian Biscotti

Yes, you read right—biscotti! Now, I know what you're thinking: how can you make biscotti without tons of eggs? Well, frankly, I threw out a lot of cookie batter before I got this one right. All I can tell you is try them; you'll like them. They are a delight with a cup of good, strong demitasse. 🍃

3/4 cup slivered almonds

3 cups whole-wheat pastry flour

1/2 cup tan sesame seeds

1 1/2 teaspoons baking powder

1/2 cup plus 2 tablespoons brown rice syrup

1/3 cup corn oil

1/2 teaspoon almond or anise extract

1/4 cup spring or filtered water

Preheat oven to 275F (135C). Arrange almonds on a baking sheet. Lightly oven-toast almonds until fragrant, about 10 minutes. Set aside 1/4 cup for garnish.

Combine flour, sesame seeds, 1/2 cup almonds and baking powder in a large bowl. Combine the 1/2 cup rice syrup, corn oil, almond extract, and water in a small bowl. Stir into flour mixture to make a stiff, kneadable dough.

Preheat oven to 350F (175C). Lightly oil a baking sheet. Divide the dough into 2 equal pieces and shape into 2 logs about 3 inches wide, 1 inch high and long enough to almost equal the length of the baking sheet. Warm the 2 tablespoons rice syrup in a small saucepan. Brush warm syrup on the tops of the logs and gently press in the remaining almonds.

Bake about 15 minutes or until golden brown. Remove from the oven and slice into 1-inch wedges while still warm. Place the wedges back on the baking sheet, cut side up, and return to the oven for 3 to 4 minutes to crisp the biscotti. 🍃

Makes about 2 dozen

Peanut Blossoms

These soft, peanuty cookies are filled to the brim with tart raspberry jam. You can use any peanut butter, but one with a crunchy texture really makes these cookies a real kid (old or young) pleaser. ✑

3 cups whole-wheat pastry flour
1 1/2 teaspoons baking powder
1/8 teaspoon sea salt
1 cup brown rice syrup
1/2 cup unsweetened, unsalted peanut butter

2 tablespoons corn oil
1 teaspoon pure vanilla extract
About 1/2 cup unsweetened raspberry jam

Lightly oil a baking sheet. Combine flour, baking powder, and salt in a large bowl. Combine the rice syrup, peanut butter, corn oil and vanilla in a small bowl. Stir into flour mixture and mix just enough to combine ingredients. Overmixing will result in tough cookies, and we want them to be chewy and gooey.

Roll the dough into 1 1/2-inch balls. Place about 1 inch apart on prepared baking sheet. Moisten your thumb and press down in the center of each cookie, making a deep indentation. Fill the hole with raspberry jam. Refrigerate the entire tray of cookies 1 hour before baking.

Preheat oven to 325F (165C). Bake 18 to 20 minutes or until cookies are set. Remove from the oven and allow the cookies to cool on the baking sheet, which allows them to finish baking but keeps the cookies soft and chewy. ✑

Makes about 3 dozen cookies

Almond Custard–Filled Torte

To make this sinfully delicious (and so-o-o-o easy) torte you really need a torte pan, which you can buy at any kitchen shop. You'll know it—the pans usually have scalloped rims with an indentation in the center for the custard or whatever. ✑

1 recipe Sure-Fire Basic White Cake
    (page 464)
1 1/2 cups almond-flavored amasake
2 tablespoons kuzu, dissolved in
    1/4 cup cold water

Strawberries, sliced, for decoration
Kiwi fruit, sliced, for decoration

Preheat oven to 350F (175C). Oil the torte pan well, being sure to get into all the creases so the cake will not stick. Dust the pan with flour. Cut a circle of waxed paper the size of the indentation in the center. Put waxed paper in place and oil it.

Prepare the cake batter as directed in the recipe. Spoon the batter carefully into the pan without moving the waxed paper around. Bake 30 to 35 minutes, until the center of the torte springs back to the touch.

Meanwhile make the filling: Heat the amasake over medium heat. Add dissolved kuzu and cook, stirring constantly, until thick and creamy, 3 to 4 minutes. You want the starch of the kuzu to cook completely so that your custard doesn't have a chalky taste.

Cool cake in pan about 10 minutes before turning out onto a serving plate to cool completely. Fill the indentation with custard and cover the top with concentric circles of strawberry and kiwi fruit slices. ✑ M a k e s 1 t o r t e , 8 t o 1 0 s e r v i n g s

VARIATIONS I like to decorate these cakes with a wide variety of fruits. I decorate the edges of the torte with toasted minced pecans and a thin ring of carefully placed nondairy chocolate chips.

NOTE Don't let the cake cool completely in the pan, as it will stick to the pan and probably break. (The same thing will happen if the cake is too hot.) So a good rule of thumb is to remove the cake from the pan when it is still warm, but you are able to hold the pan with no hot pads.

And how exactly do you turn a cake out of a pan? Run a sharp knife around the edge of the pan, then place your serving plate squarely over the cake and, holding the pan and plate firmly on both sides, flip it quickly. The cake should drop onto the plate. If you sense it sticking, gently tap the pan. If that doesn't work, flip it back over, loosen the cake and try again.

Praline Pumpkin Pie

The simple addition of sweet, crunchy pecans gives new meaning to decadent holiday treats.

(I know it's called pumpkin pie, but winter squash is so much sweeter than pumpkin.)

1 recipe Pastry Dough (page 466)

1/3 cup barley malt

2 tablespoons corn oil

1/2 cup pecans, minced

2 cups 1-inch pieces butternut squash
   or pumpkin

Sea salt

2/3 cup brown rice syrup

1 teaspoon pumpkin pie spice

1/2 teaspoon ground ginger

1 cup amasake

4 tablespoons agar-agar flakes

3 tablespoons kuzu, dissolved in
   1/4 cup cold water

Preheat the oven to 400F (205C). Prepare pie dough. Roll out thinly between sheets of waxed paper into a 10-inch circle. Lay over a 9-inch pie pan, pressing it into the pan without stretching the dough. Trim the excess dough around the edges, leaving an even 1/2-inch overhang. Turn the excess dough up toward the edge of the pie and crimp or flute to form a decorative edge. Prick with a fork. Bake the pie shell 10 minutes. This prevents a soggy crust when serving the finished pie. Allow to cool completely after baking.

Combine barley malt and corn oil in a saucepan and cook until foamy. Immediately stir in the pecans. Spread evenly over the bottom of the pie shell and set aside to cool to room temperature.

Add the squash and 1/2 inch water to a pressure cooker. Add a pinch of salt, seal and bring to full pressure over medium heat. Reduce heat and cook squash 20 minutes. Remove from heat and allow pressure to reduce naturally. Puree the squash in a food mill or food processor until smooth.

Reduce oven heat to 350F (175C). Combine rice syrup, pie spice, ginger, amasake and agar-agar with cooked squash in a heavy pot. Simmer over low heat about 15 minutes, until agar-agar completely dissolves. Stir in dissolved kuzu and cook, stirring, until mixture thickens, 3 to 4 minutes. Pour filling carefully into pie shell over the pecans. Bake 30 to 35 minutes. Remove pie from oven, cover completely with foil, and allow to cool completely before serving. Covering the pie while hot prevents the top from cracking as it cools. ✐ M a k e s 6 t o 8 s e r v i n g s

Antico Dolce Torte
An Italian tradition at most Christmas morning feasts, this confection was always a favorite of mine. So when my eating habits turned to healthier choices, I couldn't bear to give it up. Here is the result of my experimentation! ✐

DOUGH

3 cups whole-wheat pastry flour

Generous pinch of sea salt

1/2 cup brown rice syrup

6 tablespoons corn oil

3/4 cup boiling spring or filtered water

FILLING

3 cups walnuts, pan-toasted
    (page 417) and minced

2 cups raisins

1 teaspoon ground cinnamon

1/4 cup corn oil

1/4 cup brown rice syrup

GLAZE

3 tablespoons corn oil

1 1/2 cups brown rice syrup

Prepare the dough: Place the flour, salt, rice syrup and oil in a food processor or heavy-duty electric mixer bowl and mix until blended. While the mixer or processor is running, add the boiling water to the flour mixture. Blend only until the particles begin to cling together. Gather dough into a ball, wrap in waxed paper and refrigerate 1 hour.

Prepare the filling: Process nuts, raisins and cinnamon in a food processor until a fine meal forms. Do not overprocess into flour. Scrape mixture into a bowl. In a saucepan, heat oil and rice syrup until it foams and stir immediately into raisin and nut mixture. Divide the filling into 3 separate bowls and set aside.

To assemble, divide chilled dough into thirds. On a floured surface, roll out 1 portion at a time into a long rectangle, about 30 × 5 inches. Trim strips evenly so the rectangles match.

Preheat oven to 350F (175C). Lightly oil a large baking sheet. Spoon filling from each of the 3 bowls lengthwise over one-half of each strip. Fold the other half of the dough over the filling, making 3 filled 30-inch-long strips.

Starting at the end of one strip, roll up tightly into a pinwheel. Overlapping slightly at the end, attach the next strip and continue to roll. Repeat with the last strip. Now, turn the assembled torte, filling side up, onto the prepared baking sheet. Tie a string midway around the diameter of the torte.

Prepare the glaze: Heat ingredients over high heat until they foam. Immediately brush the sides of the torte with glaze, spooning the remaining glaze over the top. Bake about 1 hour, until golden brown.

When cooled, remove the string from the torte and replace it with a holiday ribbon. Serve sliced in thin wedges with strong demitasse or tea for a festive Christmas morning treat. ✧ Makes 1 torte, about 8 to 10 servings

Raspberry Pinwheels

These delightful cookies are almost as fun to make as they are to eat. A great recipe to get the kids involved in, or to prepare with friends. 🌿

2 cups whole-wheat pastry flour

1 teaspoon baking powder

1/8 teaspoon sea salt

2/3 cup corn oil

1 teaspoon pure vanilla extract

1/4 to 1/2 cup cold spring or filtered water

About 1/2 cup unsweetened or fruit-sweetened raspberry jam

1/2 teaspoon grated lemon zest

1/4 cup walnuts, pan-toasted (page 417) and minced

Combine flour, baking powder and salt in a bowl. Blend in oil, vanilla and enough cold water to make a stiff, pliable dough. Gather dough into a ball, wrap in waxed paper and chill 1 hour.

Preheat oven to 350F (175C). Lightly oil a baking sheet. Divide dough into 2 pieces and roll out each between waxed paper into 10-inch squares. Cut each square into 5 (2-inch) squares. Place small squares on prepared baking sheet.

Cut 1-inch slits from each corner toward the center, but not all the way to the center. Place a small amount of jam in the middle of the square and top with lemon zest and a sprinkling of nuts. Fold every other corner toward the center and pinch, forming the pinwheel shape.

Bake 10 minutes, until lightly golden. Remove from the oven and carefully transfer cookies to a cooling rack. 🌿 M a k e s a b o u t 2 0 p i n w h e e l s

VARIATION To glaze the cookies, heat a small amount of rice syrup over high heat until it foams and quickly spoon over the cooling pastries. Allow to stand several minutes to set the glaze before serving.

Cranberry Pear Relish

A different approach to traditional cranberry relish, this dish combines the natural tartness of cranberries with the delicate sweet taste of ripe autumn pears. ✑

1 cup brown rice syrup
3 cups fresh cranberries, sorted
    and rinsed
2 ripe pears, peeled, if desired,
    and cut into cubes

1/2 teaspoon grated nutmeg
1/2 teaspoon ground allspice
Pinch sea salt
2 teaspoons grated lemon zest

Heat rice syrup in a large saucepan over medium heat until foamy. Add cranberries, pears, spices and salt. Return to a boil and stir in 1 teaspoon lemon zest. Reduce heat and simmer 25 to 30 minutes, until the cranberries pop. Transfer to a serving bowl and chill. Before serving, garnish with remaining lemon zest. ✑

M a k e s   a b o u t   5   s e r v i n g s

No-Meat Mincemeat Pie

I never liked mincemeat pie when I was a kid, but everyone raved about my mother's version at our Thanksgiving feasts. For Robert's and my first holiday season together, I asked him what pie he'd like and he voted for mincemeat. Well, as anyone who has been in love, and especially in new love, can tell you, you bend over backwards to impress and accommodate. Referring to my mother's recipe and praying for inspiration, I came up with a recipe that still wows Robert to this very day. 🌱

1 cup raisins

1 cup dried apricots

3 cups apple juice

Pinch of sea salt

4 cups chopped tart apples

2 tablespoons red miso

1/2 teaspoon ground allspice

2 tablespoons kuzu, dissolved in
    1/4 cup cold water or juice

2 tablespoons grated orange zest

1 tablespoon grated lemon zest

2 tablespoons fresh orange juice

1/2 cup walnuts, pan-toasted (page
    417) and broken into small pieces

1 recipe Pastry Dough (page 466)

Soak the raisins and apricots together in the apple juice 6 to 8 hours. In an uncovered pot, combine the soaked fruit, the soaking juice, salt and apples and cook over medium heat, stirring occasionally, 1 hour. Remove about 2 tablespoons of hot juice and use to dissolve the miso. Stir mixture into the pot and simmer 15 minutes. Stir in allspice, then stir in dissolved kuzu and cook, stirring, until the mixture thickens, 3 to 4 minutes. Stir in the orange and lemon zests, orange juice, and walnuts. Set aside to cool as you prepare the pie crust.

Preheat the oven to 400F (205C). Prepare pie dough. Roll out thinly between 2 sheets of waxed paper into a 10-inch circle. Lay over a 9-inch pie pan, pressing it into the pan without stretching the dough. Trim the excess dough around the edges, leaving an even 1/2-inch overhang. Turn the excess dough up toward the edge of the pie and crimp or flute to form a decorative edge. Prick crust with a fork.

Bake the pie shell 10 minutes. This prevents a soggy crust when serving the finished pie.

Reduce oven temperature to 350F (175C). Pour filling into pie shell. Bake 30 to 35 minutes or until filling is set. ✍ M a k e s   6   t o   8   s e r v i n g s

VARIATIONS When making this pie, I like to prepare it as a single-crust pie, but you may also double the pastry recipe and make a lattice top. This recipe also makes really beautiful miniature tartlets.

Would You Believe Tiramisu? Anyone who has

indulged in the real version of this dessert won't be fooled for a minute by this one. A decadent dessert in its own right, it is a spin-off of the original and is so delicious, you will use it to create a new tradition of your own.

Mirin lends the amasake a slight resemblance to mascarpone, the soft, sweet cheese normally associated with this dessert. Cooking mirin removes just about all the alcohol, leaving you with just its essence. ✍

2 recipes Sure-Fire Basic White Cake
  (page 464)

2 cups almond-flavored amasake

2 to 3 tablespoons mirin

3 tablespoons kuzu, dissolved in
  1/4 cup cold water

1 cup grain coffee, brewed and cooled

1 cup slivered almonds, pan-toasted
  (page 65)

1/4 cup nondairy, malt-sweetened
  chocolate chips

Bake the cake in 2 round cake pans as directed on page 464 and allow to cool completely before continuing the recipe.

Prepare the filling: Mix together amasake and mirin in a saucepan over medium heat and warm amasake mixture thoroughly. Stir in dissolved kuzu and cook, stirring, until thick and creamy, 3 to 4 minutes. Set the amasake custard aside to cool. Start assembling the tiramisu when the amasake custard has just begun to set.

To assemble, slice the cakes in half horizontally to make 4 layers. To make even layers, insert a serrated knife and turn the cake while slicing. Place a cake layer on a serving platter. Spoon grain coffee lightly over it—do not saturate. Top with a layer of amasake custard and sprinkle with slivered almonds. Add the next cake layer and repeat the process. The top layer of the cake should be covered with amasake and almonds. If you have enough custard, you may spread it around the sides of the tiramisu as well and then press almonds into the custard as decoration. Decorate the top of the tiramisu with chocolate chips and allow to stand 30 minutes or chill 15 minutes before slicing. 🌿

Makes 10 to 12 servings

Fresh Fruit Kanten

This basic dessert is a tried and true winner. Light and refreshing, it can be simple or profoundly elegant. It's up to you and your imagination. ✑

3 cups apple juice or other fruit juice

3 tablespoons agar-agar flakes

Pinch of sea salt

1 to 2 cups bite-size pieces seasonal fruit

Combine juice, salt and agar-agar in a saucepan and bring to a boil over low heat. If you boil too quickly, the agar will simply sink to the bottom of the pan and not dissolve. Simmer 10 to 15 minutes, stirring occasionally, until agar-agar completely disappears.

Arrange fruit in individual dessert cups or on the bottom of a 13 × 9-inch dish. Pour juice mixture gently over fruit. It should set up in about 1 1/2 hours, but if you would like to speed up the process, allow to stand 30 minutes and then refrigerate. ✑

Makes 6 to 8 servings

NOTE If you are using softer fruits, like berries, cherries, melon or peaches, you do not need to cook the fruit in the kanten mixture; if using firm fruit, like apples or pears, you will need to cook them in with the agar-agar and juice mixture, so that they soften.

VARIATION A different twist on basic kanten is to simply whip it into a mousse when it has completely set up. This adds a bit of elegance and style to your presentation. Serve garnished with fresh berries and mint leaves.

Pear-Almond Clafouti

Clafouti is a traditional French dessert. This version is light and elegant, a joy to create and, of course, eat! ✎

2 cups whole-wheat pastry flour

2 1/2 teaspoons baking powder

1/4 teaspoon sea salt

1 1/2 cups almonds, ground into a
    fine meal

1/2 cup brown rice syrup

1/2 cup spring or filtered water

1 teaspoon pure vanilla extract

2 teaspoons fresh orange juice

2 firm pears, cored and thinly sliced
    lengthwise

GLAZE

2/3 cup red wine

1/3 cup brown rice syrup

4 tablespoons arrowroot, dissolved
    in 4 tablespoons cold water

Preheat the oven to 375F (190C). Lightly oil and flour a 9-inch round cake or quiche pan. Sift the flour, baking powder and salt into a bowl. Mix in almond meal and gently stir in the rice syrup, water, vanilla, and orange juice, mixing well. Pour the batter evenly into the prepared pan.

Arrange pears on top of the batter in a decorative spiral pattern. Bake 35 to 40 minutes, until a wooden pick inserted in the cake's center comes out clean and the cake springs back to the touch.

Prepare the glaze: Heat the wine and rice syrup in a saucepan over medium heat until foamy. Stir in dissolved arrowroot and cook, stirring, until the glaze thickens, about 5 minutes. Carefully turn the clafouti out of the pan and brush with glaze while still warm. ✎ M a k e s a b o u t 8 s e r v i n g s

VARIATION You may use kuzu to thicken your glaze, but in this case, the arrowroot gives the cake top a shinier look.

Watermelon Freeze

What would summer be without watermelon? Try this refreshing dessert to beat the heat. ❧

4 cups seeded and cubed watermelon

2 cups cubed cantaloupe

Pinch of sea salt

3 fresh mint leaves or 1 mint tea bag

1 cup spring or filtered water

Juice of 1 fresh lemon

Lemon Sauce (page 490) (optional)

Puree the melons in a food processor until smooth. Place in a saucepan with the salt and simmer 15 minutes.

Meanwhile, in another saucepan simmer the mint leaves or tea bag in the water about 3 minutes. Strain and add this infusion to the cooked melons. Turn off the heat and stir in the lemon juice.

Line a muffin pan with cupcake paper liners, pour melon puree into each one and freeze. When beginning to firm up, you may insert flat wooden sticks into each treat. Freeze until completely hard or the papers will not peel easily away. Remove papers before serving. I like to serve these frozen treats on a pool of chilled Lemon Sauce.

Makes 12 to 18.

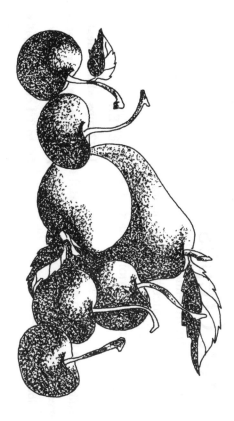

Strawberry-Lemon Terrine

There is nothing more refreshing in hot weather than a silky, lemony pudding swirled through with naturally sweet strawberries—a new take on a cool summer classic. 🌿

2 cups apple juice or water

Pinch of sea salt

2 to 3 tablespoons agar-agar flakes

Juice of 2 lemons

1 cup amasake

1 tablespoon kuzu, dissolved in

1/8 cup cold water

2 cups sliced fresh strawberries

1 cup Strawberry Sauce (opposite)

Fresh strawberry slices and mint leaves, for decoration

STRAWBERRY SAUCE

1 cup apple juice

1 pint fresh strawberries, sliced

2 teaspoons kuzu, dissolved in

1/8 cup cold water or juice

Combine apple juice, salt and agar-agar in a medium saucepan and bring to a boil over low heat. Simmer, stirring occasionally, until flakes dissolve, 10 to 15 minutes. When the flakes have dissolved, remove from heat and stir in lemon juice.

Heat amasake until hot in a small saucepan over medium heat. Stir in dissolved kuzu and cook, stirring, until it thickens, 3 to 4 minutes. Fold gently into lemon mixture.

Lightly oil a 9 × 5-inch loaf pan. Pour half the lemon mixture evenly into the pan. Refrigerate until almost set, 15 minutes. Top with strawberries, covering the entire surface of the terrine by slightly overlapping the berry slices. Return to the refrigerator until completely set. Whisk the remaining lemon pudding to loosen it and spread it carefully over the strawberries. Refrigerate until firmly set, at least 1 hour.

Prepare sauce: Heat apple juice and strawberries until hot in a saucepan over medium heat. Stir in dissolved kuzu and cook, stirring, until mixture thickens, 3 to 4 minutes. Push through a strainer to remove any pulp and seeds, so that the sauce is smooth. Chill before using.

Turn terrine out on a plate and cut into slices. Spoon a pool of sauce on each dessert plate. Place a terrine slice on the sauce. Decorate each plate with strawberries and mint leaves. 🌿 Makes 6 to 8 servings

Blueberry Pie

Nothing says summer quite like a pie laden with succulent sweet berries. Serve this pie any time to delight friends, family and, of course, yourself!

2 recipes Pastry Dough (page 466)

2 pints blueberries, sorted and rinsed

1/2 cup plus 3 tablespoons brown rice syrup

3 tablespoons kuzu, dissolved in

1/4 cup cold water

1 teaspoon fresh lemon juice

1 teaspoon grated lemon zest

Prepare dough and separate into 2 pieces. Roll out thinly between waxed paper and lay 1 crust over a pie plate. Press into position, without stretching the dough, trimming the excess flush with the sides of the pan. Keep other piece of dough wrapped in waxed paper until ready to use.

Preheat the oven to 400F (205C). Combine the berries and the 1/2 cup rice syrup in a medium saucepan and heat over low heat until hot. Stir in dissolved kuzu and cook, stirring, until the mixture thickens, about 3 minutes. Remove from heat and stir in lemon juice and zest. Spoon into pie shell, filling completely.

Moisten the edge of the bottom crust with water. Lay the other crust over top. Trim excess dough, leaving about 1/2-inch overhang. Fold the overhang under the rim of the bottom crust and, by pinching dough between your thumb and forefinger, pushing the dough between your fingers with the other forefinger, flute the edge of the crust. Next, with a sharp knife, cut a 4-inch X shape in the center of the top crust. Fold back the points of the X to make a square opening in the center of the pie.

Heat the remaining 3 tablespoons rice syrup in a small saucepan over high heat until it foams. Remove from heat and quickly drizzle over the top of the pie. Bake 40 minutes, until the filling is bubbly and the crust is golden. Cool pie completely before slicing. ❧ Makes 6 to 8 servings

Cran-Apple Crumb Tart

The soft pastry dough for this sweet and tangy tart is not rolled but simply pressed into the pan. Rice or maple syrup granules are a great natural alternative to sugar and achieve the same delicious crumb topping that is so traditional in a pastry like this.

DOUGH

1/2 cup corn oil
1/4 cup brown rice syrup
1 cup whole-wheat pastry flour
2/3 cup unbleached white flour
Pinch of sea salt

FILLING

1 1/2 pounds Granny Smith apples
1 cup fresh cranberries, sorted and rinsed
2 1/2 tablespoons arrowroot

1/2 teaspoon ground cinnamon
2/3 cup brown rice syrup

CRUMB TOPPING

1 cup rolled oats
1 cup walnuts, broken into small pieces
3/4 cup whole-wheat pastry flour
Pinch of sea salt
2/3 cup brown rice syrup granules or maple syrup granules
6 tablespoons corn oil

Lightly oil an 11-inch fluted tart pan with a removable bottom.

Prepare the dough: Whisk together the corn oil and rice syrup. Combine the flours and salt in a bowl and slowly add the liquid, mixing until the dough just comes together. Turn it out onto a lightly floured surface and knead 3 or 4 times, just enough to form a soft, smooth ball. Pat the dough gently into a thick round. Press the dough evenly into the sides and bottom of the pan and prick all over the surface with a fork. Refrigerate 1 hour.

Preheat oven to 375F (190C). Place the chilled tart shell on a baking sheet and bake, in center of oven, 10 to 15 minutes, until just beginning to color. Set aside to cool.

Prepare the filling: Peel, quarter, and core the apples and then cut lengthwise into thin slices. Toss the apples and cranberries with arrowroot and cinnamon. Mound the filling into the tart shell and drizzle with the rice syrup.

Prepare the topping: Combine the oats, walnuts, flour, salt and rice syrup granules in a food processor. Pulse to form a coarse meal. Combine mixture and corn oil in a bowl and crumble the mixture with your fingers, forming a coarse, sandy mixture. Spread topping on top of the apples, covering them completely.

Bake tart about 40 minutes, until the top is golden, the filling is bubbly and the apples are tender when pierced. Cool slightly before serving warm. ✑

Makes 8 to 10 servings

NOTE If the topping is browning too quickly, simply cover the tart with foil during the last half of the baking time.

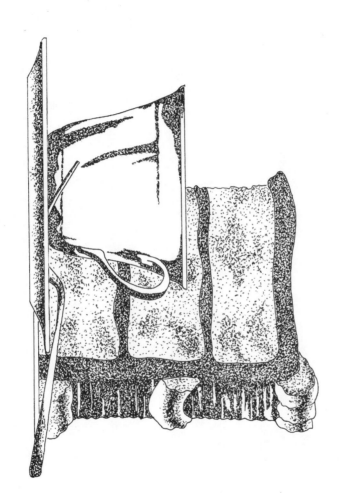

Chocolate-Hazelnut Torte

This sinful torte is so rich that the tiniest sliver will satisfy your wildest chocolate cravings. Besides, can you think of a better combination than chocolate, creamy custard and hazelnuts? Personally, I can't. Enjoy the indulgence! Go ahead, it's still low-fat. Hard to believe: decadence without guilt. ✒

PASTRY DOUGH

1/2 cup corn oil

1/4 cup brown rice syrup

2 tablespoons almond butter

1 cup whole-wheat pastry flour

1/4 cup unsweetened cocoa powder

Pinch of sea salt

CUSTARD

1/2 cup almond-flavored amasake

2 tablespoons kuzu, dissolved in
   1/4 cup cold water

1/2 cup brown rice syrup

2 tablespoons barley malt

CHOCOLATE CREAM

1/2 to 2/3 cup nondairy, malt-sweetened
   chocolate chips

1 teaspoon grain coffee, dissolved in

   2 tablespoons cold water

1/2 cup almond-flavored amasake

1 cup hazelnuts, lightly toasted and
   minced (page 323)

Prepare the pastry: Whip together the oil, rice syrup and almond butter in a bowl. Sift together the flour, cocoa powder and salt into the oil mixture. Mix until dough comes together. Gather the dough into a ball and flatten it slightly. Wrap in waxed paper and chill 2 hours.

Preheat the oven to 325F (165C). Lightly oil an 8-inch tart pan. Roll out the chilled dough into a thick round on a lightly floured surface or between sheets of waxed paper. Transfer the pastry to prepared tart pan, gently pressing the dough into the sides and bottom to create an even crust about 1/8 inch thick. Prick all over with a fork and freeze 10 minutes.

Bake pastry shell 12 to 15 minutes. The crust will still feel soft upon removal from the oven; it will set up as it cools. Set aside to cool.

Prepare the custard: Heat the amasake in a saucepan over low heat until hot. Stir in dissolved kuzu and cook, stirring, until mixture thickens, about 3 minutes. In a separate saucepan, heat the rice syrup and barley malt until they foam. Immediately stir into the custard. Set aside to cool.

Prepare the chocolate cream: Place the chocolate pieces in a heat-resistant bowl and stir in the grain coffee. In a small saucepan, bring the amasake to a boil and pour it over the chocolate. Stir until the chocolate melts and the mixture is smooth.

To assemble, reserve a small handful of hazelnuts for decoration. Pour the cooled custard into the tart shell and spread evenly. Sprinkle the remaining hazelnuts over the custard. Carefully pour the chocolate cream on top and spread evenly over custard. Arrange reserved hazelnuts around the edge of the tart to form a decorative edge. Chill until firm, about 1 hour. ☙ Makes 8 servings

Squash & Pear Pie

This unique flavor combination requires a deep-dish pie pan to accommodate its abundant filling. This is one of those rare autumn pies that actually tastes better cold than warm. ☙

1 recipe Pastry Dough (page 466)

2 medium acorn squash (about

   3 lbs. total)

Spring or filtered water

1 1/4 cups plus 2 tablespoons brown

   rice syrup

1/4 cup corn oil

Pinch of sea salt

1 cup amasake

1 teaspoon ground ginger

2 teaspoons ground cinnamon

3 tablespoons agar-agar flakes

2 to 3 tablespoons kuzu, dissolved in

   1/4 cup cold water

3 pears

Preheat oven to 400F (205C). Prepare the dough and roll it out thinly between sheets of waxed paper into about an 11-inch circle. Peel away 1 sheet of waxed paper and transfer crust to pie plate. Press crust into plate, without stretching dough too much. Cut away excess dough, leaving 1/2-inch overhang. Roll the excess dough up toward the edge and crimp to create a decorative edge. Prick all over the surface with a fork. Bake 10 minutes. Set aside while preparing the filling.

Halve the squash and scoop out the seeds. Place the halves, cut side up, in a large baking dish. Pour in 1/2 inch of water. Drizzle with the 2 tablespoons rice syrup and corn oil and sprinkle with salt. Cover and bake 45 minutes, until the squash is very soft.

Remove the squash flesh and process in a food processor until smooth. Combine squash puree, amasake, remaining 1 1/4 cups rice syrup, ginger, cinnamon and agar-agar in a saucepan over low heat. Simmer 10 minutes to dissolve agar-agar. Stir in dissolved kuzu and cook, stirring, until mixture just thickens, 3 to 4 minutes. Set aside.

Peel, quarter and core the pears. Cut lengthwise into thin slices and arrange in concentric circles in the pie shell. Pour the squash filling carefully over the pears and spread evenly, smoothing the surface. Bake on the lower rack of the oven 15 minutes. Decrease oven temperature to 350F (190C) and bake 45 minutes, until the crust is golden and the filling is just set. The center of the pie will continue cooking while the pie cools, so don't be concerned if the center seems soft when you first remove it from the oven. Cover hot pie with foil to prevent cracking and cool completely or refrigerate briefly before serving. ✒ M a k e s a b o u t 8 s e r v i n g s

Tangy Chocolate Chip Cookies
As a former chocolate addict, I can assure you that, in my past, I mastered just about every chocolate recipe that I could get my hands on. This variation on a classic cookie has stayed with me, changing and evolving as much as my eating habits. ✒

3 1/2 cups whole-wheat pastry flour
2 teaspoons baking powder
Pinch of sea salt
1 cup brown rice syrup
1/3 cup fresh orange juice
1/4 cup corn oil

1 teaspoon pure vanilla extract
2 teaspoons grated orange zest
1/2 cup coarsely diced pecans
1 cup malt-sweetened, nondairy
    chocolate chips

Preheat oven to 350F (175C). Lightly oil 2 baking sheets. Mix together flour, baking powder and salt in a bowl. Whisk together rice syrup, orange juice, corn oil, vanilla and orange zest until creamy and stir into dry ingredients. Stir in nuts and chocolate chips.

Drop cookie dough by heaping teaspoonfuls about 2 inches apart onto prepared baking sheets. Bake 18 to 20 minutes, until cookies are golden and firm. Remove to a cooling rack. ~ M a k e s   a b o u t   3   d o z e n

Blueberry Coffeecake

I love brunch, especially in the summer because of the abundance of fruit at hand and the fact that we can eat in the garden. Tartlets, strudels, kantens and custards laden with fresh fruit are a tasty addition to any brunch table. But my favorite, really, is coffeecake. And this one, well . . . ~

1 recipe Sure-Fire Basic White Cake (page 464)

1 1/2 cups fresh blueberries, sorted, rinsed and well-drained

TOPPING

5 tablespoons maple syrup granules

3 tablespoons walnuts, minced

Generous pinch of ground cinnamon

2 to 3 tablespoons corn oil

Preheat the oven to 375F (190C). Oil and flour an 8-inch round cake pan. Prepare the cake batter and fold in the blueberries. Take care not to overmix, or the cake will become tough. Spoon the batter evenly into the cake pan.

Prepare the topping: Combine the maple syrup granules, nuts, cinnamon, and corn oil in a small bowl. Sprinkle topping over the cake. Bake 35 to 40 minutes, until the top is golden and a wooden pick comes out clean when inserted in the center of the cake. Allow to cool in the pan 10 minutes before turning out. Serve warm. ~

M a k e s   1   c a k e ,   6   t o   8   s e r v i n g s

Pear-Spice Coffeecake

Remember upside-down cakes? In my version, juicy pears are covered with a spicy gingerbread cake. This beautiful cake will win you raves, and no one has to know how easy it is to make. We love it on crisp, autumn Sunday mornings with hot tea and the Sunday paper. ✎

1 tablespoon corn oil
3 tablespoons maple syrup granules
3 firm but ripe Bosc pears
1 tablespoon fresh lemon juice
1 1/2 cups whole-wheat pastry flour
Pinch of sea salt
1 teaspoon baking powder

2 teaspoons ground cinnamon
1/2 teaspoon *each* nutmeg, ginger and allspice
1/2 cup brown rice syrup
1/4 cup barley malt
1/2 cup unsweetened applesauce

Place oven rack in the lowest position and preheat the oven to 375F (190C). Oil and flour an 8-inch square baking dish.

Drizzle the corn oil over the bottom of the prepared baking dish and sprinkle with maple syrup granules. Peel, halve and core the pears. Cut a pear half, crosswise, into 1/8-inch-thick slices. Keeping the slices together, slide a spatula underneath, invert the pear half onto your hand and press lightly to fan the slices. Place it, cut side up, in the maple syrup mixture in the baking dish. Repeat with the other pear halves, filling the bottom of the dish. Drizzle with lemon juice. Bake, uncovered, 15 minutes.

Meanwhile, sift together flour, salt, baking powder and spices into a bowl. Whisk together the rice syrup, barley malt and applesauce. Stir applesauce mixture into flour mixture until just blended. Spoon batter carefully over baked pears, covering them evenly.

Bake 30 to 35 minutes, until a wooden pick inserted in the center of the cake comes out clean. With a sharp knife, loosen the edges of the cake from the pan. Place a serving platter over the pan and invert the cake onto the platter. Remove any pear slices that adhere to the cake pan and replace them on top of the cake. Allow to cool about 10 minutes before slicing. This cake is really great served warm. ✎

Makes 1 cake, 6 to 8 servings

Baked Apples with Creamy Chestnut Filling

This unique twist on a traditional dessert is especially good served with the warm, spicy cooking juices spooned over the top just before serving. 🍃

1 pound fresh chestnuts	**1/3 cup currants**
1/4 cup amasake	**6 to 8 Granny Smith apples**
1/3 cup apple juice	**Juice of 1 lemon**
6 tablespoons brown rice syrup	**1/3 cup mirin**
Generous pinch *each* of cinnamon and nutmeg	**1 cinnamon stick**

Preheat oven to 350F (175C). Lightly oil a 13 × 9-inch baking dish. Make a slit in the flat side of each chestnut. Cook in boiling water over high heat 15 minutes. Drain the chestnuts and run under cool water. Using a sharp knife, peel off the flat top and scoop out the meat.

In a food processor, puree peeled chestnuts, amasake, apple juice, 4 tablespoons of the rice syrup, cinnamon and nutmeg. Fold in currants. Core the apples and, using a spoon, scoop out the insides, leaving a 1/2-inch-thick shell to stuff. Mince apple pulp and mix into chestnut mixture along with lemon juice. Fill apple shells with chestnut mixture and arrange in prepared baking dish. Pour mirin and remaining rice syrup over apples. Place cinnamon stick in the baking dish.

Bake 30 to 40 minutes, basting occasionally with the cooking juices, until apples are tender. Place apples on a serving platter. Spoon any remaining cooking juices over apples. Serve warm. 🍃 M a k e s 6 t o 8 s e r v i n g s

VARIATION Substitute 4 ounces dried chestnuts for fresh chestnuts. Soak dried chestnuts 6 to 8 hours and pressure-cook in a small amount of water 25 minutes.

Pear Galette

This free-form pie has a delicate crust, so be sure to bring it to the table whole. It will crumble when sliced. Delicious made with any fruit, it is just the best with the delicate sweetness of ripe pears.

CRUST

1 1/2 cups whole-wheat pastry flour

1/8 teaspoon sea salt

1/4 cup corn oil, chilled

2 tablespoons brown rice syrup

1/4 cup cold water

PEAR FILLING

1/3 cup maple syrup granules

1/4 cup arrowroot

Pinch of ground cloves

6 medium-size, ripe Bosc pears

Prepare dough: Combine flour and salt in a bowl. Stir in chilled oil and rice syrup until mixture resembles coarse cornmeal. Slowly add water, mixing just until dough combines. Do not gather into a ball. Press two-thirds of the mixture into a thick round on waxed paper and cover with another sheet. Repeat with remaining dough. Roll the larger portion into an 11-inch circle and freeze 5 minutes (to release waxed paper easily).

Preheat oven to 375F (190C). Lightly oil a baking sheet or pizza pan.

Turn dough out onto prepared pan and remove top sheet of paper. Combine maple syrup granules, arrowroot and cloves in a small bowl. Peel, halve and core the pears, then cut into 1-inch wedges. Sprinkle dough with one-third of the maple mixture and arrange half the pear wedges over the dough, leaving a 2-inch border around the edge. Sprinkle pears with some of the maple mixture. Layer remaining pears on top and sprinkle with the remaining maple mixture. Roll out remaining dough into a 10-inch round. Freeze 5 minutes and remove 1 sheet of waxed paper. Place dough over pears and remove remaining paper. Pull up edges of bottom dough to meet the top layer. Pinch edges to seal. Cut 6 slits in the top of the galette to allow steam to escape.

Bake 45 minutes or until lightly browned. Allow to cool 20 minutes before slicing. Makes 8 to 10 servings

VARIATION This galette is even more delicious served with warm amasake and ginger juice (page 242) spooned over the top.

Crispy Chewies

Remember crisp rice cereal treats? Well, they got nothin' on these babies! ✎

1 cup brown rice syrup
1/2 cup almond butter

1/2 cup malt-sweetened nondairy chocolate chips
3 cups crispy brown rice cereal

In a large saucepan, heat rice syrup and almond butter over low heat until creamy. Stir in chocolate chips until they melt. Remove from heat and stir in rice cereal until coated. Press into a shallow, square casserole dish. Allow to set until firm. Cut into squares and serve. ✎ M a k e s a b o u t 1 d o z e n .

VARIATIONS Any nut butter is fabulous in this treat: peanut butter, cashew or hazelnut butter, . . . yummy. Omit chocolate and create a decadent nutty-flavored rice treat.

Raspberry Poppers

These light, flaky miniature cookies are the perfect size and the perfect taste to do justice to their name. Once you start popping these bite-size beauties, you'll be hooked. ✎

2 1/2 cups whole-wheat pastry flour

1/8 teaspoon sea salt

2 teaspoons baking powder

1/4 cup soy or canola margarine, chilled

2 tablespoons brown rice syrup

2/3 cup rice milk

1 teaspoon pure vanilla extract

About 3/4 cup unsweetened or fruit-sweetened raspberry jam

GLAZE

1/2 cup brown rice syrup

1 teaspoon unsweetened or fruit-sweetened raspberry jam

Combine flour, salt, baking powder, margarine and rice syrup in a food processor. Pulse until mixture resembles coarse cornmeal; do not overmix. Add rice milk and vanilla and pulse again until dough gathers into a ball. Again, do not overmix, just pulse until the dough gathers.

Preheat oven to 350F (175C). Lightly oil a baking sheet. Place a sheet of waxed paper on a dry work surface. Flour paper lightly. Flatten dough into a rectangular shape. Dust with flour and top with another sheet of waxed paper. Roll dough into a rectangle, about 1/8 inch thick. Remove the top sheet of paper.

With a sharp knife, cut the rectangle in half, lengthwise. Spread both halves with a thin layer of jam. Roll each piece, jelly-roll style, into a long cylinder. Cut into 1/2-inch rounds and place, cut side up, on prepared baking sheet. Bake 20 to 22 minutes, until puffy and the edges are a bit golden.

Make glaze: Heat rice syrup and jam in a small saucepan over medium heat until they foam. Quickly spoon over warm cookies. Allow to stand until glaze sets a bit before serving. ✎ Makes about 3 dozen

Chestnut Kanten

A delicately sweet and creamy dessert. Pan-toasting the dried chestnuts before soaking brings out their natural sweet taste.

1 cup dried chestnuts, pan-toasted
   (page 142) and then soaked 6 to
   8 hours
3 cups spring or filtered water
Pinch of sea salt

3/4 cup agar-agar flakes
2 cups apple juice
1/2 cup fresh orange juice
Fresh orange slices, for decoration

Place the chestnuts and water in a saucepan and bring to a boil. Cover and cook over low heat about 1 hour. Add salt and simmer 10 minutes more. Drain chestnuts. Process chestnuts in a food processor until smooth.

Combine the agar-agar and the juices in a saucepan and simmer over low heat 10 to 15 minutes. Stir in chestnut puree and mix until smooth. Rinse a shallow dish with cold water and pour in chestnut mixture. Set aside to cool until firm. After 30 minutes of setting time, you may refrigerate until set. Serve decorated with orange slices. ✐

Makes 4 to 6 servings

Apple Focaccia

A dessert pizza that I like to make during the holiday for brunches or other get-togethers when I want a lovely dessert with a minimum of fuss. ✑

1/2 recipe Basic Sourdough Bread
(page 435)

1 apple, cored and pureed in a food
processor

Pinch of ground cinnamon

2 teaspoons brown rice syrup

1/3 cup raisins

FILLING

4 apples, cored and cut into
paper-thin slices

Juice of 1 lemon

Pinch *each* of ground nutmeg,
cinnamon and ginger

1/3 cup brown rice syrup

Dash of pure vanilla extract

1/4 cup barley malt

1 tablespoon kuzu, dissolved in small
amount of cold water

GLAZE

2 tablespoons unsweetened apricot or
raspberry jam

1 tablespoon brown rice syrup

Prepare the basic dough, omitting 1/4 cup of the water. Knead in apple puree, cinnamon, rice syrup and raisins. Knead 10 minutes. Place in a lightly oiled bowl and allow to rise as directed in recipe.

When the dough is ready, preheat oven to 400F. Lightly oil a 13 × 9-inch baking pan. Turn dough onto a floured work surface and knead 1 to 2 minutes. Press dough into prepared pan. Cover with a damp kitchen towel and allow to rise at room temperature while preparing the filling.

Toss apple slices in lemon juice to prevent discoloration. Stir in remaining filling ingredients and mix well. Spread filling evenly over surface of dough.

Bake 20 minutes. Reduce oven temperature to 375F (190C) and bake another 20 minutes, until apples are browned and crust is golden. Heat glaze ingredients in a small saucepan over high heat until foamy. Immediately drizzle over warm focaccia. Cool slightly before serving. ✑ M a k e s 6 t o 8 s e r v i n g s

Resource Guide

I am sure you have noticed that in more than a few recipes you have discovered ingredients with which you are completely unfamiliar. So rather than leave you dazed and confused as to where you might find these more exotic foods, I thought I would supply you with a comprehensive list of mail-order companies that can easily supply the ingredients in question. See, I told you I would make this painless. . . . Just call the company of your choice and request a catalog. Life couldn't be easier.

DIAMOND ORGANICS
Freedom, California
800-922-2396
SUPPLIES: organic produce, shipped direct
to customer

EARTH FIRE MISO
Gays Mills, Wisconsin
800-267-6918
SUPPLIES: organic miso products

FLORA
Lynden, Washington
360-354-2110
SUPPLIES: organic, cold-pressed oils, non-
food items

GOLD MINE NATURAL FOOD CO.
San Diego, CA
800-475-FOOD, 619-234-9711
SUPPLIES: macrobiotic and natural food
items, non-food items

GRANUM CO.
Seattle, Washington
206-525-0051
SUPPLIES: macrobiotic and natural food
items, non-food items

GREAT EASTERN SUN
Asheville, North Carolina
704-252-3090
SUPPLIES: macrobiotic and natural food
items, non-food items

HARVEST TIME NATURAL FOODS
Eaton Rapids, Michigan
800-628-8736, 517-628-2506
SUPPLIES: macrobiotic and natural food
items

IVY FOODS
Salt Lake City, Utah
800-943-7311
SUPPLIES: seitan (wheat meat) and various
related products

KING ARTHUR FLOUR BREAD BAKER'S CATALOGUE
Norwich, Vermont
800-827-6836
SUPPLIES: bread-baking equipment, whole-grain flour, books, kitchenware

KUSHI INSTITUTE STORE
Becket, Massachusetts
413-623-5741
SUPPLIES: macrobiotic and natural food items, non-food items

MAINE COAST SEA VEGETABLES
Franklin, Maine
207-565-2907
SUPPLIES: American and imported dried sea plants

MAINE SEAWEED COMPANY
Steuben, Maine
207-546-2875
SUPPLIES: American and imported dried sea plants

MOUNTAIN ARK TRADING COMPANY
Asheville, North Carolina
800-643-8909
SUPPLIES: macrobiotic and natural food items, non-food items

NATURAL LIFESTYLE SUPPLIES
Asheville, North Carolina
800-752-2775
SUPPLIES: macrobiotic and natural food items, non-food items

NESHAMINY VALLEY NATURAL FOODS
Ivyland, Pennsylvania
215-443-5545
SUPPLIES: macrobiotic and natural food items, organic produce, non-food items

SOUTH RIVER MISO COMPANY
Conway, Massachusetts
413-369-4057
SUPPLIES: organic miso, soy sauce and tamari

TATRA HERB COMPANY
Morrisville, Pennsylvania
215-295-5476
SUPPLIES: natural herbal formulas, tinctures, supplements, etc.

WALNUT ACRES NATURAL FOODS
Penns Creek, Pennsylvania
717-837-0601
SUPPLIES: natural food items, non-food items

WELLSPRING
Amherst, Massachusetts
800-578-5301
SUPPLIES: macrobiotic and natural food items, non-food items

Recommended Reading

To further your study of macrobiotics, whole foods cooking and other holistic practices, please check out any or all of these volumes.

The Macrobiotic Diet by Michio and Aveline Kushi with Alex Jack

Aveline Kushi's Complete Guide to Macrobiotic Cooking with Wendy Esko

The Changing Seasons Cookbook by Aveline Kushi and Wendy Esko

Mostly Macro by Lisa Turner

Practically Macrobiotic by Keith Mitchel

Sugar Blues by William Dufty

Diet for a New America: How Your Food Choices Affect Your Health, Happiness and the Future of Life on Earth by John Robbins

May All Be Fed by John Robbins

The Natural Gourmet by Annemarie Colbin

The Rise and Fall of the Cattle Culture by Jeremy Rifkin

Recipes From an Ecological Kitchen by Lorna Sass

Confessions of a Kamikaze Cowboy by Dirk Benedict

The Cancer Prevention Diet by Michio Kushi

Macrobiotic Home Remedies by Michio Kushi with Marc Van Cawenberghe, M.D.

Diet for a Strong Heart by Michio Kushi

Recalled by Life by Anthony Sattilaro, M.D., with Tom Monte

The Macrobiotic Way by Michio Kushi

Energetics of Food by Steve Gagne

The Magic Mirror by William Tara

Diet for a Poisoned Planet by David Steinman

You Are All Sanpaku by George Ohsawa

Natural Guidebook for Living by George Ohsawa

Eco-Cuisine by Ron Pikarski

Magazines

MacroChef
243 Dickinson St., Philadelphia, PA
19147

E, The Environmental Magazine
PO Box 699, Mt. Morris, IL 61054

Natural Health
PO Box 1200, Brookline Village, MA
57320

Vegetarian Gourmet
PO Box 7641, Riverton, NJ 08077-7641

Vegetarian Times
PO Box 570, Oak Park, IL 60303

Bibliography

The following books have served me well over these last years—and for this work—for information, facts and statistics, and inspiration.

Abehsera, Michel, *Cooking for Life* (New York: Avon, 1970).

Baggett, Nancy, *Dream Desserts* (New York: Stewart, Tabori & Chang, 1993).

Blackman, Jackson F., *Working Chef's Cookbook for Natural Whole Foods* (Vermont: Central Vermont Publishers, 1989).

Colbin, Annemarie, *The Natural Gourmet* (New York: Ballentine, 1989).

Gagne, Steve, *Energetics of Food* (New Mexico: Spiral Science, 1990).

Kushi, Aveline, *The Complete Guide to Macrobiotic Cooking* (New York: Warner, 1985).

Levy, Faye, *Sensational Pasta* (California: HP Books, 1989).

Pikarski, Ron, *Eco-Cuisine* (California: Ten Speed Press, 1995).

Rubin, Maury, *Book of Tarts* (New York: William Morrow & Co., 1995).

Somerville, Annie, *Fields of Greens* (New York: Bantam, 1993).

Spencer, Colin, *The Heretic's Feast: A History of Vegetarianism* (London: Fourth Estate, 1993).

Steinman, David, *Diet for a Poisoned Planet* (New York: Ballentine, 1990).

Metric Conversion Charts

When You Know	Symbol	Comparison to Metric Measure Multiply By	To Find	Symbol
teaspoons	tsp	5.0	milliliter	ml
tablespoons	tbsp	15.0f	milliliters	ml
fluid ounces	fl. oz.	30.0	milliliters	ml
cups	c	0.24	liters	l
pints	pt.	0.47	liters	l
quarts	qt.	0.95	liters	l
ounces	oz.	28.0	grams	g
pounds	lb.	0.45	kilograms	kg
Fahrenheit	F	5/9 (after subtracting 32)	Celsius	C

Fahrenheit to Celsium

F	C
200–205	95
229–225	105
245–250	120
275	135
300–305	150
325–330	165
345–350	175
370–375	190
400–405	205
425–430	220
445–450	230
470–475	245
500	260

Liquid Measure to Liters

1/4 cup	=	0.06 liters
1/2 cup	=	0.12 liters
3/4 cup	=	0.18 liters
1 cup	=	0.24 liters
1-1/4 cups	=	0.30 liters
1-1/2 cups	=	0.36 liters
2 cups	=	0.48 liters
2-1/2 cups	=	0.60 liters
3 cups	=	0.72 liters
3-1/2 cups	=	0.84 liters
4 cups	=	0.96 liters
4-1/2 cups	=	1.08 liters
5 cups	=	1.20 liters
5-1/2 cups	=	1.32 liters

Liquid Measure to Milliliters

1/4 teaspoon	=	1.25 milliliters
1/2 teaspoon	=	2.50 milliliters
3/4 teaspoon	=	3.75 milliliters
1 teaspoon	=	5.00 milliliters
1-1/4 teaspoons	=	6.25 milliliters
1-1/2 teaspoons	=	7.50 milliliters
1-3/4 teaspoons	=	8.75 milliliters
2 teaspoons	=	10.0 milliliters
1 tablespoon	=	15.0 milliliters
2 tablespoons	=	30.0 milliliters

Index

514   Index

522 🍃 Index

Photo © Amanda Stevenson

Christina Pirello became a vegetarian at the age of fourteen. In 1983, after being diagnosed with terminal leukemia, she decided to forgo conventional medical therapies and turned to nutrition—and whole foods cooking—to cure herself. For the past eight years, Christina has been teaching whole foods cooking classes, catering, and lecturing nationwide. She and her husband also publish a bi-monthly natural foods magazine, MacroChef. Christina has been featured in the weekly food column in the Philadelphia Inquirer Magazine, on Cherie Banks' Health Watch, and on The Discovery Channel's Home Matters.